Kafka for the Twenty-First Century

Studies in German Literature, Linguistics, and Culture

Kafka for the Twenty-First Century

Edited by
Stanley Corngold and Ruth V. Gross

Rochester, New York

First published 2011 by Camden House
Transferred to digital printing 2012
Reprinted in paperback 2015

Camden House is an imprint of Boydell & Brewer Inc.
668 Mt. Hope Avenue, Rochester, NY 14620, USA
www.camden-house.com
and of Boydell & Brewer Limited
PO Box 9, Woodbridge, Suffolk IP12 3DF, UK
www.boydellandbrewer.com

Paperback ISBN-13: 978-1-57113-931-3
Paperback ISBN-10: 1-57113-931-1
Hardcover ISBN-13: 978-1-57113-482-0
Hardcover ISBN-10: 1-57113-482-4

Library of Congress Cataloging-in-Publication Data

Kafka for the twenty-first century / edited by Stanley Corngold and Ruth V. Gross.
p. cm. — (Studies in German literature, linguistics, and culture)
Includes bibliographical references and index.
ISBN-13: 978-1-57113-482-0 (hardcover : acid-free paper)
ISBN-10: 1-57113-482-4 (hardcover : acid-free paper)
1. Kafka, Franz, 1883–1924—Criticism and interpretation.
I. Corngold, Stanley. II. Gross, Ruth V. III. Title. IV. Series.

PT2621.A26Z75846 2011
833'.912—dc22

2011008049

This publication is printed on acid-free paper.

Contents

Preface vii

List of Abbreviations for Kafka Citations xi

Introduction 1
Stanley Corngold and Ruth V. Gross

1: Running Texts, Stunning Drafts 24
Roland Reuß

2: "Torturing the Gordian Knot": Kafka and Metaphor 48
Mark Harman

3: Nietzsche and Kafka: The Dionysian Connection 64
Walter H. Sokel

4: What Kafka Learned from Flaubert: "Absent-Minded Window-Gazing" and "The Judgment" 75
Uta Degner

5: Kafka's Racial Melancholy 89
Katja Garloff

6: Strange Loops and the Absent Center in *The Castle* 105
Jacob Burnett

7: Proxies in Kafka: *Koncipist* FK and *Prokurist* Josef K. 120
Doreen Densky

8: Kafka, Goffman, and the Total Institution 136
Ritchie Robertson

9: Kafka in Virilio's Teletopical City 151
Rolf J. Goebel

10: Kafka's Visual Method: The Gaze, the Cinematic, and the Intermedial 165
Peter Beicken

11: "Samsa war Reisender": Trains, Trauma, and the Unreadable Body 179
John Zilcosky

12: The Comfort of Strangeness: Correlating the Kafkaesque and the Kafkan in Kazuo Ishiguro's *The Unconsoled* 207
Robert Lemon

13: Kafka's Journey into the Future: Crossing Borders into Israeli/Palestinian Worlds 222
Iris Bruce

14: Kafka and Italy: A New Perspective on the Italian Literary Landscape 237
Saskia Elizabeth Ziolkowski

Bibliography 251

Notes on the Contributors 273

Index 277

Preface

TO JUDGE BY THE AMOUNT OF KAFKA SCHOLARSHIP that has appeared in the last few years, it is safe to say that Franz Kafka is alive and well in the twenty-first century. This fact should not surprise us, since we know that Kafka was the most widely read German author in the last half of the previous century and that there has hardly been a period since the Second World War in which Kafka scholarship has not thrived. But with all the extant criticism and interest in this author whose published works are a nano-fraction of the material that has been published about them, there is, of course, always also a danger. From the beginning, Kafka was the new, the different, the true representative of modernity. We have read his works through religious, existentialist, structuralist, and more recently, postmodern perspectives. The "period of slackening" that Jean François Lyotard described decades ago as the beginning of a certain version of postmodernism entails an "end to experimentation," and in our discourse of literature this lull suggests the possibility of what one might call "Kafka exhaustion." Can there be a permanent avatar of the avant-garde? How does the indisputable status of a classic accord with the indisputable role of a disruptor, an instigator of the new? The paradoxes of Kafka's position in world culture lead to the same question — "Kafka, again?" The answer, of course, has always been, and continues to be, "Yes, Kafka, again."

Why these thoughts now? Although it could be argued that turns-of-century are artificial markers, we tend to give them considerable attention and look to them as signposts of cultural change. In this spirit a conference with the subject "Kafka at 125" — a celebration of Kafka's 125th birthday — was held in the Research Triangle of North Carolina in April 2009. Clayton Koelb, James Rolleston, and Ruth V. Gross, the organizers of the conference, each a member of one of the three research universities in the Triangle and each a veteran Kafka scholar, felt that the concerns of a new century called for a fresh look not only at what Kafka meant to the preceding century but also at what challenges his works might offer to the decades ahead. Their idea was to assemble a number of distinguished Kafka researchers from North America and Europe to examine together the ways in which this extraordinary writer, who so decisively shaped our conception of the twentieth century, might suggest fruitful strategies for coping with the twenty-first.

From its inception, this conference was to be different: the intention was to create a model that would allow participants to engage in lengthy round-table discussions around certain topics and thereby connect to and expand upon the current critical discourses concerning and surrounding Kafka. No papers, other than the keynotes, were read: the conference was all discussion. Individual papers and abstracts were posted to a website before the conference and therefore needed only brief summaries before commentary at the actual conference could begin. What ensued was a productive synergy arising from the conversations that took place. To be sure, the presentations enhanced the Kafkan critical base, but there was also a healthy expression of differing views and insights that allowed participants opportunities to refine and rethink arguments in keeping with the challenges posed by their colleagues.

We asked a number of broad questions in our initial call for papers — What have we learned about the context surrounding Kafka's literary production, and what more can we hope to learn? How does understanding that context affect how we read his stories? What are the consequences of new critical editions that offer the general reader unprecedented access to Kafka's works in their original manuscript form? How does our view of Kafka change in response to changes in the priorities and fashions of literary scholarship? What are the elements in Kafka's fiction that are likely to find resonance in the altered historical context of a new millennium? How do we compose a complete and coherent account of a personality with so many often contradictory aspects: the writer, the Bohemian Jew, the bachelor son, the would-be celibate, the lover of many women, the lawyer, the frustrated bureaucrat, the successful business executive, the German, the Austrian, the Czech, and the failed novelist who is perhaps the most influential novelist of the twentieth century? The response to our call for papers was enthusiastic; presenters were then selected from the many abstracts proposed. In the proposals we immediately saw a number of intriguing answers that, in true Kafkan fashion, generated further questions. At the same time we invited four keynoters to begin each of the four half-day discussion sessions: Roland Reuß from Germany, Walter Sokel from the United States, Ritchie Robertson from the United Kingdom, and John Zilcosky from Canada. Representing not only four different international regions but four very different approaches to Kafka in the twenty-first century, their essays are included in the present collection.

The variation in their methodologies was only one of the ways in which the conference bridged divides and provided new syntheses of thought. From emeritus professors to graduate students and all academic levels in between, the conference participants, building on the rich body of Kafka criticism of the past decades, presented new connections and possibilities of reading the Kafkan oeuvre that — appropriate to the occasion — often made familiar texts unfamiliar again. The "Kafka world" in the academic sense has been a remarkably open and welcoming discourse. And so it continues to be. Those of us who turned to Kafka or began with him many years ago recall and will always be grateful for this community and its support. A nonagenarian and a graduate student can speak to the problems of Kafka and learn from each other, which is an unusual thing and, to many of us, characteristic of Kafka studies. We asked conference participants to expand their papers for possible publication and finally selected approximately one half for inclusion here. Contributors were able to take arguments from other papers in the volume into account in writing theirs through a website that was established for this purpose. In this way we hope to have maintained the "dialogical" texture so vividly present at the conference. In other words, our intention was to produce a volume preserving the collegial, interactive spirit of our celebration of Kafka.

Without help from the DAAD, North Carolina State University, Duke University, and the University of North Carolina, Chapel Hill, the conference and subsequently this volume, could not have happened, and the editors would like to thank those institutions for their generous support.

Meanwhile, the great question remains: "How can Kafka be so unique as to escape the logic of human attention and the fickleness of academic fashion, as he continues to draw us toward the future and the new?" The answer to this question can be found nowhere else than in the ongoing Kafka discourse. Only one decade into the twenty-first century, it is, of course, too soon to know for sure but certainly not too soon to predict that — for reasons that should be clear from the essays in this volume — Kafka will remain, as he was in the twentieth, its most widely read German author.

Ruth V. Gross, Raleigh, NC

Abbreviations for Kafka Citations

A — *Amerika: The Missing Person*. Translated by Mark Harman. New York: Schocken, 2008.

AS — *Amtliche Schriften*. Edited by Klaus Hermsdorf and Benno Wagner. Frankfurt am Main: S. Fischer, 2004.

B1 — *Briefe, 1900–1912*. Edited by Hans-Gerd Koch. Frankfurt am Main: S. Fischer, 1999.

B2 — *Briefe, 1913–März 1914*. Edited by Hans-Gerd Koch. Frankfurt am Main: S. Fischer, 1999.

BF — *Briefe an Felice*. Edited by Erich Heller and Jürgen Born. Frankfurt am Main: S. Fischer, 1967.

BM — *Briefe an Milena*. Edited by Jürgen Born and Michael Müller. Frankfurt am Main: S. Fischer, 1983.

Br — *Briefe, 1902–1924*. Edited by Max Brod. Frankfurt am Main: S. Fischer, 1958.

C — *The Castle*. Translated by Mark Harman. New York: Schocken, 1998.

CS — *The Complete Stories*. Edited by Nahum Glatzer. New York: Schocken, 1971.

D — *The Diaries of Franz Kafka, 1910–1923*. Edited by Max Brod. New York: Schocken Books, 1975.

D1 — *The Diaries of Franz Kafka, 1910–1913*. Translated by Joseph Kresh. New York: Schocken, 1948.

D2 — *The Diaries of Franz Kafka, 1914–1923*. Translated by Martin Greenberg (with the assistance of Hannah Arendt). New York: Schocken, 1949.

DL — *Drucke zu Lebzeiten*. Edited by Wolf Kittler, Hans-Gerd Koch, and Gerhard Neumann. Frankfurt am Main: S. Fischer, 1994.

E — *Erzählungen und andere ausgewählte Prosa*. Edited by Roger Hermes. Frankfurt am Main: Fischer, 1996.

KSS — *Kafka's Selected Stories*. Norton Critical Edition. Edited and translated by Stanley Corngold. New York, Norton, 2007.

L — *Letters to Friends, Family, and Editors*. Translated by Richard Winston and Clara Winston. New York: Schocken, 1977.

LF — *Letters to Felice*. Translated by James Stern and Elizabeth Duckworth. New York: Schocken, 1973.

LM *Letters to Milena.* Translated by Philip Boehm. New York: Schocken, 1990.

M *The Metamorphosis.* Translated and edited by Stanley Corngold. New York: Norton, 1996.

MP *The Metamorphosis, In the Penal Colony, and other Stories.* Translated by Willa Muir and Edwin Muir. New York: Schocken, 1975.

NS1 *Nachgelassene Schriften und Fragmente I.* Edited by Malcolm Pasley. Frankfurt am Main: S. Fischer, 1990.

NS2 *Nachgelassene Schriften und Fragmente II.* Edited by Jost Schillemeit. Frankfurt am Main: S. Fischer, 1992.

OW *Franz Kafka: The Office Writings.* Edited by Stanley Corngold, Jack Greenberg, and Benno Wagner. Translated by Eric Patton and Ruth Hein. Princeton, NJ: Princeton UP, 2009.

P *Der Proceß.* Edited by Malcolm Pasley. Frankfurt am Main: S. Fischer, 1990.

S *Das Schloß.* Edited by Malcolm Pasley. Frankfurt am Main: S. Fischer, 1982.

T *The Trial.* Translated by Breon Mitchell. New York: Schocken, 1998.

Ta *Tagebücher in der Fassung der Handschrift.* Edited by Michael Müller. Frankfurt am Main: S. Fischer, 1990.

V *Der Verschollene in der Fassung der Handschrift.* Edited by Jost Schillemeit. Frankfurt am Main: S. Fischer, 1983.

Introduction

Stanley Corngold and Ruth V. Gross

The lament: If I shall exist eternally, how shall I exist tomorrow?
— Kafka[1]

FRANZ KAFKA WAS BORN on July 3, 1883, into a German-speaking Jewish family in Prague, the capital of the Czech Lands of the Austro-Hungarian Empire. He died at the age of forty-one with the dubious luck of one who died too soon to experience the Nazi terror. His favorite sister, Ottla; his second fiancée, Julie Wohryzek; and his lover, Milena Jesenská, a brilliant Czech writer, were all murdered in concentration camps. Kafka never married — though he fell in love easily, and was easily loved — despite having been engaged three times, twice to the same woman, Felice Bauer. Felice survived the terror and left an extraordinary, voluminous collection of Kafka's letters, which are testimony to her courtship by one of the century's strangest cavaliers, as eloquent in his charm as he was insistent on his unsuitability. Kafka broke off his second engagement to Felice after he had contracted tuberculosis, which in the end consumed his larynx and caused him excruciating pain, so that he could barely speak and literally starved to death.

Kafka pursued many different paths to fulfill a life lived under intense self-scrutiny and, especially in the later years, considerable moral precision. His many friends testify to his unfailing courtesy, good humor, readiness to help — and exquisite phrasing. In response to his bullying father's complaint that his behavior was "crazy, meshuggah, not normal," Kafka replied, "Not being normal is not the worst thing. What's normal, for example, is world war."[2]

Kafka's moral qualities only added to the attractiveness of his person: he was a handsome man, some six feet tall, athletic, and at 135 pounds able to wear beautiful clothes to advantage. He was much valued for these qualities, as well as for his lawyerly brilliance, especially at the Workmen's Accident Insurance Institute for the Kingdom of Bohemia in Prague, where he rose to a high official position, becoming Senior Legal Secretary shortly before his death; and yet all the substantial good he did there could never amount to his justification. He read voraciously in nine languages, thought intensely, cared passionately for the welfare of Jewish refugees, and even pursued gardening seriously, but the path he followed — and to judge from his posthumous fame, found — was, with several interruptions, the way of writing. Only a few of his stories were published in his lifetime, and the novels for which he is most famous — *Amerika: The Missing Person* (*Der Verschollene*, 1927); *The Trial* (*Der Process*, 1925); and *The Castle* (*Das Schloss*, 1926) — appeared after his death. But from the "enormous world I have in my head," from his traffic with "spirits to darkness bound,"[3] he has enriched and frightened our imagination with imperishable figures like Gregor Samsa, the feckless traveling salesman, who wakes up one morning to find himself changed into a verminous insect; Joseph K., a high-ranking bank official, accused of a nameless crime for which he is stabbed to death in a quarry; the prisoner on a remote penal colony, strapped down on a writing machine designed to cut his sentence into his flesh; a pretend land surveyor, who, lost in the snow, desperately seeks entrance to the Castle; and countless others.

The penetration of Kafka into the public mind has steadily expanded. His audience of readers is vast; it is worldwide in scope: his works have finally been translated properly into Czech and Russian and other East European languages. Kafka scholars in America receive emails from Kafka scholars in China, asking for an exchange of ideas. For palpable proof of his appeal, one has only to visit the Franz Kafka Bookshop in the Old Town Square of Prague (also called "the Goltz"), just yards away from the Kinsky Palace where Kafka went to high school and his father had his business in ladies' finery. Here you will see visitors from all over the world poring over the copious new editions and translations of Kafka's work. And to this audience of readers add an audience of theatergoers and connoisseurs of new music, as witness the ongoing performances of Philip Glass's chamber opera *In the Penal Colony* and György Kurtág's song cycle *Kafka Fragments* for soprano and violin — works that in their own way constitute incisive readings of Kafka. Kafka's audience is by no means limited to high-culture devotees. Casual spectators of the media circus will hear his name; expert readers of current legal discourse will see his name appear in the most serious contexts, where it — or the adjective "Kafkaesque" — is regularly invoked by learned judge or counsel to excoriate unjust procedure. Many prominent cases figure in the pages of Westlaw, the online resource for case law, in which the sufferings of the accused appear to have leapt from the pages of *The Trial* and are acknowledged as such. There have been trials in American courts conducted in a language that the accused cannot literally understand; others in which the condemned was not present in court when his sentence was read. In one such case, counsel alludes plainly to the penultimate paragraph of *The Trial:* "Where was the judge he'd never seen?" (*T*, 31).[4] In a situation we find poignantly relevant, in O'Brien v. Henderson,

> the *pro se* petitioner claimed that the Board of Parole had violated his due process rights by revoking his parole without the proper explanation that was constitutionally required. The District Court granted his habeas corpus and mandamus petitions. Commenting on the unusual volume and vagueness of the petitioner's pleadings, Circuit Judge Edenfield noted that not even the most skilled of counsel, finding himself in the Kafkaesque situation of being deprived of his liberty by a tribunal which will adduce no reasons for its decision, can complain concisely and clearly of his objections to such a decision. . . . [Such a situation] leaves the prisoner no recourse but to approach the court with an attempted rebuttal of all real, feared, or imagined justifications for his confinement.[5]

Kafka is extraordinary not only for the volume of citation he has provoked; he is extraordinary for having attracted virtually endless interpretation. The power of his work to compel interpretation seems inexhaustible. In the words of the critic Theodor Adorno, "To read a story of Kafka's appears to *require* from the reader that he or she interpret it" (emphasis added).[6] This challenge has tended to produce answers involving vast quantities of information: in this sense Kafka criticism cannot fail to be instructive. This small, seemingly introspective body of work turns out to have responded seismographically to a wide range of intellectual, cultural, political, and social real-world forces.[7] Hence interpretations that might be characterized as theological, economic, biographical, existential, gender-political, psychoanalytic, neo-Gnostic, Marxian, and so on, have all proved rewarding in their own way.

Did Kafka at any point intuit his reception? The stereotypical answer is: of course not. He was just "a little clerk," the author of works whose central figures are colorless nobodies, a writer unknown in his own time, a failure in life and art. None of this is true. The first thing to say about him is that he is a genius, and he would be the last person to dispute this fact. (Readers uncomfortable with this category may prefer Mark Harman's ascribing to Kafka "the intuitive certainty of a somnambulist" [*C*, xv]). In regard, however, to extraordinary powers, there would seem to be no two ways about it, nothing "irrationally exuberant" about this claim. In a book titled *Paganism, Christianity, Judaism*, Max Brod — Kafka's friend, editor, and fervent booster — called Kafka a "Diesseitswunder" — a miracle occurring down here, on this side of the heavens — adding that the existence of Kafka — as a miracle — *and a Jew* — argued for the superiority of Judaism as a religion. Kafka read this book, saw this claim, and replied to Brod, stating that none of the evidence that Brod had adduced argued for the superiority of Judaism but — notice! — he did not bother to rebut the description of himself as a down-here miracle. In fact, such claims were not entirely a novelty to him:

In 1911, even before he had published a line of any significance, he wrote in his diary:

> The special nature of my inspiration — in which I, the happiest and unhappiest of men, now go to sleep at two in the morning [perhaps [this inspiration] will remain — if only I can bear the thought of it, for it exceeds all that came before [~~and — without a doubt — I am now the midpoint of the intellectual & spiritual life of Prague~~] — this inspiration is this, that I can do everything, not only with respect to a particular piece of work. If I write down a sentence at random, for example. "He looked out the window," it is already perfect. (*KSS*, 195, *D*1, 45)[8]

Readers may have seen this diary page on display in Oxford's Bodleian Library — Kafka's claim to be "im Geistigen der Mittelpunkt von Prag." It is inked through again and again. Kafka saw what he had written — and blushed. In black ink.[9]

But not for long — or forever. A glorious passage in the middle of Kafka's oeuvre reads:

> You lead the masses, big, tall field marshal, lead the desperate ones through the mountain passes, which are under snow, discernible to no one else. And who gives you the strength? He who gives you the clarity of your gaze.[10]

"Clarity of your gaze" (die Klarheit des Blickes) is a phrase that recurs throughout Kafka's confessional writings. It is the central virtue and, along with patience, the great bulwark against the thousand mortifications of daily life to which Kafka was subject — as a Jew in an anti-Semitic climate; as a bureaucrat (of which more later) sensitive to the outrage of a by-and-large disenfranchised working class; as a German-speaker, the target of Czech animosity, especially in the years of the disintegration of the Austro-Hungarian Empire; and, worst of all, as a grown man somehow self-condemned to live most of his life with his parents and sisters in a crowded apartment, under the sway of an angry father.

If it were possible to rationalize Kafka's genius, it might be said to consist, first of all, in the force of his literary imagination, his power to metamorphose the remains of the day. In Prague he lived alongside a river, the Vltava — or Moldau — and he would have seen or read of persons who drowned, by accident or otherwise. "In the course of the 1870s," writes Benno Wagner,

> statistics, accumulated with increasing precision, identified the Habsburg Monarchy — in comparison with the rest of Europe and according to the then current trend — as a "breeding ground of suicide."[11] Especially in Bohemia, this trend to an abnormal increase in

> suicides persisted into the 1880s as well, where Prague once again emerges as the statistical capital.[12]

But few would have been able to transform such an event into the aphorism, as Kafka does: "The man in ecstasy and the man drowning — both throw up their arms. The first does it to signify harmony, the second to signify strife with the elements" (*NS2*, 53).[13]

We spoke of Kafka's piercing intellect. His readers cannot fail to note the precision of his thought throughout the many verbal discussions — interpretations, all — in Kafka's fiction: the later chapters of *The Castle* consist almost entirely of them, to the point where even K., the protagonist, throws up his hands and cries: "Stop interpreting everything!" (*C*, 205).[14] Though self-confessedly no philosopher — as he wrote in his diary — having had to renounce "meditation" (Nachdenken) in order to concentrate on his writing, his literary prose enshrines the lucidity of his gaze.

In thinking of Kafka's genius, we will also insist on the hidden scope and depth of his erudition. We noted earlier that he read in nine languages; his letters and diaries report that he discussed with Prague friends at least the following dialogues of Plato *in Greek*: *Apology*, *Charmides*, *Crito*, *Euthydemus*, *Euthyphro*, *Ion*, *Lysis*, *Phaedo*, *Phaedrus*, *Protagoras*, *Symposium*, and *The Republic*. Indeed, the current working hypothesis of Kafka scholars is that no book published in Kafka's day and age can be excluded as a figure in or under the carpet of his prose. We do not know for certain of any book that Kafka did *not* read; the explicit absence or bare mention of the names of great contemporary literary figures in Kafka's oeuvre does not prove that they went unread. At no point does the name "Nietzsche" appear in any of Kafka's published works or in the documents that have survived him, and yet proof of Kafka's acquaintance with Nietzsche is incontestable. Kafka studied him, a fact that can be read from patterns of imagery and persiflage plainly evident in Kafka's early work "Description of a Struggle" ("Beschreibung eines Kampfes," 1936); they point to an intimate knowledge of *Thus Spoke Zarathustra*. It cannot be an accident that the haunting figure of the hunter Gracchus in the prose fragment of this name fell to his death while in pursuit of a chamois. One need only consult "The Other Dancing Song" from *Zarathustra* to find the (astonishing) lines: "I am the hunter; would you be my dog or my chamois. . . ."[15]

Kafka mentions Thomas Mann only twice — once in his travel diaries and once in a letter — but in the latter Mann is "one whose writings I hunger for." The surmise arises that *The Metamorphosis* (*Die Verwandlung*, 1915), with its famous imagery of hungering, might allude to a scandalous short story by Mann. At the close of *The Metamorphosis*, Kafka describes Gregor's way of experiencing music as his *use* of music. On hearing his sister's violin playing, Gregor heads directly for his sister's shapely neck, which he intends to kiss while remaining on aggressive alert for intrusive strangers as she plays her violin entirely for him. When Gregor was a man, and he had money, he was a music-philistine; without money, he is a music-lover, or more precisely, the decadent lover of a musician. It is at this point that we detect a wild parody of the final scene of Mann's story "The Blood of the Walsungs," which tells of incestuous lovemaking between brother and sister after they have been enthralled by the music of Wagner's opera "The Valkyries."[16]

As a final remark on Kafka's genius, we would simply advertise to readers who have not yet learned German that reading Kafka in the original ought to be a great incentive: the power of his work depends greatly on the understated elegance and refinement of his writing. His prose in German is unlike that of any of his contemporaries. Even when he complains of arrested inspiration, the lament is beautiful.

All these components of Kafka's genius must be understood as creative under very great duress. While other minds caught up in the swiftly expanding industrial modernity of Bohemia, called "the Manchester of Central Europe," produced so much coal, so to speak, in Kafka that pressure produced diamonds that (not to coin a phrase) "burn always with this hard, gem-like flame."[17] We are signaling here the hardship and oppression under which he wrote, which testifies to extraordinary inner resources. He was ill from tuberculosis, as we have mentioned, especially during the last decade of his short life, an ailment much aggravated in 1918 by the Spanish flu — the pandemic that killed some 50 million people worldwide. Without that additional trauma, he might well have been cured.[18]

Furthermore, there was Kafka's professional life: he was gainfully employed. From the beginning he wrote his stories and novels — his copious letters and diary entries — at night, after having slept only a little and after having put in six consecutive hours of concentrated work at his extremely demanding day job as a high-ranking lawyer and bureaucrat. But this "pressure" is again a very mixed affair. On the one hand, his work in the office was grueling, even "hellish";[19] on the other hand, his office experience nourished his fiction, a fact not sufficiently appreciated but which several essays in this volume point out. Kafka had significant responsibilities, which also constituted a field for creativity at the law. Indeed, during the years of the First World War, he was virtually the CEO of the Workmen's Accident Insurance Institute for the Kingdom of Bohemia in Prague, a post he was able to occupy because, although at first accepted for military service, he was afterward deferred on grounds of his indispensability to the firm.[20] Our new knowledge of the demanding nature of Kafka's day job matters enormously for our sense of how Kafka came to his night's work. Kafka's prose poetry arises, not after a day's finger-tapping at an anonymous office desk but typically after writing or dictating intricate briefs of genuine social importance. Many lives and livelihoods depended on Kafka's success in introducing such safety measures as cylindrical lathe shafts less inclined to chop off workers' fingers, and prohibiting brandy-drinking and pipe-smoking in the immediate vicinity of dynamite sheds in quarries.[21]

The office writings play an important role in Kafka's fiction. They move spectrally through his fiction, an adverb to be taken quite literally, since, in a letter to his lover Milena Jesenská, Kafka describes the office as not a machine in which workers like himself might be "a little cog" or "a big wheel." Rather, "to me," he wrote, "the office is a human being — watching me with innocent eyes wherever I am, a living person to whom I have become attached in some way unknown to me." The office, in his words, "is not dumb, it is phantasmal" (*LM,* 126).[22] These phantasms might also refer, as Paul North has noted, to "the sociological, political, and legal concepts regularly left out of Kafka criticism — including empirical psychology, theories of mass behavior, developments in industrial machinery, accident statistics, social insurance laws, and actual court battles."[23] Kafka's experience in the office — and on-site — undergoes the transformations of Kafka's "dream-like inner life" but still emerges as recognizable for what it once was.

Consider a few examples, beginning with farms and quarries: they are two of the workplaces that preoccupied Kafka. One aspect of insuring farms seems to have had a lasting impact on Kafka. For a number of pragmatic reasons, the institute proposed the solution of offering small farmers flat insurance rates, simply related to acreage and the kind and number of machines in operation.

In his report for 1908, Kafka wrote that a prerequisite for flat-rate insurance is "to establish the particulars pertaining to the extent of the fields and pastures as well as of the net income" of the individual farms. But in a note of protest sent to the Ministry of the Interior in 1911, he declared that this project was foundering on the issue of competent land surveying. Many small farmers had complained about the resulting flat-rate calculations, arguing that, owing to the mountainous nature of their land, the surveys were invalid. Lacking reliable data, Kafka's note concludes, the institute would have to operate in "complete darkness" until new legislation for comprehensive insurance was passed.[24]

A number of Kafka's oblique diary entries bearing on his fictional work arise from this situation. He writes of "a connoisseur, an expert, someone who knows his *field*, knowledge, to be sure, that cannot be imparted but that fortunately no one seems to stand in need of" (*D*2, 197).[25] Here he is thinking, surely, of his inner life and the writings that come out of it. But what he had had to deal with in early days were pretend-experts, who did *not* know their *fields* — did not have the knowledge, to be sure, that can be imparted and that unfortunately "everyone" seems to stand in need of.

This situation of incompetent land surveying throws light on the hero of *The Castle* who, as we know, is also a pretend land surveyor. Kafka scholars, very few of whom have bothered to familiarize themselves with Kafka's tribulations with flat-acreage taxation, have had to take a long way round to get to the truth of the hero's situation and pretensions. The German word for this functionary is "Landvermesser," which means "surveyor" — someone who measures the land. Some critics have preferred to break down the word into its components: *Land* (country) and *Vermesser* (measurer) but, by dint of the prefix *Ver-*, also *mis*-measurer, with the result that we have in the character K. a country bumpkin mismeasurer, a dense misapprehender of things — a figure that might then hark back to Kafka's interest in Hasidic fables, which speak of the "Mann vom Lande," the countryman who comes to hear the Rabbi's elliptical wisdom but does not get *it* or, as in Kafka's great parable "Before the Law," the man who comes seeking entrance to the Law and who does not get *in*. But there is a certain chutzpah in that effort to gain entry, a notion tipped off by the ghostly presence in the word for surveyor (Landvermesser) of the German word "Vermessenheit" — hubris, insolence, overweening ambition — so we now have — in lieu of a land surveyor — a country bumpkin hugely impudent mis-measurer of things.

Now this reading, which like almost any reading of Kafka of a certain ingeniousness is bound to be at least a bit right, might still be brought down to earth, as it were, by a knowledge of Kafka's early experience of pretend farmland surveyors.

In the case of the quarries, we have one more instance of a vivid and suggestive congruence between Kafka's work world and his literary dream world, owing to the clarity of the legal scholar Jack Greenberg's gaze. "One visit to a quarry site," Greenberg has written,

> may have imprinted itself on Kafka's memory and found its way into *The Trial*. The 1914 report on quarry safety describes a quarry in which there was "a loose block of stone 1 cubic meter" and accompanied the text with a photograph. That year, Kafka began writing *The Trial*, which ends in a chilling execution scene in a quarry . . . . As the executioners lead K. to his execution, the author relates that: "the other man searched for some suitable spot in the quarry. When he had found it, he waved, and the other gentleman led K. over to it. It was near the quarry wall, where a loose block of stone was lying." It is not difficult to surmise that the loose 1 cubic meter block of stone of the quarry report prompted Kafka's imagination of the loose block of stone of *The Trial*. At that spot, they executed K. with a knife to the heart. He died "like a dog." (*OW*, 357–58)

This is a find that gives us a great deal of morbid pleasure but also gives us work to do when we try to grasp the meaning of the spin that Kafka has put onto the stone. In the quarry report, the stone presented a mortal danger to workers: it lay in the path of their wagons. It would be easy to stumble over it and then crash onto steep rock. It is a kind of danger inherent to the life of the worker. Now Kafka's hero in *The Trial* is a high-ranking bank bureaucrat who, by all appearances, has given little thought to the working conditions of the underclass — or for that matter, to anything other than his normal pleasures and normal progress upward through society. Is Kafka expiating pangs of social conscience when he has this average bourgeois (in certain respects not unlike his author), insufficiently attentive to the pain of others, stabbed to death, *Inferno*-like, on that very stone?

The essays by many hands that follow fall with a sort of scholarly naturalness into five categories: each is liberally, and we hope exemplarily, represented. They are, very briefly, philology, rhetoric, influence, culture (institutions, machinery), and global echoes (from Israel, from England, from Italy). Along with their variety of theme and content, these essays feature a variety of generational standpoints: several have been written by some of the most mature and well-established Kafka scholars; others, by younger scholars (even, in a few cases, advanced graduate students) representing a new wave of Kafka scholarship.

We begin our account of these chapters by pointing out that the focus — literally and figuratively — of Kafka scholarship has changed dramatically at the start of the new century; this change is owed in large part to the interest in the handwritten texts that went unpublished during Kafka's lifetime. These were the drafts used by Max Brod, as well as later editors, as a basis for Kafka's posthumously published books. Roland Reuß is the textual critic who, more than any other, has made us aware of the ways in which literal misreadings of text can lead to figurative misreadings. As editor of the *Historisch-kritische Franz Kafka-Ausgabe*, the first volume of which appeared in 1997 with subsequent volumes appearing and continuing to appear, Reuß offers unprecedented insights into the creative process of Kafka's writing. After all, Kafka was a (hand)writer! And as such, his total text — that is, crossed-out words, substituted words, markings over and under lines — bears interpretation, not just the words that were ultimately extracted from these labyrinths by editors bent on producing readable books. Dealing with the works that Kafka did not publish himself is like dealing with drafts on their way to becoming text, which is Reuß's especially cogent observation, since this transformation is precisely what occurred in the case of his own essay. The essay we print developed from a video transcript of a free-style talk that we worked into a "running text" — Ruth Gross transcribed it, Stanley Corngold rewrote and shaped it — in a way similar to Reuß's idea of a Kafkan running text.

Mark Harman attends with comparable precision to Kafka's rhetoric, prompting him to address the question of metaphor in Kafka anew. Writing against what has been the idée reçue that Kafka's avowed repugnance for metaphor meant that his work was devoid of metaphor, Harman puts the matter in a different light: Kafka's resistance to metaphor was the product of his very facility, a response to the torrent of metaphor that assailed him. His work is replete with metaphors, which surge up uncontrollably in inappropriate places, notably the very places where Kafka denounces the cognitive unreliability of such figures. Kafka was said by his friend Johannes Urzidil to have identified prowess in metaphor as the very hallmark of the poet, and Kafka did not take pains to exclude himself from this company. At the same time he might well have feared, like goodness, dying in his own too much (*Hamlet*, act 4, scene 7, lines 116–17). Kafka's suspicion of metaphor abides in tension with his rich incorporation of the figure. It is quite untrue that his repugnance for metaphor amounts to a systemic "purification" of his prose. Proust remarked about Flaubert that one could look in vain for a single lustrous metaphor; on the strength of Kafka's adoration of Flaubert, critics have inclined to attribute the same deliberate poverty to Kafka, but this idea is demonstrably false. Recall, for example, the narrator's formulation of Georg Bendemann's absentmindedness:

> A long time ago he had firmly decided to observe everything very exactly so as to avoid being taken by surprise in some devious way, from behind or from above. Now he remembered that long-forgotten decision once again and forgot it, the way one draws a short thread through the eye of the needle. (*KSS*, 10)[26]

Comparisons of such elegance cannot be referred to a casual slippage of attention by the purist author: Kafka was not nodding; he was allowing his prowess to show.

According to Max Brod, Nietzsche "was the almost mathematically exact opposite pole" to Kafka. Brod continues his polemic by excoriating the "instinct" of those Kafka critics who "do not stop at putting Kafka and Nietzsche on the same level — as if even the vaguest of possible connections or comparisons rather than pure contradiction were possible here."[27] Walter Sokel, the author of the chapter on Kafka's "Dionysian Connection," needs no defense of his formidable instinct for the reading of Kafka: he is by common consent the most powerful and original interpreter of Kafka of the last century. We use the latter category advisedly, as Walter Sokel now approaches the full century of his life as a scholar and thinker. Far more in tune with intellectual currents of this century than Brod might ever have been, Sokel propounds the view, in the words of Benno Wagner, that Kafka's work is "engaged almost line by line with Nietzsche, in the most intimate and intense dialogue."[28] Sokel's reading of the Dionysian element in Kafka gives concrete evidence of the rightness of the view.

Working with Nietzsche's distinction between "ego and "deep self," Sokel reads "The Judgment" (Das Urteil, 1913), Kafka's breakthrough story, as the story of a breakthrough of the deep self (of Georg Bendemann) though the crust of the joyless empirical ego; in this light Kafka's breakthrough is enabled by the breaking in of Nietzsche's Dionysianism. Georg's ecstatic leap into a river very like Kafka's Vltava at a moment when the flux of vehicular traffic, commodity exchange, and sexual intercourse is "nothing short of infinite" is Dionysianism *pur sang*. The same logic of the usurpation of the sway of the empirical ego by something deeper and more nearly connected to the biological self bent on power informs Gregor Samsa's metamorphosis. As the family invalid and hence family tyrant who exults in the new-found capacities of his body, he emerges, despite appearances, as a figure of Dionysus.

Uta Degner proposes a reading of "The Judgment" as well, now as a contest of literary styles. Her approach takes one into the main current of Kafka studies that might be summed up in the slogan "Only contextualize." Here, Pierre Bourdieu's historical sociology of literary form stands the critic in good stead. Bourdieu sees the state of the art of writing in Kafka's early years as a contest of literary modes — realist versus aestheticist — and Degner puts this thesis to work in "The Judgment" with surprising results. Statements by the protagonist Georg Bendemann suggest his indifference, his lack of attention to real world details, an attitude signaled from the start that shows him neither observing the world carefully through his window nor concentrating on the task at hand: instead, he "toys" with the crucial letter to a friend. In this way he displays the qualities of the relaxed, "aestheticist" mind, at home in its own imaginary universe. On the other hand, in this contrast of types, Bendemann's father comes forth chiefly as the realist, as situated (or once upon a time situated) in the real world of commerce: he is a businessman who established the firm that Georg has made flourish: it is Georg's patrimony. Degner's idea is to see this contest of types as allegorizing the style-types singled out by Bourdieu as dominant in Kafka's literary world. But Kafka, who is famously averse to antitheses, promotes their opposition only long enough to ironize it by showing that each of these characters in fact shares qualities of his putative opposite. This ironical turn also conveys the empirical truth that Kafka's early work *mingles* both styles. His works abound in the exact perception of real world details at the same time that they enact the aestheticist stance via the musical and visual charm of his prose.

Katja Garloff studies another primal scene of contestation: she reaches deep into current theorizing on gender to conjure a formative moment of sexual repression that illuminates the plight of the ape Rotpeter in "A Report to an Academy" ("Ein Bericht für eine Akademie," 1919). His predicament might be reconstructed from a scene of racialization, in which the creature is forced to suffer the consciousness of an ethnic object of desire forever prohibited to him. In the case of the ape, it is the desire fostered in him by his teachers and masters — "a desire for the human that is at once solicited and prohibited." He will never be permitted to mate with a human being; the reader is struck by the melancholy tone with which he reports his nightly encounters with a half-crazed chimpanzee. There is an unmistakable subtext or parallel to this narrative; it is that of the Jew whose assimilation, in the anti-Semitic climate of the time, is limited by the prohibition on interracial marriage. Both Kafka and his vice-exister the ape are stuck in a melancholy that also empowers an uncanny facility for imitation, for mimicry. But when Rotpeter's ascent into full species hybridity is examined, one feels an exhilaratingly witty undermining of these various suppositions about the species divide. The acts that the ape is encouraged to imitate are the acts of apish human beings. Furthermore, there is an uncanny play in these concepts provided by Kafka's extreme literalization, through the ape, of alleged Jewish mimicry. The stereotypical figure, the metaphor, of the Jew as mimic is, as it were, driven to distraction by Kafka's relentless "orchestration of variations on [his] theme" (*D2*, 184).[29] The same rhetorical tactic of extreme literalization also allows Kafka to undo the notion of a "blood community," embedded in the racialist discourse of the time.

Jacob Burnett brings in another sort of cultural reference with unexpected results: topology, the "strange loop." The loop is famously illustrated by the Möbius strip: one advances only to return to one's starting point. The cogency of this figure to K.'s peregrinations around Kafka's Castle is evident. Modern literature as a whole is rife with such loop-figures, with their connotations of irony and paradox and self-undoing; what we have here are the markings of a world picture light-years removed from the medieval, with its spiritual topography of center, circle, and transcendence. This loss of a firm orientation might not be an occasion for despair — not at all. The "loop" points up "a new dimension of existence," the modern stairway that has its own logic of apparent hierarchy and its own allure as a path accessible to a higher good. But that good is only its perpetual untenability as a spur to interpretation en route, a circuit that always ends in a return to "self" reflecting on its own waiting-for-Godot-like predicament. Roland Barthes famously saw that the verb "to write," in the hands of the moderns, is an *intransitive* verb. This mutation, for Burnett, also applies to the verb "to interpret," which marks an ineluctable way of being in the world. Kafka is the poet of the modern mode of existence *as* the interpretation of the loss of firm categorical distinctions.

The new century has seen the attention of many Kafka scholars shift to the hitherto underestimated element of Kafka's intellectual universe supplied by his professional life, a topic further developed by Doreen Densky. Her essay revisits the symbiotic relation of Kafka's work life to his literary work and thought. The chief connecting figure is the proxy, the stand-in, the representative. Just as Kafka, who held "Prokura" (proxy power), was entitled to sign and thereby authorize documents of which he was not the author (nor, as he confesses, on occasion not even the reader), Kafka's literary protagonists assume proxy functions. They do so by performing actual proxy-like acts, presuming to stand in for whole classes of men. Think of Karl Rossmann in *Der Verschollene*, blindly assuming the role of advocate in the predicament of the proletarian stoker; think of Joseph K., mounting a platform during his own interrogation to speak on behalf of those whose pleas go unheard by the court. In another sense, these proxies are often figural narrators: they stand in for the putatively absolute authority of the absent author but do so only deficiently. For that absent wholeness of vision, they introduce an only partial perspective. As communicators they are essentially liars, on the principle, following Kafka, that the truth of what is the case cannot be "communicated." "It is," however, "only in the chorus that a certain truth might lie."[30] Densky's account of the many intermediators, communicators, representatives, stand-ins — in short, proxies — throughout Kafka's work conveys the irrefutable truth of Kafka's own being in the world, for consider the famous aphorism:

> He does not live for the sake of his personal life; he does not think for the sake of his personal thoughts. It seems to him that he lives and thinks under the compulsion of a family, which, it is true, is itself superabundant in life and thought, but for which he constitutes, in obedience to some law unknown to him, a formal necessity. (*GWC*, 269)[31]

What is generally clear is that today's conversation on Kafka has turned from the ever-central psychological and inward world of his protagonists to the traumatic state of the material, though human, world around them — and, by extension to *us*. It is as if in reading Kafka we were sounding out what he has to say about our world from his art of describing *his* world in prescient ways. In addressing the institutional structures of the state, the abolition of space and time in the age of perennial "telepresence," the trauma inflicted by rapid travel, and even the impact of the movies on the modern text, the critical discourse of the moment finds Kafka at the center.

Turns-of-the-century — artificial markers of change, at best — engender thoughts of futurism and the new; at the same time they call for perspectives on the significant movements of previous decades. Looking back from the twenty-first century, Ritchie Robertson, in "Kafka, Goffman, and the Total Institution," observes that one of the qualities attributed to Kafka by non-scholarly readers is an ability to prophesize the future, to foresee developments in the century that followed his death. But Robertson, like Rolf Goebel in his essay on Paul Virilio's "teletopical" city, observes as well that if Kafka seems to have understood what would happen later in the twentieth century, it was not his "prevision of the future but his perception of his present" that enabled him to do so. Kafka is especially lucid about mechanisms of power, authority, and violence — in short, the total institution that, as Erving Goffman would later maintain, aims to supervise and dictate totally the behavior of its inhabitants. For Kafka, the original total institution is the family, "the place where power, guilt, law, and punishment originate." The patterns of oppression and subservience that Kafka felt he experienced as a child and later excoriates in "Letter to his Father" recur not only, as we might expect, in his prose texts set in family circles, like *The Metamorphosis* and "The Judgment," but reappear, much elaborated, in his texts on bureaucratic organizations, such as *The Trial* and *The Castle*. In an opposing thrust, Kafka also created moments — the most lyrical — at which certain characters, like Frieda or K. in *The Castle*, in a kind of resistance to an enveloping institution, dream of escape. Kafka himself persistently envisioned a "way out" of the institutionalization of both his professional and personal life, first with his break from the family when he and Dora moved to Berlin and then with his unfulfilled dream of emigrating to Palestine.

Institutions of the twentieth century have morphed into those of the twenty-first, and their power continues to reside in their pervasiveness, illusory or real, as well as our willingness to acquiesce to them. But because they are virtual and reside in a non-place of time and space, according to Paul Virilio — the controversial theorist of space, speed, and telecommunication — they are also inescapable: no matter how strenuously we desire to free ourselves from institutional control, the citizen of the "teletopical city" will be enslaved.[32]

In "Kafka in Virilio's Teletopical City," Rolf Goebel examines Virilio's work as it relates to Kafka's prescient texts. The miracle that allows Kafka criticism to thrive and take on new directions is, as we have come to understand, the uniquely Kafkan text. Goebel points to the dynamic process of continuing exploration that never reaches "interpretive closure": this is the reality of Kafka the writer, insuring new readings and investigations "far into the future." Kafka's uncanny insight into his present provokes the idea that he is "anticipating" the future, here the "technocratic universe of a post-humanistic age." Read through Virilio's conceptual lens, Kafka emerges as a seer, but just because Kafka's narratives and descriptions are ambiguous and always elusive does not mean that they can be taken as prophetic. Still, Virilio foresees the ultimate oncoming abolition of space and time in a world of telepresence; and yet again hasn't Kafka already experimented with the human experience of such a reality and, indeed, with the abolition of its rules, in "An Everyday Confusion"?[33]

Kafka encountered the electronic immediacy of our telepresent world in the cinema; his visual narrative and experience of early movies have been a subject of interest for some time. In the 1990s, with scholars building on the tradition of interarts studies, the concept of "intermediality" took hold, especially in the German-speaking research community, and this term can be fruitfully applied to Kafka's unique modes of seeing. Although an umbrella term that has different nuances in different fields, intermediality serves to heighten awareness of medial border-crossings and hybridization in works of art. In "Kafka's Visual Method: The Gaze, the Cinematic, and the Intermedial," Peter Beicken expands this discourse to include Kafka's utilization of innovative strategies in narrative perspective that leads to what he calls the cinematic quality of his texts, a quality developed even before Kafka actually "went to the movies." In his earliest texts, techniques reminiscent of camera shots or views through a lens abound — among them the fascinated gaze, gaze guidance, changing angles of perspective, and zooming in on a subject. Once Kafka was able to experience film as a real medium, he began to employ cinematic devices directly in his narrative perspectives. In this way, he creates a kind of literary screen — a "trans-form" — the intermedial event that places the reader/viewer into the situation of experiencing a scene as if she were seeing it through the camera eye.

What lifts the discrete images on a strip of film from their position laid out in space is speed, the speed with which they are spun through a projector creating a single moving image. Speed that transforms the fundamental elements of modernity is a crucial and accelerating category, and so it was for Kafka, who persistently recorded his anxieties about rapid train travel. In John Zilcosky's "'Samsa war Reisender': Trains, Trauma, and the Mechanized Body," we are reminded that humans have had to make hard adjustments, both physical and mental, to technological advances as they occurred; speed has always come at a cost to bodily and psychical well-being. Medical reports from Kafka's time record the debilitating effects to the body and nervous system seemingly caused by railway travel — claims of "railway spine" and "railway brain." Seen through this lens of cultural studies, *The Metamorphosis* illustrates how Gregor's symptoms at the opening of the novella — horrible dreams, a vague sense of alarm, unusual loquacity and excitability, and even blurred vision — typify the symptoms of railway-crash victims. Because travelers did not understand how these vehicles worked, they increasingly felt alienated — like commodities. As an insurance lawyer, Kafka read railway accident reports; and as the representative of his institute, he frequently had to take trains himself to provincial courts and businesses. This came at a cost: he was deeply disturbed by their vibrations and turbulence, anxieties that he then transferred to his protagonist Gregor Samsa. These are Gregor's "readable" symptoms, at the same time that he has been endowed with a full panoply of "unreadable" symptoms — signs that have been read in different ways in every decade since the vermin's first appearance in print. Zilcosky's focus on the damaged body and brain provides our speed-obsessed new century with yet another possibility of interpretation.

In the twenty-first century speed is a virtue, at least in the world of commerce, communication, and transportation. Virilio has noted that speed is not merely a concept of effective travel but in a telepresent society applies to all seeing, hearing, and perceiving. We conceive our modernity through the fact and demand of speed, which, to say the least, increases the opportunity for Kafkaesque effects: "He has forecast the multiplication of the opportunities for unintelligibility in what is called the media" (*OW*, 10).

Speed shrinks the world. The concept of the "global" applies to almost every realized project, be it commercial or artistic. And whether in Prague or London, in Jerusalem or Rome, Kafka's prose has become a touchstone. In the twentieth century there was often talk of Kafka's "universal" appeal, a term to which many scholars rightly objected.[34] In the twenty-first, "Global Kafka" is all the rage. Our collection includes three essays that reflect this consciousness while at the same time illuminating the source texts.

In "The Comfort of Strangeness: Correlating the Kafkaesque and the Kafkan in Kazuo Ishiguro's *The Unconsoled*," Robert Lemon applies a Kafkan (not Kafkaesque!) scholarly lens to an English novel that, from its explicit indebtedness to Kafka, has not surprisingly been called "frustrating," "difficult," "confusing," and "absurd." Ishiguro's novel, with its indeterminate setting, dream-like tone, and absence of conventional narrative resolution, welters in Kafkan themes, such as music, ethnology, and familial conflict. There is a significant difference, however, between this postmodern work and Kafka's narratives: Ishiguro eschews the "comfort" of a recognizable diegetic form — an avoidance that has the paradoxical result of propelling the novel to an unexpected conclusion and resolution. In this way, Ishiguro creates what might sooner be considered a modernist work, precisely because it provides the reader with a recognizable resolution or what Lyotard calls modernist "good form." Kafka, on the other hand, in both his short fictions and his longer novels, offers his readers traditional "good forms" but "missing contents" and leaves his readers perplexed by an unresolved ending. His works, more like standard examples of postmodern fiction, withhold narrative resolution; and, hence, it is Kafka, not Ishiguro, who leaves his readers "unconsoled." Just as the Kafkan mode has crossed geographic borders, modern and postmodern fiction have exchanged characteristics and crossed boundaries of their own.

Iris Bruce's essay "Kafka's Journey into the Future: Crossing Borders into Israeli/Palestinian Worlds," takes Kafka on the journey he wished for himself. Kafka's desire to emigrate to Palestine went unfulfilled, but we learn from recent newspaper reports that many Israelis now consider him part of their cultural heritage: they argue that because Kafka was Jewish, his works belong "at home." Bruce points out that while Israelis may well claim him as their own, it is significant that in the 125 years since his birth, they have yet to name a street after him.

Bruce reads Kafka's "Jackals and Arabs" ("Schakale und Araber," 1917) as a critical representation of Jewish racial prejudice in early Palestine. The jackals express the views of the indigenous religious Jews; the Arabs express the documented Arab sentiments of Kafka's day. In this light, Kafka's story feeds the traditional Israeli resistance to Kafka, given the perpetual climate of ethnic conflict, adding yet another difficulty to the shadow of uneasiness cast by the diasporic Jew. Nonetheless, Kafka's works stand behind the works of Israeli writers on both sides of the Israeli/Palestinian divide, notably Emile Habiby, an Israeli Palestinian, who is the only writer to have won major literary prizes from both the PLO and the Israeli government, and the eminent novelist and philosopher A. B. Yehoshua. Their novels display Kafka's stories as vivid intertexts. The ambiguity and dialogical nature of his prose appeal to their sense of irony and satire, devices that both writers employ, despite their different perspectives, to criticize life in contemporary Israel.

We know that on several occasions Kafka went by train to Northern Italy. His experiences in Brescia and Riva del Garda figure not only in his travel writings but also in his fiction. While scholars have examined what Kafka took from his Italian experiences, few have explored the converse: what Italian literature has taken from Kafka. In "Kafka and Italy: A New Perspective on the Italian Literary Landscape," Saskia Ziolkowski sets out to map a distinct but unexamined Kafkan tradition in Italian literary modernism. From animal imagery to representations of identity crises, alienation, haunting spaces, and repressive bourgeois relations, Italian literature is shot through with Kafka's obsessive themes. A wide range of modern authors, including Italo Svevo, Elsa Morante, Cesare Pavese, Tomaso Landolfi, Primo Levi, Italo Calvino, and Claudio Magris, all acknowledge Kafka as a compelling, influential, or beloved writer. A notable exception is Dino Buzzati, who has refused to admit any family resemblance to Kafka in his work, revealing his anxiety of influence: to be called Kafkaesque is to vacate all claims to originality. Though this reaction may seem misplaced, it testifies to Kafka's pervasive presence in modern Italian writing. Ziolkowski focuses on Svevo's "Argo and his Master," a story that until now has not often been connected to Kafka, despite its protagonist, a man who learns to understand "dog-language." The comparison to "A Report to an Academy" illuminates both works. Italian modernism in a Kafkan key suggests that, as his work has informed the work of twentieth-century Italian authors, the study of Kafka criticism will usefully inform the work of twenty-first century Italian scholars.

Let us reconsider in 2011 the celebrated remark made in 1945 by the English poet W. H. Auden: "Had one to name the artist who comes nearest to bearing the same kind of relation to our age that Dante, Shakespeare and Goethe bore to theirs, Kafka is the first one would think of."[35] Kafka, Auden says, stands in the same relation to the past hundred years as Dante, Shakespeare, and Goethe stood to their centuries — he is our representative, the poet who gives us shape and form.

It has become natural to see Kafka as Auden did, as the inevitable expression of our modernity — and more: he is said to have intuited its catastrophes and its scars, visible already in this infant twenty-first century. But there is a dialectical side to the question of a Kafka for the twenty-first century — the question of Kafka's relation to the centuries that precede the twenty-first, indeed that precede his birth.

We have heard and read about Kafka's "forward looking," his "foreshadowing" of the present and recent past — a claim that owes much to a questionable "backshadowing" in the sense given this term by the literary scholar Michael Bernstein. Armed with hindsight, we invest early events — here, Kafka's consciousness of small disasters — with a profound significance.[36] But now we are interested in asking the shadow side of this question: If Kafka is so often held to be forward-looking (into the face of the disasters of the twentieth century, above all, into its fatal marriage of technology and terror), why is his imagination so often backward-looking, in the quite literal sense that it analytically reimagines ancient and past civilizations? He locates stories and parables in Old Testament settings (viz. Abraham as a rag-and-bone man) and in a mythicized Greece (viz. the Sirens, Prometheus enchained, Poseidon harassed). He alludes to the world of Alexander the Great, and in several "Chinese stories" he sinks deeply into old China. We encounter the early medieval figure of the hunter Gracchus and later medieval settings of pieces about the law.

Are we helped to understand this gesture by the motive termed "the escapist turn to myth" allegedly on display in modernist literature? No. Kafka's treatment of the Chinese empire, for one, is not so much a conjuring of myth as an analytic study of the relation of the Chinese people to *their* myths.

Kafka's relation to ancient Greece is more than a borrowing of a myth to lend structure to a narrative foundering in the chaos of modern experience; it is more than a borrowing of detail for the sake of scenic color. Consider his surprising treatment of the Greek mind, their fate, and their gods apropos his response to Brod's book, *Paganism, Christianity, Judaism* mentioned above. It is an expression of sympathy for a religion that concedes a "democratic" possibility of happiness in daily life without the need to strive for the divine — an ideal of happiness, incidentally impossible for us, which thereafter haunts Kafka's Zürau aphorisms.

It is here that we wish to turn in a different direction by asking a tributary question. What if, as a thought experiment, we reverse the direction of the question posed above? What if we ask not only about what Kafka teaches us of the past; not only about the imaginative obligation that Kafka felt to the past — to which his historical dislocation of character, scene, thought, and action is a response. What if we oblige ourselves to think not only of the past *in* Kafka, the past into which he inserts himself imaginatively, but of the Kafka who emerges *when we, his legatees, think him into the past*? Can we, being true to Kafka's own adventurous historical spirit and to the discourse on Kafka, imagine a Kafka in other eras . . . and with what results?

In "'I Always Wanted You to Admire My Fasting'; or, Looking at Kafka," Philip Roth made a start in alienating Kafka into an unlikely time and place; he has him reappear as a Newark Hebrew teacher and mooted suitor to an Aunt Rhoda a decade or more after his real death. But we are asking rather about Kafka in the times before his birth.

A Greek Kafka seems natural, since we have heard of his familiarity with that myth-saturated world; Roman literature knows a Kafka of sorts in Petronius at Trimalchio's surrealistic banquet. One can imagine a Renaissance Kafka decked out in Florentine doublet and hose (perhaps because he was a clothes horse), briefly at home at the Medici court before his exile. Kafka as a nineteenth-century officer or official and writer is easy to conceive. We think of his "blood relative" Kleist, who, as Dr. Kleist, the dentist, "pumps air into me like a pig's bladder"; on better evidence, Kafka's elective affinity with Kleist seems assured.[37] There are his other nineteenth-century "blood relatives": Grillparzer, Dostoevsky, and, above all, Flaubert; we see Kafka in conversation with them while standing in an archival office in Vienna or strolling along a leaf-strewn path in Baden-Baden or facing the sea wind on a Norman bench.

A medieval Kafka might be harder to envision at first; a world without highly developed bureaucracies would seem to have little to offer him, until we shift the author of "The Problem of our Laws" to twelfth-century Córdoba — a brilliant adjunct to Averroës and Maimonides. Further north, a century later, at the University of Paris, we find him debating questions of natural theology, at the cost of being called a *murmurante*.

Most challenging, perhaps, is an Enlightenment Kafka, so different is his tone from the confident mockery of Voltaire or the bluntness of the late Kant, say, on marriage. There is Kafka's vitalism, his skepticism as to the curative value of knowledge acquisition. But Kafka and Rousseau share the same religion of the imagination . . . . Our task seems endless, and endlessly interesting.

Kafka as a lamp onto "what will have been" sets us on a track to a different understanding of our intellectual history;[38] and as he does so, he gives us evidence of his perennial freshness. Kafka and the twenty-first century is “what will be.” Kafka in a tunic or a rabbi’s robe is “what will have been” if the Kafka discourse that has proven so rich continues its work. And why not? It is a discourse that seems to have no boundaries. So perhaps this is how Kafka will exist, or will have existed, tomorrow.

Notes

[1] “Die Klage: Wenn ich ewig sein werde, wie werde ich morgen sein?” (*NS* 2, 71).

[2] Reiner Stach, *Kafka: Die Jahre der Erkenntnis* (Frankfurt am Main: Fischer, 2008), 244.

[3] “Die ungeheuere Welt, die ich im Kopfe habe” (*Ta,* 562); “den dunklen Mächten, diese Entfesselung von Natur aus gebundener Geister” (*Br,* 384).

[4] “Wo war der Richter den er nie gesehen hat?” (*P,* 312).

[5] Amanda Torres, “Kafka and the Common Law: The Roots of the ‘Kafkaesque’ in *The Trial*,” unpublished seminar paper for “Kafka and the Law,” Columbia U School of Law, 7 May 2007, 10–11.

[6] Theodor Adorno, “Notes on Kafka,” in *Prisms*, trans. Samuel Weber and Shierry Weber (London: Spearman, 1967), 246.

[7] This sentence was contributed by Ritchie Robertson to the “Proposal” for the Princeton-Oxford-Humboldt Kafka Consortium. http://www.princeton.edu/international/doc/GCRF-KAFKA-network.pdf.

[8] “Die besondere Art meiner Inspiration in der ich Glücklichster und Unglücklichster jetzt um 2 Uhr nachts schlafen gehe [sie wird vielleicht, wenn ich nur den Gedanken daran ertrage, bleiben, denn sie ist höher als alle früheren], [~~und zweifellos bin ich jetzt im Geistigen der Mittelpunkt von Prag~~] ist die, daß ich alles kann, nicht nur auf eine bestimmte Arbeit hin. Wenn ich wahllos einen Satz hinschreibe z.B. Er schaute aus dem Fenster so ist er schon vollkommen” (*Ta,* 30), also *Kritische Kafka-Ausgabe: Tagebücher; Apparatband* (1990), 169.

[9] Readers who have not been fortunate enough to visit Kafka’s manuscript at the Bodleian library should consult its facsimile on p. 56f. of the Oxforder Quartheft 1 [2001], in Roland Reuß and Peter Staengele, eds., *Franz Kafka, Historisch-Kritische Ausgabe sämtlicher Handschriften, Drucke und Typoskripte* (Frankfurt am Main: Stroemfeld, 1995–).

[10] “Du führst die Massen, großer langer Feldherr, führe die Verzweifelten durch die unter dem Schnee für niemanden sonst auffindbaren Passstraßen des Gebirges. Und wer gibt dir die Kraft? Wer dir die Klarheit des Blickes gibt” (*Ta,* 903). Kafka admired a few other rival field marshals: Alexander the Great — and Napoleon — but from a considerable height; both generals, according to expert opinion, were 5 feet 6 inches; Kafka was six feet tall.

[11] J. C. Nyíri, "Einleitung," in *Der Selbstmord als sociale Massenerscheinung der modernen Civilisation,* by Thomas G. Masaryk (Munich: Philosophia Verlag, 1982), 7.

[12] Benno Wagner, "'. . . in der Fremde, aus der Sie kommen . . .': Die Geburt des Schreibens aus der Statistik des Selbstmords," in *Odradeks Lachen: Fremdheit bei Kafka,* ed. Hansjörg Bay and Christof Hamann, Litterae, 136 (Freiburg: Rombach, 2006), 193–228.

[13] "Der Verzückte und der Ertrinkende — beide heben die Arme. Der erste bezeugt Eintracht, der zweite Widerstreit mit den Elementen" (*NS2*, 53).

[14] "Laß die Deutungen!" (*S,* 324).

[15] Friedrich Nietzsche, *Thus Spoke Zarathustra: Third Part,* in *The Portable Nietzsche,* trans and ed. Walter Kaufmann (New York: Viking, 1969), 337.

[16] Mann's story was composed in 1905 and due for publication that year in the *Neue Rundschau.* It was already typeset when Mann suddenly withdrew it, finally realizing that its anti-Semitic tenor would give grievous offense to his wife and her Jewish family. He eventually published it privately in 1921. How then can Kafka have known of it? As early as 1906 Mann sent copies of the story to Arthur Schnitzler and Jakob Wassermann, among others. The story then circulated in samizdat, and news of the scandal was bruited about in Vienna and thereafter, it might well be supposed, in Prague. Kafka was a devoted reader of the *Neue Rundschau* and of the works of Schnitzler and Wassermann and would have perked up at any mention of writings coming from their desk. (Wassermann was one of the several authors whom Kafka declares he was "thinking of" apropos of "The Judgment.")

[17] Walter Pater, *The Renaissance: Studies in Art and Poetry,* ed. Adam Phillips (Oxford: Oxford UP, 1986), 152.

[18] This is the view of Kafka's foremost biographer, Reiner Stach. In an interview published in the *Jerusalem Post,* Stach declares: "I suspect that [in October 1918] Kafka had already recovered from tuberculosis, and for him the Spanish flu presented the real threat." Kafka was very ill from the flu for weeks after he was infected but recovered, while millions of other patients died. http://jewishnews.at/jewish-news-from-austria-21/the-impossibility-of-being-kafka.html. Further details are found in Stach, *Kafka: Die Jahre der Erkennntis.*

[19] ". . . (*real hell is there in the office, no other can hold any terror for me*)" (LF, 238); "(*dort im Bureau ist die wahre Hölle, eine andere fürchte ich nicht mehr*)" (*B2,* 158).

[20] In a book review of *OW,* the Kafka expert Louis Begley wrote, "We are told [by the editors] that 'during the war years [Kafka] was [the institute's] virtual CEO [ix].' A virtual CEO, indeed: he was on the verge of a nervous breakdown most of 1915, and, after the hemorrhage he suffered in August 1917." Begley, *The New Republic,* "Books: *Before the Law,*" 6 May, 2009. This is the reviewer's sarcastic way of disputing the claim, but the objection is unfounded. Until his breakdown in August 1917 Kafka worked constantly and on overtime for the institute. His efforts are evident from a number of documents, especially those concerning his work for

the care of wounded veterans. In fact, he was supposed to be awarded an Imperial "Orden" for his special engagement in this field in 1918, an honor he managed to escape thanks only to the collapse of the empire. Furthermore, in the light of the documents newly presented in *OW*, Kafka's visit to the Frankenstein psychiatric hospital in 1915 almost certainly was related to the institute's search for a site for shell-shocked veterans, a campaign he *organized* (all this notwithstanding, of course, his own personal fate as a nervous patient). This clarification is contained in a communication from Benno Wagner, coeditor of both the German and American editions of Kafka's office writings.

[21] The latter sentences are adapted from *OW*.

[22] "Unter-Unter-Rad" . . . "Ober-Ober-Rad . . . mir aber ist das Bureau . . . ein lebendiger Mensch, der mich, wo ich auch bin, mit seinen unschuldvollen Augen ansieht, ein Mensch, mit dem ich auf ingendeine mir unbekannte Weise verbunden worden bin (*BM*, 169). Kafka's letter to Milena is dated Saturday evening, 31 July 1920.

[23] Paul North, in an unpublished review of Stanley Corngold and Benno Wagner, *Franz Kafka: The Ghosts in the Machine* (Evanston, IL: Northwestern UP, 2011).

[24] This matter is discussed at length in *OW*, 77–79.

[25] "Ein Kenner, ein Fachmann, einer der seinen Teil weiß, ein Wissen, allerdings, das nicht vermittelt werden kann, aber glücklicherweise auch niemandem nötig zu sein scheint" (*Ta*, 869).

[26] "Vor einer langen Weile hatte er sich fest entschlossen, alles vollkommen genau zu beobachten, damit er nicht irgendwie auf Umwegen, von hinten her, von oben herab überrascht werden könne. Jetzt erinnerte er sich wieder an den längst vergessenen Entschluß und vergaß ihn, wie man einen kurzen Faden durch ein Nadelöhr zieht" (*DL*, 50).

[27] Max Brod, *Über Franz Kafka* (Frankfurt am Main: Fischer Bücherei, 1966), 259.

[28] Benno Wagner, "Der Bewerber und der Prätendent: Zur Selektivität der Idee bei Platon und Kafka." *Hofmannsthal Jahrbuch zur europäischen Moderne* 8 (2000): 274.

[29] "Mir immer unbegreiflich . . ., daß ich z. B. im Unglück . . . jemandem schriftlich mitteilen kann: Ich bin unglücklich. Ja, ich kann noch darüber hinausgehn und in verschiedenen Schnörkeln je nach Begabung, die mit dem Unglück nichts zu tun zu haben scheint, darüber einfach oder antithetisch oder mit ganzen Orchestern von Associationen phantasieren. . ." (*Ta*, 834).

[30] "mitteilen kann man nur das was man nicht ist, also die Lüge. Erst im Chor mag eine gewisse Wahrheit liegen" (*NS2*, 348).

[31] "Er lebt nicht wegen seines persönlichen Lebens, er denkt nicht wegen seines persönlichen Denkens. Ihm ist, als lebe und denke er unter der Nötigung einer Familie, die zwar selbst überreich an Lebens- und Denkkraft ist, für die er aber nach irgendeinem ihm unbekannten Gesetz eine formelle Notwendigkeit bedeutet" (*Ta*, 857).

[32] Paul Virilio, "The Third Interval: A Critical Transition," in *Rethinking Technologies*, ed. Verena Andermatt Conley (Minnesota: U of Minnesota P, 1993), 11.

[33] Ruth V. Gross, "Rich Text, Poor Text: A Kafkan Confusion," *PMLA* 95 (1980): 168–82.

[34] Evelyn Beck, "Kafka's Traffic in Women: Gender, Power, and Sexuality," *Literary Review* 26 (1983): 577–87.

[35] W. H. Auden, *Prose, 1939–1948*, in *The Complete Works of W. H. Auden*, ed. Edward Mendelson (Princeton, NJ: Princeton UP, 1986), 2:110.

[36] Michael Bernstein, *Foregone Conclusions: Against Apocalyptic History* (Berkeley: U of California P, 1994).

[37] Walter Hinderer, "'Kleist bläst in mich wie in eine alte Schweinsblase,'" in *Kafka und die Weltliteratur*, ed. Manfred Engel and Dieter Lamping (Göttingen: Vandenhoeck & Ruprecht, 2006).

[38] Jean-François Lyotard, "Answering the Question: What is Postmodernism?" in *The Postmodern Condition: A Report on Knowledge*, trans. G. Bennington and B. Massumi (Minneapolis: U of Minnesota P, 1984), 81.

1: Running Texts, Stunning Drafts

Roland Reuß

During the 1960s, 1970s, and 1980s, Paul Raabe's edition of Kafka's stories titled *Sämtliche Erzählungen* sold a million copies in Germany alone and functioned as the main textual source for many Kafka scholars. This edition contains a curious emendation that has a certain exemplarity. Both the manuscript and all the authorized published versions of Kafka's story "The New Lawyer" ("Der neue Advokat") contain the sentence "Im Allgemeinen billigt das Barreau die Aufnahme des Bucephalus" (In general the bar approves the admission of Bucephalus, *KSS* 60). If any sentence of Kafka's might be termed authentic, it is this one: it is found in the manuscript, in an early printing in Theodor Tagger's journal *Marsyas* (1917) and in the first book version, *A Country Doctor: Little Stories, 1920* (*Ein Landarzt: Kleine Erzählungen*). But there was something about the word "Barreau" (a clear importation from the French "barreau") that evidently disturbed Paul Raabe; without consulting a dictionary, he chose to change the word "Barreau" to "Bureau." For long time this travesty could be found in Raabe's edition, which remained definitive until the 1990s, when Kafka's true word was happily restored. Meanwhile, such emendations are not harmless: this one generated more than one dissertation based on the fantasy of an entire bureaucratic apparatus involved in the authentication of Bucephalus. So if you do not want your reading to be based on philological sand, you must have a reliable editorial basis for your interpretation. Otherwise you are writing about a topic of your own — or in this case, Paul Raabe's — invention.

What I have to say is directed against a tradition of exegesis that takes Kafka's wording for granted. At the same time it is a plea for taking seriously the interdependence of edition and interpretation. A few premises need to be discussed in this context.

First, consider the meaning of a word. The meaning is never something separate from the material sign. Not only is the material basis of the word the one and only proper source of an edition, but it is also the indispensable *point de repère* for every interpretation.

Second, in Kafka's case, the verbal object we interpret when we address the material basis of the octavos and the quartos — including *Amerika: The Missing Person* (*Der Verschollene*, 1927), *The Trial* (*Der*

Process, 1925), and *The Castle* (*Das Schloss*, 1926) — is not so much text as *draft* on its way to becoming text. Texts that Kafka delivered in his publications are one thing — his handwriting is another. Here we have an especially acute instance of a philological difference, which we can define as the difference between a linear text and everything that occupies a place in the manuscript. In the case of handwriting, words crossed out, written above and under the line, and ostensibly deleted from the manuscript — and thereafter restored — call for interpretation. As a consequence, passages that seem to be eliminated are no less important than passages that remain. It is a (hand)writer's thing.

Meanwhile, the Fischer edition of Kafka's works, allegedly produced on the "basis of the manuscripts," implies that no words crossed out by Kafka belong to the constituted text. This publishing decision has had at least one very peculiar consequence: Fischer's text of *The Trial* has three fewer chapters than Max Brod's earlier idiosyncratic version. The Fischer argument is based on the fact that certain chapters in the manuscript, though readable, are crossed out with diagonal strokes. But the important idea has to be grasped that, for example, *the entire text* of *Der Process*, and not only the parts that are crossed out, is a *fragment*. The whole handwritten heritage of Kafka was crossed out by his so called "testaments." To get in touch with the "Nachlass" (the author's surviving documents, unpublished in his lifetime), one is forced to think about the notion of omission and cancellation from a new perspective.

A second consequence of this state of affairs is that the undecidability of passages in the manuscript calls for reflection in its own right. It is not a defect but a philological fact, demanding a very patient, vigilant textual scrutiny and not decisionism.

If you perceive doubts and hesitations in the thought flow of the handwriting, this is a phenomenon that is *by itself* important and not something to be considered regrettable, as something that should never have happened, as in the traditional "scriptive" view of the autograph. You must be careful not to bruise the tissue of the text.

I turn now to the octavo notebooks and their new poetics. Here, Kafka's approach makes use of material parameters to experiment with semantics (I mean by "material parameters" such things as page size, line length, the width of the pencil stroke, and so on). The craft of reading these pages runs contrary to every traditional hermeneutics, which in the end returns to a confident assertion of the author's intention. In Kafka's case, on the other hand, we see an author *experimenting* with language when language is confronted with the reality of page layout. As we know, Kafka began writing in octavos when his sister Ottla rented him the flat in the Alchemistengasse. He walked over the bridge on the Vltava every day and not incidentally changed his modus from pen and ink to pencil. This movement in the material implies a movement to a different type of poetics.

The traditional concept of writing, somehow Platonic, sees it as a process of putting preformed thoughts into script(ure) as their afterwords, so to speak. Kafka abandoned this concept and sought a type of communication involving the semantic effects that the accidental line and page breaks accidentally produced in his writing. This means that he really hadn't a clue as to what might result from the process of writing before he had written his words and marks down. For example, there are certain passages in the octavos where you can see that a new line does not just continue the preceding one but reflects back on it, on both its material and semantic character. This relationship has an analogy in Freud's analysis of speech acts, in which he reflects on the breaks and intervals within the utterance. (This is a line of thought that I cannot now draw out).

What finally lies behind Kafka's literary experiments is the question of power. In chapter 3 of this volume we read some very relevant remarks by Walter Sokel on Nietzsche and the will. The will to power was something Kafka was very interested in. As we know, together with Otto Gross he developed the plan of a journal to which he pledged his active participation. The magazine had an odd name, *Blätter zur Bekämpfung des Machtwillens* (Pages for Combating the Will to Power). This idea is quite extraordinary and altogether pertinent to our philological quest, because this combat is precisely what we see now in Kafka's notebooks: the octavos are literally pages for resisting the will to power. For one of the main instances of power in Kafka's world is, in a word, the "Erzählinstanz" (narrative instance) — the writerly posture that allegedly holds everything together in its grasp. This idea entails one of the most substantial realizations of power in literary texts. Kafka's deliberately non-intentional writing in the octavo notebooks pointedly undercuts it.

My argument now is twofold — the first is exoteric, the second, esoteric. I begin with the exoteric one. One of the main cruxes in the philology of Kafka's octavos is the story "Prometheus," which is not Kafka's title but one that Brod gave to Kafka's narrative. This story, in the Brod version, figures prominently in a long chapter at the end of Hans Blumenberg's great work *Arbeit am Mythos* (*Work on Myth*).[1] But an editorial problem arises from the fact that Brod edited it one way and the editors of the Fischer edition, wanting to separate themselves from Brod, another way.

First, note that in the manuscript the entire story is crossed out (see figs. 1.1, 1.2, and 1.3). This is quite bemusing if you will imagine the rather nervous, consternated look on the faces of the Fischer editorial team. After all, they had decided to publish nothing in the main printed book that Kafka had crossed out in manuscript; such passages would be included only in the apparatus. Without a doubt they will have imagined that were the whole Prometheus story not in the main volume, every clued-in reader would think that they had overlooked it. So they decided to proceed tacitly — to put it in the main text, even though it had been

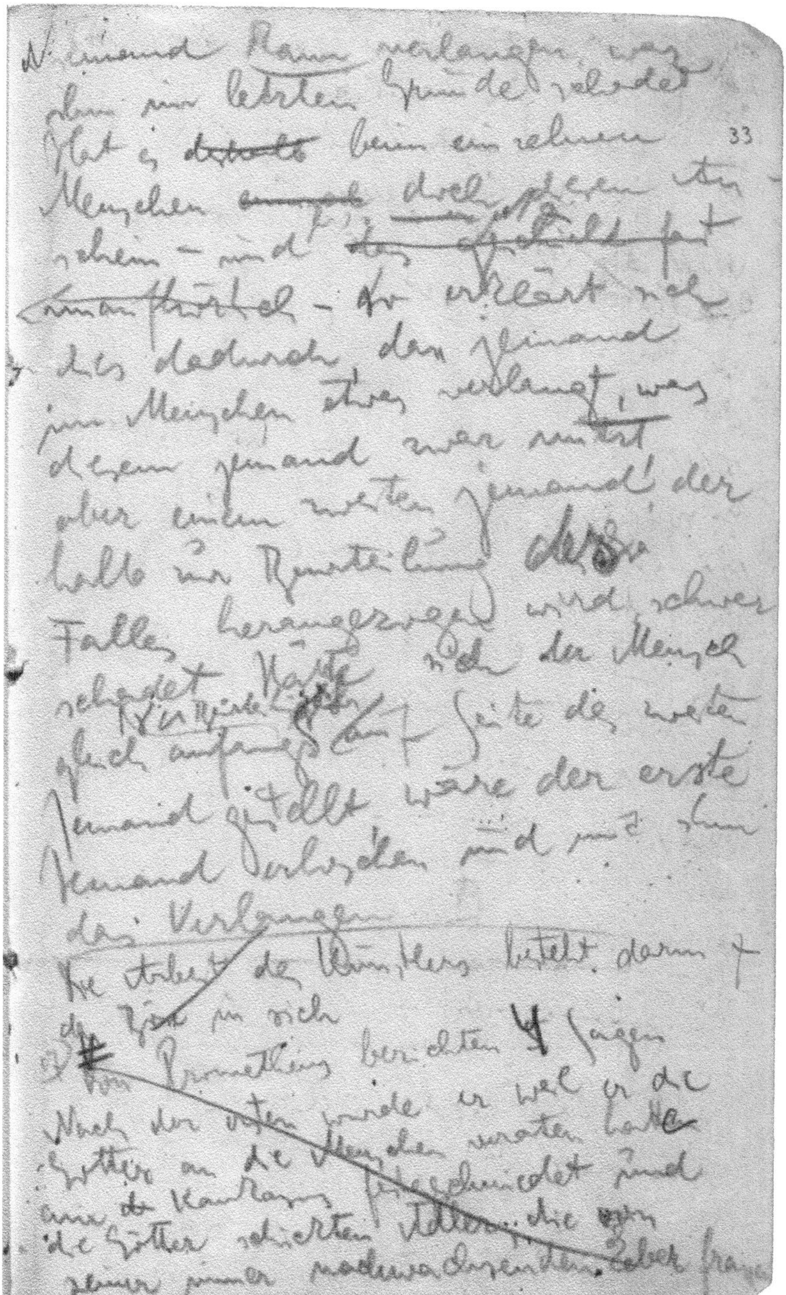

Fig. 1.1. From: Franz Kafka-Ausgabe. Historisch-kritische Ausgabe, *ed. Roland Reuß and Peter Staengle. Oxforder Oktavhefte 7, 33 recto. Mss. facsimiles © Copyright Bodleian Library Oxford & Stroemfeld Verlag, Frankfurt/Main and Basel.*

Fig. 1.2. From: Franz Kafka-Ausgabe. Historisch-kritische Ausgabe, *ed. Roland Reuß and Peter Staengle. Oxforder Oktavhefte 7, 33 verso. Mss. facsimiles © Copyright Bodleian Library Oxford & Stroemfeld Verlag, Frankfurt/Main and Basel.*

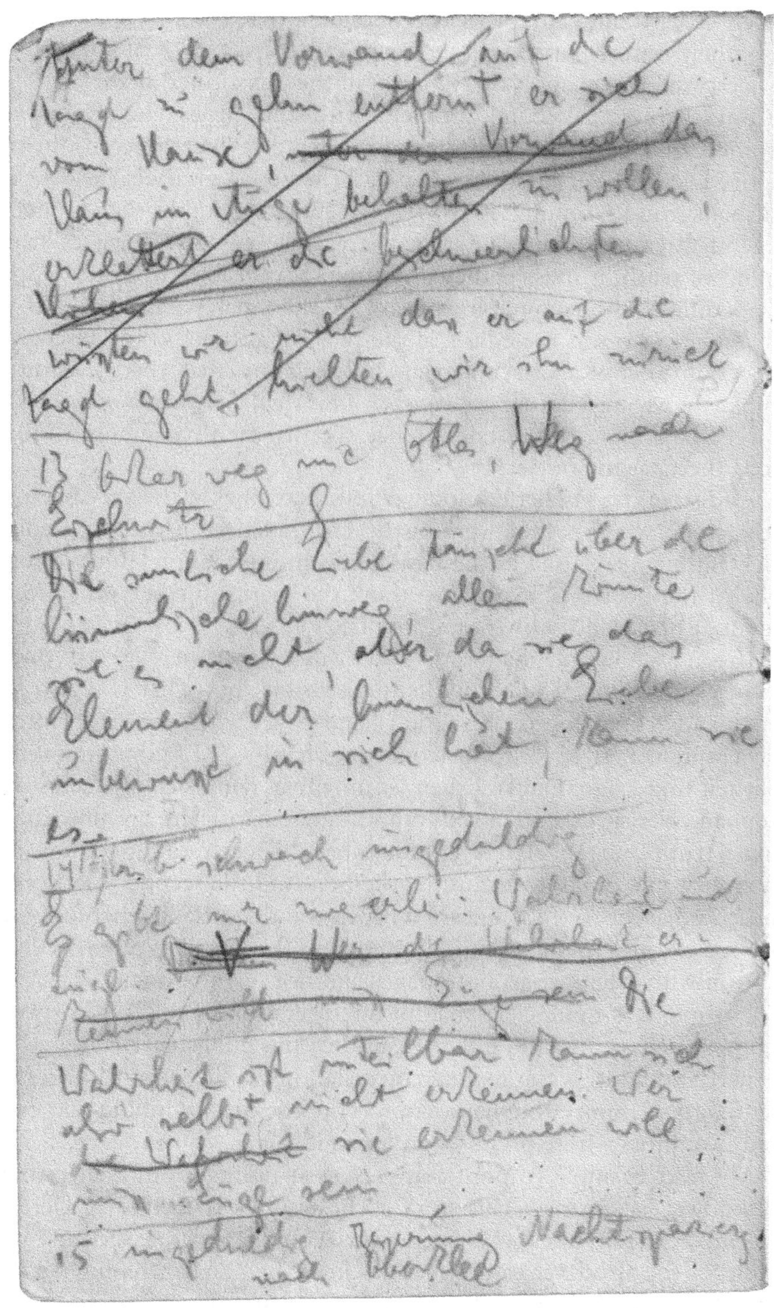

Fig. 1.3. From: Franz Kafka-Ausgabe. Historisch-kritische Ausgabe, *ed. Roland Reuß and Peter Staengle. Oxforder Oktavhefte 7, 32 verso. Mss. facsimiles © Copyright Bodleian Library Oxford & Stroemfeld Verlag, Frankfurt/Main and Basel.*

entirely crossed out. This procedure should have led to a complete rethinking of their editorial principles and made evident the error of not including every crossed-out chapter of *The Trial* in the constituted text.

But there is a second problem with this little tale. The specific "Prometheus" crux in the editions of Brod and Fischer concerns the paragraph, "Die Sage versucht das Unerklärliche zu erklären; da sie aus einem Wahrheitsgrund kommt, muss sie wieder im Unerklärlichen enden" (Legend attempts to explain the inexplicable; because it arises from a ground of truth, it must end again in the inexplicable, *KSS*, 129). In the Brod edition this paragraph appears as the final paragraph. But Jost Schillemeit, who was the editor of the relevant volume in the Fischer edition, confronted Kafka scholarship by declaring that this decision was completely wrong because *we have an insertion sign in the manuscript* at the very beginning of the tale. Hence the disputed paragraph should be placed there, at the outset.

And so in the Fischer edition we find these lines at the very beginning of the story, whereas they were in the final position in the Brod edition, which Blumenberg used as the basis of his interpretation. But the topography of the octavo obliges us to think the matter further; what seemed evident at first glance now raises doubts.

If you examine the manuscript, you will see that there are not one but two insertion signs. The second is quite visible, but what you also see is that this insertion sign is on the left-hand page, where we have, interestingly enough, a reference to the concept of truth — "Es gibt nur zweierlei: Wahrheit und Lüge. Die Wahrheit ist unteilbar, kann sich also selbst nicht erkennen. Wer sie erkennen will, muß Lüge sein" (There are only the two things: truth and lie. Truth is indivisible; hence it cannot know itself. Whoever wants to know it must be the lie). And the second insertion sign is nearly adjacent to these lines. So if you want to decide where the insertion sign belongs in the text of "Prometheus," you will have to decide this question with reference to both pages and not just the one.

For me, it is quite clear that an interpretation of this kind of writing cannot be reduced to the interpretation of the published "running" text but needs to address the textual constellation on the original pages. It is essential to scrutinize the manuscript as opposed to a running text constituted by editors whose premises are opaque.

My next example is more complex — it points to another crux in a well-known Kafka story. This story, "The Hunter Gracchus" ("Der Jäger Gracchus," 1917), has always been a very complicated one, because in the middle of the Brod version it changes from an "Er-Erzählung" (a third-person narrative) to an "Ich-Erzählung" (a first-person narrative). The text that Brod prints is the result of a contamination by several sources. It is hard to fathom the logic of the version he produced: it is the product of a transgression — a violent boundary-crossing. But you will not begin to understand what Kafka wrote if you do not read this text as a *writing process.*

Note the last lines on this page: "Ich bin der Jäger Gracchus, meine Heimat ist der Schwarzwald in Deutschland" (I am the Hunter Gracchus, my homeland is the Black Forest in Germany; see fig. 1.4 — Gracchus 1). These are the last lines associated with this particular verbal corpus. They are then followed by a drawn line separating it from the famous sentence, "Niemand wird lesen was ich hier schreibe" (No one will read what I write here, *KSS,* 112). But at this point we cannot know whether the text *following this sentence* belongs to the previous "Gracchus the Hunter" scheme, or whether it is a second step, the beginning of another story written from an entirely different perspective. The interesting thing is that it is only *after you turn the page* that you see that these lines do explicitly refer to "Gracchus the Hunter."

If you read just the bottom of the page in figure 1.5 (Gracchus, 2) — "und mir vergegenwärtige, wo ich bin und — das darf ich wohl behaupten —" (and remember where I am and — this is something I can say with certainty —, *KSS,* 112) — you will see nothing that identifies it as part of the "Gracchus the Hunter" ensemble of fragments. But now turn the page (fig. 1.6 — Gracchus, 3), and with the next words on the new page — "seit Jahrhunderten" ("for centuries") — which is the beginning of the conclusion to the sentence at the bottom of the preceding page — "seit Jahrhunderten wohne" (where I have been living for centuries, *KSS,* 113) — you will see that the text does explicitly return to "Gracchus the Hunter." It was not evident to Kafka from the very beginning that the lines at the bottom of the previous page were part of the Gracchus ensemble (and neither should it be for us). It was while writing the conclusion to this sentence at the beginning of the new page that Kafka decided to bring the story back to — I hesitate to use the possessive case — *its* beginning. You cannot understand this textual maneuver if you do not abide by the *process* of writing. The rest of the text then unfolds within the metaphoric field of the "Jenseits" (Beyond, Hereafter) — or literally, "auf der anderen Seite" (on the other, the far side); this trope dominates the consciousness of the hunter Gracchus, viz.

> Hier liege ich seit damals, als ich, noch lebender Jäger Gracchus, zuhause im Schwarzwald eine Gemse verfolgte und abstürzte. Alles ging der Ordnung nach. Ich verfolgte, stürzte ab, verblutete in einer Schlucht, war tot und diese Barke sollte mich ins Jenseits tragen.
>
> [I have been lying here ever since the time when I, still the living hunter Gracchus, at home in the Black Forest, chased a chamois and fell. Everything went in order. I gave chase, fell, bled to death in a gulch, was dead, and this sailboat was supposed to carry me into the hereafter. (*KSS,* 112)]

Fig. 1.4. From: Franz Kafka-Ausgabe. Historisch-kritische Ausgabe, *ed. Roland Reuß and Peter Staengle. Oxforder Oktavhefte 2, 9 verso. Mss. facsimiles*

Kopf geschlagen, eine nächtliche 10
Herberge die ganze Erde. Das
hat guten Sinn, denn niemand weiß
von mir, und wüßte er von mir
so wüßte er meinen Aufenthalt
nicht und wüßte er meinen Aufent-
halt so wüßte er mich dort
nicht festzuhalten und wüßte er
mich dort festzuhalten so wüßte
er nicht wie ihm helfen. Der
Gedanke mir helfen zu wollen
ist eine Krankheit und muß im
Bett geheilt werden.
Das weiß ich und schreibe also
nicht um Hilfe herbeizurufen selbst
wenn ich in Augenblicken unbeherrscht
wie ich bin z. B. gerade jetzt
sehr stark daran denke. Aber
es genügt wohl zum Austreiben
solcher Gedanken, wenn ich
umherblicke und mir vergegen-
wärtige, wo ich bin und
– das darf ich wohl behaupten –

Fig. 1.5. From: Franz Kafka-Ausgabe. Historisch-kritische Ausgabe, *ed. Roland Reuß and Peter Staengle. Oxforder Oktavhefte 2, 10 recto. Mss. facsimiles © Copyright Bodleian Library Oxford & Stroemfeld Verlag, Frankfurt/Main and Basel.*

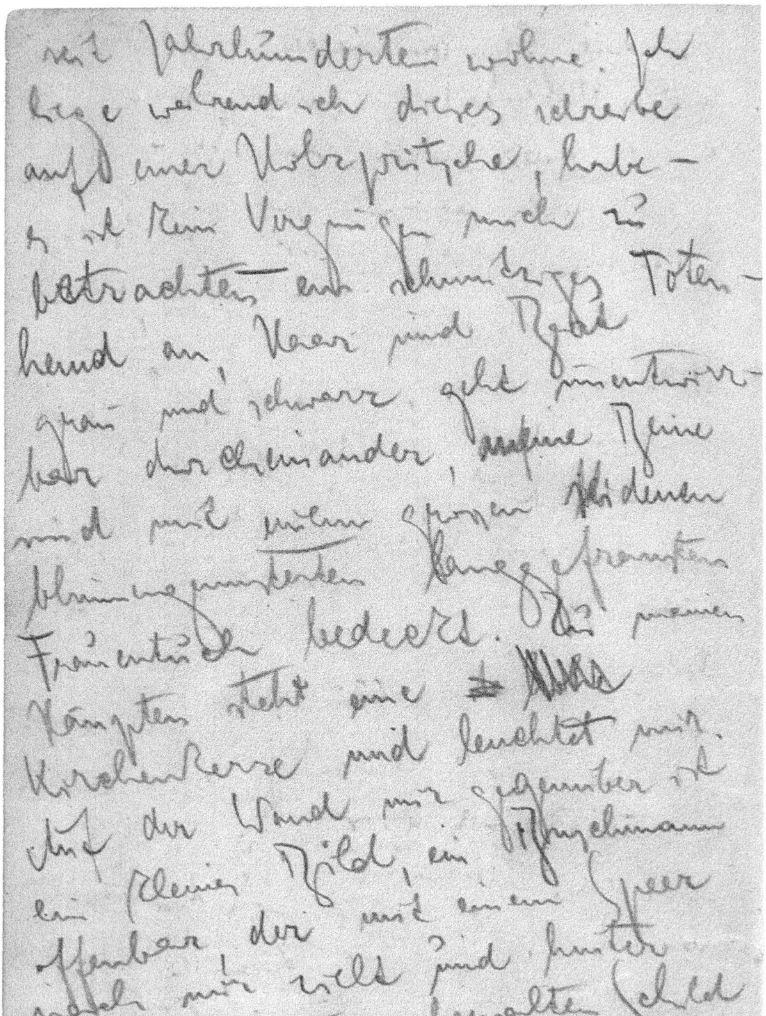

seit Jahrhunderten wohne. Ich
liege während ich dieses schreibe
auf einer Holzpritsche, habe –
es ist kein Vergnügen mich zu
betrachten – ein schmutziges Toten-
hemd an, Haar und Bart
grau und schwarz geht unentwirr-
bar durcheinander, meine Beine
sind mit einem großen seidenen
blumengemusterten langgefransten
Frauentuch bedeckt. Zu meinen
Häupten steht eine
Kirchenkerze und leuchtet mir.
Auf der Wand mir gegenüber ist
ein kleines Bild, ein Buschmann
offenbar der mit einem Speer
nach mir zielt und hinter
einem großartig bemalten Schild
sich möglichst deckt. Man
begegnet auf Schiffen manchen
dummen Darstellungen, diese ist

Fig. 1.6. From: Franz Kafka-Ausgabe. Historisch-kritische Ausgabe, *ed. Roland Reuß and Peter Staengle. Oxforder Oktavhefte 2, 10 verso. Mss. facsimiles © Copyright Bodleian Library Oxford & Stroemfeld Verlag, Frankfurt/Main and Basel.*

Observe that this part of the story proceeds from a "Jenseits," a Beyond, on the other side . . . *of the page*. Kafka finds his way to the other side of the page and with it the way back to the original content of "Gracchus the Hunter." But with this movement he also finds its inverse again, the problematic geography of the Beyond, to which the author but not the hunter can find his way.

Be that as it may, no interpretation is possible that does not scrupulously follow *the process of writing*. This process is completely relative to the fixed parameters of the page layout and its intentional-accidental production of sense; the meaning of the material is very specific to the page. That is one of the great challenges in the interpretation of the octavos.

The next problem concerns the many drawn separation lines. There are countless such lines in the octavo notebooks, but they do not have one specific function; their function changes. Sometimes the separation mark is found between drafts of different texts, and sometimes it is used to indicate the shift to another speaker in dramatized speech. There is such a line in "A Report to an Academy" ("Ein Bericht für eine Akademie," 1919), which Kafka now wants to stage as a kind of dialogue. At the beginning we have a conventional Er/Ich-Erzählung (a third-person/first-person narrative), which then shifts into a dialogue. To mark the change of speakers, Kafka uses this line. The sense of the separation line varies according to its different functions in the octavos. This is not a crucial editorial issue: in our Stroemfeld edition, *Die historisch-kritische Ausgabe sämtlicher Handschriften, Drucke und Typoskripte Franz Kafkas*,[2] we simply print the separation marks as they appear.

Here is another editorial crux: Brod edited a story to which he gave the title "The Knock at the Courtyard Gate" ("Der Schlag ans Hoftor"). This title, again, was not supplied by Kafka; it is Brod's invention (see fig. 1.7). The end of the left-hand page reads: "Die Stube sah einer Gefängniszelle ähnlicher als einer Bauernstube. Große Steinfliesen, dunkelgraue kahle Wand, irgendwo eingemauert ein eiserner Ring, in der Mitte etwas, das halb Pritsche halb Operationstisch war" (The room looked more like a prison cell than like a tavern parlor. Large flagstones, a dark gray, bare wall, an iron ring cemented somewhere into it, at the center something that was half plank bed, half operating table, *KSS*, 125). On the right-hand page (fig. 1.8), you see a separation mark and then the lines, "Könnte ich noch andere Luft schmecken, als die des Gefängnisses? Das ist die große Frage oder vielmehr sie wäre es, wenn ich Aussicht auf Entlassung hätte." (Could I still sense any air other than that of a prison? That is the great question — or rather, it would be the question if I had any prospect of being released, *KSS*, 125). Brod ignores the separation mark and treats these lines as the end of the story that was begun on the left-hand page. But these lines may very well be the beginning of a *different* story. This is an excellent example of a philological dilemma.

Fig. 1.7. From: Franz Kafka-Ausgabe. Historisch-kritische Ausgabe, *ed. Roland Reuß and Peter Staengle. Oxforder Oktavhefte 3, 33 verso. Mss. facsimiles © Copyright Bodleian Library Oxford & Stroemfeld Verlag, Frankfurt/Main and Basel.*

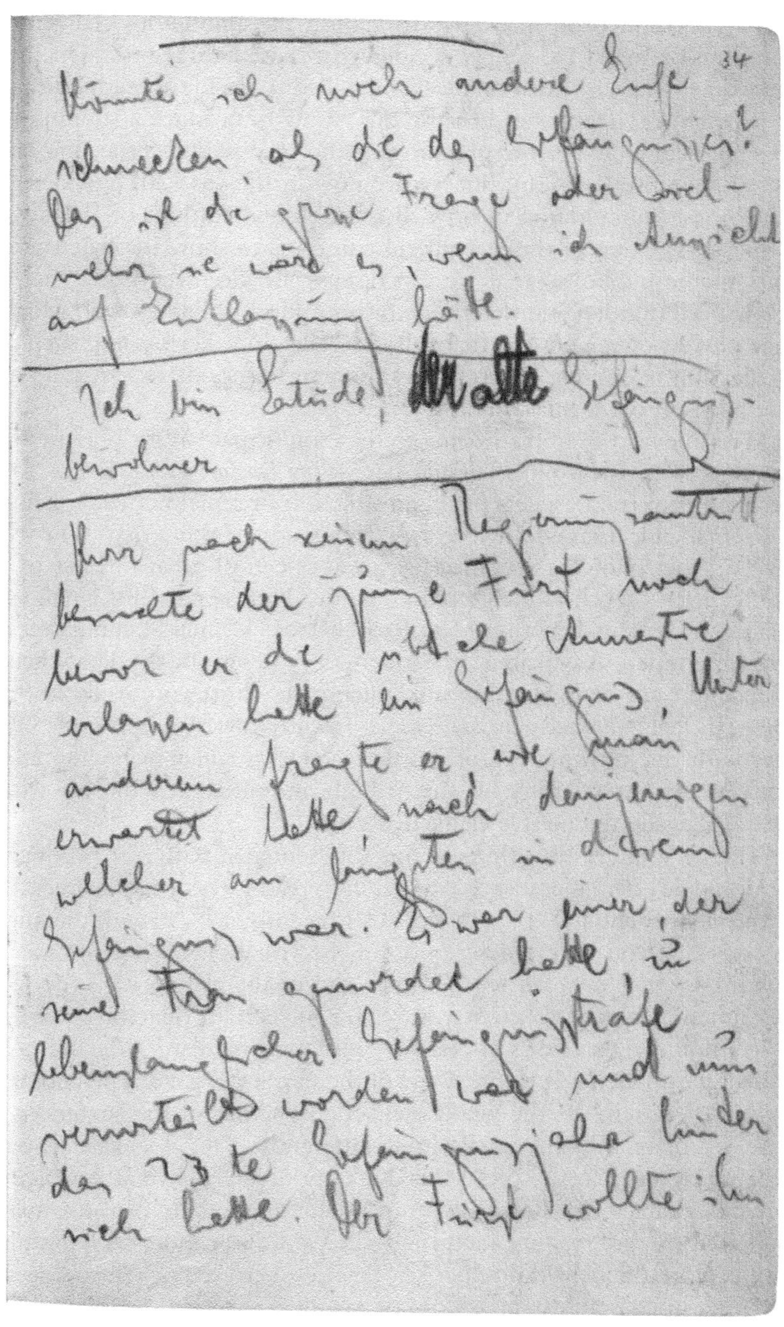

34

Könnte ich noch andere Luft schmecken als die des Gefängnisses? Das ist die große Frage oder vielmehr sie wäre es, wenn ich Aussicht auf Entlassung hätte.

Ich bin Student, der alte Gefängnisbewohner

Kurz nach seinem Regierungsantritt besuchte der junge Fürst noch bevor er die übliche Amnestie erlassen hatte ein Gefängnis. Unter anderem fragte er, wie man erwartet hatte, nach demjenigen welcher am längsten in diesem Gefängnis war. Es war einer, der seine Frau gemordet hatte, zu lebenslänglicher Gefängnisstrafe verurteilt worden war und nun das 23te Gefängnisjahr hinter sich hatte. Der Fürst wollte ihn

Fig. 1.8. From: Franz Kafka-Ausgabe. Historisch-kritische Ausgabe, *ed. Roland Reuß and Peter Staengle. Oxforder Oktavhefte 3, 34 recto. Mss. facsimiles © Copyright Bodleian Library Oxford & Stroemfeld Verlag, Frankfurt/Main and Basel.*

The decision Brod made was to abolish the ambiguous character of the separation mark. He simply decided that these lines are to be included in the story. But why must one feel compelled to decide something that is not decidable? The answer: because one wants to produce a running text and only negligibly an interpretation of the manuscript. True, the latter task was not Brod's to do, but we are now in the year 2011, and so we have to raise the question of how these published editions of Kafka were produced. The aim of the Stroemfeld edition is to show the true state of affairs to the public, so that we can discuss, besides everything that has already been decided and determined, this undecidability as well, which is a factor of its own, and one that calls for reflection. Performing such acts of reflection is entirely different from issuing decisions in order to turn these pages into a formal running text.

With the next example I come to the esoteric part of my presentation, beginning with the volume titled *A Country Doctor: Little Stories.* I am interested in certain aspects of the production of semantic fields. I find a very remarkable example in the first paragraph of the story "The New Lawyer"; the following sentence has always been of great interest to me (see fig. 1.9): "Doch sah ich letzthin auf der Freitreppe selbst einen ganz einfältigen Gerichtsdiener mit dem Fachblick des kleinen Stammgastes der Wettrennen den Advokaten bestaunen, als dieser, hoch die Schenkel hebend, mit auf dem Marmor aufklingendem Schritt von Stufe zu Stufe stieg" (In fact, on the main staircase I recently saw a quite simple court usher with the knowing eye of a little racetrack regular marveling at the lawyer as the latter, lifting his thighs high, mounted step by step with a stride that made the marble clang, *KSS,* 60).

The very interesting thing about this sentence is that it produces a kaleidoscopic effect, because as you begin to read — "doch sah ich letzthin . . . mit dem Fachblick . . ." (In fact . . . I recently saw . . . with the knowing eye . . .), you have a description of the visual process of the speaker himself. But it is only on reaching the end of the clause, with the word "bestaunen" (marveling), that you realize for certain that this "knowing eye" is not the narrator's (he is no "racetrack regular," after all). The "knowing eye" belongs to the *object* of the narrator's gaze. The ending of the clause reassembles the whole syntactic structure of the sentence; the entire set of relations arranges itself differently. This is a kaleidoscopic effect visible even in the prose that Kafka printed. It is vital to grasp the *processual* character of Kafka's writing — the temporality of the semantic field and the act of reading adequate to it. We will see more such examples as we explore the octavo notebooks.

Here, now, is an example from octavo "C" (see figs. 1.10 and 1.11). The lines that we see at the bottom of the first page of this notebook reflect a certain rich textuality. You will be inclined to read the word "Absätze" with a material referent in mind — stair landings — since the passage is all

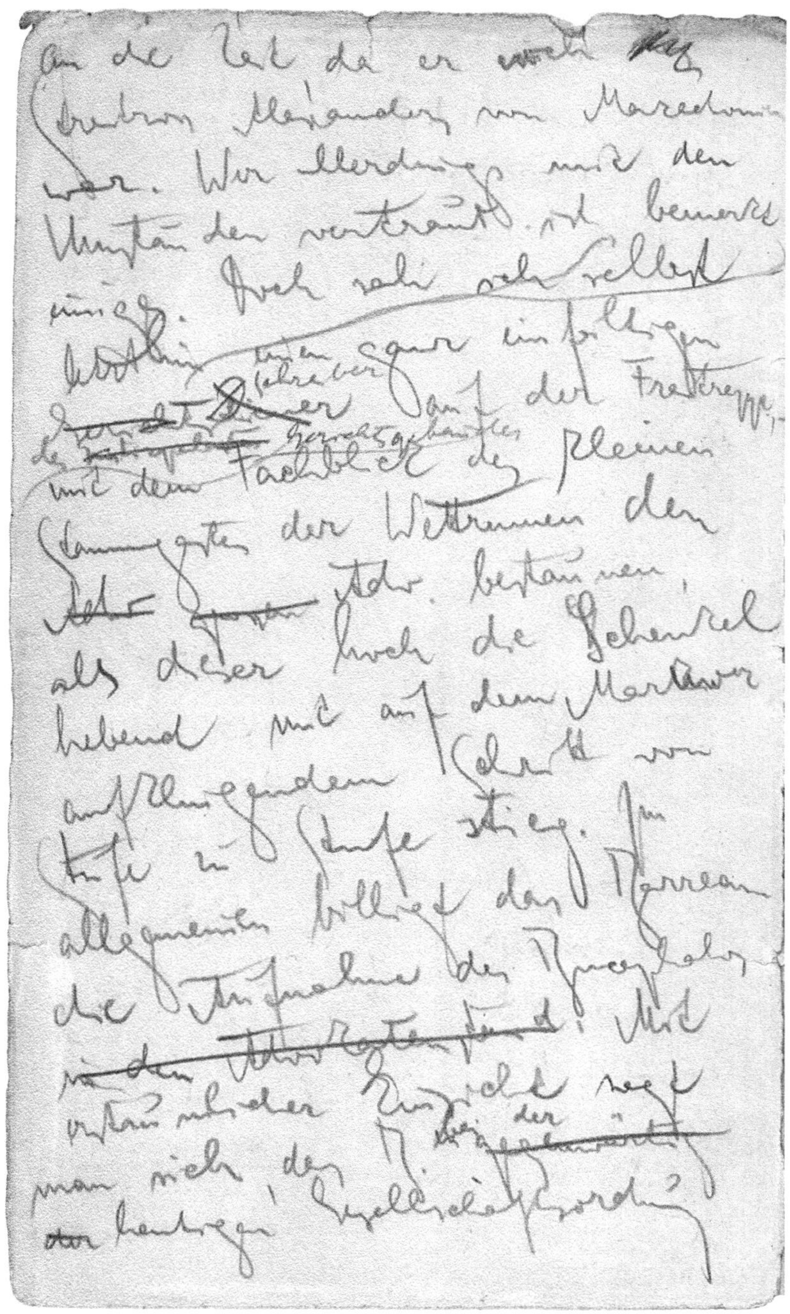

Fig. 1.9. From: Franz Kafka-Ausgabe. Historisch-kritische Ausgabe, *ed. Roland Reuß and Peter Staengle. Oxforder Oktavhefte 2, 27 verso. Mss. facsimiles*

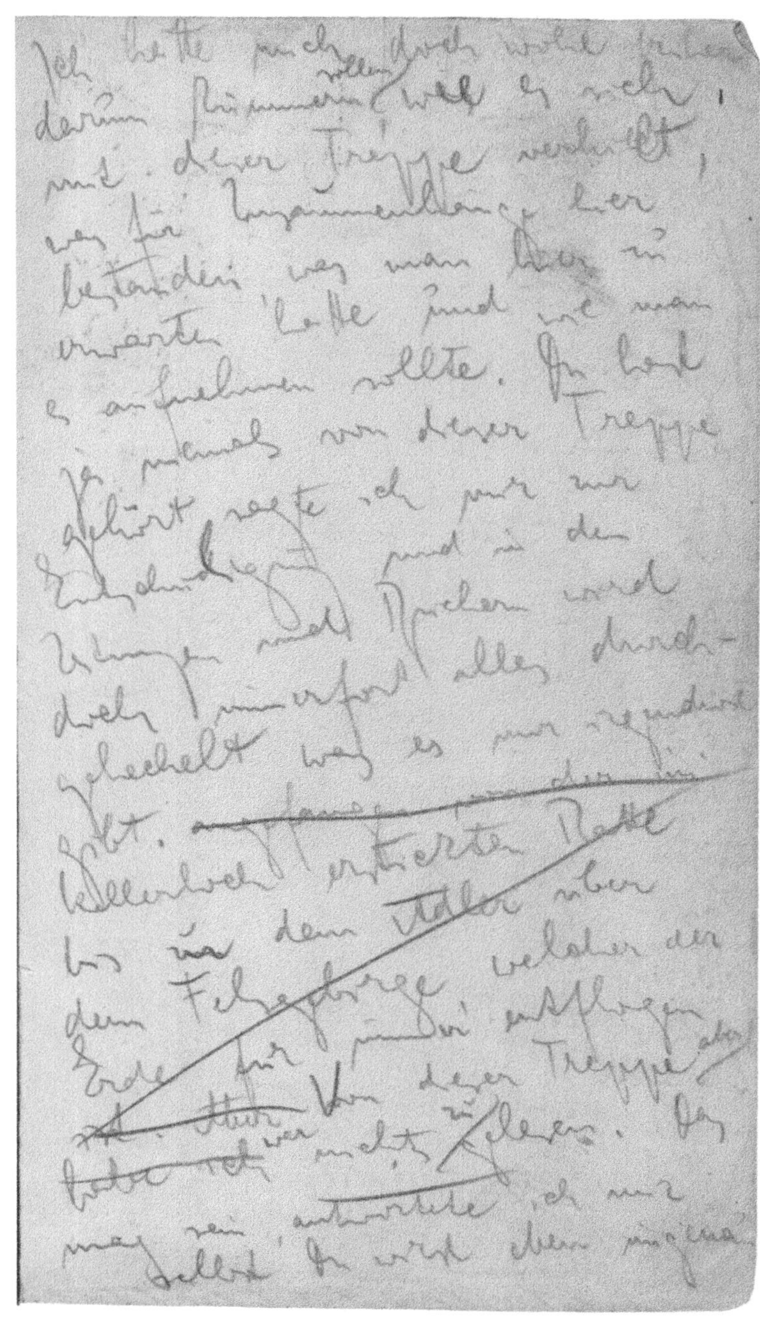

Fig. 1.10. From: Franz Kafka-Ausgabe. Historisch-kritische Ausgabe, *ed. Roland Reuß and Peter Staengle. Oxforder Oktavhefte 3, 1 recto. Mss. facsimiles © Copyright Bodleian Library Oxford & Stroemfeld Verlag, Frankfurt/Main and Basel.*

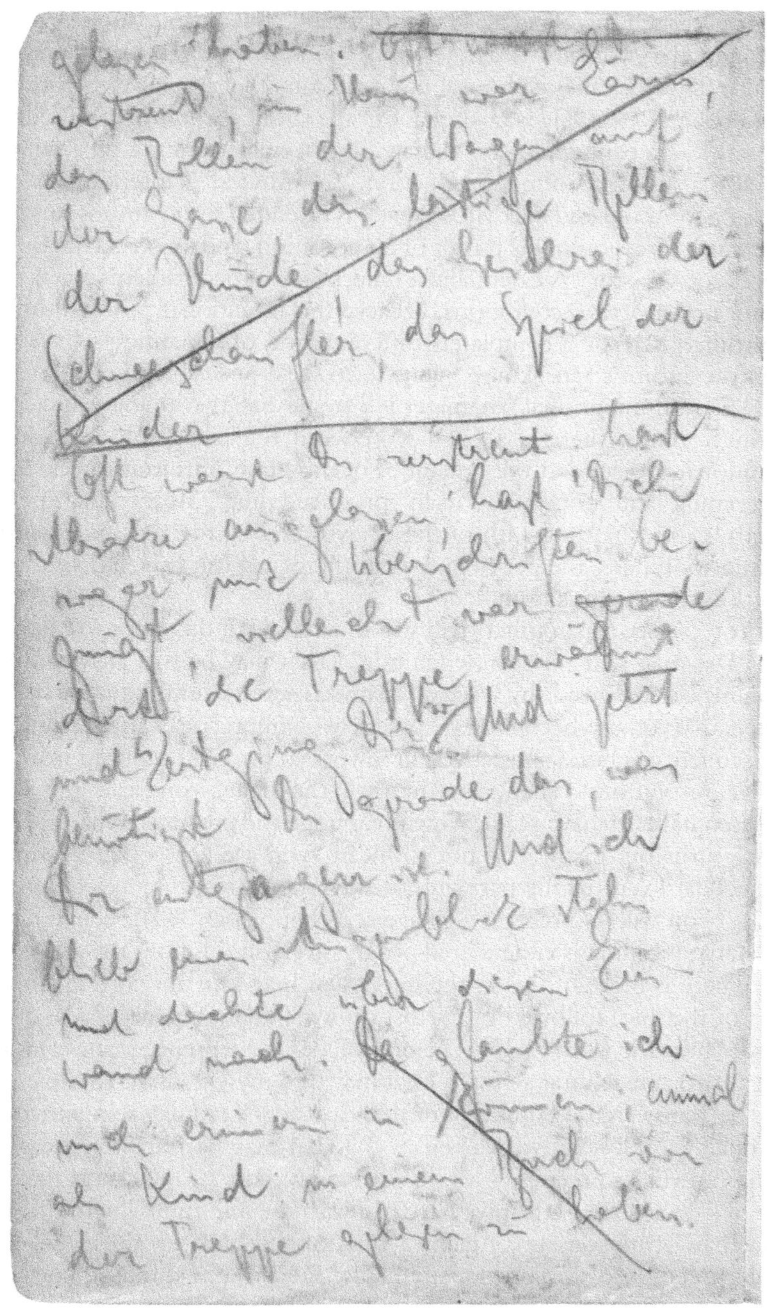

Fig. 1.11. From: Franz Kafka-Ausgabe. Historisch-kritische Ausgabe, *ed. Roland Reuß and Peter Staengle. Oxforder Oktavhefte 3, 1 verso. Mss. facsimiles © Copyright Bodleian Library Oxford & Stroemfeld Verlag, Frankfurt/Main and Basel.*

about a certain "Treppe" (a flight of stairs); but if you do so, you will conclude that you are dealing with a nonsensical text, and rightly so, because Kafka is talking about a flight of stairs that has never before been seen on land or sea. He is talking about the specific *semantic field* called an "Absatz" — a paragraph. An "Absatz" is not only a landing on a staircase; it is also a structure in text production. An "Absatz" is intentionally composed, a form of language whose shape is intended by an author (and so it is also an expression of his power of composition, and so on). The thought process of this story is essentially a reflection on the problems faced by an author under octavo conditions, because this intentionally formed unity is confronted here by a completely different kind of semantics, which arises from the author's "speaking" freely, so to speak, *while writing.*

The non-intentional parameter is a single *line* that follows the flow of writing. Hence, there is a conflict between the paragraph as a kind of intentional project and the semantics of the "free," arbitrary, accidentally intervening and non-intentionally produced line. Meanwhile, the line length is fixed by the width of the octavos and by the specifically chosen writing tool, here, the pencil and what the pencil can do. And so the line length is materially determined.

You can see this conflict vividly in the middle of this story. We have the line "Das mag sein antwortete ich mir" (That may be so I answered me); this line is followed by "selbst" (myself/even) and "du wirst eben ungenau" (you are becoming — precisely — imprecise). The semantics of this sequence is not a substance but a work in progress built up from successive resolutions. Then, as you turn the page, you read the words "gelesen haben" (have read), which rearrange the previous semantics. "Du wirst" turns out in the end not to mean "you are becoming"; "wirst" is the auxiliary verb to the participle at the end of the sentence, which now reads: "You will — precisely — have read imprecisely." The semantics are not static: meaning is engendered progressively throughout the act of writing. There is more of this in the line: "Das mag sein antwortete ich mir" (end of the line) followed by "selbst du wirst eben ungenau." We do not know where the word "selbst" belongs. Does the sentence read, "Das mag sein antwortete ich mir selbst" (That may be I myself answered me / That may be I answered me myself), or does it read, "Das mag sein antwortete ich mir [—] selbst du wirst eben . . ." (That may be I answered me [—] even you will — precisely — have read imprecisely . . .)? This is the same sort of kaleidoscopic effect we have had with the line ending with the word "ungenau" (imprecisely). Again, a turn of the page produces an entire reinterpretation of the previous semantic set. What a stunning line: "Das mag sein antwortete ich mir selbst du . . . ." (That may be I [myself] replied to me [myself] [even] you . . .).

We now have, I hope, a lively sense of the effect — which I have called kaleidoscopic — that Kafka's art produces. I think a musician would have

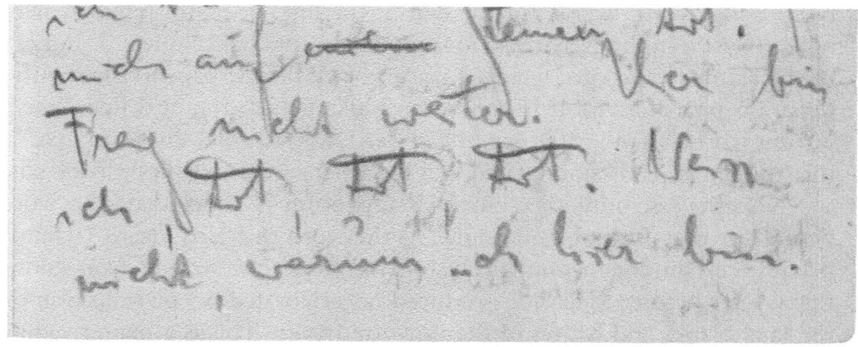

Fig. 1.12. From: Franz Kafka-Ausgabe. Historisch-kritische Ausgabe, *ed. Roland Reuß and Peter Staengle. Oxforder Oktavhefte 4, 19 recto. Mss. facsimiles © Copyright Bodleian Library Oxford & Stroemfeld Verlag, Frankfurt/Main and Basel.*

no difficulty appreciating this practice. Musicians try to set certain parameters, and then they become experimental and inventive within them. This impulse produces a conflict between these parameters and the flow of invention. The collision becomes apparent, like water rushing against stones; the water becomes spectacular when it collides with these scruples (lat. *scrupulus*: bit of sharp stone); the collision reveals something hitherto unseen. The effect cannot be calculated in advance, and that is the interesting thing about it.

We have papers in this volume employing the rhetoric of psychoanalysis; in a way Kafka's experiments with page and paragraph constitute a psychoanalytic practice, by bringing to light something unintended, something of which he was not aware. This revelation is produced by the constraints of line- and page-length within the paragraph. We have an interaction between the page layout and the free authorial thought flow. But this latter intention does not control the whole; instead we have semantic incidents, and that is the important thing: they occur at the end of the lines.

I will now offer a very striking graphic example from the fourth Oxford Octavo (fol. 19r; see fig. 1.12). Look at the page on the right, at the last two lines. We are in the midst of the "Hunter Gracchus" ensemble. This, I think, is especially interesting: the words "Ich" (I) and "weiss" (know) stand opposite to one another on the line; preceding the words "nicht, warum ich hier bin," we have this very striking ensemble in one line: "ich tot tot tot. Weiss."

The word "tot" (dead) is repeated three times, with a line running through both the "t"s in every "tot." This is a constellation in Kafka's writing reflecting, though not intentionally, the whole adventure of the handwriting: writing within the horizon of black and white. That is because the word "weiss," at the end of the line, does not refer, trivially, only to *wissen* (to know); it also means "white" and hence refers, I suggest, to the status of the ego, which is not in black on the paper. (I know this remark is provocative.) It is only when Kafka gets to the next line, "nicht warum ich hier bin" ("[I, dead dead dead, know] not why I am here"), that the phrase is disambiguated and the abstract constellation dissolved.

Nonetheless, until the semantic suspension is concluded, the word "weiss" projects a double meaning. As the word that also means "white," it has a certain cogency in the history of modernist writing, you know: thirty years before, Mallarmé produced his celebrated poetic reflection on the fatal blanks and whites of the unwritten page. This is a matter calling for study.

A final example (see fig. 1.13). In the third octavo, we have the text of a tale titled by Kafka "A Page from an Old Document" (Ein altes Blatt) and published by Kafka during his lifetime in *Ein Landarzt: Kleine Erzählungen*. On the pages of the third Oxford Octavo, this story precedes by a little the fragment edited by Brod and called by him "The Knock on the Courtyard Gate" ("Der Schlag ans Hoftor"). "A Page" is a longer story, and at the end Kafka does something that is unique in the octavos: he stresses the omission of text. You can see these brackets — they are now evident in our edition, because we reproduce the manuscript: we are not obliged to produce linear text.

There is nothing between these brackets; they speak of the *absence* of linear text. The brackets fall below the lines following the conclusion to "A Page" as published by Kafka; these lines are separated from the conclusion by a drawn line. They too speak of the absence of linear text, reading: "[. . .] Es ist ein Bruchstück. Hoffnung, daß die Fortsetzung gefunden werden könnte besteht nicht" (It is a fragment. Hope that the continuation could be found is non-existent). Then you see the brackets enclosing empty space. Thereafter, the following lines again take up the absence of linear text. If you read without attending to the line breaks and the parameters of handwriting, you get: "Hier folgen noch einige Seiten, die aber allzu beschädigt sind, als daß ihnen etwas bestimmtes entnommen werden könnte" (This is followed by several pages, which, however, are much too damaged for anything definite to be extracted from them). Then comes a line of separation and, as mentioned, the beginning of the story that Brod was to publish with the title "The Knock at the Courtyard Gate."

But above the brackets we have "Es ist ein Bruchstück" (It is a fragment), which is *crossed out*; then, in the same line (unit), the word "Hoffnung." Thereafter, Kafka rescued "the fragment" by restoring it with dots under the line. This is an archetypical manuscript constellation, which as such requires interpretation. You can literally read about the constellation of fragmentariness and hope.

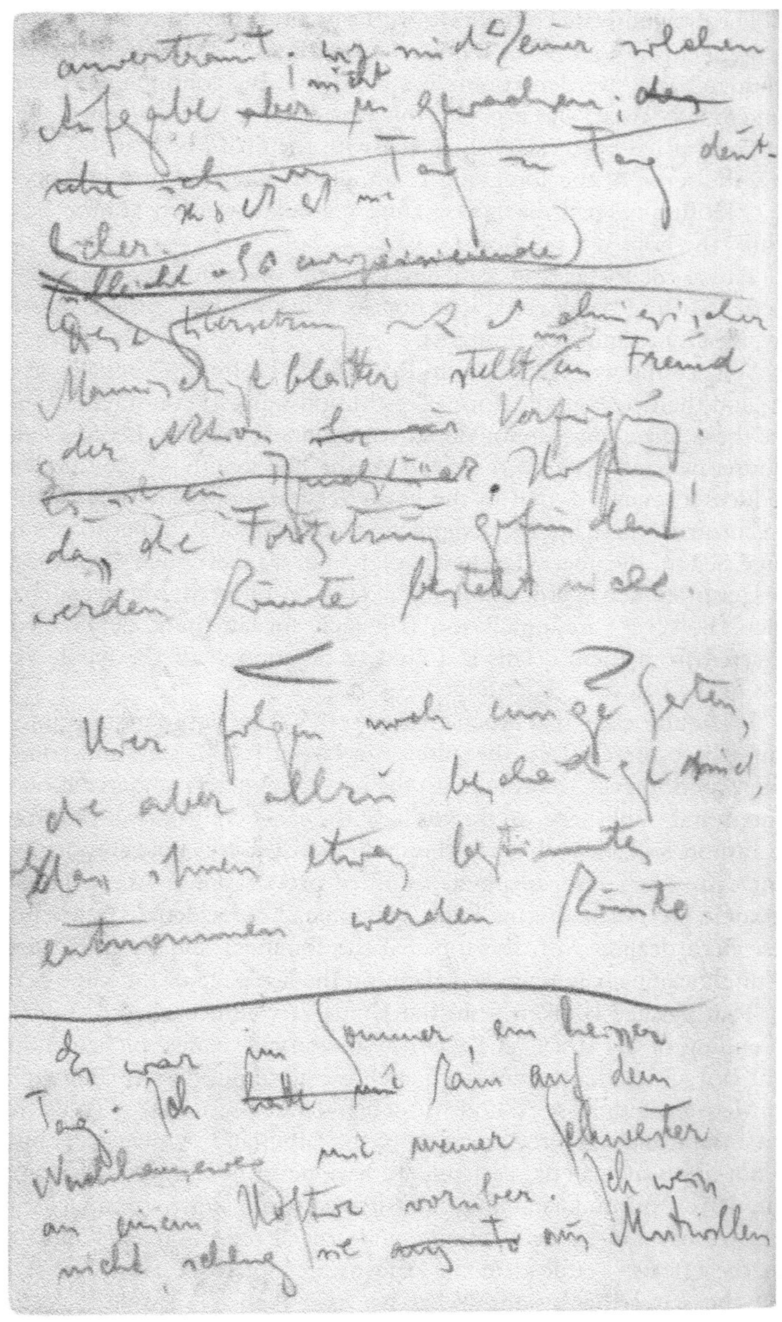

Fig. 1.13. From: Franz Kafka-Ausgabe. Historisch-kritische Ausgabe, *ed. Roland Reuß and Peter Staengle. Oxforder Oktavhefte 3, 31 verso. Mss. facsimiles © Copyright Bodleian Library Oxford & Stroemfeld Verlag, Frankfurt/Main and Basel.*

The previously deleted phrase — "Es ist ein Bruchstück Hoffnung" (It is a fragment of hope) — is followed by the lines — "daß die Fortsetzung gefunden" and "werden könnte besteht" (that the continuation could be found [. . .] exists); and it is into this new context that it wanders, before that context has been established. For with the final word "nicht" ([does] not), the sense of the foregoing is completely changed into its opposite, viz., "Hoffnung, daß die Fortsetzung gefunden werden könnte besteht nicht" (the hope does not exist).

This is all to be read as a development of meaning constrained by external writing parameters; it is not an "after-writing" of already (mentally, ideally) formulated thoughts.

You see the words "Es ist ein Bruchstück Hoffnung" initially crossed out, and then you see the dots — restitution signs. If you intend to interpret these lines, you cannot do so with a linear version, because on the manuscript page, sense is restricted by the line length — the line length produces a semantics that in the linear version, unlike the manuscript, is transformed. These lines are completely self-referential: "Hier folgen noch einige Seiten, die aber allzu beschädigt sind, als daß ihnen etwas bestimmtes entnommen werden könnte" (This is followed by several pages, which, however, are much too damaged for anything definite to be extracted from them). This is a kind of description of the whole verbal mass of the octavos. "Hier folgen . . ."

It is quite clear that when this story "A Page" appears in print, you cannot have these effects, because print layout is different, and you, as a writer, cannot react accordingly to the print parameters; and as editors and printers and publishers, we do not have the same control over the story as the author. Kafka just changed this ending *because* it is not reproducible in print (consider this remark as another provocation). After this story appeared, in 1918, during Kafka's lifetime, he decided to rework only these lines dealing with the topic of the fragment and the lost hope of definite meaning. He reworked them on the last page of the same octavo.

That passage is taken from the Landarzt volume, where it figures as the ending of the story "A Page": "Wir sind aber einer solchen Aufgabe nicht gewachsen; haben uns doch auch nie gerühmt, dessen fähig zu sein. Ein Missverständnis ist es, und wir gehen daran zugrunde" ([To us craftsmen and businessmen the salvation of the fatherland is entrusted;] but we are not up to such a task; certainly we have never boasted of being capable of it. It is a misunderstanding, and it means our destruction, *KSS,* 67). Here we have an explicit, unique, and crucial reflection on Kafka's part that the effects produced in the octavos are not to be carried over into print; he states this insight! What we have then is a subtle dialectic of manuscript and print.

If you want to study Kafka's writings, you must be keenly aware of the technique that informs them. It becomes clear that Kafka's chief predilection is to see himself producing work through not wanting it to be produced by himself qua a powerful ego. It is a kind of deep self-discovery achieved by writing under strict material conditions, since, as we have seen in every case, these semantic incidents come about through the constraints of page width and length. It remains for us to explore the kinds of semantic incidents that occur on the contact of the free line with the recalcitrant parameters of the page layout. This sort of exploration is of course confined to the manuscript and not the printed version; it is a key optic through which to study the Kafka of the manuscripts — and there is no other Kafka.

Notes

[1] Hans Blumenberg, *Arbeit am Mythos* (Frankfurt am Main: Suhrkamp, 1984). In English, *Work on Myth*, trans. Robert M. Wallace (Cambridge, MA: MIT Press, 1985).

[2] Roland Reuß and Peter Staengle, eds., *Die historisch-kritische Ausgabe sämtlicher Handschriften, Drucke und Typoskripte Franz Kafkas* (Frankfurt am Main: Stroemfeld, 1995–).

2: "Torturing the Gordian Knot": Kafka and Metaphor

Mark Harman

Yes, torturing is extremely important to me. . . . Torturing is pathetic too, of course. After all, Alexander didn't torture the Gordian knot when it wouldn't come untied.
— Kafka

What, then, is truth? A mobile army of metaphors, metonyms, and anthromorphisms.
— Nietzsche

ALTHOUGH KAFKA DISTRUSTS his own gift for metaphor, he resorts to metaphorical language both in his fiction and in his autobiographical writings. Metaphors occur to him in what W. B. Yeats called the "foul rag and bone shop of the heart,"[1] and his fiction often germinates from intensely personal images. We can watch him experimenting in his diaries with a tangle of often tormented images, which he, metaphorically of course, likens to the Gordian knot.

In Kafka studies, where there has been much discussion about metaphor, the pendulum can swing too far, obliterating the partial validity of previous perspectives. Thanks to Stanley Corngold,[2] few of us are now likely to accept without qualification Günther Anders's once widely accepted notion that Kafka's narratives are literalized metaphors.[3] Yet if we carry this rejection of the role of figurative language to extremes, we risk losing sight of Kafka's gift for metaphor. This debate in Kafka studies parallels the lively discussions about metaphor in recent decades, not only in literary studies but also in philosophy, linguistics, and cognitive science. Heeding the philosopher Paul Ricoeur's insistence on the need to recognize "the place and role of feeling in the metaphorical process,"[4] I shall focus here on the manner in which Kafka brings self-conscious craft to bear on intimate obsessions, thereby transforming private images into enduring metaphors.

Kafka's explicit comments about metaphor might admittedly seem to undermine the case for the centrality of metaphor in his creative process. His criticism of images can be trenchant, as in the often-quoted diary entry of 6 December 1922, prompted by a metaphor in a letter in which he had likened writing to a fire that gives off warmth:

> Metaphors are one among many things which make me despair of writing. Writing's lack of independence of the world, its dependence on the maid who tends the fire, on the cat warming itself by the stove. . . . All these are independent activities ruled by their own laws; only writing is helpless, cannot live in itself, is fun and despair. (*D*, 397–98)[5]

Since metaphors are dependent on such fortuitous circumstances as the state of the room in which the writer sits, they lack the aesthetic autonomy that Kafka wishes to achieve. However, if he dwells on the questionable nature of figurative language, it is precisely because similes and metaphors occur to him constantly.

One exception to the generally scathing tone of Kafka's remarks about metaphor occurs in a conversation reported by his Prague friend, Johannes Urzidil:

> Once Kafka said to me: To be a poet means to be strong in metaphors. The greatest poets were always the most metaphorical ones. They were those who recognized the deep mutual concern, yes, even the identity of things between which nobody noticed the slightest connection before. It is the range and the scope of the metaphor which makes one a poet.[6]

Corngold suggests that this comment about metaphor must be ironic since Kafka is "the writer par excellence who came to detect in metaphorical language a crucial obstacle to his own enterprise."[7] However, the fact that Kafka finds metaphors problematic does not mean that he is averse to using them. After all, he was nothing if not ambivalent in life as well as in art. Of course, while Urzidil may be a more reliable witness than Gustav Janouch, author of the notoriously untrustworthy *Conversations with Kafka*,[8] this reported remark should not be accorded the same authority as Kafka's direct utterances. Still, even if he never used those exact words, Kafka was indeed strong in metaphor.

Rather than pitting Kafka against metaphor, I would suggest that in much of his writing there is a tension between his gift for thinking in metaphors and his doubts about their adequacy. This tension is already apparent in his earliest extant writing. As a seventeen-year-old writing in a girl's keepsake album, he is already questioning the efficacy of language:

> How many words there are in this book! They are meant for remembrance! As though words could remember! For words are poor mountaineers and poor miners. They cannot bring down the treasure from the mountains' peaks, or up from the mountains' depths. (*L*, 1)[9]

This skepticism about language will become a mainspring of Kafka's literary creativity.[10] Through the analogy with mountaineers and miners he suggests that words cannot articulate profound thoughts or feelings. However, in conveying his distrust of language, he resorts to metaphors, which he comes to see as fundamentally unreliable figures of speech. Although these skeptical phrases can certainly be read against the backdrop of the well-known crisis of language in turn-of-the-century Austro-Hungary, it is worth keeping in mind that Kafka wrote them in 1900, two years before Hofmannsthal's powerful depiction of that crisis in his *Letter to Lord Chandos* (1902).[11]

Kafka has a congenitally associative mind. Yet rather than taking pleasure in his enviable ability to think in images, he castigates himself for this alleged deficiency: "All those things, that is to say, those things which occur to me, occur to me not from the root up but rather only from somewhere about their middle" (*D*, 12).[12] He goes on to criticize this penchant for thinking in images on account of its slipperiness: "Let someone then attempt to seize them, let someone attempt to seize a blade of grass and hold fast to it when it begins to grow only from the middle." In other words, thoughts expressed through the medium of metaphor are inherently elusive. However, it is telling that in critiquing this supposed weakness, he cannot help resorting to metaphor.

The metaphors in the early letters reflect a raw need for self-expression. Only through his writing could Kafka overcome his isolation, sustain relationships with friends, and develop an awareness of his potential. Take, for instance, his letters to Oskar Pollak, whom he avowedly preferred to engage not face-to-face but through correspondence: "When we talk together, the words are hard; we tread over them as if they were rough pavement. The most delicate things acquire clumsy feet and we can't help it" (*L*, 1).[13] The intensity of the imagery in these letters to Pollak recalls earlier eras of letter-writing, such as the sentimental language of the *Sturm und Drang*, which Goethe infuses with such vibrancy in *Die Leiden des jungen Werther* (*The Sorrows of Young Werther*).

Although couched in irony, the lachrymose sentiments of young Kafka emerge in a passage about a small package of his writings he is about to send to Pollak: "Well, why all the fuss, eh — I am taking a piece (for I can do more than this and I shall — yes), a piece of my heart, packing it neatly in a few sheets of inscribed paper, and sending it on to you" (*L*, 9).[14] The jocose disclaimers cannot entirely conceal the fact that, as Walter Sokel has rightly noted, young Kafka subscribes to Romantic notions of sincerity and authenticity.[15]

While it could be argued that Kafka's fiction from "The Judgment" ("Das Urteil," 1913) onward is — at least on the surface — largely devoid of figurative language, Corngold alerts us in his study *Lambent Traces* to the dramatized theory of the explosive potential of metaphor underlying this breakthrough story.[16] Moreover, Kafka's decision to keep regular diaries in 1910 was, as is widely acknowledged, a decisive turning point in his development as a writer. In the diaries he gives free rein not only to his tendency to think in images but also to his need to interrogate such thinking. The diaries and letters certainly abound in powerful images: in a letter to Pollak he claims that "a book must be the axe for the frozen sea inside us" (*L,* 16);[17] on a postcard to Max Brod, after a casual remark about a visit to a dentist, he jots down the remarkable metaphor: "Kleist blows in me as in an old pig's bladder" (*L,* 71);[18] he conveys his revulsion for literary preening through an olfactory image: "Writers speak a stench" (*D,* 12).[19] These metaphors are memorable instances of what the French linguist Jean Cohen has called "semantic impertinence."[20]

In the early diaries Kafka describes the situation that inspired him to begin keeping a regular diary with a combination of metaphors and direct observations about his internal and external state. He uses metaphors quite self-consciously to discipline himself and to create a semblance of order. Castigating himself for his inability to write anything during a five-month period, he invokes the image of a heap of straw: ". . . there was always something in me to catch fire, in this heap of straw that I have been for five months and whose fate, it seems, is to be set afire during the summer and consumed more swiftly than the onlooker can blink his eyes" (*D,* 12).[21] Not satisfied with implicit self-flagellation, he switches from metaphor to plain speech to deliver the *coup de grâce*: "If only that would happen to me!" He is determined to cling to his diary: "I won't ever give up the diary again. I must hold on here, it is the only place I can" (29).[22] Ten days later, on 26 December 1910, he begins to notice the benefits of regular diary keeping: "A slight ordering of my interior begins to take place and I need nothing more, for disorder is the worst thing in small talents" (33).[23] He wishes to find a circle within which he could confine himself:

> Why don't I stay within myself . . . You can achieve nothing if you abandon yourself, but what do you miss, aside from this, in your circle? To this appeal I answer only: I too would rather submit to blows within the circle than myself deal the blows outside it — but where the devil is this circle? For a time, indeed, I did see it lying on the earth, as if sprayed in lime, but now it just seems to hover about me, indeed does not even hover. (14)[24]

Here Kafka scrutinizes the circle metaphor and finds it wanting: How could he possibly hope to find such a circle? After all, however we may choose to classify that perhaps hallucinatory outline in chalk, the circle is only a metaphor. But it is an enduring image. In August 1913, amid another attempt to achieve focus by turning inward, he writes: "In me, by myself, without human relationship, there are no visible ties. The limited circle is pure."[25] Still, regular entries will keep his potentially unruly and chaotic self under surveillance. He even likens his entries to the telescopes scouring the heavens for Halley's comet: "But every day at least one line should be trained on me, as they now train telescopes on the comet" (12).[26] Yet while such images might appear to suggest that he can plumb his inner life by writing regular diary entries, he remains skeptical about the ability of language, and metaphors in particular, to describe what occurs within.

Elsewhere I have suggested that the diary imagery can be divided into two groups: obsessive metaphors and workshop selves.[27] The former are phrases that emerge from Kafka's subconscious. Take, for instance, the reference to the nucleus of future works such as *The Trial* (*Der Process*, 1925): "I have continually an invocation in my ear: Would that you came, invisible tribunal" (31).[28] In the following observation about his own body one can detect seeds of *The Metamorphosis* (*Die Verwandlung*, 1915): "For a moment I felt myself cased in armor" (umpanzert) — "How far from me are, for example, my arm muscles" (39).[29] In the opening paragraph Gregor Samsa awakens to find himself lying on his back, which is now "armor-like" (panzerartig).

Kafka found a way to make creative use of the tension between his gift for metaphor and his skepticism about figurative language by shifting from musings about his life to entries that blend biographical and fictional material.[30] He realizes that the best way to forge a consistent literary persona is by tackling the issue of his troubled childhood, which he had first broached in a lost early literary effort, a collection of short prose, "The Child and the City" ("Das Kind und die Stadt," *B1*, 29).

The emotional origins of Kafka's seminal metaphors emerge forcefully in a sequence of diary passages in which he — or rather a first-person narrator who at times seems identical to the biographical Kafka and at others not — reproaches those who allegedly harmed him as a child and hindered his subsequent development. He grieves for the confidence in his abilities and the natural zest for life that he was tempted to regard as the natural birthright of human beings. A series of revealingly repetitive entries in June 1910 begins with a vision of an alternative childhood as a survivor among the ruins: "I should prefer most of all to have been such a little dweller in the ruins . . . even though I might have been weak at first under the pressure of my good qualities, which would have grown tall in me with the might of weeds" (15).[31]

This metaphorically resonant passage implies that the child has survived a catastrophe that has swept away his parents and family. Far from seeing this *tabula rasa* as a disaster, Kafka, or rather the first-person narrator, presents the deserted setting as the most propitious environment for raising a child, or rather for allowing a child to raise itself. No directions are needed for this little dweller in the ruins. In the raw state of nature, unimpeded by the power-lust of authority figures, his young alter ego can soak up the life-giving sun. The disaster that struck may have obliterated not only the family of this rustic Franz but all other human beings. In any case, the absence of tyrannical adults ensures that the good qualities of this little ruin-dweller can sprout like weeds.

How seriously are we supposed to take this escapist thinking? As the negative introduction ("I was not") and the metaphorical alignment of good qualities with weeds surely suggest, this daydream of an alternative childhood is written tongue-in-cheek. After all, such fantasies about an alternative childhood would not allow Kafka to build the literary-existential foundation that he needs if he is to create work of lasting value. So, starting from scratch, he begins to name those who supposedly damaged him.

Through metaphors he constructs a persona that draws on biographical material and yet is also fictional. One of the most potent images to emerge in subsequent elaborations of this initial paragraph is that of a "dead bride" — a metaphor for a potential self that had been crushed during the course of his upbringing: "The reproach for having after all spoiled a part of me — for having spoiled a good, beautiful part (in my dreams sometimes it appears to me the way a dead bride appears to others)" (18).[32]

Envisaging a fate he wishes to avert, Kafka imagines himself as a forty-year-old in whom these emotions have become calcified: "The reproaches lie around inside me like strange tools that I hardly have the courage to seize and lift any longer" (19).[33] He fears becoming an ineffectual middle-aged bachelor who will have failed to transform raw emotions about his childhood into the "tools" of his art. However, by experimenting with these images he gradually learns how to make use of these implements. His identity as a person lies in the force with which he articulates those reproaches: "What I still am now is revealed most clearly to me by the strength with which the reproaches urge their way out of me" (19).[34] This awareness makes him all the more determined to channel emotions triggered by memories of childhood into images.

At the same time he reveals the limits of such similes and metaphors by allowing the narrator to undermine his own indictment of those who have supposedly harmed him. The more he writes, the greater the number of culprits he finds. Soon they include not only those who played major roles in his childhood but also chance acquaintances who made him feel miserable. The comic absurdity of these belated attempts to settle scores becomes evident once the number of defendants becomes so large that he has difficulty recalling them. While this litany may reflect real emotions triggered by childhood memories, it is tinged with irony and humor. The manner in which the narrator lumps the defendants together is risible: he yokes those, such as his parents, whom he believes — or affects to believe — did him serious harm, with those whose offenses were so slight that he cannot even recall their identities. When one hears this extensive diary entry read well aloud — for instance, Susan Sontag's reading of it in 1998 at a Kafka event in New York's Town Hall — it is difficult to suppress one's laughter.[35]

Yet, as often in Kafka, the humor has a serrated edge. In one variant we learn that a grievance "twists through society like a dagger" (15).[36] Those disinclined to perceive social criticism in Kafka would do well to ponder this simile. This image of a dagger projects outward onto society the violence inherent in his often masochistic metaphors: "This morning, for the first time in a long time, the joy again of imagining a knife twisted in my heart" (101).[37]

Far from seeking to justify himself retrospectively, the narrator frequently allows doubts about the veracity of his perspective to seep into his account. He openly acknowledges the increasingly fictional quality of his accusations against those who may have injured him as a child. As a result, he begins to depict those supposedly tormenting adults not as flesh-and-blood individuals but as ghostly memories or even opaque metaphors: "Forgotten energy may hold these persons fast in memory, but they would hardly have any ground left under them and even their legs would have already turned to smoke. . . . Like tired dogs they stand there, because they use up all their strength in remaining upright in one's memory" (17).[38] The image of "tired dogs" evokes a metaphor that Kafka would later apply to his alter ego, Josef K., in *The Trial*, who in the final sentence of the novel describes himself as dying "like a dog." The first-person narrator is no longer filled with the intense anger that once drove him to accost complete strangers: "There were times when I had nothing else inside me except reproaches driven by rage, so that, although physically well, I would hold on to strangers in the street because the reproaches inside me tossed from side to side like water in a bowl that was being carried rapidly" (19).[39]

Although Kafka mistrusts individual images, he retains faith in the power of metaphor to transform the raw material of life into art. Hence, perhaps, the narrator's belief that his reproaches, however dubious, are nourished by sound theory: "That is the reproach that I have to make. It has a healthy core, theory supports it" (17).[40] While the narrator does not explain this tantalizing reference to theory, the outline of such a theory might resemble James Olney's characterization of autobiographical metaphors as "order-produced and order-producing, emotion-satisfying theories and equations . . . something known and of our making, or at least of our choosing, that we put to stand for, and so to help us understand, something unknown and not of our making."[41] However, since Olney focuses mostly on classic autobiographical writers such as Montaigne and John Henry Newman, some of his generalizations about metaphor can seem less applicable to literary modernists. Take, for instance, the following assertion: "We do not see or touch the self, but we do see and touch its metaphors: and thus we 'know' the self, activity or agent, represented in the metaphor and the metaphorizing" (34). Neither Kafka — nor for that matter Beckett[42] — is so confident that the self can be truly known.

Kafka's metaphors can never quite conjoin — to use the customary rhetorical terms — tenor and vehicle. Indeed, he often builds into his metaphors an acknowledgement of his inability or unwillingness to make any such connection. This "failure" need not be seen in exclusively negative terms; indeed he himself did not see it so. For instance, during a walk on Prague's Laurenziberg — described in a remarkable diary entry of 15 February 1920 — he describes wishing to construct a paradoxical table that would at the same time be nothing at all:

> This is the problem: many years ago I sat one day, in a sad enough mood, on the slopes of the Laurenziberg. I went over the wishes that I wanted to fulfill in life. I found that the most important or the most delightful was the wish to attain a view of life . . . in which life, while still retaining its natural full-bodied rise and fall, would simultaneously be recognized no less clearly as a nothing, a dream, a dim hovering . . . . Considered as a wish, somewhat as if one were to hammer together a table with painful and methodical efficiency, and simultaneously do nothing at all, and not in such a way that people could say: "Hammering a table together is nothing to him" but rather: "Hammering a table together is really hammering a table together to him, but at the same time it is nothing," whereby certainly the hammering would have become still bolder, still surer, still more real, and if you will, still more senseless. (*GWC*, 267–68)[43]

The thirty-seven-year-old Kafka writing these lines is aware that resentment and defiance fuels those youthful reveries. Others' reactions merely spurred him to hammer furiously, thereby rendering his paradoxical carpentry all the more "senseless." That paradoxical table surely stands for the literary works that Kafka will eventually construct and de-construct. His urge to create and at the same destroy certainly anticipates the shape of his self-obliterating fictions.

An early example of this technique can be seen in a short text in "Observation" (*Betrachtung*, 1902), "The Trees" ("Die Bäume"), which opens with a seemingly straightforward simile:

> For we are like tree trunks in the snow. Apparently they lie flat on the ground and with a little push one should be able to push them aside. No, one can't, for they are firmly connected to the ground. But look, even that is merely apparent.[44]

Since the tree trunks are simply lying on the ground, it might seem easy to move them. If these trunks can be easily pushed aside, the simile would imply that we humans are creatures without roots, who can easily be blown away. However, the narrator goes on to withdraw the initial statement by insisting that the trees are in fact solidly connected to the ground and cannot be readily dislodged. But the next, and final, sentence withdraws this alternative interpretation: "But look, even that is only apparent." This bewildering conclusion cancels the possibility of attributing any conclusive meaning to the initial analogy between the tree trunks and the human condition.[45]

In *The Castle* (*Das Schloss*, 1926), the hero's interpretative struggles mirror the reader's frequently futile quest to find meaning. As in the case of the late short text "On Parables," the significance of Kafka's final novel may lie precisely in the way it refutes all attempts to assign any fixed interpretation. Take, for instance, the first detailed description of the castle, in which Kafka uses metaphors that simultaneously invite and deflect interpretation. Although K. is eager to project lofty meanings onto what he sees, the ramshackle buildings comprising the castle complicate and at times even undermine his efforts (*C*, 8). Toward the end of this well-known passage he comes up with alternative similes and metaphors. Whereas the vertical thrust of the tower compares favorably with the church tower in his hometown, the battlements remind him of a child's tentative drawing:

> The tower . . . was a monotonous round building, in part mercifully hidden by ivy, with little windows that glinted in the sun — there was something crazy about this — and ending a kind of terrace, whose battlements, uncertain, irregular, brittle, as if drawn by the anxious or careless hand of a child, zigzagged into the blue sky. It was as if some melancholy resident, who by rights ought to have kept himself locked up in the most out-of-the-way room in the house, had broken through the roof and stood up in order to show himself to the world. (8)[46]

So this intricate passage, which began with K.'s hopes of finding an imposing edifice that would surpass the church tower in his hometown, ends with the image of an enclosed occupant finally breaking through the roof, conjuring up thoughts of imprisonment and rebellion.

The repeated comparisons in the passage cited above between K.'s home town and the castle on the hill echo a recurrent preoccupation of Kafka's. He claimed to have embarked on his artistic odyssey in order to find a metaphorical substitute for home. While working on *The Castle*, he invokes in a letter to Max Brod of 12 July 1922 a metaphor that suggests the depth of this preoccupation with home ("Heimat"): "I am away from home and must always write home, even if any home of mine has long since floated away into eternity. All this writing is nothing but Robinson Crusoe's flag hoisted at the highest point of the island" (340).[47] Although Kafka sought to build a substitute — much like Defoe's Robinson Crusoe on his island — he became increasingly aware that the metaphors underlying literature can never be an adequate substitute for home.

According to Max Brod, Kafka spoke of concluding the novel on an ironically conciliatory note: on his deathbed K. would be denied official permission to settle in the village but on account of auxiliary circumstances would receive provisional permission to stay. On the evidence of the incomplete novel as it stands, however, the prospect of K.'s finding anything resembling home would seem poor, especially since he spurns Frieda's attempts to establish a common household.

In works such as *The Castle,* Kafka constructs his metaphorical edifices along lines envisaged by Jacques Derrida, who offers a useful gloss on passages such as K.'s first extensive contemplation of the castle: "It (deconstruction) is not simply the technique of an architect who knows how to deconstruct what has been constructed, but a probing which touches upon the technique itself."[48] Although Derrida wrote these words for an audience of architects, he could just as well be describing Kafka's narrative strategy. As we saw above, Kafka continually constructs and deconstructs his metaphorical table. These deconstructions always contain an implicit reflection not only on the inherent deceitfulness of figurative language but on any fiction built upon such faulty cornerstones.

Kafka's remarks about metaphor after 1920 must be seen in the context of his increasing disillusionment with life and literature. In his diaries and letters he complains about the artificial nature of writing: "There is an artificial, miserable substitute for everything, for forebears, marriage, and heirs. Feverishly you contrive these substitutes, and if the fever has not already destroyed you, the hopelessness of the substitutes will" (*D,* 402).[49] Whether consciously or not, he reprises metaphors from the early diaries, such as the circle:

> It was as if I, like everyone else, had been given a point from which to prolong the radius of a circle, and had then, like everyone else, to describe my perfect circle round this point. Instead, I was forever starting my radius only constantly to be forced at once to break it off. (Examples: piano, violin, languages, Germanics, anti-Zionism, Zionism, Hebrew, gardening, carpentering, writing, marriage attempts, an apartment of my own) the center of my imaginary circle bristles with the beginning of radii, there is no room left for a new attempt, and no new attempt means the end. (404)[50]

Here Kafka's tone is very different from that in the early entries, in which the image of the circle conveyed a degree of hope. In 1910 he still believed that if he confined himself to an imaginary circle, he could establish a solid sense of self and achieve the focus he needed to write convincingly. However, the examples of his abortive efforts to strike out on his own suggest that he no longer places writing and literature on the pedestal it once occupied. Now he can simply list it among such failed forays as gardening or carpentry. So low in status has writing sunk that it is now merely one among his supposed failures.

Also, in these late entries he revisits the theme of the damage supposedly inflicted on him as a child, which he had explored in June 1910. Now he is longer willing to blame himself or anyone else for his unhappiness: ". . . I cannot grant that the first beginnings of my unhappiness were inwardly necessitated, they may have indeed had a necessity, but not an inward one, they swarmed down on me like flies and could have been as easily driven off" (405).[51] In an evident effort to avoid ritual self-castigation, he resorts to the passive voice, thereby avoiding blaming himself directly for his failure to ward off those metaphorical flies.

Critics often use the previously cited diary entry of 6 December 1921, in which Kafka describes his frustration with the referential quality of metaphors, to illustrate his aversion to metaphor. However, that seeming indictment of his own metaphor-inspired form of writing is worth parsing carefully: "only writing is helpless, cannot live in itself, is fun and despair" (397–98). If one focuses exclusively on the final word, despair, one misses the fun or *Spaß*. Despair, fun, and literary ambition remain as inseparable in Kafka's writing as they were in his early experiments with autobiographical metaphors in June 1910.

In an often-cited diary entry of 16 January 1922, Kafka famously characterizes his literary efforts as an "assault on the frontiers" (*D*, 399)[52] that could have developed into a new Kabbalah. While these words are quoted tirelessly, less attention has been paid to the way in which Kafka substitutes one metaphor for another, building up slowly to the final image of metaphysical assault.

The passage begins with the image of two clocks that attempt to convey the contrast between the calm pace of outer reality and the rapid tempo of his thoughts, which have made him experience "something like a breakdown." The speed with which thoughts pass through his mind, threatening his mental equilibrium, evokes the somewhat predictable image of a chase (*Jagd*). However, since "chase" is simply a metaphor, he can always replace it with another:

> "Pursuit," indeed, is only a metaphor. I can also say "assault on the last earthly frontier," an assault, moreover, launched from below, from mankind, and since this too is a metaphor I can replace it by the metaphor of an assault from above, aimed at me from above. (399)[53]

This fundamental interchangeability of metaphors allows Kafka to switch effortlessly back and forth between conceptually diverse themes, from psychological self-analysis to metaphysics, religion, and literature. In such passages in the diaries and letters we can observe him creating an acutely self-aware web of metaphors, revealing a "coherent vision of all reality, the point through which the individual succeeds in making the universe take on his own order."[54]

Toward the end of his life Kafka, who was always fond of military metaphors, declared a truce in his life-long struggle with figurative language. Like Nietzsche in his remarkable polemic about metaphor, "On Truth and Lie in an Extra-Moral Sense," he could employ metaphors adroitly while continuing to profess doubts about their veracity. No longer tempted to torture the Gordian knot, even amidst the crises of his final years he managed to have a little fun deploying his mobile army of metaphors.[55]

Notes

[1] W. B. Yeats, *Collected Poems* (London: Macmillan, 1961), 336.

[2] Stanley Corngold, *Franz Kafka: The Necessity of Form* (Ithaca, NY: Cornell UP, 1988), 47–104.

[3] Günther Anders, *Kafka Pro und Contra* (Munich: Beck, 1951).

[4] Paul Ricoeur, "The Metaphorical Process as Cognition, Imagination, and Feeling," in *On Metaphor*, ed. Sheldon Sacks (Chicago: Chicago UP, 1979), 153.

[5] *D*1, 397–98; "Die Metaphern sind eines in dem Vielen, was mich am Schreiben verzweifeln läßt. Die Unselbständigkeit des Schreibens, die Abhängigkeit von dem Dienstmädchen, das einheizt, von der Katze, die sich am Ofen wärmt. . . . Alles dies sind selbständige, eigengesetzliche Verrichtungen, nur das Schreiben ist hilflos, wohnt nicht in sich selbst, ist Spaß und Verzweiflung" (*Ta*, 875).

[6] Johannes Urzidil, "Recollections," in *The Kafka Problem*, ed. Angel Flores (New York: New Directions, 1946), 22.

[7] Corngold, *Necessity of Form*, 51.

[8] Mark Harman, "Kafka's Unreliable Friend," in *New York Review of Books* 55.16, 82 — a letter in response to Zadie Smith's review of Louis Begley's biographical essay, *The Tremendous World I Have inside My Head* (New York: Atlas, 2008).

[9] "Wie viel Worte in dem Buche stehn! Erinnern sollen sie! Als ob Worte erinnern könnten! Denn Worte sind schlechte Bergsteiger und schlechte Bergmänner. Sie holen nicht die Schätze von den Bergeshöhn und nicht die von den Bergestiefen!" (*B*1, 380). The translation has been changed here and elsewhere to bring out certain features in the German.

[10] Unfortunately, the editors of the critical edition place this keepsake album entry at the end of the first volume of letters, thereby obscuring the significance of these precocious thoughts. (See *B*1, 380).

[11] The *Letter to Lord Chandos* first appeared in the Berlin daily *Der Tag* under the title "Ein Brief" ("A Letter") in 1902.

[12] "Alle Dinge nämlich die mir einfallen, fallen mir nicht von der Wurzel aus ein, sondern erst irgendwo gegen ihre Mitte. Versuche sie dann jemand zu halten, versuche jemand ein Gras und sich an ihm zu halten das erst in der Mitte des Stengels zu wachsen anfängt" (*Ta*, 14).

[13] "Wenn wir miteinander reden: die Worte sind hart, man geht über sie wie über schlechtes Pflaster. Die feinsten Dinge bekommen plumpe Füße und wir könnnen nichts dafür" (*B*1, 10).

[14] "Nur warum soviel Aufhebens, nicht — ich nehme ein Stück (denn ich kann mehr, als ich dir gebe, und ich werde — ja) ein Stück von meinem Herzen, packe es sauber ein in ein Paar Bogen geschriebenen Papiers und gebe es Dir" (*Bl*, 26).
[15] See, for instance, Walter H. Sokel, "Zur Sprachauffassung und Poetik Franz Kafkas," in *Franz Kafka: Themen und Probleme* (Göttingen: Vandenhoeck, 1980), 26–47; Sokel, "Kafka as a Jew," in *New Literary History* 30.4 (1999), 837–53.
[16] Corngold, *Lambent Traces: Franz Kafka* (Princeton, NJ: Princeton UP, 2004), 13–36.
[17] ". . . ein Buch muß die Axt sein für das gefrorene Meer in uns" (*Bl*, 36).
[18] "Kleist bläst in mich, wie in eine alte Schweinsblase" (*Bl*, 132).
[19] "Schriftsteller reden Gestank" (*Ta*, 13).
[20] Jean Cohen, *Structure du langage poétique* (Paris: Flammarion, 1999), 143.
[21] ". . . hier war noch immer etwas aus mir herauszuschlagen, aus diesem Strohhaufen, der ich seit fünf Monaten bin und dessen Schicksal es zu sein scheint, im Sommer angezündet zu werden und zu verbrennen" (*Ta*, 13–14).
[22] "Ich werde das Tagebuch nicht mehr verlassen. Hier muß ich mich festhalten, denn nur hier kann ich es" (*Ta*, 131).
[23] "Eine kleine Ordnung meines Innern fängt an sich herzustellen und nichts brauche ich mehr, denn Unordnung bei kleinen Fähigkeiten ist das Ärgste" (*Ta*, 139).
[24] "Warum bleibe ich nicht in mir? . . . Du kannst nichts erreichen, wenn Du Dich verläßt, aber was versäumst Du überdies in Deinem Kreis. Auf diese Ansprache antworte ich nur: auch ich ließe mich lieber im Kreis prügeln, als außerhalb selbst zu prügeln, aber wo zum Teufel ist dieser Kreis? Eine Zeitlang sah ich ihn ja auf der Erde liegen, wie mit Kalk ausgespritzt, jetzt aber schwebt er mir nur so herum, ja schwebt nicht einmal" (*Ta*, 16).
[25] "In mir selbst gibt es ohne menschliche Beziehung keine sichtbaren Lügen. Der begrenzte Kreis ist rein" (*Ta*, 581).
[26] "Aber jeden Tag soll zumindest eine Zeile gegen mich gerichtet werden wie man die Fernröhre jetzt gegen den Kometen richtet" (*Ta*, 14).
[27] Mark Harman, "Biography and Autobiography: Necessary Antagonists?" *Journal of the Kafka Society* 10.1/2 (1986): 56–62.
[28] "Ich habe immerfort eine Anrufung im Ohr: Kämest du unsichtbares Gericht!" (*Ta*, 135).
[29] "Einen Augenblick fühlte ich mich umpanzert" — "Wie fern sind mir z.B. die Armmuskeln" (*Ta*, 149).
[30] For a detailed consideration of Kafka's creation of literary personae, see Mark Harman, "Life into Art: Kafka's Self-Stylization in the Diaries," in *Franz Kafka (1883–1983): His Craft and Thought*, ed. Roman Struc and J. C. Yardley (Waterloo, Ontario: W. Laurier UP/Calgary Institute for Humanities, 1986), 101–16.
[31] ". . . am liebsten wäre ich jener kleine Ruinenbewohner gewesen . . . wenn ich auch im Anfang schwach gewesen wäre unter dem Druck meiner guten Eigenschaften, die mit der Macht des Unkrauts in mir emporgewachsen wären" (*Ta*, 17).

[32] "Der Vorwurf darüber, daß sie mir doch ein Stück von mir verdorben haben ein gutes schönes Stück verdorben haben — im Traum erscheint es mir manchmal wie andern die tote Braut . . ." (*Ta*, 22).

[33] "Die Vorwürfe liegen in mir herum, wie fremde Werkzeuge, die zu fassen und zu heben ich kaum den Muth mehr habe" (*Ta*, 25).

[34] "Was ich jetzt noch bin, wird mir am deutlichsten in der Kraft mit der die Vorwürfe aus mir herauswollen" (*Ta*, 25).

[35] An audio recording of Sontag's reading from the 1910 diary is available through the Jewish Heritage Online Magazine website: http://jhom.com/bookshelf/kafka/index.html.

[36] "windet sich wie ein Dolch durch die Gesellschaft" (*Ta*, 18).

[37] "Heute früh zum erstenmal seit langer Zeit wieder die Freude an der Vorstellung eines in meinem Herzen gedrehten Messers" (*Ta*, 220).

[38] "Diese Personen mögen mit einer vergessenen Energie in der Erinnerung festgehalten werden, einen Fußboden werden sie kaum mehr unter sich haben und selbst ihre Beine werden schon Rauch sein . . . Wie müde Hunde stehn sie da, weil sie alle ihre Kraft dazu verbrauchen um in der Erinnerung aufrecht zu bleiben" (*Ta*, 21).

[39] "Es gab Zeiten wo ich in mir nichts anderes als vor Wuth getriebene Vorwürfe hatte, daß ich bei körperlichem Wohlbefinden mich auf der Gasse an fremden Leuten festhielt, weil sich die Vorwürfe in mir von einer Seite auf die andere warfen, wie Wasser in einem Becken, das man rasch trägt" (*Ta*, 25).

[40] "Das ist der Vorwurf, den ich zu erheben habe. Er hat ein gesundes Innere, die Teorie erhält ihn" (*Ta*, 22).

[41] James Olney, *Metaphors of Self: The Meaning of Autobiography* (Princeton, NJ: Princeton UP, 1972), 30.

[42] See Mark Harman, "Terminal Fantasies: Beckett and Kafka," in *That Other World: The Supernatural and the Fantastic in Irish Literature and Its Contexts*, Princess Grace Irish Library 12 (Gerrards Cross, UK: Colin Smythe, 1998), 2:177–87; "'At least he could garden'": Beckett and Kafka," in *Partisan Review* 66.4 (1999): 574–79.

[43] "Es handelt sich um folgendes: Ich saß einmal vor vielen Jahren, gewiß traurig genug, auf der Lehne des Laurenziberges. Ich prüfte die Wünsche, die ich für das Leben hatte. Als wichtigster oder als reizvollster ergab sich der Wunsch, eine Ansicht des Lebens zu gewinnen . . . in der das Leben zwar sein natürliches schweres Fallen und Steigen bewahre aber gleichzeitig mit nicht minderer Deutlichkeit als ein Nichts, als ein Traum, als ein Schweben erkannt werde . . . Etwa als Wunsch einen Tisch mit peinlich ordentlicher Handwerksmäßigkeit zusammenzuhämmern und dabei gleichzeitig nichts zu tun undzwar nicht so daß man sagen könnte: "ihm ist das Hämmern ein Nichts" sondern "ihm ist das Hämmern ein wirkliches Hämmern und gleichzeitig auch ein Nichts," wodurch ja das Hämmern noch kühner, noch entschlossener, noch wirklicher und wenn Du willst noch irrsinniger geworden wäre" (*Ta*, 854–55).

[44] "Denn wir sind wie Baumstämme im Schnee. Scheinbar liegen sie glatt auf, und mit kleinem Anstoß sollte man sie wegschieben können. Nein, das kann man nicht, denn sie sind fest mit dem Boden verbunden. Aber sieh, sogar das ist nur scheinbar" (*DL*, 30).

[45] For a related development of this thought, see the essay in this volume by Jacob Burnett, "Strange Loops and the Absent Center in *The Castle*."

[46] "Der Turm . . . war ein einförmiger Rundbau, zum Teil gnädig von Epheu verdeckt, mit kleinen Fenstern, die jetzt in der Sonne aufstrahlten — etwas Irrsinniges hatte das — und einem söllerartigen Abschluß, dessen Mauerzinnen unsicher, unregelmäßig, brüchig wie von ängstlicher oder nachlässiger Kinderhand gezeichnet sich in den blauen Himmel zackten. Es war wie wenn irgendein trübseliger Hausbewohner, der gerechter Weise im entlegensten Zimmer des Hauses sich hätte eingesperrt halten sollen, das Dach durchbrochen und sich erhoben hätte, um sich der Welt zu zeigen" (*S*, 18).

[47] "Ich bin von zuhause fort und muß immerfort nach hause schreiben, auch wenn alles Zuhause längst fortgeschwommen sein sollte in die Ewigkeit. Dieses ganze Schreiben ist nichts als die Fahne des Robinson auf dem höchsten Punkt der Insel" (*Br*, 392).

[48] Jacques Derrida, "Architecture: Where the Desire May Live," in *Rethinking Architecture: A Reader in Cultural Theory*, ed. Neil Leach (New York: Routledge, 1997), 302.

[49] "Für alles gibt es künstlichen, jämmerlichen Ersatz: für Vorfahren, Ehe und Nachkommen. In Krämpfen schafft man ihn und geht, wenn man nicht schon an den Krämpfen zugrunde gegangen ist, an der Trostlosigkeit des Ersatzes zugrunde" (*Ta*, 885).

[50] "Es war so als wäre mir wie jedem andern Menschen der Kreismittelpunkt gegeben, als hätte ich dann wie jeder andere Mensch den entscheidenden Radius zu gehn und dann den schönen Kreis zu ziehn. Statt dessen habe ich immerfort einen Anlauf zum Radius genommen, aber immer wieder gleich ihn abbrechen müssen (Beispiele: Klavier, Violine, Sprachen, Germanistik, Antizionismus, Zionismus, Hebräisch, Gärtnerei, Tischlerei, Litteratur, Heiratsversuche, eigene Wohnung). Es starrt im Mittelpunkt des imaginären Kreises von beginnenden Radien, es ist kein Platz mehr für einen neuen Versuch, kein Platz heißt Alter, Nervenschwäche, und kein Versuch mehr bedeutet Ende" (*Ta*, 887).

[51] "Ich kann . . . auf keine Weise zugeben, daß die ersten Anfänge meines Unglücks innerlich notwendig waren, sie mögen Notwendigkeit gehabt haben, aber nicht innerliche, sie kamen angeflogen wie Fliegen und wären so leicht wie sie zu vertreiben gewesen" (*Ta*, 889–90).

[52] "Ansturm gegen die Grenze" (*Ta*, 878).

[53] "'Jagd' ist ja nur ein Bild, ich kann auch sagen 'Ansturm gegen die letzte irdische Grenze' und zwar Ansturm von unten, von den Menschen her und kann, da auch dies nur ein Bild ist, es ersetzen durch das Bild des Ansturmes von oben, zu mir herab" (*Ta*, 878).

[54] James Olney, *Metaphors of Self: The Meaning of Autobiography* (Princeton, NJ: Princeton UP, 1972), 30. The sequence of metaphors in the diary entry of 28 January 1922 brings to mind Dylan Thomas's description of the way he creates chains of metaphors: "I make one image . . . let it breed another, let that image contradict the first, make of the third image bred out of the other two together, a fourth contradictory image." *The Collected Letters of Dylan Thomas*, ed. Paul Ferris, vol. 2 (London: J. M. Dent, 1985), 397.

[55] A spirited discussion after the presentation of an early version of this essay at *Kafka at 125* suggests that this topic may be far from exhausted. I would like to thank the conference organizers — Ruth Gross, Clayton Koelb, James Rolleston — and also the audience at that session, especially Stanley Corngold and Walter Sokel, as well as the moderator, John Zilcosky.

3: Nietzsche and Kafka: The Dionysian Connection

Walter H. Sokel

"NIETZSCHE AND KAFKA" is a significant but many-sided topic. That Kafka was always a Nietzschean from the beginning is confirmed by Max Brod, when he tells us about their first meeting. They indulged in a philosophical argument, in which Brod took the side of his favorite philosopher, Arthur Schopenhauer, while Kafka took Nietzsche's side. Kafka was a Nietzschean from way back, and he remained one throughout his work in many differing ways.

Their relationship is by no means simple. Nothing is simple where those two — Friedrich and Franz — are concerned. There are several distinct aspects and areas in which Kafka's writing relates to Nietzsche's in a very striking way. I have counted at least five distinct areas where Kafka texts show significant analogies to Nietzschean thought.

I cannot do justice here to more than one of them, but I should at least like to list the others before I deal with one in detail.

The area that is first and foremost fundamental to both authors I should like to term the Dionysian. The most relevant Nietzschean text here is *The Birth of Tragedy*, but Dionysianism, as I have tried to show elsewhere, remains fundamental to Nietzsche in all phases of his thought.[1] The second area of at times stunning agreement deals with the ironization of asceticism and ascetic values. A third common area links the birth of the continuous individual to the infliction of painful suffering as mnemotechnic instruction. A fourth and fifth area center around a complex and problematic view of "truth" and what Nietzsche termed "the spirit of gravity."

Having sketched this rough idea of the multiplicity of Kafka's relationship to Nietzsche, I should now like to concentrate on what I have termed the Dionysian. According to Nietzsche's *Birth of Tragedy*, the Dionysian orgies of the ancient world celebrated the oneness of being by impersonating it in orgiastic dances. As mentioned before, even though Nietzsche never explicitly returned to the topic in his later work, he remained faithful to the belief in the oneness of being throughout his thinking life. In the four central ideas of his later thought — the Overman, the Eternal Return, the war upon ascetic ideals, and his aesthetic approach to existence — Nietzsche remained a faithful Dionysian. All existence is one, and individuation is ultimately illusionary.

However, we have to distinguish radically Nietzsche's conviction of the oneness of being from traditional pantheism as we find it, for instance, in Spinoza. Dionysian oneness is not static but dynamic. It is not substance but cosmic energy. What is One is not a static substantive being but an ever-active, ever-creative, and ever-destructive energy that Schopenhauer, with misleading anthropomorphism, had called the Will. "The Will" is a misnomer insofar as it seems to imply a quasi-conscious desiring, a setting up of objectives and attempts to attain them. That is not Nietzsche's notion of what Schopenhauer called the Will. The Will can best be thought of as a restless unceasing force that perpetually creates everything there is, constantly transmutes and re-forms, and eventually destroys it. All phenomena are embodiments of the Will and inwardly filled with and driven by it. Whatever the Will brings forth, it likewise destroys, making room for ever-new creations. This seemingly senseless cycle of creation and destruction, which knows no end, no goal, no reason, inspired in Schopenhauer his famous radical pessimism.

Nietzsche inherited from Schopenhauer this structure of being as restless becoming, but reversed its evaluation. By a radical change of perspective from the individual to the whole, Nietzsche, instead of feeling overwhelmed by the Will's destructiveness, celebrated its never-ceasing creativeness. With a basically identical content, this change of perspective made Nietzsche an enthusiastically affirmative yea-saying thinker.

The Dionysian key to the unity of all existence is the view that it is a perpetual series of creations. With that in mind, its destructiveness hardly counts for more than a stimulus, an enabler of new creations. The Dionysian unity lies in being as an interminable becoming, a flow of ever-changing, ever-new creations, with unceasing destruction secondary, subordinate to primal ubiquitous creation. Unity of being as the oneness of the creative energy of the universe is fundamentally an artistic or aesthetic one. Being so considered is ultimately art, a creative activity. Creation not only precedes but also outlives destruction.

For Nietzsche, Greek tragedy reflects that perfectly. The hero or protagonist, individuation par excellence, goes under, to be sure, but in the chorus, occupying the stage at the end, the continuity and endurance of life and its ultimate triumph over mortal individuation manifests itself. Thus Greek tragedy is the perfect portrayal of existence with its duality of negation and affirmation, affirmation asserting its supremacy over tragic mournfulness. Schopenhauer would stop with the tragic hero, but Nietzsche goes on, striding over the corpse, as it were, toward the dancing chorus. Viewed in this fashion, Attic tragedy is a faithful mimesis of being.

As he sees ultimate being as a process or an activity akin to art, Nietzsche's view of being can rightly be called aesthetic, as his well-known saying makes clear: "It is only as an *aesthetic phenomenon* that existence and the world are eternally *justified*."[2] This aestheticism also informs Nietzsche's value system, which his subsequent work as a moralist propagates. The connection, often overlooked, between Nietzsche's early *Birth of Tragedy* and his later works as a critic, analyst, and pioneer of moral values lies in the aestheticism common to both.

In the early work, Nietzsche's Dionysian aestheticism rests on the view of being as creation and thus, in the broadest sense, art. That perspective is, as it were, that of the Will itself, which Nietzsche's writing intends to make manifest. In his later work, Nietzsche also writes from the perspective of the spectator, the beholder and critical judge of the creation, the "work of art," as which the world is to be seen and judged.

He devotes all his intellectual energy to the endeavor of helping to make the world as aesthetically satisfying a spectacle toward which it might and could possibly, and in many as yet unimaginable ways, evolve. Allied to this extension of perspective from artist-creator to evaluating spectator is a shift in the temporal dimension from the eternal present of Dionysus to the future as envisaged and promoted by Zarathustra.

Thus Nietzsche's aestheticist — equally: aesthetic — morality bifurcates into two aspects. One is the spectator's morality, which seeks to aid the Will in bringing into being ever-grander, ever more interesting and fascinating forms of life to witness and enjoy. The other one is the imitation of the Will as artist embodying the ever-outward-bound and other-directed activity of the universe, a modem secular version of the medieval "imitatio Dei."

Zarathustra's ideal of "the giving virtue" (die schenkende Tugend), which exhorts man to imitate the sun that shines upon and gives himself to all without regard to any advantage accruing to the giver and without any consideration of whether one's beneficiaries merit the gifts, exemplifies the morality of the creative artist. Giving is not a means to something else; giving is the manifestation of one's being. It is the expression of a richness of energy that is self-overflowing, self-transcending by its very nature. Its being is *having to* give, having to add to and to enhance being. Energy cannot contain itself. This artist's morality has as its only law the need to squander itself and thus to enrich being.

It is the opposite of judgmentalism, because it is entirely future-bound. Here it converges with the other element of Nietzsche's morality, the spectator's perspective, which complements the creative artist's ethics. For aiming toward an ever-heightened quality of spectacle, it too looks toward the future. It is future-bound, as the creator-artist's morality is outward-bound, other-directed. Both strain away from the ego, the individual, as it is here and now. Both seek to transcend the status quo. Thus the creation of an Overman, to whom man will be what the ape has been to man, becomes a moral duty.

The giving up of the present for the future, of the ego for the other, can likewise take the sun as an appropriate metaphor. The sun of the day not only rises; it also sets; it yields to night as the presently attained self is to yield to death to give way to a more glorious tomorrow.

The priorization of the future in the aestheticist morality of the spectator closely corresponds to the priorization of the other, the non-ego, in the aestheticist morality of the creator-artist. The future is the time dimension of otherness, and it is in his service of otherness that Zarathustra's morality is anchored. As Walter Kaufmann has often pointed out, close analogies to Christian morality should not be overlooked, and they acquire special relevance when we consider the common ground between Nietzsche and Kafka.

One important sign of the future-directedness of Zarathustrian morality is the crucial importance it gives to childhood and children. Favoring the future over the past and the present, Zarathustra exhorts us to look toward the "Kinderland" (children-land) instead of the fatherland.[3] The purpose of sexual union between husband and wife, he exhorts married couples, should be the child as a bridge toward the Overman of an as yet unimaginable future. As we shall see, the extolling of childhood and children as a signifier of the future closely relates Zarathustrian morality to Kafka's *The Metamorphosis* (*Die Verwandlung*, 1915).

Indeed the very word "Verwandlung" (metamorphosis, transformation) plays a crucial role in the story of Zarathustra. Zarathustra is referred to as "verwandelt" and calls himself a "transformed" being, and one of his key parables is called "Von den Verwandlungen." This very obvious verbal link to Kafka's story will serve as our starting point in comparing the two authors.

What does the term "Verwandlung" mean when applied to Zarathustra? Its most obvious and primary meaning designates Zarathustra's change from a hermit disgusted with, and therefore withdrawn from, human beings as they are, to one willing and eager to help them and to sacrifice himself in the quest of aiding them to go beyond themselves. His "Verwandlung" is a transformation from self-indulgence to active concern for his fellow humans, from a self-centered to an other-directed life. It is a form of self-sacrifice, and that will lead us directly to Kafka's story *The Metamorphosis.*

I propose to unravel Gregor's story in *The Metamorphosis* from its end point beyond Gregor's death. An anticipatory glimpse of the "Kinderland" appears after, and because of, Gregor's voluntary dying. The whole story describes a *transformation* toward that point, beginning with Gregor's waking up physically *transformed.* In Zarathustrian terms, Kafka's narrative of Gregor Samsa enacts its protagonist's conflict between ego and self in a series of battles in which the self always wins out over the ego, till it triumphs completely in the prospect of Grete's future children taking Gregor's place.

To understand *The Metamorphosis* in its amazingly close connection to Nietzsche's Zarathustrian thought, we have to look closely at Zarathustra's radical distinction between the ego and the self. Consistent with his Dionysian holism, Nietzsche derives the notion of the ego from the concept of individuation, the fleeting phenomenon based, according to Schopenhauer, on the illusionary Ideas dreamed by the Will. As such, individuals are fleeting illusions. Inheriting from Schopenhauer this low regard for the individual as fleeting and illusionary, on the one hand, Nietzsche combines it with the highest regard for the great individual, on the other hand. How can we account for such a dual evaluation? What makes individuals great is the Will working in and through them. Individuals are great as the vessels and manifestations of the energy forming them and pulsating in them.

However, the individual as ego is the reification and idolizing of split-off individuation, and as such the ego is illusory, and undue concern for it is fatuous and contemptible. Egotism, self-regard, or more accurately ego-regard, is the basest self-alienation. It is sheer idolatry. Based on delusion and a fundamental misreading of existence, it is betrayal of the universal Will for the worship of an utterly illusionary idol. It degrades the dynamic subject into a static object, a morally reprehensible desertion and betrayal of the Will within the body.

While the ego is illusionary and undue regard for it reprehensible, what Zarathustra calls the self is an entirely different story. The self is the secret mover of the individual and its link to the cosmos. We might view it as the representative of the Will working in and through the individual. Here the link to Kafka's *Metamorphosis* becomes clear. In Nietzschean terms, Gregor's metamorphosis can be seen as the taking over and displacement of Gregor's ego by his self.

Gregor's dominant position in his family as its breadwinner and thus its head, the successor of his failed and seemingly near-senile father, is felt by the family as oppressive. This elevation of Gregor's ego, however, has paradoxically also enslaved Gregor to the treadmill of the business he serves. His metamorphosis as the eruption of Gregor's unconscious self eliminates him as head of the family and, by the same token, as slave of the business. By the same paradox, while he liberates his family from his oppressive dominance, which is felt as a usurpation, he also burdens them now with his parasitic dependence, heaping disgrace and shame on them. The true logic of his metamorphosis would be the completion of his self-removal from his ego-driven life with them, the ultimate crowning of his ego-transcendence in death.

Initially, however, the eruption of Gregor's self in the metamorphosis of his body leads to a liberation of the physical Will in him, an aimless free activity, a passionately energetic crawling on the walls and ceiling of his room in which the triumph of the Will-driven energy of the body over the timid rational ego celebrates itself. His body's new hitherto undreamt-of self-command and daring would have been utterly impossible for his ego in its human form. In that we can see the first triumph of the self over the self-reflective, defensively fretful ego. It is the first stage of Gregor's ego-transcendence but not yet his self-overcoming, his self-sacrifice.

Gregor's mother, who loves him, notes this liberation in her son and wants to make it easier for his self by removing the furniture from his room. But faced with that, Gregor recalls his threatened ego, which rebels against this well-meaning dehumanization. His ego seeks to reassert itself and return to its former status, his life as an individual in a position of self-respect and command, shown by his desperate defense of the picture of the lady, which had served his ego's masturbatory degradation of Dionysian eros.

The Dionysian expression of his self, however, comes to the fore in the new meaning that music, transmitted by his sister's violin playing, assumes for him. In this new significance of music, the Dionysian emerges in Gregor.

Music, his sister's playing the violin, reminds Gregor of his humanity, his community with his sister, his family, his oneness with his species, shown in his inward rhetorical question: "Was he an animal if music could grip him so?"[4] But Gregor's ego reasserts itself in his erotic daydream of his sister playing only for him. By wanting his sister and her music for himself alone, he violates the communal Dionysian spirit of music.

His desire to keep Grete a prisoner in his room amounts to a fatal self-contradiction and repudiation of the universalist meaning and function of both music and eros.

Owing to his aggressively defensive, isolationist daydreaming, Gregor forgets the actuality of his situation and by his advance toward Grete destroys the potential community of family and lodgers meeting through music. Shock, horror, disgust, and indignation take the place of a dawning togetherness, and Gregor will pay with his life for his self-assertive assault upon the community-forming, Dionysian spirit of music. After Grete's outburst against his egocentric parasitism, Gregor realizes that the real meaning of his fate is to cease to be himself, cease to be an ego, and abandon himself for the future of his family. The ultimate message music gives him through his sister is to cease to be an individuated self. He dies emotionally reunited with his family, giving way to their future awakening through his sister's nubile body.

The conflict between the spirit of music and the ego is basically analogous in Kafka's last text, "Josephine, the Singer, or the Mouse People" ("Josefine, die Sängerin, oder das Volk der Mäuse," 1924). However, before turning to it, we shall examine the text of Kafka's "breakthrough," as he famously called "The Judgment" ("Das Urteil," 1913).

In contrast to *The Metamorphosis*, which it closely preceded, "The Judgment" lacks not only the Dionysian element of music but also the Zarathustrian time dimension, futurity.

However, it exhibits an even more striking closeness to the dramatic and tragic function of the Dionysian as presented in Nietzsche's analysis of Attic tragedy. Driven by his ego, Georg Bendemann, protagonist of "The Judgment," is bent on displacing his father as the center of familial power in all its aspects — economic, social, and sexual. Financial and erotic aspects of power merge in Georg's case, as he boasts of having become engaged to a girl of a well-to-do family. However, in the course of the narrative, what we might see as Georg's self compels his ego to surrender to his father. Initially, Georg is at the point of breaking with his self, represented by his childhood friend who, rather than challenging and succeeding his own father, has chosen to eschew ego-assertive struggle and exile himself to economic failure and permanent bachelorhood in Russia. Georg's self has been drawn to this childhood friend. But he is about to cut his tie to his self when, in a letter, he confronts his friend with his desertion of the latter's way of life, choosing worldly success culminating in his engagement to a girl of a well-to-do family.

However, instead of sending off his letter, he seeks out the realm of his father, who has been relegated to the dark back room of their apartment, to inform him of his intended break with his childhood, as embodied in the bachelor friend in Russia. In light of what happens subsequently, we can discern the dual, ambiguous, and self-contradictory nature of Georg's act of self-assertion. For while Georg's conscious intention, his ego, challenges his father, his self literally seeks out his father's judgment of Georg's intent. The plot of the story presents the self-refutation of the ego's attempt at emancipation. Georg's instantaneous and utterly surprising obedience to his father's verdict — his death by drowning, purely self-administered, without any external compulsion — enacts the victory of the child-like self in Georg over his adult ego.

His self is the vessel and instrument of the Dionysian. It makes Georg submerge his ego in the river. For Nietzsche's favorite thinker in the Dionysian aspect of his thought, Heraclitus, the notion of the river represents something closely akin to what Schopenhauer was to call the Will, an ever-flowing dynamism leading toward the unbounded, all-uniting sea. In Kafka's text, death by drowning in the river enacts the submersion and dissolution of the ego and its rejoining the totality of being. The German word for river, "Fluss," which Kafka's text uses, signifies "flow." "Flow" expresses much more clearly than "river" the flow of being that Heraclitus's metaphor of the river signifies in Nietzsche's Dionysian thought. In Kafka's story, the flow of the river below finds its exact equivalent in the "unending" flow of traffic or sexual intercourse — in German the word "Verkehr" used by Kafka has both meanings — on the bridge above. Finally both signifiers of flow — river and traffic — are linked in Kafka's text to the flow of procreation, the semen, to which Georg owes his existence and to which his father alludes with his rhetorical question: "Don't you think I have loved you, I from whom you issued?"[5] invoking both aspects of eros — sex and love — in one. Georg's immediate compliance with his father's death sentence affirms his father's love by reciprocating it. His last words are his avowal of love for his parents. With his reaffirmation of his own love for them, he rejoins them in love, canceling his ego, his independent, individuated existence as an aberrant illusion.

Uniting with his family in love, Georg also reconnects to the whole of being — the "unendlicher Verkehr" on the bridge above the river of his extinction, with the dual meaning of "Verkehr" as intercourse in both its erotic and its communal-commercial meaning. By submerging his life in the "flow," Georg becomes one with the intercourse, the all-connectedness that makes up the cosmos. Death, understood as a cancellation of the ego, brings about the union of the deep self with life. In obeying his father, Georg symbolically reunites with his parents in the stream of love. By the same token, Georg reunites with the world of which that love is a part by ceasing to be a separate individual, an ego.

"The Judgment," the text of Kafka's "breakthrough," constitutes his Dionysian text par excellence. It was written in a Dionysian vein, in a single uninterrupted stream of words, a flow, the act of writing exactly reflecting its idea, the flow filling the space-time of one night, without break, without interruption, in a single continuous whole. In "The Judgment," Kafka's Dionysian vein approximates, even more closely than in *The Metamorphosis*, Nietzsche's idea of tragedy and the tragic. In "The Judgment," the individual as self-important, arrogantly confident, rebelliously assertive, as hero, is ultimately driven to surrender to the stream of life that, according to Nietzsche's *The Birth of Tragedy*, is located in the dancing chorus. In "The Judgment," the chorus is not merely the family, as in *The Metamorphosis*, but the unending traffic of the world, the flow of being also embodied in the river with which the protagonist merges. He literally immerses himself in the flow. In terms of structural function, the flow of the river in which Georg drowns himself is the same flow of being as his father's semen through which Georg had once issued into individuated existence. But Georg has allowed the principle of individuation, his ego, to take over his being.

In Nietzsche's view in *The Birth of Tragedy*, the individual can ultimately be only illusionary, and this is what Georg discovers and acts upon when he adopts his father's judgment as his own and ceases to be a separate individual.

"The Judgment" conforms to the structure of Attic tragedy, as seen by Nietzsche. It reenacts the same relationship between the individual, the hero, and collective life as represented by the chorus. As the chorus survives the fall of the hero, so the "infinite intercourse" of collective life on the bridge survives the literal fall of Georg into the flow. The "intercourse" on the bridge outlives Georg. It signifies the victorious continuation of life, not only outlasting the life of the individual but in a sense reuniting him with the life that outlives him.

In "The Judgment," the Dionysian inheres in the flow with which Georg, in the end, merges. In *The Metamorphosis*, it resides potentially in music as well as in the stream of life's generations suggested in the end by Grete's nubile body. In Kafka's last text, "Josephine, the Singer, or the Mouse People," music and the collective life of the people are one.

The title of the story shows both the contrast between the individual and the collective and their ultimate synonymy. For the "or" in the title both separates and unites Josefine and the mouse people. As conveyor of music — song — the individual, the heroine, is literally the mouthpiece and medium of the Dionysian force. Through and in her singing, Josefine unites her people in their dreaming of a childhood they never knew in actuality.

Music frees them from the reality principle, the struggle for existence, which is the curse of individuation. In Josefine's singing the individuals forget themselves and are united in their collective self. Music leads individuals back to their shared being, the dream of their childhood in which they are one.

At the bottom of Josefine's art lurks a paradox. Does Josefine really sing, or is not her apparent "song" really a whistling or piping, a sound all mice produce, but which her brazen self-confidence, her forwardness, her chutzpah, make sound like song? What this shows is a kind of convergence of the Dionysian and the Apollonian in her art. Josefine's singing in its effect is Dionysian insofar as it unites the people, but as dreaming it is also Apollonian. In communal dreaming, the Dionysian and the Apollonian merge. Her singing leads, not to orgiastic dance, but to the mouse folk's dream of childhood; and dreaming, according to Nietzsche, rather than drunken revelry, is the Apollonian in art. Josefine's art as a conjuring of dreams is a *Schein*, a semblance, whistling disguised as song, and thus eminently Apollonian. It is an art not of intoxication but of conjuration, an art based on illusion, engendering dreams. It is an individual's creation of collective effects.

Insofar as Josefine is able to create illusions, she is the Apollonian artist par excellence and as such is bound to the principle of individuation. Like many great artist-divas, primadonnas, master geniuses, she insists on her uniqueness, the uniqueness of genius. She insists on being different from all other mice, on being special and incomparable, and therefore exempt from the common lot of all mice — the duty of communal labor service to which each and every mouse is subject without exception. By insisting on her exemption from it, because of her exceptional achievement, Josefine undermines the Dionysian foundation of her art, her dream-engendering songs that speak to all and thus embody the Dionysian nature of music. By demanding a special status she excludes herself from the community and thereby undercuts the foundation of her art as universal appeal. Rather than merging with the rest of the people, she chooses silence in protest at her treatment, and silence becomes her fate. Her self-chosen isolation is literally the end of her art. For her art was an appeal to the common nature of all mice. By insisting on her uniqueness, she represses what had made her art. She has become nothing but an ego, individual, and she will share the fate of all individuals, she will cease to be, eventually forgotten, submerged, like all heroes, in the stream that is collective life. The narrator calls that her redemption. Only by forgetting and being forgotten can the individual attain — what is impossible for individuated life — ultimate happiness as submersion in the universal. The creative Will will continue to individuate in others, not in Josefine.

Her singing provides the bond that unifies her public with itself and with her. She is one with them in her singing but nothing when apart from them. For, as we have seen, her singing is not something special but the evocation and recreation of what all mice share. It is nothing apart from the people, the listeners, and in that sense, Josefine's art is Dionysian, a communal experience par excellence. But what enables her piping to be perceived and experienced as song is Josefine's unique attitude, her nerve, her chutzpah, as we have called it, her audacity that transforms what all mice do into something unique, into song. As mentioned before, one might see in that the Apollonian element in her art, for it is semblance, illusion, dream. It transforms the common into the special, the life of the species into art. Thus in Josefine the two fundamental drives of art, as seen by Nietzsche, Dionysian intoxication and Apollonian magic, unite. Their union is art, as seen by Nietzsche in Attic tragedy.

In a development, likewise explicable in Nietzschean terms, the Apollonian in Josefine veers over too far toward the egocentric. Josefine perverts aesthetic illusion to a cult of personality, an illusion of the individual as incomparable and absolute. Thereby she undermines and destroys the Dionysian foundation of her art.

As in *The Metamorphosis*, the drive to gratify the ego and its desire for isolation and desire for splendid uniqueness rules out the communal essence of music. In both texts, there can eventually be no coexistence between musical art and egocentricity. The claims of the ego ultimately make music a self-contradiction that is enacted in both stories. Without the Dionysian community there can be no musical art. As she ceases to be the Dionysian artist, Dionysianism takes over Josefine's life. Her individuation gradually ceases, and she is obliterated in universal forgetfulness. No memory is left of Josefine or any of the heroes of the mouse people.

The end of Dionysian art is the triumphant fulfillment of Dionysian being. Like all the heroes of her nation, like all great and distinguished individuals, Josefine too cannot escape the common fate of all individuated existence, its merging with and disappearance in the universal stream of being.

At this point, the close analogy between the ending of the work of Kafka's "breakthrough" and his very last text — between "The Judgment" and "Josefine" — becomes evident. The two texts end in an analogous way. The protagonist, defeated in and by the assertion of his, respectively her, ego, ends by immersion in and union with the stream, the "infinite" flow of total being, which outlasts and reabsorbs all existence that has sought to emancipate and separate itself from it — to no avail. However, in this remerging with the universal, the individual, in both texts, finds a kind of redemption, a homecoming to existence as a whole.

Notes

1 Walter Herbert Sokel, "On the Dionysian in Nietzsche," *New Literary History* 36.4 (Autumn 2005): 501–20.

2 Friedrich Nietzsche, *Basic Writings of Nietzsche*, ed. and trans. Walter Kaufmann (New York: Modern Library, 1968), 52.

3 "Was Vaterland! *Dorthin* will unser Steuer, wo unser *Kinder-Land* ist! Dorthinaus, stürmischer als das Meer, stürmt unsre große Sehnsucht! —." Friedrich Nietzsche, "Von alten und neuen Tafeln," in *Also sprach Zarathustra,* in *Werke in drei Bänden*, ed. Karl Schlechta (Munich: Hanser, 1954), 3:28.

4 "War er ein Tier, da ihn Musik so ergriff?" (*DL*, 185).

5 "Glaubst du, ich hätte dich nicht geliebt, ich von dem du ausgingst?" (*DL*, 50).

4: What Kafka Learned from Flaubert: "Absent-Minded Window-Gazing" and "The Judgment"

Uta Degner

> Education sentimentale *is a book that for many years has been as dear to me as are only two or three people; whenever and wherever I open it, I am startled and succumb to it completely, and I always feel as though I were the author's spiritual son, albeit a weak and awkward one.*
>
> — Kafka, *Letters to Felice*

KAFKA'S REPEATED DECLARATION about an "elective affinity" with the French writer Gustave Flaubert — here in a letter of November 1912 to Felice Bauer — has led to various suggestions from scholars about how to interpret Flaubert's role in Kafka's writing.[1] Attention has primarily focused on psychoanalytical and narratological parallels between the two authors. Indeed, it is apparent that Kafka models his letters to Felice Bauer on Flaubert's letters to Louise Colet; and Kafka's narrators might have learned from the French model and its "impassiveness." However, while these suggestions are useful in highlighting some aspects of Kafka's writing and personality, they fail to explain the full measure of the literary identification declared by Kafka.

Kafka's affinity with Flaubert can be considered along structural lines by taking into account the state of the literary field of their time. In his major study, *The Rules of Art*, the French cultural sociologist Pierre Bourdieu analyzes Flaubert's authorial practice as an art of positioning himself against contemporary literary conventions.[2] He describes Flaubert's writing in terms of a "double rupture" that breaks with both sides of the most entrenched literary conflict of his time, "realistic" writing versus the "high" style.[3] The "realist" Flaubert does not follow the conventions of realist writers, who chose to accompany their socially rather "humble" characters with a certain stylistic anonymity. On the contrary, he submits the realistic subject to a cult of form, as it was practiced in the poetry of his time, and which focuses the attention of the reader on the "how" of the narration itself, requiring from her a scrutiny of every word. Flaubert was well aware of this revolutionary pairing and reflected it in letters to Louise Colet, which Kafka read in a 1904 translation.[4] In this vein, while writing *Madame Bovary*, Flaubert remarks: "The whole value of my book, if it has one, will consist in its capacity to have walked upon a hair that is spanned between the double abyss of Lyricism and the Vulgar (I want to melt both into a narrative analysis)."[5] Later he states: "To want to give prose the rhythm of verse (allowing it to remain prose and very much prose); to write the ordinary life as one writes history or epic (without making the subject unnatural), might be absurd — this I ask myself sometimes; but maybe it is also a great and very original attempt."[6]

Flaubert summarized his combination of two conventionally incompatible styles as "bien écrire le mediocre" — to "write the mediocre well." Bourdieu comments:

> This formula in the form of an oxymoron concentrates and condenses his whole aesthetic program. It gives a fair idea of the almost impossible situation in which he has placed himself in trying to reconcile contraries — that is, requirements and experiences ordinarily associated with opposing regions of the social space and of the literary field, and hence sociologically irreconcilable ones. And thus he is going to establish, in the lowest and most trivial forms of a literary genre held as inferior — that is, to say, in the subjects commonly treated by the realists . . . the highest requirements that had ever been asserted even in the noble genre par excellence.[7]

The result of Flaubert's style is a "totally paradoxical (almost 'impossible') position" in the literary field of his time.[8] By combining two literary opposites, Flaubert questions the very fundamentals of writing, "the common principles of vision and division that . . . ground the consensus about the common meaning of the world: poetry against prose, the poetic against the prosaic." With his own "impossible" "mixture of genres," "prose applied to the poetic and especially poetry applied to the prosaic," Flaubert "revokes the limits and the incompatibilities that ground the perceptual and communicative order."[9]

Kafka, who read Flaubert at least partly in French, was sensitive to the formal aspects of the art of Flaubert. In a letter to Felice, he enthusiastically highlights the stylistic beauty of a sentence from *Madame Bovary*: "Dear God! Read that, dearest, do read it! 'Elle avoua qu'elle désirait faire un tour à son bras, dans les rues.' What a sentence! What a construction!"[10] In terms of content, the line from Flaubert is not very remarkable: "She confessed that she would like to go for a walk through the streets on his arm." But it has indeed the rhythm of poetry in the repetition and variation of one and three syllables: "Elle avoua" is taken up in "qu'elle désirait," followed by three groups of three monosyllables: "faire un tour" — "à son bras" — "dans les rues." Kafka had surely perceived Flaubert's "collision of opposites" as he began developing a generative formula structurally homologic with Flaubert's. Like Flaubert, Kafka relates to the literary field of his time in a form of "negative contact." His "radical originality" can therefore not be understood outside its literary context: "It is by completely historicizing it that one can completely understand how he tears himself away from the strict historicity of less heroic destinies."[11]

In the case of Kafka scholarship, however, we can detect a reluctance to relate the author to the literature of his time.[12] As if to preempt this reception, Kafka seems to playfully allude to contemporary literary productions with "Bendemann," the last name he gave to the protagonist of his story "The Judgment" ("Das Urteil," 1913), which he saw as his literary breakthrough. "Bendemann" sounds like a variation on "Beer-Hofmann" and binds together all the "Manns" current in the literary field of the time — on the one hand, realist writers like Jakob Wassermann[13] and Gerhart Hauptmann; on the other hand, aestheticist writers like Hugo von Hofmannsthal and Richard Beer-Hofmann, and in between the two poles, Thomas Mann. The name of Kafka's protagonist lets us read him as a "spiritual child" of all these different writers.[14] Moreover, in the first syllable of Bendemann, one can also hear an echo of Gottfried Benn, who in 1912 had caused a minor scandal with the publication of his first collection of poetry, *Morgue*, because of its drastic representation of death and decay in poetic form.[15]

In "The Judgment" one can see particular traits of the literary styles in use at Kafka's time: it recounts a story, that — except for the conclusion — appears familiar from realist writers. In the beginning the narrator apparently cites the conventional realist narrator's voice. Yet at the same time he tells this story in a way that encourages the reader to reflect upon each individual word and its meaning. The modernity of Kafka lies not in a stylistic radicalization of one of the competing literary styles but in the unique mixture of opposing features that distances itself from all of them. To illustrate this, I would like to consider how the conflict between father and son in "The Judgment" can be read as an allegory of the conflict between different writing modes. However, to contextualize this argument, we will first turn to an early example of Kafka's short prose to highlight the genealogy of his particular style of writing.

Writing Prose like Poetry: "Absent-minded Window-gazing"

In his earliest writings, Kafka works on blending the two stylistic modes. His first publication consists of eight short prose texts, which appeared in 1908 under the title "Observation" (*Betrachtung*, 1912) in the exclusive journal *Hyperion*, edited by Franz Blei. Here the young and still unknown writer appeared in the company of prominent aestheticist authors such as Rilke and Hofmannsthal. A book edition of these short texts, now with individual titles and with some new pieces added, was published with the same title four years later. One of these texts was "Absent-minded Window-gazing" ("Zerstreutes Hinausschaun"):

> What are we to do with these spring days that are now fast coming on? Early this morning the sky was gray, but if you go to the window now you are surprised and lean your cheek against the latch of the casement.
>
> The sun is already setting, but down below you see it lighting up the face of the little girl who strolls along looking about her, and at the same time you see her eclipsed by the shadow of the man behind overtaking her.
>
> And then the man has passed by and the little girl's face is quite bright. (*CS*, 387)[16]

At first glance, this is a little sketch, as the title suggests: a momentary impression upon looking out of the window, and the observation of the (non-)encounter of two human beings. If one looks attentively, however — not "absent-mindedly" — and if one not only looks but also reads the text out loud, its strong lyrical sound quality comes to the fore. The title already has a certain phonetic effect: the two three-syllabic title words are put in relation by the repetition of the sounds "shhh" and "s," in a form of inverted, or mirrored reduplication: 'ZerSHHtreuteS HinauS-SHHaun. This inversion will also be significant for the poetics of the text, mirrored semantically in the shifting of gazes. A sign that Kafka used this principle of "harmonic opposition" intentionally is the elision of the "e" of "Hinausschauen," which shortens the word to three syllables, establishing the equal balance of syllables and the impression of sound-contiguity between the title words.

Figures of phonetic repetition organize the text throughout, in various forms: alliterations like "Was werden wir," "Frühlingstagen tun," "sinkende Sonne"; the echoes of "Früh" in "Frühling," of "rasch" in "überrascht" and "rascher"; identical repetitions like "jetzt," "Fenster," "Gesicht," "sieht man"; varying repetitions like "kommen" and "kommt"; partial repetitions like "ich" in "Licht," "Gesicht," "kindlich"; rhyming structures like "Klinke" and "sinkenden," "dann" and "Mann"; metrical repetitions like the adoneus in "Klínke des Fénsters," "sínkenden Sónne," "kíndlichen Maédchens," and "Schátten des Mánnes" — all draw the reader's attention to the linguistic character of the text. Not only does the sound accompany the narrative, but the narrative fundamentally unfolds from its sound material. From the twofold repetition of the indefinite pronoun "man," which does not refer to a real-existing entity, there arises

— by a kind of *creatio ex lingua* — a "man" (Mann), a visible male human being, who even throws a shadow, thereby proving his "realness." Kafka interrelates two conventionally distinguishable poetics: while attention is focused on what is told, there is a constant shift toward the linguistic form, which in the latter part comes vividly into the story. The mixture of the different stylistic devices of "pure art" and more traditional realistic writing leads to the provocative effect "that the relationships among narrative elements in Kafka's fiction are intimately linked to relationships at the level of the verbal signifier."[17] By linking together these mutually exclusive tendencies of the literary field, Kafka's narratives come to life. If one accepts the logic of related sounds, one can read the poetic character of the texts by borrowing from elements close to one another. If "Wange" and "Klinke" exchange "g" and "k," one gets to the "Klinge[n]" and "Wanke[n]": we see that the sound of the text is one of the artist's tools to establish meaning and the effect of a certain textual wavering. One senses a wavering between the referential level of the signifiers, which is also present in the text, and the accentuation of sound, with its effects of dispersion.

In this way, "Absent-minded Window-gazing" is organized in a twofold manner on several levels — the many phonetic doublets are an indication that the text cannot be resolved in favor of a "simple" coherence. This double nature also applies to two different figures and their different forms of movement as well as to their ways of looking: the "coming" movement of spring days ("die jetzt rasch kommen"), introduced by the adverb "rasch," meaning "quick, fast," is absorbed by the movement of the man in the later part of the text, who "overtakes her." Although the man has already "passed by" the girl in the end, she is still standing there. Opposite to his speed, she follows a different velocity: "das so geht," says the text, although it does not clarify exactly what this "so" means. The only additional information we get is that she looks around ("sich umschaut"). "Umschauen" can indicate a change in the direction of the view or also, in a more colloquial sense, a looking around that is unspecified in direction and intent. In comparison with a look that has a definite direction, the "looking about her" is a "gazing" as through the window of the title. "So gehen" can colloquially also mean an analogously undirectional movement of the body, opposite to the movement of the man, who at the conclusion has walked out of the picture.

Kafka scholarship in recent decades has extensively revealed the tendency of Kafka's text to allegorical self-reflection.[18] This scriptive habit can also be seen here: the two figures — man and girl — are readable as allegories of two different classes of reader-types, which correspond to the stylistic diversity present in Kafka's text. The man embodies a linear reader, who passes through the text quickly; the girl follows a more sedate model of reading, looking around, back and forth, embodying a kind of "lectio difficilior." The way the girl perceives corresponds to the aestheticist perception, which digresses from conventionally emphasized objects to more peripheral ones. It is an experience described by Lord Chandos in Hugo von Hofmannsthal's *Chandos Letter*, a famous astheticist text, in which not only words fall apart like moldy mushrooms in the mouth but in which this decomposition also opens the way to a new seeing where the hierarchic order of what is worthy of perception and representation is dissolved.[19] Lord Chandos finds pleasure in things "past which the eye ordinarily glides with natural indifference," a

> watering can, a harrow left in a field, a dog in the sun, a shabby churchyard, a cripple, a small farmhouse — any of these things can become the vessel of my revelation. Any of these things and the thousand similar ones past which the eye ordinarily glides with natural indifference can at any moment — which I am completely unable to elicit — suddenly take on for me a sublime and moving aura which words seem too weak to describe.[20]

The negative experience of the decomposition of (conventional) language, the loss of coherence,[21] corresponds to a positive experience of a "free" perception. Kafka's texts imitate such a shift of perception by working not only on the side of the signified but also on the signifier. The partial suspension of linear meaning at the level of the *histoire* that goes with it has often earned aestheticist literature the onus of being hermetic. The tension between *obscuritas* and *claritas* as it appears in Kafka's text has been described by Mallarmé as the relation between light and shadow.[22] In "Absent-minded Window-gazing," this effect is metaphorized by the dynamic changing of light and by the face of the child onto which "light" and "shadow" fall "at the same time." The change between different stages of brightness is already included in the second sentence: "Early this morning the sky was gray, but if you go to the window now you are surprised and lean your cheek against the latch of the casement." According to the logic of the text, the reason for surprise can consist only in the sky's not being "grau" anymore, but otherwise — as the latent rhyme suggests — in its being "blau" and therefore brighter. A reduction of light then takes place in the next sentence, with the "sun . . . already setting." The diminished sun, however, lights up the face of the girl, where the changes in light reflect the oscillation of Kafka's stylistic principles: the specific aesthetic obscurity and the clarity of more realistic parentage. Their mixture both forms and performs the matchless voice of his writings.

Kafka's text also stages a little *histoire* and with the man a more "realistic" reading model. It is just as possible to read it as an impressionistic sketch — as a short prose piece — as it is possible to read it as a symbolist poem. Gerhard Kurz was therefore not wrong to evoke the genre of "prose poetry."[23] Indeed, "one is surprised" (*CS*, 387) to observe how Kafka's writing creates a space in which prose and poetry are no longer distinguishable.

Poetic Struggle in "The Judgment"

These stylistic features, usually considered incompatible, are also active in Kafka's "The Judgment," written in 1912, in the same year as the publication of "Meditation." However, while in "Absent-minded Window-gazing" they were blended together, in "The Judgment" we can perceive what Bourdieu calls "negative contact": now they are on display not as two possibilities but as two impossibilities. Where "Absent-minded Window-gazing" might satisfy the expectations of either a realist or aestheticist reading, "The Judgment" disappoints both, as each style is constantly undermined. We can attempt to read the conflict between the father and Georg as a struggle between a realist and an aestheticist approach, as I will show, but Kafka's narrator adds the irony that both protagonists repeatedly fail to emulate their own principles, and he shifts their identity constantly throughout the text. In the end, neither of them has our sympathy, and the end appears less tragic than absurd.

Here Kafka encounters, albeit in a new stylistic way, the effect of Flaubert's writing: the ironic exposure of the defects and the limitations of both stylistic schools by allowing them to collide into incoherence.

The father expresses the rivalry between two different modes of writing when he admits to being a writer himself and designates the Russian friend as a reader of two different kinds of texts. This scene functions as a *mise en abime* for the literary conflict of "The Judgment":

> Oh, how you amused me today when you came to ask me whether you ought to write to your friend about your engagement. He knows everything, you foolish boy, he knows absolutely everything! I've been writing him, because you forgot to take my writing things away from me. That's why he hasn't come for years now, he knows everything a hundred times better than you. He crumbles up your letters in his left hand without reading them, while in his right he holds up my letters to read! (*KSS*, 11)[24]

We as readers cannot know if this scene, which we read as an uncommented direct speech from the father's mouth, corresponds to the fictional reality. But even if it is only the father's invention, it is illuminating to understand his negative judgment of his son as based on an opposition *within* writing: his letters are the right ones — analogously held in the friend's right hand — as they reveal the facts "a hundred times better," whereas Georg's are "lying little letters" (*KSS*, 9).[25] According to the father, they are also judged negatively by the friend, who refuses to read them (any more); this judgment would correspond to his opinion of Georg's worthlessness, which will lead to the son's death sentence.

Two different genres of writing appear here: Georg wrote letters about "insignificant events in the way they accumulate pell-mell in one's memory when one reflects on a quiet Sunday" (*KSS,* 5),[26] of which we are given the following example: "Three times, in letters fairly far apart, Georg announced to his friend the engagement of some inconsequential fellow to an equally inconsequential young woman, until his friend, completely contrary to Georg's intentions, actually began to take an interest in this curious fact (*KSS,* 5).[27] "Insignificant" and "inconsequential" are two attributes of Georg's writing until the day of the narration: it is "inconsequential" about his own reality, about which it keeps quiet, and it contains "keine eigentlichen Mitteilungen" (*DL,* 45; no actual messages). These are attributes that bring to mind the aestheticist mode, its self-distancing from conventional reality. The repetition ("three times") stresses the formal aspect of this writing and increases the contrast between the insignificance of the content and Georg's treatment of it as something important. Indeed, it affects the reader-friend, who "actually began to take an interest in this curious fact."

Opposed to that kind of writing is the father's authorship, which follows the reality principle: telling what is real, so that the distant friend "knows absolutely everything" (*KSS,* 11).[28] Indeed, the main reproach of the father against his son is his ignorance of reality: "So now you know what else there was in the world beside you, until now you knew only about yourself! True, you were an innocent child, but truer still, you were a devilish man!" (*KSS,* 12).[29] The adjective "devilish" is a hint as to Georg's nature, etymologically deriving from the Greek *diábolos,* which is composed of "dia-," "across," and "ballein," "to hurl." Disorder and incoherence are the main defects of Georg in his father's eyes, as he once makes explicit: "You probably meant to say that before. Now it doesn't even pertain" (*KSS,* 12).[30] Not only the father but also the narrator gives us various hints in that direction: Georg's usual way of writing letters is a reflection of his attitude toward the world in general, which consists in a disinterestedness about its actual state, "toying with it" (*KSS,* 3).[31] We encounter this stance as early as the first paragraph, in the way Georg deals with the envelope, which forecasts his general attitude: he looks "out the window" (*KSS,* 3), but indeed, he does not see the outer world, as the narrator says precisely: "his face [was] turned to the window" but he "had barely responded with an absentminded smile to an acquaintance passing by who had greeted him from the street" (*KSS,* 6).[32] Throughout the text, the narrator repeatedly stresses Georg's forgetfulness, his habitual blindness to his environment. So he sees his father and does not see him at the same time:

> Georg looked up at this bogeyman of a father. The St. Petersburg friend, whom his father suddenly knew so well, gripped his imagination as never before. He saw him lost in far-off Russia. He saw him at the door of his empty, plundered establishment. He was just barely able to stand among the wreckage of his shelves, the ransacked goods, the collapsing gas brackets. (*KSS,* 10)[33]

Georg looks up to his father — but he does not actually see him. Instead, he fantasizes about his Russian friend, with all the details that normally characterize a "reality effect" that resembles Lord Chandos's vision of "distinct images of absent objects" in "the fullest, most sublime present."[34] The father is aware of his son's absent-minded state and tries to call him to order: "'Look at me, will you!' shouted the father" (*KSS,* 10)[35] but without success: "Georg ran almost distractedly to the bed in order to grasp everything but halfway there stopped short" (*KSS,* 10).[36]

The narrator lets us know that Georg's absent-mindedness, his *Zerstreutheit,* is not a temporary but a habitual state:

> A long time ago he had firmly decided to observe everything very exactly so as to avoid being taken by surprise in some devious way, from behind or from above. Now he remembered that long-forgotten decision once again and forgot it, the way one draws a short thread through the eye of the needle. (*KSS,* 10)[37]

Not only does Georg repeatedly forget to observe, but he even keeps forgetting his decision to do so. His perception and thinking is without order; it stops halfway and then shifts to something else, without any logic, taking its path "in some devious way": "He thought so for only a second because he kept forgetting everything" (*KSS,* 11).[38] Georg's digressions perform the anti-logical "logic" of the aestheticist artwork, which does not admit reality but subverts it by establishing its own mode of perception. Georg does not consider the whole of his father's words, their meaning, but adheres to details of the formulation: "'He knows everything a thousand times better,' he shouted. 'Ten thousand times!' said Georg" (*KSS,* 11).[39]

These remarks display the aestheticistic and the realistic approach as irreconcilable attitudes. However, the narrator's distance from both of them and their relation becomes clear in the way he portrays them: not affirmatively but critically, highlighting their deficiencies and inconsistencies: Georg's "aestheticism" is not a voluntarily thing, it is not a mastered art but something he cannot control: the condition "contrary to Georg's intentions" bears not only on the reaction of his friend, not only on the course of his conversion with his father, but even on his own assertions and their effects:

> "Play actor!" Georg *could not help shouting,* immediately saw the harm he had done . . . *except too late.* (*KSS,* 10; emphasis added)
>
> "Ten thousand times!" said Georg, to make fun of his father, but while still in his mouth, the words took on a deadly serious note. (*KSS,* 11)[40]

It is its way of being involuntary that invites the negativity of the narrator's reference to aestheticism. As Georg has no other guiding principle, he has to stick to the words, words over which he has no control but which control him; and they will, ironically enough, drive him to death: "while still in his mouth, the words took on a *deadly serious* [emphasis added] note." It is the very opposite of autonomy that Georg gains by taking words so seriously. At the end, the difference between words and "the real" is itself abolished. From "a devilish man" Georg turns into "Jesus," if we understand the exclamation of the cleaning woman as addressing him. "Jesus" embodies the paradigm of the "Word made flesh," words performing reality. While aestheticist poetics claims to assume a distance from reality, in Georg's perspective language substitutes for reality, it becomes reality. The violent way language affects his body is already expressed when his words "play actor" make him "bit[e] his tongue so hard . . . — his eyes gaped — that he staggered from the pain" (*KSS,* 10).[41] That Georg's death is word-driven becomes even more evident after the father's death sentence, as his immediate reaction is to perform it, in a manner between passivity and activity: "Georg felt himself driven from the room," "he raced as if down a ramp," "he leaped out of the gate, across the avenue, driven on toward the water" (*KSS,* 12).[42] We can thus read Georg's end as Kafka's implicit distancing from aestheticist poetics.

The realistic approach of the father, however, is not much more convincing. It also shows a similar fatal self-contradiction. Regarding Georg's friend, he twice announces different "realities." While at first he denies the existence of the friend in an absolute way — "You have no friend in St. Petersburg" (*KSS,* 8) — he afterward states: "I know your friend all right" (*KSS,* 9).[43] While realism claims to make language transparent to reality, the father (ac)claims reality thanks to speech acts, with the help of the narrator, who does not guarantee their reliability. So not only is Georg's dependence on words problematic, as, denying reality, they gain the power of reality; moreover, his father's "reality principle" is soon inverted: instead of words representing reality, it appears that reality, for him, is an effect of his words. In this dimension of word-dependence, Georg and his father are finally less opponents than members of one family. It is surely ironic that the catastrophe takes place just after Georg has started to reconsider his attitude to the world and to address his father. Recall that on deciding to write the truth to his friend, he had begun to see things he had not noticed before. For example: "Georg was amazed at how dark his father's room was, even on this sunny morning. So, the high wall that rose up on the far side of the narrow countyard cast so much shadow!" (*KSS,* 6).[44] Or, again: "At the sight of the not especially clean underwear, he blamed himself for having neglected his father" (*KSS,* 9).[45]

As the narrator retains Georg's perspective throughout (with the exception of the final sentence), we might be allowed to think that Georg had reached this state before and had merely forgotten it, "as he kept forgetting everything" (*KSS,* 11). Nevertheless, it is Georg's perception that continually presents us with details from a (fictive) reality. Just as the father is revealed to be a "play actor," and thereby assimilates to Georg's "comedian"-like existence, so, with this observation, Georg assimilates to the reality of his father — an act that only intensifies the conflict. The narrator does not lend his sympathy to either of the two men, nor does he justify their attitudes. But he increasingly makes space available for their direct articulation. He stages the conflict and seems to let their words enact their struggling lives. The poetic struggle in Kafka's "Judgment" is therefore ironized by the way in which the narrator allows the two antagonistic sides to intertwine and contradict themselves. The narration stresses the conflict — but the narrator's perspective reveals both sides as dependent upon what they seek to oppose.

Does Kafka, the implicit author, pass judgment? His narrator's final sentence can be read in both registers: "At the moment, the traffic going over the bridge was nothing short of infinite" (*KSS,* 12).[46] It is a description of reality, a mere observation; but in comparison with the previous sentence — the catastrophe of Georg's fall into the river — it also produces a provocative digression of the narrator's gaze. Kafka shifts from his protagonist to the traffic on the bridge, although there is no evident coherence between the two. The effect is a final disturbance of the reality effect, without nullifying it completely. Even as it focuses on the details of reality, it reminds us that what we have read is only a story.

Notes

[1] In another letter to Felice dated 2 September 1913, Kafka describes Flaubert as one of his "eigentlichen Blutsverwandten," one his "proper blood relatives" (*BF,* 460). On the relationship of Kafka's writing to Flaubert's, see Charles Bernheimer, *Flaubert and Kafka: Studies in Psychopoetic Structure* (New Haven, CT: Yale UP, 1982); Klaus Pape, *Sprachkunst und Kunstsprache bei Flaubert und Kafka* (St. Ingbert, Germany: Röhrig, 1996); Manfred Schmeling, "Kafka und Flaubert: Perspektive, Wirklichkeit, Welterzeugung," in *Kafka und die Weltliteratur,* ed. Manfred Engel and Dieter Lamping (Göttingen: Vandenhoeck & Ruprecht, 2006), 109–24.

[2] Pierre Bourdieu, *The Rules of Art: Genesis and Structure of the Literary Field* (Cambridge: Polity, 1996). A "field" is a net of relations between distinct positions as developed in a historical process. At a certain historical moment, every position differs in symbolic and economic power according to the quantity possessed, and there is a continous struggle between the actors to keep their position or conquer new more powerful ones.

[3] Bourdieu, *Rules of Art,* 77.

[4] Gustave Flaubert, *Briefe über seine Werke,* vol. 7 of *Gustave Flauberts Gesammelte Werke,* ed. E. W. Fischer (Minden: Bruns, 1904).

[5] Flaubert, *Briefe*, 35, my translation.
[6] Flaubert, *Briefe*, 79, my translation.
[7] Bourdieu, *Rules of Art*, 94–95.
[8] Bourdieu, *Rules of Art*, 92.
[9] Bourdieu, *Rules of Art*, 92.
[10] Letter of 16 Jan. 1913 (*LF*, 157). "Du lieber Gott! Ach lies das, Liebste, lies das nur! . . . Was ist das für ein Satz! Was ist das für ein Gebilde!" (*BF*, 252).
[11] Bourdieu, *Rules of Art*, 96.
[12] Cf. Mark M. Anderson, *Kafka's Clothes: Ornament and Aestheticism in the Habsburg Fin de Siècle* (Oxford: Clarendon, 1992), 10.
[13] It is no coincidence that the protagonist of Kafka's *Metamorphosis*, written shortly after "The Judgment," borrows his name from a Wassermann novel, *Die Geschichte der jungen Renate Fuchs* (cf. *M*, 3n1). The name "Gregor" can also be understood as a new combination of the elements of "Georg."
[14] Kafka wanted "Sons" to be the title of a collection uniting "The Judgment," *The Metamorphosis*, and "The Stoker."
[15] Such a reading might be regarded as an overinterpretation, if Kafka himself had not practiced such a "nomenology" in relation to "The Judgment" in a letter to Felice Bauer and stated relations to contemporary texts in a diary entry. Cf. *BF*, 394/*LF*, 265; and *The Diaries of Franz Kafka, 1910–1923*, ed. Max Brod (Minerva: London, 1992), 219 (entry for 23 Sept. 1912).
[16] Zerstreutes Hinausschaun

> Was werden wir in diesen Frühlingstagen tun, die jetzt rasch kommen? Heute früh war der Himmel grau, geht man aber jetzt zum Fenster, so ist man überrascht und lehnt die Wange an die Klinke des Fensters.
>
> Unten sieht man das Licht der freilich schon sinkenden Sonne auf dem Gesicht des kindlichen Mädchens, das so geht und sich umschaut, und zugleich sieht man den Schatten des Mannes darauf, der hinter ihm rascher kommt.
>
> Dann ist der Mann schon vorübergegangen und das Gesicht des Kindes ist ganz hell. (*DL*, 24–25)

[17] Clayton Koelb, *Kafka's Rhetoric: The Passion of Reading* (Ithaca, NY: Cornell UP, 1989), 122.
[18] Hans-Thies Lehmann, "Der buchstäbliche Körper: Zur Selbstinszenierung der Literatur bei Franz Kafka," in *Der junge Kafka*, ed. Gerhard Kurz (Frankfurt am Main: Suhrkamp, 1984), 213–41; Stanley Corngold, *The Necessity of Form* (Ithaca, NY: Cornell UP, 1988), and Koelb, *Kafka's Rhetoric*.
[19] It is known that Kafka had read Hofmannsthal's text by 1905. See Gerhard Kurz, "Einleitung: Der junge Kafka im Kontext," in Kurz, *Der junge Kafka*, 19; on Kafka and Hofmannsthal, see also Dorritt Cohn, "Kafka and Hofmannsthal," *Modern Austrian Literature* 30.1 (1997): 1–19.
[20] Hugo von Hofmannsthal: "A Letter," in *The Lord Chandos Letter and Other Writings*, trans. Joel Rotenberg (New York: New York Review of Books, 2005), 117–28; here 123.

[21] "I have completely lost the ability to think or speak about anything in a *connected* way" (my translation, my emphasis). Hugo von Hofmannsthal, "Ein Brief," in *Erzählungen, Erfundene Gespräche und Briefe. Reisen,* vol. 7 of *Gesammelte Werke in Einzelausgaben*, ed. Herbert Steiner (Frankfurt am Main: Fischer 1979), 465.

[22] Karlheinz Stierle, "Möglichkeiten des dunklen Stils in den Anfängen moderner Lyrik in Frankreich," in *Immanente Ästhetik, ästhetische Reflexion: Lyrik als Paradigma der Moderne*, ed. Wolfgang Iser (Munich: Fink, 1966), 157–94 (=Poetik und Hermeneutik, vol. 2).

[23] Kurz, "Einleitung," 23.

[24] "Wie hast du mich doch heute unterhalten, als du kamst und fragtest, ob du deinem Freund von der Verlobung schreiben sollst. Er weiß doch alles, dummer Junge, er weiß doch alles! Ich schrieb ihm doch, weil du vergessen hast, mir das Schreibzeug wegzunehmen. Darum kommt er schon seit Jahren nicht, er weiß ja alles hundertmal besser als du selbst. Deine Briefe zerknüllt er ungelesen in der linken Hand, während er in der rechten meine Briefe zum Lesen sich vorhält!" (*DL*, 59).

[25] "falsche[n] Briefchen" (*DL*, 56).

[26] "bedeutungslose Vorfälle . . ., wie sie sich, wenn man an einem ruhigen Sonntag nachdenkt, in der Erinnerung ungeordnet aufhäufen" (*DL*, 47).

[27] So geschah es Georg, dass er dem Freund die Verlobung eines gleichgültigen Menschen mit einem ebenso gleichgültigen Mädchen dreimal in ziemlich weit auseinanderliegenden Briefen anzeigte, bis sich dann allerdings der Freund, ganz gegen Georgs Absicht, für diese Merkwürdigkeit zu interessieren begann" (*DL*, 47).

[28] "er weiß doch alles!" (*DL*, 59).

[29] "Jetzt weißt du also, was es noch außer dir gab, bisher wußtest du nur von dir! Ein unschuldiges Kind warst du ja eigentlich, aber noch eigentlicher warst du ein teuflischer Mensch!" (*DL*, 60).

[30] "Das wolltest du wahrscheinlich früher sagen. Jetzt paßt es ja gar nicht mehr" (*DL*, 60).

[31] "in spielerischer Langsamkeit" (*DL*, 43).

[32] "Einem Bekannten, der ihn im Vorübergehen von der Gasse aus gegrüßt hatte, hatte er kaum mit einem abwesenden Lächeln geantwortet" (*DL*, 49). Compare also the motivic parallel to "Absent-minded Window-gazing."

[33] "Georg *sah* zum Schreckbild seines Vaters auf. Der Petersburger Freund . . . ergriff ihn, wie noch nie. Verloren im weiten Rußland *sah er ihn.* An der Türe des leeren, ausgeraubten Geschäftes *sah er ihn.* Zwischen den Trümmern der Regale, den zerfetzten Waren, den fallenden Gasarmen stand er gerade noch" (*DL*, 56; emphasis added).

[34] Cf. Hofmannsthal: "Letter," 124.

[35] "'Aber schau mich an!' rief der Vater" (*DL*, 57).

[36] "Georg lief, fast zerstreut, zum Bett, um alles zu fassen, stockte aber in der Mitte des Wegs" (*DL*, 57).

[37] "Vor einer langen Weile hatte er sich fest entschlossen, alles vollkommen genau zu beobachten, damit er nicht irgendwie auf Umwegen, von hinten her, von oben herab überrascht werden könnte. Jetzt erinnerte er sich wieder an den längst vergessenen Entschluß und vergaß ihn, wie man einen kurzen Faden durch ein Nadelöhr zieht" (*DL*, 57).

[38] "Nur einen Augenblick dachte er das, denn *immerfort vergaß er* alles." (*DL*, 59; emphasis added). Compare also "because you forgot to take my writing things away from me" (*KSS*, 11); "weil du vergessen hast, mir das Schreibzeug wegzunehmen" (*DL*, 59).

[39] "'Er weiß alles tausendmal besser!' rief er. 'Zehntausendmal!' sagte Georg" (*DL*, 59).

[40] "'Komödiant!' konnte sich Georg zu rufen nicht enthalten, erkannte sofort den Schaden . . ., nur zu spät" (*DL*, 58); "'Zehntausendmal!' sagte Georg, um den Vater zu verlachen, aber noch in seinem Munde bekam das Wort einen todernsten Klang" (*DL*, 59).

[41] "und biß, nur zu spät, — die Augen erstarrt — in seine Zunge, daß er vor Schmerz einknickte" (*DL*, 58).

[42] "Georg fühlte sich aus dem Zimmer gejagt," "er . . . eilte" — "Aus dem Tor sprang er, über die Fahrbahn zum Wasser trieb es ihn" (*DL*, 60–61).

[43] "'Du hast keinen Freund in Petersburg.'" (*DL*, 53) — "Wohl kenne ich deinen Freund." (*DL*, 56).

[44] "Georg staunte darüber, wie dunkel das Zimmer des Vaters selbst an diesem sonnigen Vormittag war. Einen solchen Schatten warf also die hohe Mauer, die sich jenseits des schmalen Hofes erhob" (*DL*, 50).

[45] "Beim Anblick der nicht besonders reinen Wäsche machte er sich Vorwürfe, den Vater vernachlässigt zu haben" (*DL*, 54).

[46] "In diesem Augenblick ging über die Brücke ein geradezu unendlicher Verkehr" (*DL*, 61).

5: Kafka's Racial Melancholy

Katja Garloff

Kafka's "A Report to an Academy" ("Ein Bericht für eine Akademie," 1919) has often been read as a parody of Jewish assimilation into German culture, in part because it was first published in Martin Buber's acclaimed Jewish monthly *Der Jude*. In this reading, the text would suggest a problematic convergence between racial antisemitism and a Zionist-inspired critique of assimilation. The parable of the African ape that becomes an almost-human European intimates that biological differences set the Jews apart despite all their efforts at acculturation. The fact that "A Report" ends by describing the ape's nightly encounters with a creature of his own kind, a half-tamed female chimpanzee, underscores this parallelism. In the antisemitic imagination of the time, interracial marriage and procreation set the limit to Jewish assimilation or reveal that assimilation has been a sham to begin with. Symptomatic of this trend is Oskar Panizza's *Der operirte Jud'*, in which a Jew undergoes a series of grotesque medical operations to acquire a perfectly Germanic body and soul, only to see his fabricated identity unravel on the night of his wedding to a Gentile woman. Does Kafka endorse this kind of racial thought? Ritchie Robertson suggests that Kafka's reflections on intermarriage in a letter to Milena Jesenská indeed put him in proximity to such racial antisemites: "There is a disturbing resemblance to the contemporary novels of Bahr, Bartsch, and even Dinter which likewise warned against marriages between Gentiles and Jews."[1]

In this essay I suggest an alternative interpretation of Kafka's ambiguous participation in racial discourses that sanction "intra-racial" love and reject "interracial love." Allusions to racial mixing and non-mixing appear not only in "A Report" but also in some of Kafka's programmatic writings that present modern Jewish culture as an emanation of the Jewish "blood community." I discuss several in detail in the latter part of this paper. My central argument is that all of these texts are an expression of racial melancholy rather than racial ideology. The term racial melancholy, which expands on Judith Butler's concept of gender melancholy, sheds light on the peculiar erotic dimension of "A Report." As I will show, the ape's transformation is fueled by his foreclosed desire for the human: he attempts to become what he must not desire. I also suggest a critical potential of melancholy that is alluded to but never fully elaborated by Butler. Kafka repeatedly revisits the scene of racialization or the moment in which racial groups are being defined and set against each other. His melancholic "stuckness" in the terms of racial discourse ultimately undermines these very terms. As we shall see, his "A Report to an Academy" dismantles the conception of sexuality as an instinctual expression of racial identity, and his programmatic writings put a subversive twist on the central metaphor of turn-of-the-century racial theories: blood.[2]

Racial Melancholy in "A Report to an Academy"

With the concept of gender melancholy, Judith Butler revisits Freud's distinction between mourning and melancholia, following the revisions of Nicolas Abraham and Maria Torok.[3] As is well known, Freud thought of melancholia as a reaction to loss that is inferior to mourning. Whereas the mourner commemorates the lost object while gradually shifting his love to new objects, the melancholic cannot come to terms with loss, because he does not even recognize the loved object as separate from himself. While Abraham and Torok agree with Freud that melancholia is a deficient mode of grief, they reflect on the reasons for the misrecognition and on the status of the lost object in a way that influences Butler's more radical rethinking of the concept. According to Abraham and Torok, what makes it impossible to acknowledge loss is the shameful secret, usually of a sexual nature, that surrounds the lost object.[4] Unspeakable loss leads to a fantasy of incorporation, by which the subject quasi-magically sustains the lost object in or on her body. This idea of incorporation is at the heart of Butler's theory of gender identity as a melancholic response to the loss of the possibility of homosexual attachments.[5] According to Butler, we cannot verbalize or metabolize the loss of our first same-sex love-objects because the social taboo against homosexuality, which precedes the incest taboo, prohibits not only the object but also the orientation of desire. This redoubled interdiction preempts the process of substitution that characterizes socially sanctioned heterosexual desire (that is, a man cannot marry his mother but can marry another woman). As a result we incorporate the lost homoerotic object by identifying with it and acquiring some of its attributes. Essentially, a woman becomes a woman because she is not allowed to desire women.

Because other forms of desire can also become the subject of redoubled interdiction, we may productively use the concept of gender melancholy to explain the formation of other kinds of cultural, ethnic, and racial identities. Butler herself has sketched out how her model might be expanded to explain racializing processes. In an interview with Vikki Bell, she describes two kinds of experiences that may lock racialized subjects into a state of melancholia. First, because racialization has historically been bound up with displacement, the attempt to visit the places of its first enactment quickly ends in an impasse. As an example Butler cites African Americans who embark on McDonald's-sponsored trips to Libya to search for their roots, yet soon find themselves absorbed in a commodity culture that turns the memories of the slave trade into objects of commerce and fetishization. Second, the foreclosure (rather than just the prohibition and repression) of interracial relationships means that certain forms of desire become unthinkable, unspeakable, and ungrievable in public discourse. The discursive aspect is crucial: "It's not a question of this ego not being able to love that person . . . . It's rather what it means to have one's desire formed as it were through cultural norms that dictate in part what will and will not be a loveable object, what will and will not be a legitimate form of love."[6] It is striking that Butler chooses two such different examples of racial melancholy, one that stems from the trauma of deportation and the other from the foreclosure of interracial love. Interestingly, she does not elaborate much on the taboo against interracial love, and other scholars working on racial melancholy have tended to drop it altogether.

Kafka's "A Report to an Academy," which depicts a process of cross-species identification fueled by displacement and blocked desire, helps fill in the lacunae left by Butler. At first glance "A Report" seems to support the notion of an indelible biological difference, in this case between apes and humans, because the ape (called Rotpeter) engages in superficial mimicry rather than genuine change. Rotpeter observes and imitates human behavior with the greatest precision but without true comprehension. However, the text gradually undermines the hierarchical distinction between apes and humans by subtly conflating apish and human behavior. Rotpeter's imitation of such "respectable" human habits as drinking, burping, and spitting exposes the dependence of human identity on the compulsive repetition of certain rituals, which moreover cannot be clearly distinguished from animal behavior. Remarks such as "Your apedom, gentlemen, to the extent that you have something of the sort behind you, cannot be more remote from you than mine is from me" suggests that the human identity of Rotpeter's interlocutors is no more stable than his own (*KSS*, 77).[7]

The critical import of "A Report to an Academy" goes beyond its emphasis on the performative character of human identity. The text also gives expression to melancholy, or a state of unresolved grief resulting from the foreclosure of certain desires. We get a first sense of the complexity of erotic desire in "A Report" when reading that Rotpeter's transformation into a human of sorts begins with a castration of sorts — a castration, however, that generates new pleasures and desires. During his capture Rotpeter incurs a wound below his hip with the result that his naked hip region now shows "nothing . . . other than a well-groomed pelt" (*KSS*, 78)[8] and a conspicuous scar. As he attempts to describe this scar and the injury that caused it, the care he takes in choosing the right adjective draws attention to a certain duplicity in the act of castration: "the scar left by a — let us choose here a specific word for a specific purpose, a word, however, that should not be misunderstood — the scar left by a profligate [frevelhaften] shot" (*KSS*, 78).[9] The German word "Frevel," with its meanings of crime, outrage, iniquity, or sacrilege, denotes the violation of a fundamental, even divine, law. But it also carries connotations of a bold and willful transgression, suggesting that the shot that castrated Rotpeter afforded the hunters some secret pleasure. Rotpeter's eagerness to show off his scar, the bodily sign of his capture and subjugation, betrays a certain pleasure on his part as well.

The shooting scene anticipates the ways in which erotic desire persists in the very act of imitation. Rotpeter's forcibly chosen self-transformation — "I, a free ape, accepted this yoke" (*KSS*, 77)[10] — is a form of subjugation that brings with it secret erotic pleasures in both the oppressor and the oppressed. His assimilation to human culture comes up against clear limits, not only because an ape cannot by definition become human, whatever his efforts, but also because his teachers seek to produce in him an "almost-but-not-quite" human, the perfect object of colonial power. The sadistic pleasure his first teacher, a sailor, takes in instructing Rotpeter reflects this conviction that the ape can never become a real human. The sailor rejoices more in the uncivilized exuberance with which Rotpeter expresses his interest in human activities than in his actual imitation of these activities. As he witnesses with malicious satisfaction Rotpeter's eagerness to learn how to drink liquor from a bottle, his behavior exemplifies what Homi Bhabha calls colonial mimicry, or the attempt to produce "a reformed, recognizable Other, *as a subject of a difference that is almost the same, but not quite.*"[11] Rotpeter responds to the teacher's injunction with a passionate attachment to the structures of power. In this scene he voyeuristically revels in the sailor's power over himself, the powerless ape:

> . . . after the bottle was uncorked, he raised it to his mouth; my glances follow him down into his gullet; he nods, satisfied with me, and puts the bottle to his lips; I, *ecstatic* with gradually dawning understanding, *squealing, scratch* the length and the breadth of me, *wherever my hand lands*; he is pleased, puts the bottle to his mouth, and takes a swig; I, impatient and desperate to emulate him, *soil myself in my cage, an act that once again gives him great satisfaction*; and now, holding the bottle at arm's length and with a swoop bringing it back up again, he leans back with exaggerated pedantry and in one gulp empties it. *Exhausted from excessive desire*, I can follow no longer and hang weakly onto the bars. . . . (*KSS*, 81–82, emphasis added)[12]

In another important scene, Rotpeter speaks his first word and experiences the applause that follows "like a kiss on my whole sweat-soaked body" (*KSS*, 82).[13] In other words, he registers his approval by the human community as an erotic sensation.[14] This occurs after he has emptied his first bottle of liquor and intoxication has loosened his tongue. There are undeniable Dionysian undertones in this scene — Rotpeter throws the empty bottle away "like an artist" (*KSS,* 82)[15] — yet this is hardly the ecstatic release of primordial energies Nietzsche had in mind. Throughout "A Report," sexual desire arises from a process of subjugation in which the ape's desire for the human is simultaneously solicited and prohibited. The fact that Rotpeter concludes his report by soberly mentioning his nightly encounters with a female chimpanzee enhances the impression that a taboo exists against the ape's desire for humans, a taboo that forms the basis of his melancholic identification with humanity. The very rigidity of Rotpeter's pseudo-scientific language is a symptom of this melancholy. He presents his report to a scientific academy, that is, an institution that represents the society that captures monkeys to display them in zoos or to make them objects of scientific research. His use of the word *Affe* (ape) in a pejorative sense and of numerous bureaucratic locutions shows that he has thoroughly assimilated the rhetoric and the biases of the institution. Yet his language remains an oddly external and detachable part of his deportment, which becomes evident in his sudden changes of linguistic register, his leaps into expressively metaphorical and crassly physical language.

To read "A Report to an Academy" through a Butlerian lens helps explain an aspect of the text critics have curiously neglected, namely, its preoccupation with Rotpeter's decision to become a human being. His inability to give an account of this decision reflects an inability to revisit the scene of his racialization, or the moment when he became human society's other. The presence of a formative yet inaccessible past is tangible throughout "A Report." Rotpeter begins his report by stating that he cannot fulfill the academy's request to provide an account of his life as an ape because becoming human required him to cut off the connection to his origins and the memories of his youth. He can in fact not even remember his own capture but rather depends on the report of others to visualize the scene. His own memories gradually set in with the moment that he woke up on a ship on the way to Europe, his back painfully pressed against the bars of a narrow cage. The bulk of the report is focused on Rotpeter's decision to seek a "way out" of this hopeless situation by becoming a human being. He cannot completely reconstruct this decision, in part because its outcome is never entirely predictable, that is, it is not a decision for something and is thus no decision at all.[16] Language itself impedes the access to Rotpeter's past state of mind because human words can only approximate ape emotions. Thus he can only surmise how he arrived at his decision to become human: "A clear, beautiful thought that I must *somehow* have *hatched with my belly*, for apes think with their belly" (*KSS,* 79, emphasis added).[17]

The ungrievable origin on which the text is focused is the moment Rotpeter was jolted into the human world as a never-completely human being. His attempt to account for his forced "decision" to become human is akin to that of the slave descendants who travel to Africa in search of memories of the beginnings of slavery. Like these travelers, Rotpeter imaginatively revisits the moment when he became society's other only to find that he can never fully recapture this moment. His report lingers over the moment when he lost his ape freedom or when this freedom became forever an object of conjecture. One indication of the text's preoccupation with an originary yet inaccessible moment is the circular movement it performs. At the end of the report Rotpeter states that by finding a way out of imprisonment, he enacted the "German expression, 'to slip off into the bushes'" (*KSS*, 83).[18] Yet the bushes were also the place where Rotpeter was caught and from which he was propelled into the human world — the hunters who captured him were lying in wait "in the bushes along the shore" (*KSS*, 78)[19] — so his transformation from ape to human equals a movement from the bushes to the bushes. It is a circular movement back to the site of capture, with the difference that this time Rotpeter appears to be initiating his own imprisonment. In Butlerian terms, his way out of imprisonment stays within the limits set by social power; his resistance owes its possibility to what it opposes. Yet the very conditions that force his subjugation to human society also give him the means to rearticulate the terms of subjugation, for instance, the ability to distance himself from pretensions of human freedom.

It is in this context that we have to read the scene that pictures Rotpeter's sexual relations with a half-tamed female chimpanzee, that is, an ape on the way to becoming more like a human. Just as he stays fixed in his position as an "almost-but-not-quite" human being, Rotpeter remains libidinally attached to an "almost-but-not-quite" ape.

> If I return late at night from banquets, from learned societies, from convivial occasions, a little half-trained chimpanzee is waiting for me, and I have my pleasure of her in the way of all apes. In the daytime I do not want to see her; she has the lunatic look of the bewildered trained animal; I am the only one who recognizes it, and I can't stand it. (*KSS*, 83–84).[20]

Like Rotpeter, the female chimpanzee is suspended between an irredeemably lost origin and an unreachable destination. Her description suggests that her madness results from this state of suspension. This description linguistically performs the opaqueness of her gaze as it foregrounds the materiality of sounds and letters at the expense of semantics: "sie hat nämlich den Irrsinn des verwirrten dressierten Tieres im Blick" ("she has the lunatic look of the bewildered trained animal"). While Rotpeter can decode his mate's gaze — is indeed so struck by its meaning that he cannot bear it — the accumulation of "s" and "r"s in its description makes the reader linger and puzzle over the phrase, attracting her attention but barring her from full understanding. Kafka seems to suggest that to have a sexual relationship means to be locked together in a state of suspension and faced with a question — in this case: Why is it that the ape at the same time must and must not become human? In linking this question to sexuality, Kafka undermines any essentialist idea of sexuality as the inalienable expression of the ape's apish nature. Rather, Rotpeter's remark "I have my pleasure of her in the way of all apes" casts sexual pleasure as something generic and imitated; when he is with his female mate, he does not express his innermost desires but rather mimes what he used to be, "in the way of all apes" (nach Affenart). The scene also suggests that Rotpeter's love for his own kind is no less secret and illicit than his desire for humans. He does not want to see the female chimpanzee during the day, we may infer, because she is his uncanny double, a ghost from the past that continually reminds him of the paradoxical injunction to which he is subject: "Become human! Know that you cannot become human!"

I have suggested that "A Report" is a response to the racialization of Jewish identity in modern anti-Semitism. By picturing the assimilating Jew as an ape, Kafka does not amplify the biological difference between "Jews" and "Aryans" and shift its level from race to species — according to one influential definition, members of different species do not mate with each other — but instead dismantles notions of biological difference altogether. The fact that Rotpeter's sexual preference remains apish is not evidence of a biological barrier separating apes and humans but rather renders the terms and conditions of Rotpeter's integration into human society legible. This is what makes the story an expression of racial melancholy rather than of racial thought. Racial melancholy means to be stuck in the discursive terms that regulate interracial desire, a kind of fixation that at the same time opens up the possibility of reconfiguring these terms. It is important to emphasize the discursive aspect of melancholy. What we hold on to in gender melancholy is not so much a lost love object but a scene of interdiction and radical foreclosure. The same is true for racial melancholy, as I have been defining it through Kafka's "A Report." Neither intra- nor interracial desire emerges in the story as an original desire that subsequently becomes repressed. Rather, Kafka's peculiar representation of both kinds of desires highlights the linguistic terms of racialization, or the ways in which the categories of "ape" and "human" become defined in relation to each other.

Literalizing the "Community of Blood"

The critical impetus of "A Report" is important because Jews occupied a special place in the norms and taboos regulating interracial desire at the turn of the twentieth century. As Sander Gilman has shown, Kafka was well aware of the dominant discourses on the dangers of racial mixing and their antisemitic implications. In his highly popular *The Foundations of the Nineteenth Century*, Houston Stewart Chamberlain describes the Jews as a "mongrel" race produced through interbreeding with Africans during the Alexandrian exile.[21] According to Chamberlain, racial mixing can have positive effects if it occurs in a limited fashion and between closely related races. The Jews, however, emerged from large-scale mixing between unrelated races and to this day pay for this *Blutschande* (defilement of the blood) with psychical imbalance and guilt feelings. Chamberlain's impact can be gauged by the fact that even those Jewish scholars who polemicized against him adopted parts of his argument and vocabulary. Nathan Birnbaum, an eloquent critic of Chamberlain and leading supporter of Yiddish language and culture in Eastern Europe, unwittingly confirmed Chamberlain's idea of racial purity when he argued that long periods of endogamy renewed and strengthened the Jewish people.[22] Other Jewish writers similarly responded to Chamberlain's construction by positing a special purity of the Jewish race. In 1909 Max Warwar published an article in the Zionist periodical *Selbstwehr*, which Kafka read regularly, about the insecurities of male Jews who reject their body as a "mixed type." Warwar admonishes his readers instead to affirm their dark "Jewish type," which he deems racially pure, and to resist their erotic attraction to other types.[23]

These discourses show what is at stake in Kafka's allusions to racial mixing and non-mixing, however obliquely. Such allusions appear not only in "A Report" but also in several texts, few in number but high in critical impact, that Kafka wrote on European Jewish literature. These programmatic texts project an idea of Jewish culture as both separate from and entwined with the surrounding majority cultures. At the same time, they are shot through with the central terms of racial theories, especially where they depict Jewish culture as an emanation of a "blood community." In what follows, I will argue that Kafka literalizes the notion of a blood community in a way that wrests it away from racial discourses.

The first example is from Kafka's diary entry on "minor literatures" from 25 December 1911. The entry has been famous ever since Gilles Deleuze and Félix Guattari argued that a minor literature, which positions itself self-consciously at the margins of a dominant culture, thwarts any attempt to map a language neatly onto a nation, territory, or ethnicity. However, their reading obscures the degree of self-containment Kafka attributes to minor literatures, in part because they erroneously apply the term to Kafka's own literary production.[24] When Kafka writes about minor literatures, he has in mind Czech literature in Prague and Yiddish literature in Poland, neither of which was composed in the language of the cultural elite. Such literatures, he believes, are collective in nature and conducive to lively debates precisely because they lack outstanding talents. Since they have fewer themes to tackle and less room to unfold, such literatures have a closer connection to public life and more immediate political effects. A minor literature is a "keeping of a diary by a nation" that leads to "the narrowing down of the attention of [the] nation upon itself and the accepting of what is foreign only in reflection" (*D*1, 191–92).[25] For all its inner heterogeneity, a minor literature is a self-contained, quasi-organic entity with limited contact to other literatures.

Kafka's concern with biological models of community becomes even more overt in two entries framing the minor literature entry, which depict circumcision scenes and in which blood quite literally helps constitute a community. The first scene occurs in Prague among assimilated Western Jews, who show a marked indifference toward the event and each other, and the second among Orthodox Jews in Russia, where the ritual still functions to usher an individual into a religious community and a meaningful life. This entry concludes with reflections on the attachment among Russian Jews, who seek out every opportunity to be together. Despite these differences, Kafka's descriptions of the two circumcision scenes betray a similar mix of fascination and disgust with the blood that flows from the circumcised penis:

> [In Prague:] . . . then the operation is performed with what is almost an ordinary knife, a sort of fish knife. One sees blood and raw flesh, the *mohel* bustles about briefly with his long-nailed, trembling fingers and pulls skin from some place or other over the wound like the finger of a glove. At once everything is all right, the child has scarcely cried. Now there remains only a short prayer during which the *mohel* drinks some wine and with his fingers, not yet entirely unbloody, carries some wine to the child's lips. Those present pray: "As he has now achieved the covenant, so may he achieve knowledge of the Torah, a happy marriage and the performance of good deeds." (*D*1, 190; translation modified)[26]

> [In Russia:] The circumciser, who performs his office without payment, is usually a drinker — busy as he is, he has not time for the various holiday foods and so simply pours down some brandy. Thus they all have red noses and reeking breaths. It is therefore not very pleasant when, after the operation has been performed, they suck the bloody member with this mouth, in the prescribed manner. The member is then sprinkled with sawdust and heals in about three days. (*D*1, 196)[27]

In the first passage, the graphic description of the baby's blood and raw flesh and the *mohel's* trembling and bloody fingers reflects the participants' alienation from the religious ritual, a state of mind Kafka diagnoses later in the passage. Once the ritual loses its religious significance, the observer focuses only on the crude physicality of the medical operation. The entry suggests that the child's future marital and communal life will be suffused with a similar spiritual meaninglessness. But why is Kafka's description of the Russian circumcision, the religious function of which is apparently still intact, also focused on repulsive physical aspects, including the smell of liquor that emanates from the *mohel's* mouth and mingles with the penis blood? One may, of course, argue that even where Kafka describes a vibrant religious experience, he cannot overcome his own inner distance from it. But there is more to this. Kafka's entry on minor literatures and the two framing entries on circumcision form a series of reflections on the grounds of Jewish communality. If the minor literature entry depicts the nation as a family of sorts, the representation of Western European and Eastern European Jewish rituals in the framing entries performs a shift from atomized individuals to a cohesive community. However, the figures of blood in both entries show that this shift is not absolute. The blood that provokes disgust signals the always-present potential of alienation from the circumcision ritual, suggesting that what constitutes a community is also what potentially tears it apart.[28] It is probably no coincidence that Kafka chooses circumcision to depict the tenuous grounds of Jewish communality. Circumcision is a religious-cultural practice that leaves a permanent physical mark on the body, and as such it encapsulates the difficulty of distinguishing between biological and cultural modes of belonging.

Another significant reference to blood appears in Kafka's address on the Yiddish language, where blood functions as a cipher of untranslatability between Yiddish and German and of the inner dividedness of the German-speaking Jew. Kafka had become interested in Yiddish after attending several theater performances staged by a Galician Jewish troupe in Prague in 1911–12, in part because it promised him the possibility of cultural authenticity and social cohesion for deracinated Western Jews. A few months after writing the diary entry on minor literature, he agreed to introduce a reading of Yiddish poetry to an audience of German-speaking Jews in Prague. In this talk he presents Yiddish as a quintessentially diasporic language that continuously absorbs words from an array of languages without ever creating a stable semantic or grammatical system. Because of its inner heterogeneity and mobility, Yiddish would easily disintegrate were it not for a mysterious force that holds it together.

One way of reading Kafka's talk is as a performance meant to draw his audience — assimilated Jews whom he did not expect to know or appreciate Yiddish — into the kind of community he found among Eastern European Jews. He alerts his listeners to two different ways in which they may approach the poems: they may either recognize the German synonyms of Yiddish or reactivate their own latent emotional connection with Yiddish culture. Whereas knowledge of German allows them to understand Yiddish from a distance, empathetic identification enables them to grasp the underlying unity of the language and of their own selves. The two approaches Kafka proposes may appear complementary in that they encourage his audience to move from a superficial, rational comprehension of Yiddish words to a deep, intuitive understanding of the culture. And yet it does not quite work this way. Rather, any attempt to understand Yiddish words via their German synonyms appears futile because, according to Kafka, Yiddish resists translation into German. Its most essential contents are inevitably lost in translation: "The links between Yiddish and German are too delicate and significant not to be torn to shreds the instant Yiddish is transformed back into German, that is to say, it is no longer Yiddish that is transformed, but something that has utterly lost its essential character."[29] Kafka thus imparts to his listeners a contradictory message: he first tells them that they *can* understand Yiddish because they know German and then that they *cannot* understand Yiddish because they know German. Ironically, Kafka attempts to foster his listeners' understanding of Yiddish poems by exacerbating the psychological split within them.

And this is where blood shows up again. As examples of Yiddish words that resist translation into German and therefore require an intuitive understanding, Kafka cites "toit" (dead) and "blüt" (blood). He does not go into further detail, so we do not learn why these specific words mark the limits of the assimilated Jew's ability to grasp Yiddish culture through his or her knowledge of German. Perhaps Kafka means to activate the associations of "dead" and "blood" with violence and destruction, thus invoking a history of Jewish suffering among Gentile neighbors, a point of view of the victims that would be lost in translation. What does not fit squarely with this interpretation, however, is Kafka's transliteration of the Yiddish word as "blüt." The common pronunciation of the Yiddish word is either "blut" or, in the Polish version, "blit." But in no case would it be "blüt" — in fact, Yiddish does not have umlauts. Kafka's decision to spell the word "blüt" may of course simply reflect his less-than-perfect Yiddish skills and the transliteration praxis of his time.[30] But it also makes the word sound like the German "blüht" (blossoms), as in "die Blume blüht" (the flower blossoms). Thus understood, the word "blüt" recalls the strange, infested wound that looks like a flower in Kafka's story "A Country Doctor" ("Ein Landarzt," 1919). Suffered by a boy the doctor cannot heal, the wound is an overdetermined signifier that connotes life and death, beauty and decay, eroticism and fatalism alike. The word "blüt" in Kafka's address on the Yiddish language functions analogously in that it both continues the connotations of death and violence in "toit" and reminds us that new life may blossom after death. In other words, "blüt" may function in Kafka's speech as a cipher of genealogical continuity. This in turn aligns Kafka with a tradition of modern German Jewish thinkers who rethink and re-signify blood as the ground of Jewish communality.

Kafka's immediate contact with this tradition was Martin Buber, who in 1909–1911 delivered three famous addresses on Judaism in Prague, of which Kafka attended at least one. Buber's first address describes the contemporary Jew as divided between the external circumstances of his life, which takes place in the midst of another nation, and his inner substance, which connects him to the Jewish people, the "community of his blood."[31] As a solution to this potentially vexing split, Buber calls upon his fellow Jews to embrace their blood community and reconnect to the chain of their ancestors. These ideas certainly have a *völkisch* ring, yet it is important to note Buber's distance from the racial ideologies of his time. He defines blood as a medium of ethnic segregation as well as of cultural exchange. Blood is "capable of being imprinted and influenced, a substance absorbing and assimilating all into its own form" (15). It would therefore be "senseless," Buber writes, "to try to shed the culture of the world about us, a culture that . . . has been assimilated by the innermost forces of our blood, and has become an integral part of ourselves" (19). Buber's interpretation of blood relations allows him to posit the existence of a Jewish people without disavowing their interaction with other peoples. Blood comes to signify permanence in the face of change, self-identity in the face of assimilation. In *The Star of Redemption* (1921), Franz Rosenzweig further develops this idea when he writes that the genealogical continuity guaranteed by blood ties enables Jews to live as a kind of messianic reminder amidst other nations.

Like Buber and Rosenzweig, Kafka reworks the notion of the blood ties and restores to it an openness lost in racial ideologies. He emphasizes the interaction between Jewish and non-Jewish cultures as well as the transience and heterogeneity of the cultural formations to which it gives rise. The Yiddish language constantly absorbs words from other languages without fully assimilating them. Minor literatures such as Yiddish literature in Warsaw are riddled by internal contradictions. However, Kafka's rhetorical strategies differ from Buber's. In Buber, "blood" serves as a metaphor to capture the simultaneity of change and constancy, self-exposure and self-identity, permeability and rigidity of communal boundaries. Kafka, too, uses "blood" to explore the nature of Jewish communality, yet in so doing he makes the word concrete, or literal, in a way not conceivable in Buber. In Kafka, blood is the substance that flows from the circumcised penis and the word that signals the divide between Yiddish and German. This concretization effectively wrests the idea of a Jewish blood community away from racial ideologies. Such ideologies operate by converting transient visual signs into intransient substance, the name of which is usually "blood." Kafka's proliferation and literalization of the signifier "blood" reverses this process. By amplifying rather than interiorizing surfaces, he renders them *unusable* for racial ideologies.[32]

Nothing illustrates the effects of this procedure better than the image of the ape that attempts to become human, another instance of literalization. On the one hand, this image amplifies an alleged difference between "races" (Germans and Jews) into one between species (humans and apes).

On the other hand, the image literalizes an ossified metaphor, namely the anti-Semitic charge that Jews can only "ape" but not truly become Germans. This literalization of a metaphor — which remains as incomplete as Gregor Samsa's famous transformation into vermin[33] — allows Kafka to linger on the image, to explore all its facets and proliferate its meanings. For this reading it does not matter that "A Report" makes no explicit reference to Jews or Judaism. In fact, this omission can itself be read as an expression of racial melancholy, understood as a productive "stuckness" in the terms of racial discourse. Dropping one half of the equation "Jew = ape," Kafka dwells endlessly on the image of the ape and grotesquely inflates the reproach of mimicry. He depicts a series of superficial imitations and ends on an allusion to an insurmountable biological barrier, namely the ape's inability to mate with a human. Yet as I hope to have shown, this emphasis on racial divisions ultimately exposes their arbitrariness. Kafka's portrayal of an ape whose sexual preference remains apish and his definition of the Jews as a blood community do not reflect an acceptance of social taboos; rather, they testify to his *melancholic* — and therefore subversive — immersion in the dominant discourses on Jewish assimilation and their racial undertones.

Notes

[1] Ritchie Robertson, *The "Jewish Question" in German Literature, 1749–1939: Emancipation and Its Discontents* (New York: Oxford UP, 1999), 368.

[2] My argument also applies to Kafka's letters to Milena Jesenská, his only non-Jewish lover. These letters show that Kafka was well aware of the role of "interracial" sex and love in the anti-Semitic imagination. In response to Milena's question of whether he is Jewish, he brings up Christian prejudice against Christian-Jewish unions, including her own marriage to Ernst Polak and his sister's impending marriage to a Gentile (*BM,* 26). At times Kafka comes close to embracing anti-Semitic stereotypes, for instance, when he suggestively links a Christian-Jewish love affair to a contemporary trial in which a Jew was accused of ritually murdering a Christian girl (*BM,* 168). This linkage recalls the tendency, in modern anti-Semitism, to transform the medieval blood libels into fantasies about Jewish sexual deviancy. Ultimately, however, the letters transform the taboo against interracial love into an opportunity for intercultural contact. While Kafka construes his relationship with Milena by way of a series of oppositions — between Jew and Christian, old and new, impurity and purity, exile and home, sexual drivenness and spiritual peace — his self-avowed "stuckness" in the first terms of these oppositions ushers in a process of religious-cultural mediation. In one instance he suspends the old-new opposition by picturing his Christian lover as a confirmation of his own Jewishness: Milena, he writes, was born shortly after his thirteenth birthday and thus given to him as a Bar Mitzvah ("eine Art jüdischer Konfirmation," *BM,* 207) present.

[3] Nicolas Abraham and Maria Torok, *The Shell and the Kernel*, vol. 1, ed. and trans. Nicholas T. Rand (Chicago: U of Chicago P, 1994).

[4] See Abraham and Torok, *The Shell and the Kernel*, 1:107–56.

[5] Butler developed the concept of gender melancholy first in *Gender Trouble: Feminism and the Subversion of Identity* (New York: Routledge, 1990), 57–72, and then in *The Psychic Life of Power: Theories in Subjection* (Stanford, CA: Stanford UP, 1997), 132–50 and 160–66.

[6] Vikki Bell, "On Speech, Race and Melancholia: An Interview with Judith Butler," *Theory, Culture & Society* 16.2 (1999): 163–74; here 170.

[7] "Ihr Affentum, meine Herren, soferne Sie etwas Derartiges hinter sich haben, kann Ihnen nicht ferner sein als mir das meine" (*DL*, 300). An earlier, shorter version of my reading of "A Report to an Academy" appeared in my article "Kafka's Crypt: W. G. Sebald and the Melancholy of Modern German Jewish Culture," *Germanic Review* 82.2 (Spring 2007): 123–40. I would like to thank Taylor & Francis for permission to reuse parts of the article here.

[8] "nichts . . . als einen wohlgepflegten Pelz" (*DL*, 302).

[9] "die Narbe nach einem — wählen wir hier zu einem bestimmten Zwecke ein bestimmtes Wort, das aber nicht mißverstanden werden wolle — die Narbe nach einem frevelhaften Schuß" (*DL*, 302).

[10] "ich, freier Affe, fügte mich diesem Joch" (*DL*, 299).

[11] Homi K. Bhabha, *The Location of Culture* (New York: Routledge, 1994), 86, emphasis by Bhabha.

[12] "nachdem die Flasche entkorkt war, hob er sie zum Mund; ich mit meinen Blicken ihm nach bis in die Gurgel; er nickt, zufrieden mit mir, und setzt die Flasche an die Lippen; ich, *entzückt* von allmählicher Erkenntnis, *kratze mich quietschend* der Länge und Breite nach, *wo es sich trifft*; er freut sich, setzt die Flasche an und macht einen Schluck; ich, ungeduldig und verzweifelt, ihm nachzueifern, *verunreinige mich in meinem Käfig, was wieder ihm große Genugtuung* macht; und nun weit die Flasche von sich streckend und im Schwung sie wieder hinaufführend, trinkt er sie, übertrieben lehrhaft zurückgebeugt, mit einem Zuge leer. Ich, *ermattet von allzu großem Verlangen*, kann nicht mehr folgen und hänge schwach am Gitter" (*DL*, 309; emphasis added).

[13] "wie einen Kuß auf meinem ganzen schweißtriefenden Körper" (*DL*, 311).

[14] Very few critics have paid attention to the erotic dimension in "A Report." One who has is the Hungarian-German-Jewish playwright George Tabori, who quotes the beginning of "A Report" in one of his speeches and comments: "So beginnt Kafkas Affenmensch eine Liebesgeschichte über den Fremdling unter den Eingeborenen: zum Beispiel eines Juden unter Deutschen" (Thus Kafka's apeman begins a love story about the stranger among the natives: for example, that of a Jew among Germans; my translation, KG). George Tabori, "Liebeserklärung: Dankrede," *Jahrbuch der deutschen Akademie für Sprache und Dichtung Darmstadt* (1992): 133. Tabori does not offer any textual evidence for his reading, but the kiss scene could be construed as such evidence.

[15] "als Künstler" (*DL*, 310).

[16] Gerhard Neumann has aptly characterized Rotpeter's transformation as the fulfillment of a promise in which the promise is only retroactively generated. See his "'A Report for an Academy': Erwägungen zum 'Mimesis'-Charakter Kafkascher Texte," *Deutsche Vierteljahrsschrift für Literaturwissenschaft und Geistesgeschichte* 49 (1975): 166–83.

[17] "Ein klarer, schöner Gedankengang, den ich *irgendwie* mit dem Bauch *ausgeheckt haben muß*, denn Affen denken mit dem Bauch" (*DL*, 304; emphasis added).

[18] "deutsche Redensart: sich in die Büsche schlagen" (*DL*, 312).

[19] "im Ufergebüsch" (*DL*, 301).

[20] "Komme ich spät nachts von Banketten, aus wissenschaftlichen Gesellschaften, aus gemütlichem Beisammensein nach Hause, erwartet micht eine kleine halbdressierte Schimpansin und ich lasse es mir nach Affenart bei ihr wohlgehen. Bei Tag will ich sie nicht sehen; sie hat nämlich den Irrsinn des verwirrten dressierten Tieres im Blick; das erkenne nur ich und ich kann es nicht ertragen" (*DL*, 313).

[21] See Houston Stewart Chamberlain, *Die Grundlagen des 19. Jahrhunders*, vol. 1. 4th ed. (Munich: Bruckmann, 1904), 389, and Sander Gilman, *The Jew's Body* (New York: Routledge, 1991), 174–76.

[22] See Nathan Birnbaum, "Über H. St. Chamberlain," in *Ausgewählte Schriften: Zur jüdischen Frage*, vol. 2 (Czernowitz, Hungary: Birnbaum & Kohut, 1910), 192–205, here 205.

[23] Max Warwar, "Die Flucht vor dem Typus," *Selbstwehr* 3 (30 Apr. 1909): 1–2. Cited in Sander Gilman, *Franz Kafka, the Jewish Patient* (New York: Routledge, 1995), 15.

[24] For an in-depth critique of Deleuze and Guattari's approach to Kafka, see Stanley Corngold, *Lambent Traces: Franz Kafka* (Princeton, NJ: Princeton UP, 2004), 142–57.

[25] "dieses Tagebuchführen einer Nation . . . die Einschränkung der Aufmerksamkeit der Nation auf ihren eigenen Kreis und Aufnahme des Fremden nur in der Spiegelung" (*Ta*, 313).

[26] "dann erfolgt mit einem fast gewöhnlichen Messer einer Art Fischmesser der Schnitt. Jetzt sieht man Blut und rohes Fleisch, der Moule hantiert darin kurz mit seinen langnägeligen zittrigen Fingern und zieht irgendwo gewonnene Haut wie einen Handschuhfinger über die Wunde. Gleich ist alles gut, das Kind hat kaum geweint. Jetzt kommt nur noch ein kleines Gebet, während dessen der Moule Wein trinkt, und mit seinen noch nicht ganz blutfreien Fingern etwas Wein an die Lippen des Kindes bringt. Die Anwesenden beten: 'Wie er nun gelangt ist in den Bund, so soll er gelangen zur Kenntnis der Tora, zum glücklichen Ehebund und zur Ausübung guter Werke'" (*Ta*, 311).

[27] "Der Beschneider, der sein Amt ohne Bezahlung ausübt, ist meist ein Säufer, da er beschäftigt, wie er ist, an den verschiedenen Festessen sich nicht beteiligen kann und daher nur etwas Schnaps herunterschüttet. Alle diese Beschneider haben deshalb rote Nasen und riechen aus dem Mund. Es ist daher auch nicht appetitlich, wenn sie, nachdem der Schnitt ausgeführt ist, mit diesem Mund das blutige Glied

aussaugen wie es vorgeschrieben ist. Das Glied wird dann mit Holzmehl bedeckt und ist in drei Tagen beiläufig heil" (*Ta*, 317).

[28] On the disruptive moments in Kafka's visions of communities, see also Vivian Liska, *When Kafka Says We: Uncommon Communities in German-Jewish Literature* (Bloomington: Indiana UP, 2009), esp. 15–33.

[29] Franz Kafka, "An Introductory Talk on the Yiddish Language," in *Reading Kafka: Prague, Politics, and the Fin de Siècle*, ed. Mark M. Anderson (New York: Schocken, 1989), 265–66. "Die Verbindungen zwischen Jargon und Deutsch sind zu zart und bedeutend, als daß sie nicht sofort zerreißen müßten, wenn Jargon ins Deutsche zurückgeführt wird, d.h. es wird kein Jargon mehr zurückgeführt, sondern etwas Wesensloses" (*NS*1, 192).

[30] I would like to thank Iris Bruce for checking the transliterations of Yiddish poems in some of Kafka's sources, including the Zionist journal *Selbstwehr* and Isser Meyer Pinès's *Histoire de la littérature judéo-allemande* (Paris: Jouve, 1911). Bruce found that even though the authors always render "blood" as "blut," they use umlauts for some other words, a praxis that possibly influenced Kafka. Bruce's book, *Kafka and Cultural Zionism: Dates in Palestine* (Madison: U of Wisconsin P, 2007), is an excellent resource for anyone interested in Kafka's relationship to his Jewish heritage. In the most recent account of Kafka's complex relationship to Eastern European Jewish culture, Dan Miron notes that the Yiddish troupes whose plays Kafka had been attending earlier likely spoke a "quasi-Germanized Yiddish." Dan Miron, *From Continuity to Contiguity: Toward a New Jewish Literary Thinking* (Stanford, CA: Stanford UP, 2010), 315.

[31] Martin Buber, *On Judaism*, ed. Nahum N. Glatzer (New York: Schocken, 1996), 17.

[32] See also John Zilcosky's argument, in his contribution to this volume, about the "unreadability" of bodies in Kafka.

[33] See Stanley Corngold's seminal reading of "The Metamorphosis" in *Franz Kafka: The Necessity of Form* (Ithaca, NY: Cornell UP, 1988), 47–80.

6: Strange Loops and the Absent Center in *The Castle*

Jacob Burnett

FRANZ KAFKA (LIKE THE REST OF US) faces the disappearance of the millennia-old Transcendent Center from European consciousness. In the absence he does not find cause for despair but from it discovers a new dimension of existence. Through the deployment of underlying narrative "strange loops" (to borrow a term from Douglas Hofstader), Kafka's work, in particular *The Castle* (*Das Schloss*, 1926), constructs an art that can survive the disappearance of a grounding center. His novel is an endless stairway on which, discovering that we are not lamed by the absence of God, we walk briskly on to meet ourselves in this new century. *The Castle*'s "strange loop" narrative leads us ever upwards, ever downwards, and always back to ourselves, always back to reality through fictions that defy the "many" who "complained that the words of the wise are over and over again merely parables and of no use in everyday life, and that's all we have"[1] (*KSS*, 161).

With the disastrous absence of the Transcendent Center — an *absent* center, not merely a central *absence* (the Gnostic's *deus absconditus*) — goes the traditional grounds of a theistic culture — or so one story goes. Resting neither on Something nor on Nothing, post-god Man can be neither a magician, manipulating through ritual and language the capricious and unfathomable forces that govern his life, nor a mystic, emptying himself out to overleap his precarious condition. If we maintain the necessity of being maintained, the situation becomes intolerable. The past century argues, in ashes more eloquent than words, that all that is left for us if we must rest on something and yet, having exhausted our gods, can rest on nothing, is the Morton's Fork of existentialism or nihilism — absurdity or self-destruction, twin parodies of priesthood and kenosis.

Nietzsche grasps this intolerable freefall into infinitude best when he writes that "we have forsaken the land and gone to sea! We have destroyed the bridge behind us — more so, we have demolished the land behind us!"[2] The intimate and disastrous consequence of this destruction follows immediately, in his parable of the madman in the marketplace who cries of the death of God:

> "How were we able to drink up the sea? Who gave us the sponge to wipe away the entire horizon? What were we doing when we unchained this earth from its sun? Are we not continually falling? And backwards, sidewards, forwards, in all directions? Is there still an up and a down? Aren't we straying as though through an infinite nothing? Isn't empty space breathing at us . . . How can we console ourselves, the murderers of all murderers!" . . . It is still recounted how on the same day the madman forced his way into several churches and there started singing his ***requiem aeternam deo***.[3]

The death of God, the vanishing of the center from Western culture — Nietzsche's madman is not alone in crying out — creates a collective consciousness of constant vertigo. Without providing even the consolation of being able to fall clearly toward some final goal, it produces the sense of a tumbling in all directions and hence in none at all.

Literature feels the impact of this *Götzen-Dämmerung* as displacement and devastation. As George Steiner writes, "Where God's presence is no longer a tenable supposition and where His absence is no longer a felt, indeed overwhelming weight, certain dimensions of thought and creativity are no longer attainable."[4] Poetics, as perceived from Plato to George Steiner, cannot be conceived of without theology — more even than that: "Any coherent account of the capacity of human speech to communicate meaning and feeling is, in the final analysis, underwritten by the assumption of God's presence."[5] Edwin Muir asserts (too late):

> There are certain beliefs which are natural to man, for they satisfy his heart and mind better than any alternative ones. The mark of such beliefs is their completeness; they close the circle. In a state of irremediable imperfection such as man's, the circle can be closed only by calling to something beyond man; by postulating a transcendent reality. So the belief in eternity is natural to man; and all the arts, all the forms of imaginative literature, since they depend on that belief, are equally natural to him . . . If that belief were to fail completely and for good, there would be no imaginative art with a significance beyond its own time.[6]

Yet it seems that belief has failed, completely and for good. The circle whose center is transcendence is broken, and in Steiner's "long Saturday" century that stretches ahead of us, the lone wan hope for literature is to act *as if*; that is, for the writer to mum the existence of what he cannot believe so as to create fictions for an audience who, although likewise incapable, will repeat from habit the motions of theocentric exegesis until their significance has been forgotten — a point at which a new age of sterile positivism is achieved and stories end.

This story, fortunately, is not true.

Those who, like Nietzsche's madman and Edward Muir and George Steiner, promulgate the myth of a disastrous Death of God, bring to mind the sage in Kafka's *On Parables*, who, when he

> says: "Go across," . . . does not mean that you ought to cross the street to the other side, something that you could manage if the result were worth the trip. But what he means is some fabulous Beyond, something we have never known, which he cannot describe more accurately and therefore can be of no help to us in this case. (*KSS*, 161)[7]

They insist we cling to the untenable, that we continue along a broken and impassable path. In Kafka's keen and witty observation, however, all their "parables merely attempt to say that the inconceivable is inconceivable, and we knew that already. But the matters we truly struggle with every day are different" (*KSS*, 161).[8] Some new way is called for, and it is by way of the "strange loop" narrative structure that Kafka creates an art that at once helps and transcends our quotidian cares.

Signifying an ancient concept, the term "strange loop" was coined by Douglas Hofstader to describe

> an abstract loop in which, in the series of stages that constitute cycling around, there is a shift from one level of abstraction (or structure) to another, which feels like an upwards movement in a hierarchy, and yet somehow the successive "upward" shifts turn out to give rise to a closed cycle. That is, despite one's sense of departing ever further from one's origin, one winds up, to one's shock, exactly where one had started out.[9]

What is key in determining whether a looped structure is "strange" or not is the appearance and sudden disappearance of progression and hierarchy — it is not sufficient that the structure simply loop back on itself. A simple loop, moreover, comprises an inner and an outer, whereas in a strange loop, inner and outer vanish — becoming only a subjective interpretation dependent on one's position along the structure.

One of the easiest strange loops to visualize is the Möbius Strip, described in the 1860s by German mathematician Augustus Möbius.[10] To create a Möbius Strip, one must "cut a long rectangular strip of paper, give the paper a half twist, and paste the ends together."[11]

Imagining ourselves progressing along the surface of a Möbius Strip, we find ourselves returned to our beginning, having passed over every point possible. At any moment we may look across the way and see another traveler above or below us (as our subjective prejudice dictates). We pursue our path upward or downward — when we reach the other's high place, he has moved across the way and below us, and when we reach that depth, he appears above us. A center from which we may gauge our progress and

Fig. 6.1. Photograph of a paper Möbius strip, by David Benbennick, March 14, 2005. From the Wikimedia Commons, http://en.wikipedia.org/wiki/File:M%C3%B6bius_strip.jpg.

a ground on which we may stake our journey's start vanish, obviated by the half-twist in the surface we travel. This half-twist creates the "strangeness" of the loop. The structure passes through dimensions in which it does not partake and thereby instantiates progress and regress simultaneously, "motion without Erhebung," to invert T. S. Eliot's formulation.

This is, of course, only the simplest of examples. Many far more complicated, strange loops lurk in the world. The iconic artwork of M. C. Escher is replete with figures proceeding along stairways that loop around on themselves, so that one figure is simultaneously upside down and right side up, moving at once (as Nietzsche's madman described it) "backwards, sidewards, forwards, in all directions" in a progression whose directionality defies the absolute.

The abstractions of mathematics perhaps lay bare strange loops best. Hofstader describes a strange loop that arises in the theory of sets when one considers sets that have themselves as members (the odd consequence of this formulation is called Russell's paradox).[12] Our intuition tells us that sets are collections of things. We may, if we wish, describe sets as being either "non-self-containing" or "self-containing." The set of all integers, for example, does not contain itself, since it is a collection only of integers, not of sets. However, if we imagine a set (call it *SoS*) of all sets which do not contain themselves, we are confronted by a quandary — which kind of set is *SoS*? If it does not contain itself, then perforce it must be a member of itself, which thereby excludes it from itself. At any point in a chain of circular reasoning, we have good reason to believe either that it is a "non-self-containing" or a "self-containing" set, yet with the slightest reconsideration, the least half-twist of sense, certainty in the firmness of our logic slips away.

Another strange loop that Hofstader describes is called "Grelling's paradox." It arises from everyday language.[13] Suppose we define adjectives as "heterological" (non-self-descriptive) or "autological" (self-descriptive). Most adjectives are heterological — the words "windy" or "insouciant" or "monosyllabic" do not evidence the qualities they describe. Some few adjectives (Hofstader offers "pentasyllabic" — "short" or "English" also fit the bill) describe themselves. The logical question to ask is whether or not the word "heterological" is an autological or heterological word. Once again, if it is self-descriptive, then it cannot by our definition be self-descriptive. Yet, if it is not-self-descriptive, then inexorably it must describe itself.

Strange loops are not, however, merely oddities of mathematical paradox, nor are they limited to the peculiarities of language. Narratives can instantiate strange loops as well. For a straightforward example (as straightforward as an infinite tangle of a strange loop can be), consider the second half of Kafka's short parable "On Parables":

> In response, someone said, "Why do you resist? If you'd follow the parables, you'd become parables yourselves and with that, free of the everyday struggle."
>
> Someone else said, "I bet that is a parable too."
>
> The first one said, "You win."
>
> The second one said, "But unfortunately only in a parable."
>
> "The first one said, "No, in reality; in the parable you lost." (*KSS*, 162)[14]

The strange loop underlying this parable hinges on the interplay between "parable" and "reality." When the first tells the second that he can rid himself of his daily cares, he is making a statement about reality — the second exists only parabolically (as a character in a narrative) and following the parable is the only real option that he has. When the second acknowledges this, he does indeed win, because he is acknowledging the reality of his existence, as the first observes. When the second says that he has won "unfortunately only in parable," he is making a statement about reality — he exists only as a parable and cannot win as anything else — yet that realistic statement is also, from another viewpoint, a parable. The reality, of course, is that the parable "On Parables" (by the very real Franz Kafka) is being read by a real reader and that, in reading, we are drawn into the strange loop, the parable contributing in its way to our reality, rendering us — at least in one sense — parabolic. Categories collapse. Whether the two speakers (or, indeed, we ourselves) are real or parabolic hinges not on a firm and objective external reality but on how, in a moment, we choose to interpret the parable — Muir and Steiner's need for a transcendent grounding absolute has been obviated by Kafka's strange loop parable.

This type of narrative construction, emblematized in such a short fragment, pervades Kafka's longest work, *The Castle*, allowing him to construct a groundless, godless art that survives the vanishing of the Transcendent Center. Moreover, this intertwining and interchanging of categories and modes is not limited to a single parable or novel; but as Stanley Corngold points out, this "double helix" likewise pervades Kafka's life and practice as a writer.[15] Corngold observes that "Kafka's affirmation of being involves a restless movement of recursive logic . . . . The recursive turn obliquely empowers the dying self."[16] One might add, it does so by subverting the untenable imperative of a divine Other to empower that dying self.

Men of the Middle Ages, Père Chenu writes, shared "the conviction that all natural or historical reality possessed a *signification* which transcended its crude reality and which a certain symbolic dimension of that reality would reveal to man's mind."[17] Matter, for medieval man, counted meaning among its necessary dimensions. Just as we might say mass-energy or position in space-time are required for a piece of matter to exist, medieval man would say that significance, too, was needed. This view created a world in which

> connatural with matter, a man's intelligence had to work through matter to attain a grasp of transcendent realities, unknowable in themselves. This *anagoge*, this upwards reference of things, was constituted precisely by their natural dynamism as symbols . . . .
> For this very reason, *anagoge* was fundamental to any true understanding of things . . . . One knew things as part of a sacred knowledge.[18]

Anagogical exegesis created anagogical art. But the medieval mode of knowing and being, so powerful and prevalent in European consciousness from late antiquity, had, by Franz Kafka's century and by our own, become untenable — untenable, but still wishfully grasped at by many. It is therefore no surprise that in *The Castle*, a novel whose central conceit is the quest for a center, Kafka constructs a setting that, with the exceptional and incomprehensible (to K.) intrusion of telephones and electric lighting, is medieval (as Elizabeth Boa notes in detail).[19] However, K. is not meant to be "the modern hero . . . in the premodern world."[20] The opposite is the case. K., with his willful insistence on a castle at the center of things, an entity that can be bargained with, that doles out meaning, and grounds the village, is a woefully premodern figure. When confronted with modernity, in the form of the telephone, he is baffled:

> From the earpiece came a humming, the likes of which K. had never heard on the telephone before. It was as though the humming of countless childlike voices — but it wasn't humming either, it was singing, the singing of the most distant, of the most utterly distant, voices — as though a single, high-pitched yet strong voice had emerged out of this humming in some quite impossible way and now drummed against one's ears as if demanding to penetrate more deeply into something other than one's wretched hearing. K. listened without telephoning; with his left arm propped on the telephone stand he just listened. (*C*, 20)[21]

Attempting to establish meaningful contact with the castle through modern means proves impossible. When K. does get through, the conversation is filled with contradictions and deceptions and ends with a firm and seemingly eternal rejection. Not only the modern fails to reach the center: the dubious messenger Barnabas appears the moment K. hangs up the phone, as if to insist on the point that premodern devices like letters and messengers, too, are ineffectual to reach a central grounding core of being.

K.'s failure to find the center does not result, however, from an intrinsic guilt or unworthiness — unlike in the case of Josef K., the dynamics of punishment does not dominate his situation. The mysterious Bureau no. X is not a tribunal. Nor is his failure the consequence of some quality of the castle, some innate ineffability that places it forever beyond reach as a truth around which man must bleakly circle forever. Kafka does not manifest the castle as a transcendent thing. As K. looks up from the village at the castle, this is what he sees: "Here the snow rose to the cottage windows only to weigh down on the low roofs, whereas on the hill everything soared up, free and light, or at least *seemed to from here*"[22] (*C*, 7, emphasis mine) — the gesture toward transcendence is immediately undercut by the narratorial interjection that insists on the ephemeral seemingness of the scene.

> On the whole the Castle, as it appeared from this distance, corresponded to K.'s expectations. It was neither an old knight's fortress nor a magnificent new edifice, but a large complex, made up of a few two-story buildings and many lower, tightly packed ones; had one not known that this was a castle, one could have taken it for a small town. (*C*, 8)[23]

From K.'s vantage point the castle appears no different from a small town — no different perhaps from the small town in which he stands, looking up at the castle. The destination has become a point of embarkation.

The text continues to collapse categories — merging the secular and spiritual, as "K. saw only one tower, whether it belonged to a dwelling or a church was impossible to tell" (*C*, 8).[24] At this moment, through a metonymic twist, Kafka reminds us of his presence through the swarms of crows that circle the tower of indeterminate purpose.

> Keeping his eyes fixed upon the Castle, K. went ahead, nothing else mattered to him. But as he came closer, he was disappointed in the Castle, it was only a rather miserable little town, pieced together from village houses, distinctive only because everything was built of stone, but the paint had long since flaked off, and the stone seemed to be crumbling. (*C*, 8)[25]

The mundanity of the castle-as-town repeats itself in the text, reiterating the point that the castle does not serve as a transcendental signifier but rather is indistinguishable from the immanent world. The text next turns, with K.'s thoughts, away from the castle and away from the town, toward a distant past.

> Fleetingly K. recalled his old hometown, it was scarcely inferior to this so-called Castle; if K. had merely wanted to visit it, all that wandering would have been in vain, and it would have made more sense for him to visit his old homeland again, where he had not been in such a long time. (*C*, 8)[26]

We do not rest in the *Heimat* of the distant past, however, but immediately move into the realm of thought, where past and present objects coexist for K.'s comparison and the categories of religious-past (bathed in the nostalgic glow of Père Chenu's "upward reference of things") and secular-present collide.

> And in thought he compared the church tower in his homeland with the tower up there. The church tower, tapering decisively, without hesitation, straightaway toward the top, capped by a wide roof with red tiles, was an earthly building — what else can we build? — but with a higher goal than the low jumble of houses and with a clearer expression than that of the dull workday. (*C*, 8)[27]

In the midst of this meditation exalting the sacred risen from the mundane, a strange interjection breaks through. "What else can we build?" The question — if it is meant to be a question and not an interrogative platitude — lacks both an identifiable speaker and a target. The universal tone of the observation leaps from the specific conditions of K.'s memory to a general judgment on humankind, yet ironizes that observation if the speaker is read not as K. but as a disembodied narrator, wryly commenting on K.'s judgment. The inclusivity of "we" calls the reader into the text to play a part, both awakening awareness of the text as an artifact and urging the forgetting of that awareness to play the game. Again, metonymically, the author appears, as the contemplation on competing architectures makes a comment on the construction of the novel. The interjection simultaneously plays the role of K.'s opinion, universal observation, narratorial irony, friendly gesture to the reader, and authorial self-commentary, vastly expanding the circle of the text. As if to call further awareness to this, the present-day tower thrusts *into* the narrative as a type *for* the narrative:

> The tower up here — it was the only one in sight — the tower of a residence, as now became evident, possibly of the main Castle, was a monotonous round building, in part mercifully hidden by ivy, with little windows that glinted in the sun — there was something crazy about this — and ending in a kind of terrace, whose battlements, uncertain, irregular, brittle, as if drawn by the anxious or careless hand of a child, zigzagged into the blue sky. It was as if some melancholy resident, who by rights ought to have kept himself locked up in the most out-of-the-way room in the house, had broken through the roof and stood up in order to show himself to the world. (*C*, 8)[28]

Following this passage from K.'s initial contemplation of the castle to the melancholy resident breaking through the text to show himself brings us, after many half-twists through dimensions in which the passage does not partake, to a representation of the writer in his work — a metaphorical miniature portrait that appears suddenly, pulling us back out of the work despite our apparent forward progress through it.

Strange loops transform hierarchy into heterarchy. Hierarchy requires a firm place to stand or to kneel — demands elevation that cannot be eliminated merely by turning around and facing the other way. In the tangled world of a strange-looped system, no title (neither Count nor Land-Surveyor) can be valid, because those who validate titles depend on the validity of titles for their own validation. K. does not see this, but then *The Castle* was not written for K., and the teacher (despite appearances) does not appear in the novel to teach to *him*. The stern young man instead proceeds by questioning and confrontation:

> "You're taking a look at the Castle?" he asked, more gently than K. had expected, but as though he did not approve of what K. was doing. "Yes," said K. "I'm a stranger here, I only arrived in the village yesterday." "You don't like the Castle?" the teacher said quickly. "What?" countered K., somewhat baffled, but then, rephrasing the question more delicately, he said: "Do I like the Castle? What makes you think I don't like it?" "Strangers never do," said the teacher. (*C*, 9)[29]

This encounter seems, on the face of it, odd — as though it is following oneiric logic, with its ominously significant insignificance. Suppose, however, it were read as follows:

> "You're taking a look at *The Castle*?" he asked, more gently than K. had expected, but as though he did not approve of what K. was

> doing. "Yes," said K. "I'm a stranger here, I only arrived in the village yesterday." "You don't like *The Castle*?" the teacher said quickly. "What?" countered K., somewhat baffled, but then, rephrasing the question more delicately, he said: "Do I like *The Castle*? What makes you think I don't like it?" "Strangers never do," said the teacher.

Replacing the object "the castle" with the title "*The Castle*" reveals the strange loop lurking beneath the surface of this interchange. A few pages into his novel, K. is being asked to comment on the putative grounds of his own existence. K. misses the insinuation (to be fair, he cannot do otherwise) and presses on in his quest for hierarchy: "'Teacher, could I call on you? I'll be staying for some time and already feel a little isolated, I don't belong among the peasants nor in all likelihood at the Castle.' 'There is no difference between the peasants and the Castle'" (*C*, 9).[30] The teacher's cryptic assertion makes sudden sense when read as: "There is no difference between the peasants and *The Castle*." Of course there isn't! They are one and the same, creating and containing one another.

Nor is K.'s encounter with the teacher the only place in the novel that invites a substitutive reading, which in turn creates a strange loop. Consider, for example, the incident in which Amalia interrupts Olga's story about the fall of their family, consequence of her refusal of a castle official's erotic attentions. In the moments before the interruption, K. attempts to lay the blame for the family's misfortunes squarely on Amalia's shoulders, which Olga denies: "'It seems significant to me that you haven't mentioned Amalia; Amalia, the one to blame for all this, probably stood quietly in the background, observing the havoc.' 'No, no,' said Olga, 'nobody should be blamed for this, nobody could behave any differently, it was all due to the influence of the Castle'" (*C*, 204–5).[31]

It is at this point that Amalia, object of K.'s blame, appears and interjects. Her echo of her sister's final words signals the start of another strange loop.

> "The influence of the Castle," repeated Amalia, who had entered unobserved from the courtyard, their parents had long since gone to bed, "telling Castle stories? Still sitting here together? But you wanted to leave right away, K., and now it's almost ten. Do you even care about such stories? There are people here who feed on such stories, they sit together as you sit here, regaling one another, but you do not strike me as one of them." "Yes I am," said K., "I am indeed one of them, whereas I am not greatly taken by those who do not concern themselves with such stories and simply make others concern themselves with them." (*C*, 205)[32]

What is evoked by Amalia's interruption is not merely the writer-reader relationship as a general phenomenon (in metafictional commentary), but the specific instantiation of that relationship between the reader of *The*

Castle (the castle story) and Kafka. Yet there are no clear indicators of how we are to take Amalia's commentary. K.'s reply can be read, given his previous condemnation of Amalia, as a rebuke to her and to those who do not "concern themselves with stories" — who do not take the time to read *The Castle*, perhaps — yet K.'s judgment has already been established as perhaps the least trustworthy in the entire novel. Therefore, his sudden identification with the reader, who feeds on *The Castle* stories, is no great compliment to the reader. Amalia's amused dismissal of the motivations of those who pore over castle stories — in the form of an anecdote about a young man who seemed fascinated by the castle, until it became clear that he was only erotically fascinated with one of the castle's scullery maids — likewise invites readers to interpret their own motivations in reading *The Castle*, and not favorably.

That said, there is something crude in Amalia's dismissal of the motivation at the heart of castle exegesis and something to K.'s blame of her for remaining aloof. Her refusal to engage with the castle (recall that the castle's original orders came to her in the form of a note, a written text from Sordini) cannot be a refusal to engage with *The Castle* — she is part of a castle story whether she wills it or no, and her status as a conscientious objector is a dubious one, K. is correct to point out. Similarly, readers of the novel may object, as K. does, that their efforts to interpret it are surely motivated by more than a simple, base eroticism.

At the heart of this exchange (the strange loop that allows Amalia to comment on her own novel without seeming to) is an ambiguity that Olga identifies, once everything goes dark and Amalia disappears. "It isn't easy to understand exactly what she is saying, for one doesn't know whether she is speaking ironically or seriously, it's mostly serious but sounds ironic" (*C*, 205).[33] The echoes with the parable called "On Parables" are obvious. Kafka goes beyond the doubling of consciousness made possible by irony and creates a new category — that which is serious but sounds ironic. What are we to make of this new category? Mathematically speaking, if serious speech has one dimension and irony has two, this new category may be said to exist in the half-twist between them — that is, to exist as a strange loop that passes through the second dimension while, at any given point, remaining unidimensional.

This half-twist drives K. to distraction, and he resorts to crying out "Stop interpreting everything!" (*C*, 205),[34] a cry that is particularly funny coming from such a relentless exegete! After a long evening spent probing every subtlety of Olga's castle story, with a sudden inversion, K. arrives at Amalia's position, refusing to interpret. That he seems entirely unaware of this and proceeds as though nothing has changed is, of course, what we would expect from his character. He can do no differently in *The Castle* story.

These substitutive readings are made possible only by acknowledging our position as readers reading a book titled *The Castle*. The teacher's initial question, therefore, sails right past K. and invites us, in the role of readers, to make a judgment on the scene. Amalia's commentary on those who feed on castle stories does likewise. All at once we are drawn into the loop, the perspective shifts onto us, and we are made to function as characters in the novel, responding to another character. Recognizing the strange loops returns us to the position of a reader, modulated upward (or downward, if you prefer) toward greater sophistication. Our roles as reader, novel character, sophisticated reader are, of course, created by Kafka's writing — although that writing itself is contingent on the agency of a reader for its existence. At any given moment, any given reading points us in a concrete direction toward *The Castle*, just as K. faces the castle from every point on his journey — yet any progress through the narrative has the potential to invert our perspective without warning. The strange loops preclude any final verdict. *The Castle* ends mid-sentence, awaiting the speech of a mysterious alcoved figure, who, like us, is reading a book.

The act of reading a narrative as rich in strange loops as *The Castle* creates, via a substrate of neurological isomorphism, the real presence of a parable in our brains. We become, in a real way, parabolic as we partake in the action of belief. We take the advice of the sage and "go across." The parable that we create by reading then creates us as readers. However, the application of the parable (the act of reading) is a real act that occurs within reality. Therefore the fiction finds an instantiation in actuality. As we realize that, we cannot help but use a figure of rhetoric to express it to ourselves, becoming writers of our own reading. This realization itself is contained within a parable written by a man named Franz Kafka, who was real. Yet the Kafka we conjecture is a matter of literature, not reality. This literary Kafka created real parables, wrote real words that we read and are created in the reading of . . . and so on it goes; and in the going, we are rid of our quotidian cares. What we win, in the Kafkan cosmos, is a way of being that encompasses both parable and reality. We win a unity of art and life, each creating the other without the need for a Prime Mover, a Central Idea that no longer exists. In Kafka's work we confront infinite riches in a little room, an unending adventure in which we may learn new things as long as we last.

Notes

[1] "Viele beklagen sich, daß die Worte der Weisen immer wieder nur Gleichnisse seien, aber unverwendbar im täglichen Leben und nur dieses allein haben wir" (*NS2*, 531).

[2] Friedrich Nietzsche, *The Gay Science*, trans. Josephine Nauckhoff (Cambridge: Cambridge UP), 119.

[3] Nietzsche, *Gay Science*, 120.

[4] George Steiner, *Real Presences* (Chicago: U of Chicago P, 1991), 229.

[5] Steiner, *Real Presences,* 3.

[6] Edwin Muir, *Essays on Literature and Society* (London: Hogarth, 1949), 150.

[7] "[Wenn der Weise] sagt: 'Gehe hinüber' so meint er nicht, daß man auf die andere Straßenseite hinübergehn solle, was man immerhin noch leisten könnte, wenn das Ergebnis des Weges wert wäre, sondern er meint irgendein sagenhaftes Drüben, etwas was wir nicht kennen, was auch von ihm nicht näher zu bezeichnen ist und was uns also hier gar nichts helfen kann" (*NS2*, 352).

[8] "Gleichnisse wollen eigentlich nur sagen, daß das Unfaßbare unfaßbar ist und das haben wir gewußt. Aber das womit wir uns eigentlich jeden Tag abmühn, sind andere Dinge" (*NS2*, 352).

[9] Douglas Hofstadter, *I Am A Strange Loop* (New York: Basic Books, 2007), 101–2.

[10] Jan Gullberg, *Mathematics: From the Birth of Numbers* (New York: W. W. Norton, 1997), 380.

[11] Gullberg, *Mathematics,* 380.

[12] Douglas Hofstader, *Gödel, Escher, Bach: An Eternal Golden Braid* (New York: Basic Books, 1999), 20.

[13] Hofstader, *Gödel, Escher, Bach,* 20–21.

[14] "Darauf sagte einer: Warum wehrt Ihr Euch? Würdet Ihr den Gleichnissen folgen, dann wäret Ihr selbst Gleichnisse geworden und damit schon der täglichen Mühe frei.

Ein anderer sagte: Ich wett daß auch das ein Gleichnis ist.

Der erste sagte: Du hast gewonnen.

Der zweite sagte: Aber leider nur im Gleichnis.

Der erste sagte: Nein, in Wirklichkeit; im Gleichnis hast Du verloren" (*NS2*, 532).

[15] Stanley Corngold, *Franz Kafka: The Necessity of Form* (Ithaca, NY: Cornell UP, 1988), in particular, the chapter "Kafka's Double Helix," 105–36.

[16] Corngold, *Franz Kafka: The Necessity of Form,* 134–35.

[17] Marie-Dominique Chenu, *Nature, Man, and Society in the Twelfth Century,* ed. and trans. Jerome Taylor and Lester K. Little (Toronto: U of Toronto P, 1997), 102.

[18] Chenu, *Nature, Man, and Society,* 123–24.

[19] Elizabeth Boa, "The Castle," in *The Cambridge Companion to Kafka,* ed. Julian Preece (Cambridge: Cambridge UP, 2002), 61–79.

[20] Boa, "The Castle," 61.

[21] "Aus der Hörmuschel kam ein Summen, wie K. es sonst beim Telephonieren nie gehört hatte. Es war wie wenn sich aus dem Summen zahlloser kindlicher Stimmen — aber auch dieses Summen war keines, sondern war Gesang fernster, allerfernster Stimmen — wie wenn sich aus diesem Summen in einer geradezu unmöglichen Weise eine einzige hohe aber starke Stimme bilde, die an das Ohr schlug so wie wenn sie fordere tiefer einzudringen als nur in das armselige Gehör. K. horchte

ohne zu telephonieren, den linken Arm hatte er auf das Telephonpult gestützt und horchte so" (*S*, 30).

[22] "Hier reichte der Schnee bis zu den Fenstern der Hütten und lastete gleich wieder auf dem niedrigen Dach, aber oben auf dem Berg ragte alles frei und leicht empor, wenigstens schien es so von hier aus" (*S*, 16).

[23] "Im Ganzen entsprach das Schloß, wie es sich hier von der Ferne zeigte, K.'s Erwartungen. Es war weder eine alte Ritterburg, noch ein neuer Prunkbau, sondern eine ausgedehnte Anlage, die aus wenigen zweistöckigen, aber aus vielen eng aneinanderstehenden niedrigern Bauten bestand; hätte man nicht gewußt daß es ein Schloß ist, hätte man es für ein Städtchen halten können" (*S*, 16).

[24] "Nur einen Turm sah K., ob er zu einem Wohngebäude oder einer Kirche gehörte war nicht zu erkennen" (*S*, 16).

[25] "Die Augen auf das Schloß gerichtet, gieng K. weiter, nichts sonst kümmerte ihn. Aber im Näherkommen enttäuschte ihn das Schloß, es war doch nur ein recht elendes Städtchen, aus Dorfhäusern zusammengetragen, ausgezeichnet nur dadurch, daß vielleicht alles aus Stein gebaut war, aber der Anstrich war längst abgefallen, und der Stein schien abzubröckeln" (*S*, 17).

[26] "Flüchtig erinnerte sich K. an sein Heimatstädtchen, es stand diesem angeblichen Schlosse kaum nach, wäre es K. nur auf die Besichtigung angekommen, dann wäre es schade um die lange Wanderschaft gewesen und er hätte vernünftiger gehandelt, wieder einmal die alte Heimat zu besuchen, wo er schon so lange nicht gewesen war" (*S*, 17).

[27] "Und er verglich in Gedanken den Kirchturm der Heimat mit dem Turm dort oben. Jener Turm, bestimmt, ohne Zögern, geradenwegs nach oben sich verjüngend, breitdachig abschließend mit roten Ziegeln, ein irdisches Gebäude — was können wir anderes bauen? — aber mit höherem Ziel als das niedrige Häusergemenge und mit klarerem Ausdruck als ihn der trübe Werktag hat" (*S*, 17).

[28] "Der Turm hier oben — es war der einzige sichtbare —, der Turm eines Wohnhauses, wie sich jetzt zeigte, vielleicht des Hauptschlosses, war ein einförmiger Rundbau, zum Teil gnädig von Epheu verdeckt, mit kleinen Fenstern, die jetzt in der Sonne aufstrahlten — etwas Irrsinniges hatte das — und einem söllerartigen Abschluß, dessen Mauerzinnen unsicher, unregelmäßig, brüchig wie von ängstlicher oder nachlässiger Kinderhand gezeichnet sich in den blauen Himmel sackten. Es war wie wenn irgendein trübseliger Hausbewohner, der gerechter Weise im entlegensten Zimmer des Hauses sich hätte eingesperrt halten sollen, das Dach durchbrochen und sich erhoben hätte, um sich der Welt zu zeigen" (*S*, 17).

[29] "'Ihr sehet das Schloß an?' fragte er, sanftmütiger als K. erwartet hatte aber in einem Tone als billige er nicht das was K. tue. 'Ja,' sagte K., 'ich bin hier fremd, erst seit gestern abend im Ort.' 'Das Schloß gefällt Euch nicht?' fragte der Lehrer schnell. 'Wie?' fragte K. zurück, ein wenig verblüfft und wiederholte in milderer Form die Frage: 'Ob mir das Schloß gefällt? Warum nehmet Ihr an, daß es mir nicht gefällt?' 'Keinem Fremden gefällt es,' sagte der Lehrer" (*S*, 18).

[30] "Könnte ich Sie Herr Lehrer einmal besuchen? Ich bleibe hier längere Zeit und fühle mich schon jetzt ein wenig verlassen, zu den Bauern gehöre ich nicht und ins Schloß wohl auch nicht. Zwischen den Bauern und dem Schloß ist kein Unterschied" (*S*, 18–19).

[31] "Besonders bezeichnend scheint mir aber, daß Du Amalia gar nicht erwähnst; Amalia, die doch alles verschuldet hatte, stand wahrscheinlich ruhig im Hintergrund und betrachtete die Verwüstung. Nein, nein, sagte Olga, niemandem ist ein Vorwurf zu machen, niemand konnte anders handeln, das alles war schon Einfluß des Schlosses" (*S*, 250).

[32] "Einfluß des Schlosses, wiederholte Amalia, die unvermerkt vom Hofe her eingetreten war, die Eltern lagen längst zu Bett, Schloßgeschichten werden erzählt? Noch immer sitzt Ihr beisammen? Und Du hattest doch gleich Dich verabschieden wollen, K., und nun geht es schon auf zehn. Bekümmern Dich denn solche Geschichten überhaupt? Es gibt hier Leute, die sich von solchen Geschichten nähren, sie setzen sich zusammen, so wie Ihr hier sitzt, und traktieren sich gegenseitig, Du scheinst mir aber nicht zu disen Leuten zu gehören. Doch, sagte K., ich gehöre genau zu ihnen, dagegen machen Leute, die sich um solche Geschichten nicht bekümmern und nur andere sich bekümmern lassen, nicht viel Eindruck auf mich" (*S*, 250).

[33] "Es ist nicht leicht sie genau zu verstehn, weil man oft nicht weiß, ob sie ironisch oder ernst spricht, meistens ist es ja ernst, aber es klingt ironisch" (*S*, 251).

[34] "Laß die Deutungen!" (*S*, 251).

7: Proxies in Kafka: *Koncipist* FK and *Prokurist* Josef K.

Doreen Densky

"I WAS NOT AT ALL CERTAIN whether I had any advocates, I could not find out anything definite about it," says a nameless narrator in the opening of a posthumously published text by Franz Kafka (*CS*, 449).[1] Neither is there any certainty about the appropriate place to search: the labyrinth of corridors and staircases around the narrator suggests places for quiet contemplation, not a law court where advocates are typically found. Asking himself why he continues to look in this unlikely place, the narrator answers: "Because I was searching for an advocate everywhere; he is needed everywhere, if anything less in court than elsewhere" (*CS*, 450).[2]

The narrator's quest for advocates or *Fürsprecher* — literally speakers for someone or something — lays bare both the importance and elusiveness of proxies in Kafka's work. Proxies claim to be authorized to act or speak for someone as agent, deputy, or substitute; in Kafka, they figure prominently but can be as easily overlooked and as difficult to grasp as the narrator implies. For two closely related reasons, the advocate-seeker's disorientation invites the tracing of the proxy figure in Kafka's professional and fictional writing. First, the narratological premise — the inherent need of narrating and narrator to have representatives — leads to questions of perspective and vocal agency. Second, the narrator's institutional situation — the ambiguity as to where advocates are required — raises broad questions around the detachment between person and function, as well as the distinction and mediation between the individual and the legal-administrative world. Does he always need to be represented by another, or can he speak for himself? How is modern narrative authority distributed within the institutional framework?

These issues permeate much of Kafka's writing in the context of what recent critical studies of his work have convincingly termed stories and poetics of the institution.[3] Central among these studies is Rüdiger Campe's identification of *The Trial* (*Der Process*, 1925) and *The Castle* (*Das Schloss*, 1926) as novels of the institution.[4] Campe also analyzes the text around the advocate-seeker, stating that in order to speak of "life," there needs to be an institutional basis or at least the search for it; and it is this construct that makes life as such a possible subject of narration.[5] Building on this fundamental observation, with a specific focus on the narrative voice that is speaking for another, one can claim that the proxy figure in Kafka's institutional fiction serves as a paradigmatic narrator or storyteller. He occupies a position in which he needs, searches for, or invents figures through which he can speak; or, if he is in the text, he himself can be seen as a first proxy of the narrative function. Moreover, the concept of proxies in Kafka's literary writing has an affinity with the administrative writing process. During his work hours, Kafka wrote legal-administrative texts for the Workmen's Accident Insurance Institute for the Kingdom of Bohemia *by proxy* or as proxy himself in his function as *Koncipist* (law clerk or legal secretary). In his fictional texts, he assigns the role of proxy to a number of characters. Notably Josef K., *The Trial* protagonist, has his proxy status already inscribed in his occupational title. As a bank *Prokurist*, his vocation stems from the Latin *procurare*, which denotes "to take care of, to manage or administer for someone" and which is etymologically related to the English term "proxy."

The following juxtaposition of *Koncipist* Kafka and *Prokurist* Josef K. is a further indication of Kafkaesque echoes in the author's *Office Writings* (*Amtliche Schriften*, 1984) and, conversely, of the resonance of his experience at the Prague bureau in the themes and topics of his literary prose. In the words of the editors of the recently translated selected *Office Writings*, both forms of writings can be considered as "a single institution, in which the factor of bureaucracy is ever present" (*OW*, xv).[6] However, the juxtaposition shifts the focus away from the often-studied topical parallels or tensions between Kafka's professional and literary life, toward the very situation of acting and writing in one's own name and in someone else's name, as their proxy. The analysis of Kafka's first brief in jurisprudence and passages from *The Trial* uncovers common procedures of delegated speech that might affect larger questions of the relation between author and narrative voice.

To correlate the bureaucratic text production and the literary work, the proxy, as he is understood here, needs to be related to other figures in Kafka's work. He is among the manifold representatives through whom Kafka's institutions — real and fictional — function and perpetuate themselves. As such, he can be compared to the intermediary figures that densely populate Kafka's oeuvre: the messengers, helpers, officials, and intercessors who often stand between the protagonist or narrator and an antagonistic force — paternal, bureaucratic, or juridical. Although the proxy shares the intermediary's conceptual position as an *in-between* figure, he cannot be reduced to the status of an intermediary. He represents one party before another and might be specified as a *stand-in*. A major distinguishing feature of the fictional proxies discussed here is their centrality in the story: they are the chief protagonists or narrators, not merely supporting actors. In their leading roles and as the carriers of the perspective, they are proxies in and of the text.

This fusion of protagonist or narrator with the textual structure becomes apparent in the prose piece I cited at the beginning of this chapter, the piece that Max Brod entitled "Advocates" ("Fürsprecher"). Following the narrator's meditation on the need for advocates and his failed search for them along the hallways of an unspecified building, there is a gradual shift toward a highly reflective, dialogic mode. From this new angle, the "I" positions himself as an external observer. Toward the end of the text another subtle twist occurs: the dialogue turns into a speech that reveals how the advocate-seeker becomes his own representative or proxy, speaking at the same time *to* himself and *for* himself. In an imperative tone, he advises himself to continue the search along the floors and on the stairs, despite the uncertain outcome of this endeavor: "As long as you don't stop climbing, the stairs won't end, under your climbing feet they will go on growing upwards" (*CS*, 451).[7] The pronominal shift from the first person "I" to the second person "you" stresses the fluctuation and volatility of narrative agency; it marks the transposition and delegation of responsibilities on a fundamental level. Kafka lets his protagonist climb out of himself and, synchronically, climb up the stairs, almost out of the story. He opens up space to explore the simultaneous possibilities and confinements of narrative perspective that constitute parts of his fictional narrating and that bear a resemblance to his administrative reporting.

Koncipist FK

The office of the Workmen's Accident Insurance Institute in Prague was the real institutional setting in which the young insurance lawyer Kafka acted as proxy. There he gained insight into institutions as sociological-anthropological entities and mechanisms of social order.[8] Only a few decades before he entered the work force, social insurance had emerged as the new principle that would organize, regulate, and administer risk.[9] A new system of circulation came into being that was based not on stories told ("Erzählungen") but rather on calculability and data collection ("Zählungen").[10] Such processes of averaging and statistical analysis had an impact on fictional narratives. Theodor Adorno writes that storytelling in the modern novel, as an art of "having something *special* to say," is outmoded because "that is precisely what is prevented by the administered world, by standardization and eternal sameness."[11]

During the fifteen years he spent writing on behalf of the institute and his superiors, Kafka composed reports, protocols, correspondence, speeches, and newspaper articles. He officially gained his title as *Koncipist* only in April 1910, after a period as assistant secretary (Aushilfsbeamter) and as a trainee (Anstaltspraktikant). However, the range of his responsibilities, such as the processing and composing of preliminary drafts (Konzepte), encompassed those of a full *Koncipist* as soon as he began his work in the summer of 1908.[12] Kafka's formidable background as a talented writer and Doctor of Laws was the reason that the director of the institute, Robert Marschner, assigned an intricate task to him after only a few months of his employment: Kafka was to draft a part of the 1907 annual report to the Ministry of the Interior in Vienna. "The Scope of Compulsory Insurance for the Building Trades" is the title and program of this first official article. Topically, it reports on recent developments in accident insurance by tracing the continuous changes to the Accident Insurance Law of 1887. Structurally, it serves as a well-suited source for examining the style of administrative proxy writing, because it fashions a net of voices while carefully weaving in the voice of the institute. Voice, in the sense of "who speaks," and here also "who is quoted," calls to mind the narratological function of the proxy. On different levels, the complex text displays the mechanisms of authorized representation, speaking, and writing.

The report's central concern is partially based on ambiguous formulations: the original regulation had left open the question as to where exactly workers were insured — only at construction sites outdoors or also in workshops indoors? At times, one and the same worker was exposed to different spatial risk groups and thus obliged to work in insured and uninsured spheres successively. Particularly interesting is *how* Kafka, as an eloquent placeholder for both his superior and the institute, tries to tackle the factually convoluted task on legally complex grounds. In well-crafted rhetoric he reconstructs the voices of all parties involved in the issue, thus immediately acknowledging that the issue could meet with divergent views.[13] The argumentative itinerary starts with several quotations and explanations, linked and set up by and large chronologically over eighteen printed pages: the relevant passage from the Accident Insurance Law of 1887, comments by the Ministry of the Interior, decisions of the Administrative Court, and reactions from the Workmen's Accident Insurance Institutes. As direct reproductions of original phrasings, the quotations show not only how the dispute is partly based on linguistic nuances but also how Kafka the bureaucrat aims for clear and objective statements. He arranges the official positions as responses to one another and describes how the Administrative Court seemingly resolved the ambiguity in 1906 toward full coverage, only to void these clarifications in 1908, shortly before the article was written.

As agent of the institute, Kafka explains how the resulting confusion prompts the institute to intervene, whereupon the tone of the report shifts. A questionnaire campaign is the institute's immediate response, to ensure direct communication with employers. Kafka quotes the open letter that informs employers of the new restrictive law and outlines the option to insure workshop labor at each company's discretion. It is thus the direct voice of the institute — the full print of the circulated letter — that takes a middle position, both figuratively and literally. A little more than halfway through the article, Kafka states that the institute has doubts about the new practices and is therefore mobilizing its own resources (*OW*, 62–63). He asks for more independence for the Workmen's Accident Insurance Institutes from the laws of the central government. At the same time, the opinion poll brings other voices into the discourse: those of the employers who were previously unheard. The resulting tension between "a 'top-down' bureaucracy based on centralized power and a 'bottom-up' model based on the voices of individuals" is significant for much of Kafka's official and literary deliberation (Commentary, *OW*, 71). Tension of this sort also informs a scene in *The Trial* — as will be detailed below — that stages protagonist Josef K. as a placeholder for those who, he seems to imply, remain unheard by the court administration. He literally steps up, on a platform, to speak to the authorities and an audience.

Along those lines, much of the remaining space of the 1907 annual report is devoted to the insured employers and their responses. Less than one-fourth of more than four thousand questionnaires were mailed back by respondents who opted out of additional insurance. Unexpectedly, many employers expressed unsolicited and enthusiastic support for maintaining their workers' compensation (*OW*, 65). While the open letter aimed to "function as a personal negotiation with the employer about his own particular firm, free from outside influences," numerous responses revealed that "particular organizations were speaking in the employers' voice, and unfortunately at times, the voice was that of an organization without the mediation of the employers" (*OW*, 65).[14] Put differently, it turned out that the system of representation was often disruptive; direct communication between employers and the institute was difficult because third parties interfered, often by default. One absurd example is that of a master carpenter on whose behalf two different organizations wrote contradictory answers: the Association of Master Carpenters claimed that additional insurance could not be maintained because the master-carpenters' current risk category was too high, while a union of building-trade professionals asked to maintain the full insurance coverage for master carpenters, because that seemed to be the better option (*OW*, 66). Kafka lists further exemplary answers — without quotation marks — to include more semi-anonymous voices. His first brief for the institute, on a cursory glance quite sober, unfolds as a sophisticated, multilayered network of proxy relations within the office world. Kafka writes as an often-intervening proxy, untangling convoluted bureaucratic communications, which many of his literary protagonists so unsuccessfully attempt.

In conclusion, while summing up the arguments for workshop insurance, Kafka spells out what reverberates across the surface of the entire report: besides the preferences of most employers and overall utility, the law itself matters — "interpreted in its intention, its history, its text, and its context" (*OW,* 69).[15] The law is the underlying, though often latent, force of the insurance institute; "speaking in the name of the law" is the ultimate proxy situation. Kafka adds that it lies equally in the interest of the workers, the employers, and the institute and serves, as well, the legislature's intention to apply insurance comprehensively. However, he also adds the amendment: "actually only two interests apply here, those of the workers and [those] of the employers, because the institute has no other interests but theirs" (*OW,* 69).[16] A few lines further down, Kafka defends the institute against resentment from either group caused by the mistaken perception that it is the source of all deficiencies in accident insurance, whereas, in reality, it only represents a "perhaps inadequate" law — and here also an "inadequately interpreted" law (*OW,* 69). This complex passage thus outlines the institute's status as a modern organization standing between employers and employees, as natural persons whose voice is obstructed by external representation, while serving equally as a connector between the state's legal administration and private industry. The role of the *Koncipist* as the institute's speaker then adds a further abstraction: he is an agent for an agency or a representative for a representative.

The last section of the report "The Scope of Compulsory Insurance for the Building Trades" suggests that the insurance institute fulfills a function between the law and all involved parties; it inherits the proxy situation of "speaking in the name of" from the law and obtains its proxy situation of "speaking for someone" from the parties. It is therefore one-sided to characterize the institute and its spokesman, the prospective *Koncipist,* as intercessors for the workers, stepping in for their rights and protection. The dominating, but competing, proxy relations "on behalf of the law," "on behalf of the employers," and "on behalf of workers" complicate matters. Kafka's essay for the institute seeks to arrange all parties' interests "by *risk calculation* in order to dissolve the conflict between capital and labor" (Commentary, *OW,* 71).

What is missing in this report, and in many other official documents, is the name "Franz Kafka." Secretarial writing typically has no name next to the published document title, and the drafter usually does not sign the circulating briefs. Kafka's authorship of the anonymously published article on workshop insurance is nonetheless evident through other sources, namely his list of qualifications and two letters he wrote — one to Felice Bauer and one to his literary publisher Franz Blei — that mention it. Yet such clear proof is the exception rather than the rule. Which papers *Koncipist* Kafka wrote in his own hand but in the name of his supervisors, as their right-hand man, remains obscure in many cases. Likewise, it is often unclear which papers he only signed, without having typed or penned them, especially toward the end of his career, after his promotion to the rank of Secretary. The official briefs are not the work of a single person but a hierarchical compilation of work stages performed by different specialized appointees. Klaus Hermsdorf observes that any official document is itself the product of a system of delegated responsibilities, from preparing the files (by *Manipulationsbeamte*) via drafting and formulating the writings (by *Konzeptsbeamte*) to signing them (by the *Direktor*).[17]

This typical feature of administrative writing was a major obstacle in compiling the critical edition of the *Amtliche Schriften* as part of Kafka's work. Responding to these concerns, the volume's coeditor Benno Wagner treats the compilation — and specifically the article on workshop insurance — as exemplary of Michel Foucault's concept of authorship, a form of writing away from the subject and toward discourse.[18] In his landmark analysis "What Is an Author?" Foucault announces a move from an author-subject to an author-function.[19] Wagner applies these terms to the annual reports, suggesting that the subject of the "institute" replaces the individual author. The "institute" is both subject and object of the official reports to the Ministry of the Interior and to employers, but in the core of the texts, the voice of the anonymous report ("Bericht-Instanz") supersedes the author-bound subject-function "in order to open up space for official objectivity."[20]

Conscious of maintaining room for objectivity, and fully aware that the institute itself fills a function "in the name of the law," Kafka tries to avoid, or at least minimize, the responsibility of signing legal briefs with his full name. An extract from a letter to Felice Bauer displays this refraining from personal authorship *in nuce*:

> I slither out of responsibility like a snake; I have to sign many things, but every evaded signature seems like a gain; I also sign everything (though I really shouldn't) with FK only, as though that could exonerate me. . . . This otherwise praiseworthy caution, however, is complemented and cancelled by the fact that I sign even the most important things with the said FK, without reading them. (*LF*, 115–16)[21]

Signing can be arbitrary, as author and signer are not always congruent. The administrative, juridical writer Kafka, who prefers his initials to his full name, acts as a *Schriftsteller*, a type or script setter, rather than as an *author* in the sense of a creator of an individual work. Stanley Corngold detects Kafka's own careful preference "of the term *Schriftstellersein* over the other words available to him: *Dichtersein* or *Autorsein*."[22] Also connected to Kafka's abstention from authoritative, subjective *Autorsein* is the opening up of multiple voices: the distribution of tasks to complete an official document allows for collective writing — and actually allows a link to the composition of some of Kafka's literary texts.

Indeed, in another letter to Felice Bauer, written only five nights after Kafka has confided to her his aversion to signing, he vividly illustrates the struggle with the writing of an unknown story:

> From the start of the story I made too many demands upon myself; at the very beginning four characters are supposed to talk and be vigorously involved in everything. But I can fully visualize as many characters as that only when they come into being and develop in the course, and from the flow, of the story. Right at the beginning I unfortunately mastered only two, but if four people are pressing forward, trying to make the floor, and the writer has eyes only for two, the result is a sad, an almost social embarrassment. These two refuse to be unmasked. But because my eyes stray all over the place, they might catch some shadows of these two, but then the two solid characters, being temporarily abandoned, become uncertain, and finally it all collapses. A pity! (*LF*, 124)[23]

The passage shows quite comically with how little authority Kafka credits himself as a literary writer and how strongly voiced his characters can be in contrast. When Kafka claims that the characters need to come into being or arise ("sich erheben") out of the flow of the story so as not to drown in representational one-dimensionality, it is not only for plain compositional reasons but probably also to underline their emancipated status. *They* have the floor and are supposed to speak, while the author slithers away; they participate dynamically in "everything." Like Kafka the bureaucrat, Kafka the literary *Schriftsteller* is conscious of how to coordinate different voices. By drafting fictional narratives, however, it becomes particularly evident to him how the system might become an "almost social embarrassment," and even collapse, when too many agents are involved. The process of delegation regarding who speaks and acts — from *Schriftsteller* to narrator to characters — is implied in the quoted passage. In the case of *The Trial*, with its principally figural narrative situation, the reflector-character Josef K. is, moreover, given the role of a bureaucratic proxy.[24]

Prokurist Josef K.

Literally a proxy at his work as bank *Prokurist*, the protagonist of *The Trial* also acts as agent and token representative for others in the legal realm.[25] Several passages from the novel fragment reveal structural transformations from the administrative writing of the *Koncipist* to the acting of the fictional *Prokurist*, as well as a major resemblance between the two: both inhabit milieux marked by the constant deferral of authority in complex, often inscrutable legal-administrative bureaucracies.

Josef K.'s entry into the dream-like story coincides with his entry into the legal sphere, when he is arrested one morning for no apparent reason. The court that prosecutes him "neither has a determinate place, nor is it everywhere, in general. It is always nearby."[26] For example, it operates in the room of his neighbor, Fräulein Bürstner, where a nightstand is used as a makeshift desk for the hearing; on the fifth floor of a poor suburban tenement house, where the first inquiry takes place; and behind the door of a junk room in K.'s workplace, where the two guards from the morning arrest are being flogged after K. reported them to the examining magistrate. K. is quick to learn that the court's presence consists of a dense network of representatives and affiliates who perpetuate its functioning. Among these delegates and substitutes are the examining magistrate, the prison chaplain, and the chain of doorkeepers within *The Trial*'s parable. As K. becomes absorbed into the court organization, he also needs intermediaries with whom to interact. Like the narrator of the "Advocates" text, he is uncertain as to why and how these intermediaries are necessary.

An important client of K.'s bank, an unnamed manufacturer, is among the people who try to provide assistance. He wants to arrange a meeting between K. and the supposedly helpful court painter Titorelli, because he believes that K. will be able to take advantage of Titorelli's advice on how to get in touch with influential people: "And even if this sort of advice is not in and of itself crucial, in my opinion it might take on great importance in your possession. After all, you're practically a lawyer. I always say: Chief Financial Officer [Prokurist] K. is practically a lawyer" (*T*, 135).[27] The manufacturer's use of a double or even triple title for Josef K. — as "Prokurist," "K.," and "practically a lawyer" — leads to the core of K.'s proxy status, with each identification referring to a different facet of what it means to be a ***stand-in***.

First of all, K.'s designated position in the bank as ***Prokurist*** classifies him as an employee entrusted with managing financial affairs for the bank, with signatory power. He works above several assistants and below the president as well as the president's substitute: the rival *Direktor-Stellvertreter*. These hierarchical distributions of work responsibilities are similar to those of ***Koncipist*** Kafka in his institutional role. Moreover, in the history of the term, the related ***Prokurator*** was a kind of legal representative for a court client. It remains speculative whether Kafka knew about the nuanced history of the profession of lawyer that Adolf Weißler laid out in a lengthy 1905 treatise, one year before Kafka received his Doctor of Laws degree. However, connections can be drawn between *The Trial*'s supposed legal representatives and Weißler's study of the profession's division into ***Advokatur*** and ***Prokuratur*** during the Middle Ages.[28] Simply put, the ***Advokat*** dealt with written work, whereas the ***Prokurator*** literally spoke for a client. Hence the ***Prokurator*** was physically present at the trial, while the advocate stayed in the background, having prepared the written pleas as the basis of the trial. K.'s legal representative *Advokat* Huld is of little help; it is mostly up to K. himself to assume the position of being his own defender, which leads to the attempt to prepare his written defense, an overview of his life.

The second proxy reference to Josef K. is "K," the abbreviated form of his last name. The "K" cipher evokes a semi-anonymous case study of a replaceable everyman, and it recalls the often-claimed proximity of the "K"–protagonists in Kafka's novel fragments: Karl Rossmann, Josef K., and K., who have been related to one another and to the author Kafka himself. In a similar vein, the letter "K" in the professional terms *Koncipist* and *Prokurist* is suggestive: Marek Nekula points to Kafka's orthographical preference for the letter "c" over "k" and "z" in foreign words, such as *Process* as opposed to *Prozess.*[29] However, this general tendency appears not to be valid for the word *Prokurist*, which is written throughout *The Trial* with "k" and never spelled in the older version as *Procurist.* It also applies less to "K" as initial letter: the spellings *Koncipist* or *Konzipist* are used frequently alongside the spelling *Concipist.* This notable exception to the beginning of words hints at a link to the idiosyncratic, calligraphic "K" in Kafka's handwriting. With their stretched, sloped final strokes, these "K" letters tend to stand out and attract attention, even in a carefully penned office letter on behalf of the entire group of *Koncipisten* — with a capital "K" — to the institute.[30] In a bracketed diary entry of May 1914, a few months before Kafka began writing *The Trial*, he notes: "(I find the letter *K* offensive, almost disgusting, and yet I use [schreibe] it; it must be very characteristic of me)" (*D2*, 33–34).[31] The process of "schreiben" — writing down — the repellent "K"s as subjective ciphers, ciphers that are "characteristic" for Kafka or his writing, surfaces here in a gestural, material, literal way: the short meditation focuses on the letter "K," whose deep, long, closing bow touches the words below in what is, playfully put, an inclusive yet authoritative movement; it resembles a hook. The "K" as hook-like focal point in the professional letter and the diary entry mirrors, on a different textual level, the "K" protagonists as both focus and anchor of the narration: in this creative sense, their proxy status is also inscribed in their name. The manuscript of *The Trial* exposes another distinct feature: its inconsistent abbreviation of several professional titles and names. Perhaps coincidentally but telling nonetheless, on the manuscript page, the manufacturer's words read: "Prok. K. ist fast ein Adv."[32] These abbreviations evoke the depersonalizing, effacing tendencies of *Koncipist* Kafka, who prefers signing with his initials only.

The third appellation given by the manufacturer to Josef K. refers in a double sense to "fast" — "almost" or "practically" — an "Adv." or a "lawyer." It is only "almost" the full title and it is only "practically" the profession. The latter holds especially true after the arrest, when K.'s life becomes an official legal affair, burdened with absurd juridical tasks that make him act as his own lawyer. Yet also in the events narrated in the fragment "Public Prosecutor," K. appears to be familiar with basic legal matters, even if he is not licensed to practice law. Public Prosecutor Hasterer, who is not part of the court system that later arrests K., is an important member of the regular gatherings of judges, prosecutors, and advocates, as well as young clerks and legal assistants. Introduced to these casual meetings by the bank's legal representative, K. is a special guest in this ensemble as the only expert in business matters but without an appointed role in the juridical sphere. It is precisely this position that makes him a unique representative in this circle, allowing him to contribute to the legal discussion as an involved-uninvolved observer.

A striking occasion to act as accuser and defender in court presents itself on a Sunday after the arrest, during the "initial inquiry" in one of the court's fleeting manifestations in a working-class tenement house. The intricate way in which institutional relations and narrative perspectives weave together is probably nowhere more explicitly played out than in this scene. K.'s theatrical speech in front of the supposed court of inquiry and the assembly, which reminds him of a precinct meeting split into parties, concentrates proxy relations in *The Trial*. The scene displays K. as a proxy who tries to orchestrate different voices and who tries to win over at least parts of the audience with the full force of a dramatic performance. His original plan to observe more than to speak is supplanted by his urge to act as a vocal proxy. When the examining magistrate mistakes him for a house painter, K. takes this blunder as his cue to speak from the slightly elevated position of the low platform, where he had climbed a moment before, taking the place of someone else who had jumped down. He corrects the error by stating that he is the first *Prokurist* of a large bank, thereby implying his status as a representative. Moreover, K. impugns the examining magistrate's error as characteristic of the proceedings to which he is subjected. He points to the opacity at play by lifting the examining magistrate's tattered notebook with his files to demonstrate that he is not afraid of it even though its content is not accessible to him. Before describing his unjust arrest at length and before pushing for transparency and communication, he declares in an automatically rising voice: "what has happened to me is merely a single case and as such of no particular consequence, since I don't take it very seriously, but it is typical of the proceedings being brought against many people. I speak for them, not for myself" (*T*, 46–47).[33] K.'s words mark a complex shift in the authoritative voice: he becomes his own legal representative through the detour of speaking for others in a performance in front of court representatives and spectators. Although he denies it, he *is* speaking on his own behalf, but this appears to be possible only because he acts as an *ad hoc*, self-appointed proxy. He assumes the role of orator for the case of many and thus also speaks for his own legal case.[34]

Nonetheless, K. clarifies that his goal is not "success as an orator" but rather "a public discussion of a public disgrace" (*T*, 47).[35] During his speech he sees the examining magistrate giving a sign to someone in the audience and comments on this instantly: "So there are those among you who are being directed from up here" (*T*, 48–49).[36] It is worth recalling the passages in the official article on workshop insurance that lament the lack of direct communication between the insurance institute and the employers. The institute's questionnaire had brought to light the fact that some of the trade associations claimed to speak on behalf of the employer but actually drowned out the employers' voices. In both cases, the proxy aims for clear articulation; K. even "publicly authorizes" the examining magistrate to give *direct* orders to the audience, "to command his paid employees below out loud" (*T*, 49).[37] He continues by pointing to the inadequacy of the entire organization, including its agents, which supports the system of judges "with their inevitable innumerable entourage of assistants, scribes, gendarmes, and other aides, perhaps even hangmen" (*T*, 50).[38] Interrupted by a shriek, he eventually jumps down from the stage and stands eye to eye with the crowd. At that moment the roles are reversed again.

Even though K.'s speech cannot save him from his ultimate execution, it shows that he is far from being a passive recipient of an unexplained charge. Instead, he becomes an accuser himself. His speech, distorted by personal indignation, actually silences the examining magistrate and dominates the occasional murmuring of the crowd around him; it is not the "public discussion" that he claimed he sought. Moreover, in the scene's turning point, K. discovers that the people in the crowd are wearing badges on their collars that identify them as members of the organization and not as public representatives to whom he intended to speak. This "initial inquiry," which is not a true inquiry after all, unfolds as both drama and farce. It is dominated by K.'s contradictory speech and accompanied by the staged assembly's mixed and partially directed reactions.

His speech also articulates outwardly what is largely inherent in the *The Trial*'s narrative situation. K.'s claim — that his "single case" is only representative for that of "many people" for whom he speaks instead of for himself — has proved only partially true with regard to his institutional and legal situation. Yet his claim is equally interesting with regard to the third-person narrative situation: like the other "K."s, he figures as a "single case" within the narration, centered but inclusive. *He* is the one through whose point of view and horizon of consciousness the events are narrated; he is always present in the course of the story. As a reflector-character whose internal perspective channels the narrative itinerary, he can stand in for the narrator. The predominant lack of another authorial voice makes K. a potential representative for "many people." Friedrich Beißner prominently calls the limitation of perspective in Kafka's novel fragments "einsinnig" (mono-perspectival) and links it to an intrinsic, formalistic reading in which "no space exists for the narrator around or above the protagonist."[39] Yet on the stage in the courtroom, the protagonist gains a temporary vantage point from which he observes and comments on the proceedings, and purports to stand in and speak for "many people." As proxy for the narrative voice, it is K. himself and his direct speech that lay claim to a comprehensive overview.

In the texts discussed above, the proxy figure reveals several multifaceted connections: between institution and narrating; between author, narrator or narrative voice, and protagonist; and between the non-fictional reports in the setting of the insurance institute, with its apparatus of proxy relations, and questions of author-function or authorship. In different discursive realms, *Prokurist* Josef K. in several scenes, and Kafka in his role as drafter of the article on workshop insurance, take on the perspectives of observers and commentators who are equally involved and uninvolved in the issues at stake. Given the institution's pervasiveness, K. acts hastily as a subjective spokesman, while the prospective *Koncipist* Kafka keeps his objectivity to offer textual space in his report for an ensemble of voices. For the narrator in the "Advocates" text, the needed representative is conspicuously absent at first. However, while he traverses the hallways of what might be a museum or library — a site of collections or books, of exhibiting, reading, or writing — and while he ascends to potentially open space, he appears to find an intercessor for himself in himself, through the very act of speaking. Constellations of proxies can thus find their way into the narrator's desires ("Advocates" text) and the protagonist's actions (*The Trial*), and they each govern a specific facet of the narrative mode. The selected passages show that modern narrating and institutional setting are linked to concerns of vocal agency and the inherent need to assign and fill positions in order to function. Yet one can go further and tentatively suggest that the proxy adds to an understanding of the distinct narrator figures in Kafka's work and converges with questions of authorship. At the same time, the proxy erodes parts of the distinction between Kafka's legal-administrative and literary-aesthetic writing. Insofar as both forms of writing reflect delegated representation, Kafka the law clerk and Kafka the literary writer refrain from exerting authority over their texts. As *Schriftsteller*, Kafka effaces himself for the sake of the voices of others.

Notes

1 "Es war sehr unsicher, ob ich Fürsprecher hatte, ich konnte nichts Genaues darüber erfahren" (*NS2*, 377). For the sake of simplicity and given the temporal, thematic, and structural proximity of this prose fragment to the later novel projects, the nameless narrator is henceforth referred to in this chapter in the third person "he," although the gender is not specified in Kafka's use of monologue and dialogue.

2 "Weil ich überall einen Fürsprecher suchte, überall ist er nötig, ja man braucht ihn weniger bei Gericht als anderswo" (*NS2*, 378).

[3] See especially *Kafkas Institutionen*, ed. Arne Höcker and Oliver Simons (Bielefeld: Transcript, 2007). Arne Höcker's contribution to *Kafkas Institutionen*, "Literatur durch Verfahren: Beschreibung eines Kampfes" (235–53), aptly shows how Kafka's writing exemplifies the disbanding of aesthetic distance, with the desk as a theater or performative site for both literary and administrative procedures.

[4] See Rüdiger Campe, "Kafkas Institutionenroman: *Der Proceß, Das Schloß*," in *Gesetz, Ironie: Festschrift für Manfred Schneider*, ed. Rüdiger Campe and Michael Niehaus (Heidelberg: Synchron, 2004), 197–208.

[5] See Rüdiger Campe, "Kafkas Fürsprache," in *Kafkas Institutionen*, 189–212.

[6] *The Office Writings* contains a translation of many important *amtliche Schriften* into English, enriched with lucid commentary that also informs my analysis. For the original German, see *Franz Kafka: Amtliche Schriften* 2004 (abbreviated in the text as *AS*).

[7] "Solange Du nicht zu steigen aufhörst, hören die Stufen nicht auf, unter Deinen steigenden Füßen, wachsen sie aufwärts" (*NS2*, 380).

[8] See Ritchie Robertson's contribution to this volume, "Kafka, Goffman, and the Total Institution."

[9] For an influential account of the emergence of the insurance state from the liberal ideology of individual responsibility, see François Ewald, *L'état Providence* (Paris: Grasset & Fasquelle, 1986).

[10] Benno Wagner, "Kafkas phantastisches Büro," in *Kontinent Kafka: Mosse-Lectures an der Humboldt-Universität zu Berlin*, ed. Klaus R. Scherpe and Elisabeth Wagner (Berlin: Vorwerk 8, 2006), 106.

[11] Theodor W. Adorno, "The Position of the Narrator in the Contemporary Novel," in *Notes to Literature,* vol. 1, ed. Rolf Tiedemann, trans. Shierry Weber Nicholsen (New York: Columbia UP, 1991), 31.

[12] For a closer look at the administrative post of the *Koncipist*, see Klaus Hermsdorf, "Schreibanlässe und Textformen der amtlichen Schriften Franz Kafkas: Eine Einführung," in *AS*, 11–104, especially 15–18.

[13] On the use of rhetorical elements and reading in the *Office Writings*, see Richard Heinemann, "The Rhetoric of Kafka's *Amtliche Schriften*," *Journal of the Kafka Society of America,* 15.1–2 (1991): 29–36.

[14] "Es sollte die Wirkung einer persönlichen, von fremdem Einflusse bewahrten Verhandlung mit dem Unternehmer über dessen konkreten Betrieb haben. . . . Die Anstalt wollte . . . den Unternehmer hören, konnte jedoch oft nur gewisse Vereinigungen durch den Unternehmer reden hören und leider manchmal nur die Vereinigung, selbst ohne Vermittlung des Unternehmers" (*AS*, 128–29).

[15] "Für die Werkstattversicherung [spricht] das Gesetz in seiner Absicht, seiner Geschichte, seinem Text und seinem Zusammenhang" (*AS*, 137).

[16] "Wobei aber die Einschränkung nicht vergessen werden darf, daß hier eigentlich nur zwei Interessen, die der Arbeiter und die der Unternehmer, gelten, denn die Anstalt hat keine anderen, als diese" (*AS*, 138).

[17] See Hermsdorf, "Schreibanlässe" (*AS*, 18).

[18] Benno Wagner, "'Beglaubigungssorgen': Zur Problematik von Verfasserschaft, Autorschaft und Werkintegration im Rahmen der *Amtlichen Schriften* Franz Kafkas," *Editio: International Yearbook of Scholarly Editing* 17 (2003): 155–69.

[19] Michel Foucault, "What is an Author?" in *Language, Counter-Memory, Practice*, ed. Donald F. Bouchard, trans. Donald F. Bouchard and Sherry Simon (Ithaca, NY: Cornell UP, 1977), 113–38. Foucault's fundamental reconstruction of the author as locus within the circulation of speech is a discourse analytical response to Roland Barthes's provocative essay "The Death of the Author." See Roland Barthes, "La mort de l'auteur" (1968), repr. in his *Le bruissement de la langue* (Paris: Seuil, 1984), 61–67.

[20] Wagner, "Beglaubigungssorgen," 164 (my translation).

[21] "Verantwortungen weiche ich aus wie eine Schlange, ich habe vielerlei zu unterschreiben, aber jede vermiedene Unterschrift scheint mir ein Gewinn, ich unterschreibe auch alles (trotzdem es eigentlich nicht sein darf) nur mit FK, als könne mich das entlasten. . . . Ergänzt und aufgehoben wird allerdings diese sonst lobenswerte Vorsicht dadurch, daß ich mit jenem FK auch die wichtigsten Sachen, ohne sie durchzulesen, unterschreibe" (*BF*, 196, letter of 20–21 Dec. 1912).

[22] Stanley Corngold, "Kafka and the Ministry of Writing," in *OW*, 1–18; here 3.

[23] "Ich habe jene Geschichte auch unter zu großen Ansprüchen an mich angefangen; gleich im Anfang sollen vier Personen reden und sich kräftig an allem beteiligen. So viele Menschen kann ich aber nur dann vollständig sehn, wenn sie sich im Laufe, aus dem Strome der Geschichte erheben und sich entwickeln. Gleich am Anfang habe ich leider nur zwei beherrscht und wenn nun vier Personen drängen und auftreten wollen, man aber nur den Blick für zwei hat, entsteht eine traurige, förmlich gesellschaftliche Verlegenheit. Die zwei wollen und wollen sich nicht demaskieren. Dadurch aber, daß mein Blick herumirrt, erhascht er vielleicht auch Schatten von diesen zweien, dafür fangen aber die zwei festen Gestalten in ihrer zeitweiligen Verlassenheit unsicher zu werden an und schließlich schlägt alles zusammen. Schade!" (*BF*, 207–8, letter of 25–26 Dec. 1912).

[24] For the terms "figural narrative situation" and "reflector-character," see Franz K. Stanzel, *A Theory of Narrative*, trans. Charlotte Goedsche (Cambridge: Cambridge UP, 1984).

[25] Further *Prokuristen* that come to mind are Felice Bauer, whose profession as sales representative for the Carl Lindström Parlograph Company fascinated Kafka — although the parlographs themselves appeared to him as rather uninspiring, lifeless proxies (see *BF*, 68–69; *LF*, 23); and Gregor Samsa's work superior, the office representative in *The Metamorphosis*. For the latter and for Gregor Samsa himself as proxies, see Kerstin Stüssel, *In Vertretung: Literarische Mitschriften von Bürokratie zwischen früher Neuzeit und Gegenwart* (Tübingen: Niemeyer, 2004), 113–16. Stüssel also analyzes bureaucracy and representation in *The Trial* (137–61).

[26] Campe, "Kafkas Institutionenroman," 205 (my translation).

[27] "Und wenn auch diese Ratschläge an und für sich nicht entscheidend sein sollten, so werden sie doch meiner Meinung nach in Ihrem Besitz von großer

Bedeutung sein. Sie sind ja fast ein Advokat. Ich pflege immer zu sagen: Prokurist K. ist fast ein Advokat" (*P,* 182).

[28] See Adolf Weißler, *Geschichte der Rechtsanwaltschaft* (Leipzig: C. E. M. Pfeffer, 1905), 110–21.

[29] See Marek Nekula, *Franz Kafkas Sprachen "... in einem Stockwerk des innern babylonischen Turmes ..."* (Tübingen: Niemeyer, 2003), 90.

[30] As spokesman for all of the institute's *Koncipisten,* "Dr. Franz Kafka" both writes and signs this appeal for salary adjustments based on statistical analysis (see *AS* Materialien, [807–14]; *OW,* 214–20, letter of 11 Dec. 1912). A facsimile of the letter, which unmistakably identifies him as writer or *Schriftführer,* and which displays several hook-like "K"s, is printed in *Kafkas Fabriken* (Marbacher Magazin 100), ed. Hans-Gerd Koch and Klaus Wagenbach, 79–96 (Marbach: Deutsche Schillergesellschaft, 2002).

[31] "(Ich finde die K häßlich, sie widern mich fast an und ich schreibe sie doch, sie müssen für mich sehr charakteristisch sein)" (*Ta,* 517; Bodleian Library, Oxford: MS Kafka 26, fol. 25v).

[32] Franz Kafka, *Der Process,* in *Die historisch-kritische Ausgabe sämtlicher Handschriften, Drucke und Typoskripte,* ed. Roland Reuß in cooperation with Peter Staengle (Frankfurt am Main: Stroemfeld, 1997), 8. "Advokat Fabrikant Maler," 60–61.

[33] "Was mir geschehen ist, ist ja nur ein einzelner Fall und als solcher nicht sehr wichtig, da ich es nicht sehr schwer nehme, aber es ist das Zeichen eines Verfahrens wie es gegen viele geübt wird. Für diese stehe ich hier ein, nicht für mich" (*P,* 64).

[34] Oliver Simons likewise points to the complexity and paradoxical gesture of representation (Stellvertretung) in this scene; see Oliver Simons, "Schuld und Scham: Kafkas episches Theater," in Höcker and Simons, *Kafkas Institutionen* (Bielefeld: Transcript, 2007), 280.

[35] "Ich will nicht Rednererfolg. . . . Was ich will, ist nur die öffentliche Besprechung eines öffentlichen Mißstandes" (*P,* 65).

[36] "Es sind also Leute unter Ihnen, die von hier oben dirigiert werden" (*P,* 67).

[37] "Ich ermächtige den Herrn Untersuchungsrichter öffentlich, seine bezahlten Angestellten dort unten statt mit geheimen Zeichen, laut mit Worten zu befehligen" (*P,* 67).

[38] ". . . mit dem zahllosen unumgänglichen Gefolge von Dienern, Schreibern, Gendarmen und andern Hilfskräften, vielleicht sogar Henkern" (*P,* 69).

[39] Friedrich Beißner "Der Erzähler Franz Kafka," in *Der Erzähler Franz Kafka und andere Vorträge* (Frankfurt am Main: Suhrkamp, 1983), 37, 42 (my translation). Subsequent studies largely support, yet further define and considerably modify Beißner's claims, detecting breaks in perspective.

8: Kafka, Goffman, and the Total Institution

Ritchie Robertson

Of all authors writing in German, Kafka is the one whose works have particularly fascinated readers throughout the world. One result is a division between what may be called the lay readers of Kafka and the professional or academic readers. The two groups are divided, in particular, by their attitude to the widespread notion that Kafka's works must in some sense prophesy the Third Reich and the atrocities of the mid-twentieth century. Writing in the *Times Literary Supplement*, and hence largely for a lay audience, in 1963, George Steiner asserted that Kafka "was, in a literal sense, a prophet." He elaborated:

> *The Trial* exhibits the classic model of the terror state. It prefigures the furtive sadism, the hysteria which totalitarianism insinuates into private and sexual life, the faceless boredom of the killers. Since Kafka wrote, the night knock has come on innumerable doors, and the name of those dragged off to die "like a dog!" is legion. Kafka prophesied the actual forms of the disaster of western humanism which Nietzsche and Kierkegaard had seen like an uncertain blackness on the horizon.[1]

Something like this is still part of the common wisdom about Kafka. In any discussion of Kafka with a lay audience, the question is likely to be raised whether he foresaw the horrors to come. Alan Bennett's intelligent and funny play *Kafka's Dick* (1986) actually makes its protagonist say: "I dream the future."[2]

At this point academic readers of Kafka are liable to become impatient. They will point out — rightly, of course — that Kafka did not have extrasensory perception and could not see into the future. In any case, the future does not lie before us, invisible yet already fixed; it is still undecided. It is not there to be foreseen.[3] Yet it is sobering to read that when Kafka's works first became available in the Soviet Union, where a version of *The Trial* (*Der Proceß*, 1925) began circulating in samizdat in 1961 before being officially published in 1965, Russian readers were convinced that the author must be writing indirectly about the Stalinist terror and the great purges, when the invasion of one's home early in the morning by men in strange uniforms was the real experience of many thousands of people.[4] Such responses cannot be dismissed as foolish or ignorant, especially as those readers came fresh to the text without the prior assumptions about Kafka that were by then standard in the West.

And yet "prophetic" readings of Kafka can hardly be accepted as they stand. If Kafka seemed so prescient about Soviet reality, the reason lay not in Kafka's prevision of the future but in his perception of his present. He had an extraordinary insight into the mechanisms of power, authority, and violence, mechanisms that are in some measure common to a wide variety of social systems. These mechanisms reside above all in institutions.

Institutions are types of social organizations serving particular purposes, such as the household, the family, the business corporation, the government ministry, the school, the hospital, the prison. The word "institution" tends to slip from its general meaning to a more specific sense, denoting especially those institutions where people are confined, allegedly for their own good and often against their own wishes, such as old people's homes, mental asylums, and jails. An institution is, on the whole, a place where one would rather not be. Randall Jarrell caught the ambivalence of the word when he gave his novel of American academic life, published in 1954, the title *Pictures from an Institution.* It implies both that a university is a home for eccentrics and that it is impersonal, run on bureaucratic lines. The concept of an "institution" is also implicitly contrasted with home. Institutional clothing means a uniform; institutional food is likely to be nasty. If one is institutionalized, it may be, by a cruel irony, in a place which euphemistically calls itself a "home," such as a "retirement home," a "nursing home," or a 'sunset home."

Some of these ambiguities also inhere in the word Kafka used, "Anstalt." He uses it to refer to the organization where he worked, the Arbeiter-Unfall-Versicherungs-Anstalt für das Königreich Böhmen (Workmen's Accident Insurance Institute for the Kingdom of Bohemia), but in different contexts it can mean an educational institution (*Erziehungsanstalt*) or lunatic asylum (*Irrenanstalt*). A well-known novel begins: "Granted, I am the inmate of a mental hospital" (*einer Heil- und Pflegeanstalt*), my keeper is watching me, he never lets me out of his sight."[5] Here nursing is equated with surveillance.

In the later twentieth century, sociologists paid close attention to institutions, particularly to those which exerted the greatest control over their inmates. We are all familiar with Michel Foucault's *Discipline and Punish* (1975), which considers how institutions associated with justice, especially the prison, and with training, such as the army, shape the very bodies of those assigned to them. Walter Müller-Seidel cited Foucault extensively in his study of "In the Penal Colony" ("In der Strafkolonie," 1914) entitled *Die Deportation des Menschen* (1986). Perhaps, however, more can be learned about Kafka from a less famous sociological work, Erving Goffman's study of mental homes, *Asylums* (1961). Here Goffman examines an instance of "total institutions," which aim to supervise and dictate the entire behavior of their inhabitants. Other examples of total institutions that he mentions in his introduction are jails, concentration camps, boarding schools, and monasteries. Kafka, however, was there before them. His work contains a deeply felt, sensitively rendered analysis of institutions, not only showing how they oppress the bodies and minds of their inmates, but also, in his later works, exploring possibilities of resistance and escape. An enigmatic sentence from *The Trial* — "Everything belongs to the Court" (*T*, 150)[6] — suggests that Kafka's court is a total institution.

As Goffman has shown, the structure of institutions is similar, whether their purposes are supposedly benign or malign. Prisons, monasteries, asylums and camps are all total institutions. On entering a total institution, the inmate is subjected to various forms of what Goffman calls "mortification."[7] One is physically separated from the outside world and from the role one played there and from whatever respect accompanied it. One loses some or all of one's possessions, wears institutional clothing, is known either by a new name or by an unduly familiar version of one's own. One must treat staff with deference signaled not only in words but in one's bodily posture, and undergo gratuitous humiliations. In a mental institution or a monastery, or wherever one has to be "reeducated," one must submit to having the history of one's life, especially shameful episodes, generally known. One has little or no recourse against maltreatment by those with power over one.

Much of this happens to Josef K. when he is arrested. A warder invades his bedroom; he is ordered about, mocked, and shouted at; his physical space is violated when the warders bump against him; his underclothes are confiscated, and he is told he must wear a much shabbier nightgown in future; he is ordered to put on a black coat to meet the inspector; and he is watched by his neighbours from across the street. Even someone less proud of his civil status would be discomposed by this treatment. On his first visit to the court, he is subjected to what Goffman calls "role dispossession" (24). That is, the dignified and respected role that he has previously played, as chief clerk of a large bank, is ignored, and the examining magistrate says to K., as though stating a fact, 'You're a house painter?" (*T*, 44)[8]

When K., indignant at being mistaken for a painter, declares his true profession, half the audience bursts into laughter. For most people in such a situation, to be surrounded by laughter would intensify their discomfort and humiliation; K., however, is so egoistic that he assumes the audience are laughing, not at him, but at the magistrate's mistake. The narrative perspective corresponds to K.'s, but that does not mean that K. has understood the situation correctly.

K.'s relations with court officialdom correspond to a feature that Goffman notes in total institutions — a "basic split" between the inmates of the institution and its staff. The two groups have no contact outside their institutional roles. They dislike and despise each other: the staff see inmates stereotypically as untrustworthy, the inmates regard the staff as condescending and wantonly unkind (18). This latent conflict has a corrosive effect on both. There are always some individuals among the staff who are inclined to maltreat the inmates if they can get away with it. We have recently seen how institutions such as Abu Ghraib prison in Iraq tend to promote such behavior. And the inmates are made to feel "inferior, weak, blameworthy, and guilty" (18); Goffman cites the case of an imprisoned conscientious objector who, owing to his subordinate position within the prison, found it difficult to retain the conviction of his moral innocence (58). In *The Trial*, the gulf separating court officials from defendants such as K. is repeatedly emphasized. The warders, on first intruding into K.'s flat, treat him high-handedly, misappropriate his belongings, and show impatience with his questions and protests. The doorkeeper in the chaplain's parable treats the man from the country in a condescending manner, asking him questions without any genuine interest. The implications of this division are further explored in the conversation between K. and the chaplain, which purports to elucidate the parable. There the chaplain points out that though the man from the country appears to be under the door-keeper's control, he actually retains his freedom inasmuch as he has come voluntarily to seek access to the law and could, in theory at least, go away again, whereas the doorkeeper is obliged to remain at his post and is not even allowed to approach closer to the law. Yet, ironically, it never occurs to the man from the country that he might make any use of his alleged freedom.

The long-term effects of a trial are shown by the defendants K. meets waiting in court offices one Sunday: though clearly from the middle and upper classes, they are poorly dressed, and when they rise to salute a court usher, they stand with bowed backs and bent knees like beggars in the street. We may suppose that even without physical maltreatment, the moral pressure of being on trial has worn them down. A partially similar development is charted in Goffman's account of "the moral career of the mental patient" (119–55). When first hospitalized, many mental patients insist that they are there only as the result of a mistake, and that they will be released very soon. They construct self-justifying autobiographical narratives, but these narratives are met with skepticism and contempt by the staff, and in the course of his confinement the patient loses his self-belief and his self-respect. We can see elements of this in K.'s determination to compose an autobiographical document detailing and justifying all the important actions he has performed in his life. Talking to the chaplain, he still maintains that he is innocent, yet he has become pitiable in his search for help from unlikely sources and in his anxiety to find a kindly human response. The chaplain's motive for telling him the parable of the doorkeeper, which centers on the respective institutional roles of a petitioner and an official, is to deter him from seeking such a response from an official.

Others suffer a more severe humiliation than K. does. He has the warning example of Block, the corn-merchant who has virtually given up his business in order to fight his case with the help of a whole group of lawyers. While K. is not placed in a physical institution, but allowed to go about his normal life at the cost of becoming psychologically obsessed by his case, Block suffers physical institutionalization in the advocate's house. Like some inmates, such as army recruits, Block is given meaningless tasks — in his case, reading documents that he does not understand, in a bad light that makes it difficult even to decipher them. He is kept in a cell-like room under the surveillance of Leni, the advocate's housekeeper. He is verbally abused, being told that he always arrives at the wrong time, even when he has actually been summoned. And he is physically abused in being made to kneel before the advocate. This prompts in K. the reflection: "He was no longer a client, he was the lawyer's dog. If the lawyer had ordered him to crawl under the bed, as into a kennel, and bark, he would have done so gladly"[9] (*T,* 195). We may again recall Abu Ghraib, where Iraqi prisoners were forced to kneel, and assume even more humiliating postures, by their captors. But Kafka's account has a further element: Josef K. thinks that Block experiences pleasure in his humiliation. This may be accurate, or it may be a projection onto Block of K.'s own feelings, but in either case it exposes how the abuse of power can be not just sadistic but sado-masochistic. It raises the question, a crucial one for Kafka, of why people allow themselves to be oppressed by others, and the explanation will be found in the logic of institutions.

Kafka's grasp of institutions enables him to disclose patterns of oppression and subservience, ultimately underpinned by violence, that are present in some measure in all institutions, the more so as the institutions approach totality. There is an immense difference between the purposes of institutions that genuinely seek to help people, like hospitals, and those that seek to destroy them, like concentration camps and death camps, and in between there are many institutions that seek to train people (schools, the army) or simply to keep them out of society's way, but what Kafka shows us is that there is not a difference in structure. Indeed the true nature of an institution entered voluntarily, such as K.'s office, is revealingly mirrored in the hierarchical structure of an oppressive institution such as the court.

The template for Kafka's understanding of institutions was his family. The family is the first institution that anyone encounters, and, for Kafka, the family is the place where oppression starts. The oppression Gregor

Samsa suffers from his family is vividly embodied in the layout of his room, which has three doors (Gregor locks them all at night), at each of which a member of his family, his father, mother, and sister, knocks, urging him to get up and go to work. Kafka spoke of parental love as smothering, and of family life as a battleground. He wrote to Felice Bauer in 1912: "I have always looked upon my parents as persecutors. . . . All parents want to do is drag one down to them, back to the old days from which one longs to free oneself and escape; they do it out of love, of course, and that's what makes it so horrible" (*LF,* 55).[10] Eight years later he described to Milena Jesenská the awfulness of family life: "Certainly living at home is very bad, but it's not just the living there — it's the life, the sinking into this circle of kindness, of love — you don't know the letter to my father — the buzzing of the fly on the lime-twig." Yet, he added, even this had its good side: "It's just that one man fights at Marathon, the other in the dining room, while the god of war and goddess of victory are omnipresent" (*LM,* 123).[11]

Kafka is not here complaining about parental unkindness or abuse. For him, it is the sticky bond created by parental affection that is so hard to resist. In his two great stories of family conflict, "The Judgment" ("Das Urteil," 1913) and *The Metamorphosis* (*Die Verwandlung*, 1915), the heroes are doomed by their love for their parents. Georg Bendemann is certainly a selfish and neglectful son, who has given no thought to how his father will fare after Georg's marriage, and his protestations of affection are clearly designed to stop his father's awkward questions about the friend in Russia, and, as the father rightly charges, to cover him up. But when, obeying his father's sentence, Georg throws himself off the bridge, he reverts to a childish identity as the outstanding gymnast who had once been his parents' pride and joy, and his last words are: "Dear parents, I really always loved you" (*KSS,* 12).[12] As for Gregor, he is so submissive that even after his family have decided that he must vanish, since he threatens their livelihood, he obediently dies, thinking back to his family not with resentment but with affection.

Kafka repeatedly complains that adults seek to suppress children's individuality. In 1910 he explored his own experience of failed individuality in a series of autobiographical sketches beginning, "When I think about it, I must say that my education has done me great harm in some respects" (*D*1, 14).[13] A photograph of him as a small boy has been memorably described by Walter Benjamin:

> There is a childhood photograph of Kafka, a rarely touching portrayal of the "poor, brief childhood." It was probably made in one of those nineteenth-century studios whose draperies and palm trees, tapestries and easels placed them somewhere between a torture chamber and a throne room. At the age of approximately six the boy is presented in a sort of greenhouse setting, wearing a tight, heavily lace-trimmed, almost embarrassing child's suit.[14]

One feels for the little boy who gazes sadly out of the frame, obviously wishing to be somewhere else, and who, as Benjamin reminds us, later wrote the escape fantasy, "Wish to be a Red Indian." But one also notes the atmosphere of coercion, which Benjamin registers with the startling term "torture chamber."

Kafka was a severe and radical critic of contemporary child-rearing. He sympathized with the radical psychoanalyst Otto Gross, whom he met through Max Brod in 1917; they discussed founding a journal to be called *Blätter zur Bekämpfung des Machtwillens (Pages on Combating the Will to Power)*. Gross took drugs, had many lovers (including Frieda Weekley, later the wife of D. H. Lawrence) and considered the conventional family the source of patriarchal authority that needed to be overthrown by revolution. He spoke from experience: in 1913 his father, a professor of criminal law whose lectures Kafka had attended at university, had Otto institutionalized in a psychiatric clinic, on the grounds that his belief in free love proved his insanity. He was released after a public outcry.

The family, for Kafka, is the place where power, guilt, law, and punishment originate. His "Letter to My Father" describes how Hermann Kafka laid down strict laws on good behavior from which he himself was exempt. From such experiences Kafka came to imagine law as a mechanism of power, going back to family relationships. Children, dependent on their parents and trapped by the bonds of love, acquiesce in the power that rules their small lives and internalize the standards of behavior, which they later pass on to their own offspring. The acquiescence that secures the law of the family is carried over into adult life as acquiescence in social institutions.

Acquiescence in authority is a central problem in *The Trial.* The novel contains no actual court proceedings. After his arrest Josef K. is summoned before the examining magistrate, to whom, instead of waiting to be questioned, he blusters about his innocence. Thereafter the court leaves him alone until the scene where, waiting in the cathedral for a business contact, K. finds himself summoned from a small pulpit by a clergyman who proves to be the prison chaplain, and who warns him that he is thought to be guilty. The court's only further move is to send K. his executioners, and K. is duly found waiting for them.

To understand why Josef K. submits to the court, we need also to consider what kind of person he is. Josef K., like other Kafka protagonists, embodies the type required and produced by modern institutions of work, commerce, and government. Such institutions are abstract, remote from manual labour, and hierarchical.

The world of abstraction and hierarchy requires a particular type of person to operate in it. Gregor, for example, is an unhappy and inadequate version of a type of which aspects are embodied in several Kafka protagonists. From Gregor, Georg Bendemann, Josef K., and the Country Doctor

("Ein Landarzt," 1919), we can distill an ideal type of the modern professional man.[15] He is orderly and calculating, as his job demands. Josef K. gets his breakfast in bed every day at eight, works in his office till 9:00 PM, and then socializes with influential officials till eleven. Even his sexual life, consisting of a weekly visit to an apparent prostitute called Elsa, is fitted into his routine.

The professional man generally works for an organization that is hierarchically structured. While Gregor has a lowly position in his firm, bullied by the chief clerk, Josef K. *is* a chief clerk, as he proudly informs the examining magistrate. His arrogance is evident from his treatment of the three junior employees who are assigned to accompany him to the bank after his arrest. They are so inferior that he does not consider them his colleagues. Toward his superiors, however, he is obsequious. He jockeys for power with his nearest rival, the deputy director, and he cultivates the society of Public Prosecutor Hasterer at the "regular table" dominated by senior officials.

As Kafka shows, success within an institution requires one to accept its rules, including its system of hierarchy, so that anything different becomes intolerable, even unthinkable. Josef K. is the supreme example of a professional man committed to order. His arrest strikes him principally as the cause of disorder, which must be tidied up:

> Without knowing exactly how, it seemed to him as if the morning's events had thrown the whole of Frau Grubach's boarding-house into disarray, and that he was the one needed to restore order. Once that order had been restored, all trace of what had happened would be wiped away, and the old routine would resume. (*T*, 21)[16]

Nevertheless, he becomes obsessed with the court, picturing it in the image of his own organization, with a vast opaque hierarchy of officials, and deciding to deal with it by submitting a lengthy document.

In his portrayal of bureaucracy, Kafka captures another characteristic of modern institutions: the invisibility of their rulers. Premodern institutions established their authority by ceremonial. Even punishment was a solemn public ceremony, in which a murderer passed through crowds, mounted the scaffold, and was exhorted to repent for the edification of the spectators. In Kafka's fiction, organizations are headed by managers and directors. Traditional rulers appear only as ineffectual figureheads, like the emperor in "A Page from an Old Document" who, unable to drive away the nomads who have invaded his city, watches them from the window of his palace. In *The Castle* (*Das Schloß*, 1926) the traditional rule of Count Westwest exists in name only. The count's flag flies from the battlements, but he never appears, and the bureaucrats, especially Klamm, enjoy the superstitious respect formerly reserved for royalty.

Punishment has likewise retreated to private spaces. In the most horrific episode of *The Trial*, the warders who arrested K., and of whose conduct K. complained to the examining magistrate, appear in a lumber-room in K.'s bank, being whipped for their misdemeanours by a man in a leather outfit. The hint of homosexual sadism here confirms that the punishment is a vicarious realization of K.'s unconscious desires. Consciously, K. is shocked by the obvious and extreme cruelty of the punishment, tries ineffectually to buy the flogger off, and at last slams the door on the screaming victim. This revelation of the violence underpinning the court's authority anticipates the final chapter, where K. is taken by his executioners to a remote quarry and has a knife twisted in his heart.

Kafka knew that in the civilized modern world violence was banished to concealed rooms in police stations and prisons and to colonial settings far from Europe. For somebody who never left Europe, he gives an astonishingly perceptive portrayal of colonialism and violence in the story "In the Penal Colony," written about the same time as the whipper scene of *The Trial*; it bears comparison with *Heart of Darkness*, which is based on Conrad's first-hand knowledge of colonial exploitation in the Belgian Congo. One of Kafka's uncles, Joseph Loewy, worked from 1891 to 1902 in the Congo as administrator on a railway that was built by forced labor; his experiences seem to have inspired a fragment in Kafka's notebook about "building the railway in the interior of the Congo" and to have shaped "In the Penal Colony" by coalescing with reports of Captain Dreyfus's unjust imprisonment in the French penal settlement of Devil's Island. Kafka would also have known from the press about the genocidal suppression by the German colonial authorities of the Herero uprising in South-West Africa (now Namibia).[17] In the story, set in a French-speaking colony, an officer shows a European visitor an "apparatus" (a word used not only for machinery but for the apparatus of administration) designed for punishment.[18]

Oppression in Kafka's penal colony may change its character, but it looks unlikely to vanish. In the past, punishment was a public spectacle. It is now conducted shamefacedly in a remote valley. Although the old commandant, to whose authoritarian legacy the officer is devoted, is dead, his successor lacks the courage to abolish inhumane punishments and is preoccupied by technical progress (building extensions to the harbor). The only sign of hope lies with the traveler from whose perspective the story is told. Urged by the officer to support traditional punishments, the traveler appears distinctly, and plausibly, unheroic as he mentally runs through the usual excuses: he is a foreigner who should mind his own business; cultural relativism suggests that European standards should not be expected in the tropics; and so on. At last, however, he pulls himself together and says firmly: "No." A courageous liberal conscience can just conceivably make a difference.

The morbid cruelty of the punishment machine again prompts the question about how Kafka's fiction has a bearing on the atrocities of the twentieth century. Kafka was exceptionally perceptive about the working of institutions in his own day. He shows how easy it is, if one works in an institution, to lose sight of any values beyond those promoted by the institution for its specific purposes. This attitude is illustrated not only by Josef K. but by the flogger, who says: "I've been hired to flog, and flog I will" (*T*, 83).[19] The concentration-camp workers who later asserted that they were only doing their job were not saying anything new; they were simply following out the logic of institutions, which Kafka had already explored.

This sounds deeply pessimistic. It seems that power and its ill-effects are omnipresent. But Kafka's vision may not be unrelievedly bleak. One of the most depressing aspects of institutions is that they gain their power from the acquiescence of their inmates. Just as the child, dependent on love and nurture from its parents, accepts their control unquestioningly and internalizes their standards, so adults inwardly acquiesce even in institutions that harm them. But that fact, which might seem to render them invulnerable, contains a germ of hope. For if one withdraws one's acquiescence, one can in theory deprive the institution of its power. In theory at least; it is much more difficult in practice. Kafka's aphorism about Atlas, the giant who in Greek mythology bore the world on his shoulders, runs: "Atlas was able to hold the opinion that if he wished he could drop the earth and slink away; but he was allowed no more than this opinion."[20] That is, Atlas's belief in freedom existed only in his head and could never have any effect on his life.

Kafka expresses obedience to authority as a double bind. An aphorism of 1917–18 formulates it like this:

> They were given the choice of being kings or king's couriers. Like children, they all wanted to be couriers. So now there are only couriers; they dash through the world, and as there are no kings, shout their meaningless messages to one another. They would gladly put an end to their wretched lives, but they dare not because of their oath of loyalty.[21]

There is no authority; it is by a human decision that there is no authority; yet people persist in living as if they were under authority, even though their lives are miserable and meaningless. But the exposure of this double bind is the first step toward overcoming it.

Still, that is only mental resistance. Does Kafka show any examples of practical resistance to authority? There is of course the traveler from "In the Penal Colony," whose refusal to support the use of the punishment machine must allow him, despite his hesitation, to count as a courageous liberal. But it is comparatively easy for him, since he comes from outside the system. A foreigner, he has not internalized the system of authority upheld by the officer. Josef K., by contrast, has been trained, as it were, by the hierarchy of the bank to slip easily into the alien hierarchy of the court. No wonder then that his initial attempts at resistance are histrionic, and that he increasingly succumbs to the power of the court, so that he is even ready and waiting for his executioners.

What about resistance in *The Castle*? Here the authority of the castle officials is supported, not by physical violence as with the court, but by ideology. The villagers are under a kind of spell that makes them believe in the quasi-magical authority of the castle officials, especially of Klamm. Klamm's name is invoked as though it were sacred. The authority of the officials seems to meet the most determined resistance, not from the combative K., but from Amalia, the sister of Barnabas. We are told how Amalia received a coarsely worded letter from a castle official, Sortini, summoning her to his bed. Unlike most village girls, who think such patriarchal condescension an honor, she refused. Ever since then her family have been ostracized by the villagers and have believed themselves to be in disfavor with the castle. They have spent many hours waiting by the roadside in the hope that an official would pass to whom they could plead for mercy. Amalia's sister Olga spends her nights in the stables with castle servants as their sexual plaything, hoping that one of them may utter something remotely helpful to the family's struggle for rehabilitation. Amalia meanwhile has become cold and withdrawn, devoted to tending her parents, who have been rendered prematurely decrepit by their grief at the family's disgrace.

Amalia's refusal has provoked much critical debate. Max Brod, who understood the castle as the abode of divine grace, thought that Sortini's invitation was a divine command that ought to have overridden ordinary morality. He compared it to God's inexplicable instruction to Abraham to sacrifice his son Isaac, which Kierkegaard in *Fear and Trembling*, a book well known to Kafka, took to illustrate the "teleological suspension of the ethical." Writing in the 1970s, in a close reading of *The Castle* that is for the most part exceptionally illuminating, Richard Sheppard questioned this interpretation but argued instead that Amalia was refusing "to live by the life forces within her personality."[22] Hence she becomes hard, cold, and reserved. For a long time I also inclined toward this view, but I now doubt it. Nor, however, do I want simply to accept the other and more obvious view that Amalia should be celebrated for her courageous feminine resistance to male tyranny, even though that would not be a false description of her conduct. I think that a more complex interpretation is possible. There is no sign that the castle has done anything to harm the family or has shown disapproval of Amalia's defiance in any concrete way. The family are the victims of their own belief in the authority of the castle. And this belief shows its destructive effects both in Olga's self-prostitution and in Amalia's emotional withdrawal. Amalia's rejection of Sortini's crude summons was indeed heroic, as her sister Olga says. It was a blow against the arrogant sexual exploitation practiced by the castle officials and sanctioned by tradition. But it was of limited value, because it was only negative. She still accepts the authority of the castle; having disobeyed that authority, she has nowhere left to go. She remains emotionally frozen, with nothing to do but tend her decrepit parents. Her refusal may have been an act of dignified self-assertion, but it is futile as long as her resistance to authority holds her trapped within the structures of authority. "Anyone who fights with monsters," says Nietzsche, "should take care that he does not in the process become a monster."[23]

But is there no other answer? Is resistance always futile? If so, another solution is suggested by Frieda, when she proposes to K. that they should simply leave the castle domain and emigrate: "If you want to hold on to me, we must leave and go somewhere else, to southern France or to Spain" (*C*, 136).[24] This reference to specific places has always struck readers as highly incongruous with the closed world of the castle and the village. We are not even told anything about where K. came from (except that it was a town with a church). It is strange to be reminded that outside the castle domain there is still our familiar geography. It feels like a sudden, unsightly tear in the otherwise seamless fabric of Kafka's fictional world. Adorno remarks that Kafka's stories take place "in the same spaceless space, and all holes are so tightly plugged that one shudders when anything is mentioned that does not fit in, such as Spain and southern France at one point in *The Castle*."[25] But perhaps this tear, this discordant reference, may reveal to us that Kafka's self-contained fictional world itself expresses the power of an institution. The institution wants to persuade its inmates that there is nothing outside, that there is no possibility of escape and nowhere to escape to. Yet this is an illusion, and one might say that it is the illusion that an ideology seeks to generate. Terry Eagleton expresses this wittily: "Ideological space is curved like space itself, and history lies beyond it as only God could lie beyond the universe."[26] Ideology, that is, seeks to persuade us not only that it is true but also that it is the *only* truth, and that any thought that disagrees with it is literally unthinkable. The institution that is the castle, with its attendant ideology of subservience to castle officials, seeks to persuade people that there is no space beyond its domains. Frieda's mention of France and Spain reminds us that there actually is a human world out there and that the worship of Klamm and Graf Westwest is a hideous illusion that one can shake off — simply by going away and turning one's back on it.

In the novel K. rejects this solution. "'I cannot go abroad,' said K. 'I came here in order to stay here.' And in a contradiction he didn't bother to explain, he added as if speaking to himself, 'Now what could have attracted me to this desolate land other than the desire to stay?'"[27] (*C*, 136). What stands out from this enigmatic passage is the word "desire." If K. is in part a rational person, trained in the mathematical technique of land surveying and keen to challenge the villagers' superstitious reverence for the castle, he is also an emotional person, subject to impulses that well up from beneath his conscious self and take him by surprise. We see this side of him, not only in this passage, but also in his self-abandonment while making love to Frieda and in the dream he experiences while dozing on Bürgel's bed. Such passages stand out by the emotional tone that Sheppard has rightly identified as "lyrical."[28] They point us to a profound emotional layer within K. that is free from the otherwise all-pervasive control of a total institution and its ideology, and can even encourage resistance to the institution.

In his recent biography, Peter-André Alt observes that Kafka's fiction sometimes anticipates events in his life.[29] The solution that Frieda urges in the novel — emigration — was the one that Kafka later adopted in reality, strengthened by a new emotional relationship. He first made the long-awaited break with Prague by moving, in the autumn of 1923, to Berlin, where he set up house with Dora Dymant. There, he and Dora made plans to emigrate to Palestine. Kafka had been interested in such plans for a long time; he had even discussed them with Felice Bauer on first meeting her in August 1912. But the importance of Palestine for him was that Zionism made it possible to escape from the tyranny of familiar institutions by establishing radically new forms of social living. Like many early Zionists, Kafka was attracted to Tolstoyan ideals of the simple, even ascetic life. As early as spring 1918 he noted down plans for a community of workers without material possessions, under the heading "The Propertyless Work-Force" (*NS2*, 105–7), which is evidently close to the kibbutz ideal.[30] His letters to Elli Hermann about progressive education confirm how keen he was to devise alternatives to the institutional structures that had dominated his own upbringing. His fiction dwells obsessively on confinement, yet his actual practice comes ever closer to a real escape from confinement — only frustrated by his death.

Notes

[1] George Steiner, "K," in *Language and Silence: Essays, 1958–1966* (London: Faber, 1967), 144.

[2] Alan Bennett, *Two Kafka Plays* (London: Faber, 1987), 9.

[3] A point forcefully made in James Hawes, *Excavating Kafka* (London: Quercus, 2008), 89.

[4] Efim Etkind, "Kafka in sowjetischer Sicht," in *Franz Kafka: Themen und Probleme*, ed. Claude David (Göttingen: Vandenhoeck & Ruprecht, 1980), 229–37.

[5] Günter Grass, *The Tin Drum*, trans. Ralph Manheim (London: Secker & Warburg, 1965), 15.

[6] "Es gehört ja alles zum Gericht." (*P*, 202)

[7] Erving Goffman, *Asylums* (1961; repr. Harmondsworth, UK: Penguin, 1968), 23–51.

[8] "Sie sind Zimmermaler?" (*P*, 61)

[9] "Das war kein Klient mehr, das war der Hund des Advokaten. Hätte ihm dieser befohlen, unter das Bett wie in eine Hundehütte zu kriechen und von dort aus zu bellen, er hätte es mit Lust getan." (*P*, 265)

[10] "Ich habe die Eltern immer als Verfolger gefühlt, . . . Nichts wollen die Eltern als einen zu sich hinunterziehn, in die alten Zeiten, aus denen man aufatmend aufsteigen möchte, aus Liebe wollen sie es natürlich, aber das ist ja das Entsetzliche" (*BF*, 112).

[11] "Gewiß das Wohnen bei den Eltern ist sehr schlecht, aber nicht nur das Wohnen, das Leben, das Hinsinken in diesem Kreis der Güte, der Liebe, ja Du kennst den Vaterbrief nicht, das Rütteln der Fliege an der Leimrute, . . . Einer kämpft eben bei Marathon, der andere im Speisezimmer, der Kriegsgott und die Siegesgöttin sind überall" (*BM*, 165).

[12] "Liebe Eltern, ich habe euch doch immer geliebt, . . ." (*DL*, 61).

[13] On these and other autobiographical constructions in Kafka, see Gerhard Neumann, "Kafka und Goethe," in *Franz Kafka und die Weltliteratur*, ed. Manfred Engel and Dieter Lamping (Göttingen: Vandenhoeck & Ruprecht, 2006), 48–65, esp. 51.

[14] Walter Benjamin, *Illuminations*, trans. Harry Zohn (London: Fontana, 1973), 115.

[15] See Hans-Ulrich Derlien, "Bürokratie in der Literatur und Soziologie der Moderne: Über Kafka und Max Weber," in *Die Modernität des Expressionismus*, ed. Thomas Anz and Michael Stark (Stuttgart: Metzler, 1994), 44–61.

[16] ". . . ohne genau zu wissen, was er meinte, schien es ihm, als ob durch die Vorfälle des Morgens eine große Unordnung in der ganzen Wohnung der Frau Grubach verursacht worden sei und daß gerade er nötig sei, um die Ordnung wieder herzustellen. War aber einmal diese Ordnung hergestellt, dann war jede Spur jener Vorfälle ausgelöscht und alles nahm seinen alten Gang wieder auf" (*P*, 30–31).

[17] See Paul Peters, "Witness to the Execution: Kafka and Colonialism," *Monatshefte* 93 (2001): 401–25.

[18] On the semantic range of "Apparat," see Astrid Lange-Kirchheim, "Franz Kafka: *In der Strafkolonie* und Alfred Weber: *Der Beamte*," *Germanisch-Romanische Monatsschrift* 27 (1977): 202–21.

[19] " . . . Ich bin zum Prügeln angestellt, also prügle ich." (*P*, 112)

[20] My own translation. "Atlas konnte die Meinung haben, er dürfe, wenn er wolle, die Erde fallen lassen und sich verschleichen; mehr als diese Meinung aber war ihm nicht erlaubt" (*NS2*, 80).

[21] My own translation. "Es wurde ihnen die Wahl gestellt, Könige oder der Könige Kuriere zu werden. Nach Art der Kinder wollten alle Kuriere sein. Deshalb gibt es lauter Kuriere, sie jagen durch die Welt und rufen, da es keine Könige gibt, einander selbst die sinnlos gewordenen Meldungen zu. Gerne würden sie ihrem elenden Leben ein Ende machen, aber sie wagen es nicht wegen des Diensteides" (*NS2*, 56).

[22] Richard Sheppard, *On Kafka's Castle: A Study* (London: Croom Helm, 1973), 157.

[23] Friedrich Nietzsche, *Beyond Good and Evil*, trans. Marion Faber (Oxford: Oxford UP, 1998), 68.

[24] " . . . Willst Du mich behalten, müssen wir auswandern, irgendwohin, nach Südfrankreich, nach Spanien" (*S*, 215).

[25] Theodor W. Adorno, "Notes on Kafka," in *Prisms*, trans. Samuel Weber and Shierry Weber (London: Neville Spearman, 1967), 256.

[26] Terry Eagleton, *Criticism and Ideology* (London: New Left Books, 1976), 95.

[27] "Auswandern kann ich nicht . . . ich bin hierhergekommen, um hier zu bleiben. . . . Was hätte mich denn in dieses öde Land locken können, als das Verlangen hier zu bleiben." (*S*, 215)

[28] Sheppard, *On Kafka's Castle*, 95–105.

[29] Peter-André Alt, *Franz Kafka: Der ewige Sohn; Eine Biographie* (Munich: C. H. Beck, 2005), 14.

[30] See Niels Bokhove, "'The Entrance to the More Important': Kafka's Personal Zionism," in *Kafka, Zionism and Beyond*, ed. Mark H. Gelber (Tübingen: Niemeyer, 2004), 46–47; Iris Bruce, *Kafka and Cultural Zionism: Dates in Palestine* (Madison: U of Wisconsin P, 2007), 170–73.

9: Kafka in Virilio's Teletopical City

Rolf J. Goebel

KAFKA'S ACTUALITY EMERGES from the ability of his texts to enlighten, explain, and subvert some of the most pressing issues in our global culture today. Nothing seems to resonate more acutely with today's culture than Kafka's persistent questioning of modern technologies of travel (railway, automobile, or airplane), audiovisual reproduction (photography, film, gramophone), and communication (telephone, telegraph).[1]

In a recent paper, Patrick Fortmann has shown how Kafka's "Little Automobile Story" elucidates the interconnections between modern traffic, circulation, and communication and his own acts of writing.[2] Moreover, Kafka's texts persistently respond to historic changes in technological media and their impact on collective ways of seeing and communicating in the age of high industrial capitalism and administrative efficiency. In his contribution to the Kafka@125 conference in April 2009 and in this volume, Peter Beicken has explored the intermedial connections between Kafka's literary writings and visual perception, focusing on how cinematic techniques and photography relate to Kafka's preoccupation with erotic desire and other psychological predispositions.[3] But instead of merely reproducing the function of other media mimetically (for example, adapting the visual montage technique of film or imitating the ambiguous verisimilitude or distortion of the gramophone's recorded voice), Kafka cites particularly (stereo)-typical details from these media's technological apparatuses, reconfiguring their possibilities and limitations through stylistic strategies that range from positivistic description without direct commentary or value judgments to satiric irony, comic exaggeration, and even slapstick. Although the technological media innovations of Kafka's age become the targets of social and moral critique, they are being employed and exploited foremost as literary material to be freely manipulated within the aesthetic parameters of the writer's artistic imagination and writing practice.

Kafka interrogates the new media technologies not through abstract theoretical reflection but through imaginary scenarios set in the minutely described hyper-realism of his preferred cities of modernity: Prague, Berlin, Paris, and New York. Here recording machines and telecommunication devices variously facilitate, impede, or manipulate human interactions, but what Kafka seems mostly interested in is the physical impact of the media's technological apparatus, which inscribes itself directly on people's psyche and even on the human body itself. By comparison, the content of these media — their processes of signification, their ideologies, and even their truth claims — appears subordinated to the media's materiality. This is why technological media messages in Kafka's works usually remain ambiguous, opaque, and elusive, evading any attempt by the denizens of Kafka's fictional cities to decipher them. Therefore, Kafka's cities of accelerated modernity are no longer primarily places for dwelling and working and for cultivating authentic experiences and lasting memories; instead, his urban spaces become rhizome-like functions of media technologies that always already exceed the individual's will, desires, and actions. In extreme cases, Kafka's media become autonomous and self-referential systems that seem to communicate among themselves for purposes not immediately discernible to the human users they no longer serve. It is this direct linkage between media diagnosis and urban topography that mediates between his time and our own, bridging the historical gap between European high capitalist modernity and the radical reconfiguration of urban space in the global age of digital communication.

One way of elucidating the anticipatory power of Kafka's modernism is by tracing the critical constellation between his media images and certain passages from Paul Virilio, perhaps the most important, if controversial, theorist of space, speed, and telecommunication today. Following (rather freely) Walter Benjamin's lead, I will work out this constellation by isolating brief but densely suggestive passages from Kafka that seem particularly predisposed to attaining their legibility today in the context of Virilio's analysis. It would be presumptuous to contend, of course, that such legibility in any way exhausts or fully unfolds the potential meaning of Kafka's passages. Virilio's theory, its assumptions, analytic statements, and prose style, carry with them their own temporal index, a specific ambience of temporality and evanescence, which marks the constellation between them and Kafka's texts as provisional, thus pointing to the continued exploration of Kafka's actuality as a dynamic process that does not reach interpretive closure in our present but reaches far into the future, where other readings and new interrogations await Kafka's work.

In *Vitesse de liberation* (*Open Sky*, 1995),[4] Virilio refers to a famous letter by Kafka to Milena Jesenská, dating from late March 1922, in which the writer self-reflexively problematizes the very act of epistolary communication.[5] Kafka suggests that letters are a treacherous form of pseudocommunication that shatters the soul and turns letter writer and recipient alike into specters. Letter writing necessitates one's perversely eroticized exhibition before these lustful ghosts who prey on their victims like vampires: "Written kisses don't reach their destination, rather they are drunk on the way by the ghosts" (*LM,* 229).[6] In the excerpt cited by Virilio (67), Kafka contends that humankind has invented the railway, the motorcar, and the airplane in order to eliminate the spectral alienation between people and to attain "natural communication" or "traffic" (Verkehr) and peace of mind. As Kafka implies, these modern means of transportation seem more natural than letters because they conquer space while preserving the integrity of the human body's experience of traveling through actual geographic territory. However, as he goes on to argue, this genuine but rapidly disappearing form of human interaction with space has been crushed by the successors to the postal service: telegraph, telephone, and wireless telegraphy. With the advent of these media, the emotional experience of bodily mobility through mechanical transport technologies gives way to the abstract (spectral) omnipresence of electrically transmitted signals, which, as Kafka suggests, disable any genuine contact among users: "The ghosts won't starve but we will perish" (*LM,* 229).[7]

For Virilio, Kafka's letter directly anticipates his own claim that "the development of telecommunication prosthetics accentuate[s] the 'ghostly dimension' of a vision of the world from now on computer-enhanced" (66). As he speculates, Kafka foreshadows the age of television and virtual reality, where the physical topography of the actual city of modernity gives way to globally interactive urbanity in hyperspace: "While the topical city was once constructed around the 'gate' and the 'port,' the teletopical *metacity* is now reconstructed around the 'window' and the teleport, that is to say, around the screen and the time slot" (26). In this transitional space from the mechanical/electric age of modernity to the electronic/digital time of postmodernity, the ontological differences between the real and the virtual, as well as the near and the far, are increasingly eliminated by instantaneous telecommunication and remote sensor/control devices. Contemporary radio technologies (digital signal, video signal, radio signal) lead to a de-realization of the human surroundings and the human body's relation to them: "For the staking out of the territory with heavy material infrastructure (roads, railroads) is now giving way to control of the immaterial, or practically immaterial, environment (satellites, fiber-optic cables), ending in the *body terminal* of man, of that interactive being who is both transmitter and receiver" (11). Virilio's stress on the "immateriality" of electronic telecommunication radicalizes Kafka's metaphor of the ghostliness of the electric precursors of these technologies, eliminating even the appearance of some kind of bodily presence still discernible in Kafka's terminology. The illusory telepresence of audiovisual information and the ability to extend one's body through long-distance control technologies in real time lead to the inability to distinguish between "here" and "elsewhere" and to the disappearance of traditional modes of traveling as a meaningful movement through actual space. For Virilio, even the transportation revolution of the nineteenth century, which for Kafka still protects the genuine experience of geographic space, devalues the notion of travel as an end in itself in favor of departure and arrival, thus anticipating the "instantaneous transmission revolution" of the twentieth century that leads to "*the generalized arrival of data*" in the technologies of television, telecommuting, and remote control (56). Ultimately, electronic devices dismantle authentic human experience altogether, which for Virilio is predicated on the sensory presence of the physical body in real urban space.

It is worth noting that Virilio cites Kafka's letter to Milena primarily to support his own critique of audiovisual telecommunication — "television and the reality of a virtual space that will allow us to interact long-distance and no matter what the distance from our neighbor" (67), whereas the letter itself focuses exclusively on modernity's text-processing and audio technologies (script, telegraph, telephone, and wireless). Virilio's shift accounts for postmodernity's predominantly visual orientation and its tendency to privilege technologies that combine visual, audio, and scriptural data (television, computer, mobile phone, and so on). In what follows, however, I will redirect this focus back to Kafka's original concern — the impact of audio technologies on human interaction and the presence of the human body and real space. This seems important, as it corrects Virilio's somewhat one-sided and decontextualizing appropriation of Kafka, and it counterbalances Kafka's own usual preoccupation with visuality, whether in the shape of textual *flânerie*, the meticulous recording of optical details and physical space, or his voyeuristic tendency to project erotic desire through intense gazing.

When read through Virilio's conceptual lens, Kafka emerges as one of the most astute observers of what one may call the disappearance of the autonomous human subject in the man-machine interface during the era of high capitalist industrialism. Kafka addresses this problem in a letter written in the night of 10–11 January 1913 to Felice Bauer, who at that time worked in the teeming capital of the German empire for the Carl Lindström Company, where she oversaw the marketing of the parlograph, an electric dictation device for office use.[8] Although Kafka is generally intrigued about the possibilities of ultramodern communication technologies, he is also afraid of them. As he notes, the parlograph exerts a stronger and crueler power over employees than a human being does. A human typist, Kafka notes, can easily be controlled, yelled at, or sent away. But when faced with the mechanical presence of the parlograph, the dictating manager is "degraded and becomes a factory worker whose brain has to serve a whirring machine."[9] By having his thoughts extracted from his brain mechanically, the dictating person is no longer the dictator in his own office. Instead he sees his authority subverted by the instrumental efficacy of a recording device that turns the medium of his administrative activities, the human voice, into lifeless electronic signals that require faraway secretaries in order to be transcribed into language again. Kafka concedes that one can regulate the speed of the apparatus at will or simply put it away, but these arguments are no refutations of the machine's lasting effects (*BF,* 149; *B2*, 30–31). Despite the seemingly lighthearted tone of his letter, Kafka senses that the dictating device has become a new dictator, that it reverses the traditional hierarchy of manager and machine, announcing not only the demise of the boss's patriarchal authority but also the end of the human subject's free agency in the administrative space of industrial modernity.

A few days later, the rather skeptical tone of this letter becomes, surprisingly, much more optimistic. In a letter to Felice dated 19 January 1913, Kafka complains as usual about the noise in his family's apartment and the unpleasant things that await him at the office next morning. Nonetheless, he is curious about specific details of Felice's own office work, such as requests from the factory foreman, telephone calls, and other such matters that preoccupy her. Then he wonders whether a public parlograph salon has already been installed in Friedrichstraße, Berlin's busy center of commerce and entertainment, and if not, when Felice will set one up. Kafka even proposes that hotels should be encouraged to offer not only telephones but also parlographs for their guests' convenience. He believes that he could have a thousand other such ideas while sitting in Felice's office with his head resting on her shoulder all day: significantly, Kafka's technological fantasies about disembodied communication devices are nurtured by, and in turn produce, his erotic projections upon Felice, whose body he does not desire and wants to keep at bay in faraway Berlin (*LF,* 162–63; *B2*, 49–50).

In the night of 22–23 January 1913, Kafka, part ironic technophile and part self-deprecating technophobe, spins out further details of his imaginative tale about the sheer endless expansion of technological communication media in the infrastructure of the modern metropolis.[10] He recounts a dream, in which, by chance, he picks up two telephone receivers from the parapet of a bridge or a quay. Pressing the instrument to his ears, he hopes to hear "news from Pontus," but hears nothing except a "sad, mighty, wordless song and the roar of the sea." He understands "that it was impossible for human voices to penetrate these sounds" (*LF,* 166).[11] As Gerhard Neumann argues, Kafka alludes here to Ovid, who was banished to the Pontus (Tomi, on the Black Sea) for his amorous literature and subsequently wrote about the unattainable world of love in distant Rome.[12] The traditional voice of poetic inspiration from antiquity, then, has been supplanted by the chance encounter with modern media technology that transmits signifiers without signification — a pure, self-referential kind of music without words that blends into the roaring of the sea, the primordial sound of nature.[13] From here on, Kafka will focus primarily on the technological apparatus of media systems, on their sheer physical materiality and direct impact on the human body rather than on the media's purported message. This focus leads him to propose some new ideas: a typing office where everything that is dictated into a Lindström parlograph is transcribed into typewritten script at cost price; coin-operated parlographs should be installed everywhere in the streets where one might find automats and mutoscopes (mechanical picture animation devices); as with mailboxes, the users should be given the exact time when the typescript of their dictation would be delivered to the post office by small cars owned by the Lindström company; parlographs should be introduced in all major post offices and even in railway carriages, on ships, in Zeppelins, and electric streetcars (*LF,* 167–68; *B2*, 56–57).

The increasing fragmentation of social life in the big city — its mass anonymity, competitiveness, incessant traffic acceleration, crime rates, and poverty — seems miraculously transfigured by a utopian dream of an immense network of interactive communication and transport media coupling technological knowhow and bureaucratic efficiency to satisfy (or create) new consumer desires. Kafka even predicts the invention of an interface between telephone and parlograph that will be of immense importance for editorial offices, news agencies, and so forth. As he admits, to add gramophones to this telephone-parlograph combination would be more difficult because "one can't understand a word the gramophone says, and a parlograph can't very well ask for clearer pronunciation."[14] In any case, he concludes, the connection between gramophone and telephone would be helpful only for people like himself, who are afraid of the telephone; unfortunately, however, since people like Kafka are also afraid of the gramophone, nothing could really help them at all (*LF,* 168; *B2*, 57). In this passage, despite the strange — and humanly estranging — ascendancy of new media networks, the human psyche and its language remain tenuously in place as criteria for measuring the success of the telecommunication system. Hinting at the psychological shortcomings of the machine-machine interface, Kafka retains his human obsession with the unequivocal transmission of the spoken word — the linguistic representation of the human soul — as the benchmark against which the self-correcting efficacy of the system reveals its limitations: the parlograph, although being able to receive dictation, cannot possibly ask the croaking and screechy gramophone for clear pronunciation.

Astonishingly, however, right in the next sentence, Kafka abandons this humanistic perspective: "Here, by the way, is a rather nice idea: a parlograph goes to the telephone in Berlin, while a gramophone does likewise in Prague, and these two carry on a little conversation with each other" (*LF,* 168).[15] As if coming straight from a Charlie Chaplin movie, Kafka's vision now no longer merely depicts the machine's uncanny tyranny over people but goes one radical step further, conjuring up the possibility of telecommunication empowering itself to annihilate its human users altogether. Kafka's scenario here is no longer preoccupied with the alienating dependency of people on machines that mechanically turn their speech into lifeless electric signals. Instead, he outlines the possibility that human agency may disappear altogether as it is being displaced by the self-sufficient alliance of robot-like parlographs and gramophones mimicking the telephone conversation that was once the prerogative of real human beings. Gerhard Neumann has noted that here living communication is being replaced by the networking of media, and the place of loving human subjects (like Kafka and Felice) is now occupied by the disembodied play of signs.[16] But what makes Kafka's scenario truly special is the idea that some privileged media (parlograph and gramophone) employ other subordinate ones (such as the telephone) to assert their own autonomy and power in the impending age of total intermediality. In Kafka's comedic snapshot, the traditional hierarchy of human user and technological medium appears to be more than simply reversed; the machines do not merely replace human agents but parody the very terms of interaction once reserved for their human predecessors: mutual instrumentalization in the name of enlightened consumer convenience and speedy communicative efficacy.[17]

What Kafka envisions in this passage is a technocratic universe of a post-humanistic age, where the only thing that counts is the self-referential technology of data transmission itself, that is, the purely formal connectivity of recording and reproduction devices for its own sake. Not the anxieties of human users or clear pronunciation or even the message itself are of any importance any longer, since Kafka does not waste a single word as to what it actually is that parlograph and gramophone may talk about. Perhaps there simply *is* no such topic; perhaps the two machines have nothing to converse about at all — at least nothing that a human being could possibly understand. Implicitly, the translation from machine language into human language (or *vice versa*) is a topic that Kafka excludes from his hyper-technocratic vision.

Here Kafka avoids any kind of morally motivated social critique; rather, he joyfully revels in his "rather nice idea" in purely aesthetic terms, even reiterating to Felice: "But dearest, the combination of parlograph and telephone simply must be invented" (*LF*, 168).[18] This willful suspension, not only of technical disbelief but of moral judgment, is important to remember for readers who — like Virilo — want to claim Kafka for their own political or ethical agendas. While the collusion of epistolary ghosts and electric telecommunication and the subordination of the office manager by the parlograph may indeed be themes that can be used to support Virilio's starkly pessimistic media critique, Kafka's fantasy of the telephone conversation between parlograph and gramophone cannot be so easily appropriated for moral ends. Kafka's discourse is always ambiguous, partial, and divided in itself, hence escaping any kind of totalizing inscription into the cultural regime of today, even if it anticipates some of our most urgent concerns.

A similarly ambivalent vacillation between social media critique and primarily aesthetic representation can be found in *Amerika: The Missing Person* (*Der Verschollene*, 1927). In the letters to Felice, the communication between gramophone and parlograph is still predicated on their physical mobility in urban space, on their imaginary ability to "go" to the telephone in Prague and Berlin for their chat. By contrast, Kafka's first novel envisions telecommunication as a means of technological efficacy that conquers metropolitan distances without having to participate in the city's economy of physical speed as it is embodied in chaotic traffic conditions in the seemingly never-ending streets.[19] The enormous business enterprise owned by Karl's uncle, the senator Edward Jakob, managing the trade of commodities and raw materials between large manufacturing cartels, relies on the "most precise and uninterrupted telephone and telegraph connections with its clients."[20] The hall is filled with the constant traffic of employees, and the doors of the innumerable telephone booths are continually opening and closing, while the ringing confuses all senses. But telecommunication itself seems to operate in a completely static manner of electrically induced efficacy. In one of the booths, Karl watches a telephone operator sitting in a "sparkling electric light," totally indifferent to the sounds coming from the door. His head is "tucked into a steel band that pressed the earpieces up against his ears. His right arm lay on a small table as if it were a heavy burden, and only the fingers holding a pencil twitched at a rapid and inhumanly regular pace" (*A*, 43).[21] Even the operator's voice no longer serves as the natural medium giving presence to the employee's thoughts and actions; instead, it is reduced to an intermittent kind of stuttering constantly stifled by the interlocutor's orders: "He spoke into the mouthpiece sparingly, and often one could even see that he perhaps wanted to object to something the speaker had said, or to ask him about something in more detail, but before he could do so, he heard further utterances that compelled him to lower his eyes and write" (*A*, 43–44, trans. modified).[22] As Karl's uncle explains, there is no real need for the operator to speak, since the transcript itself is simultaneously recorded by two other employees and then compared with the operator's own notes so as to avoid any errors (*A*, 44; *V*, 67).[23]

Kafka's novel marks the precise moment in modern urban history when the tangible dynamics of people and vehicles moving about in streets and office buildings is increasingly displaced by what Virilio calls the immateriality of telecommunication technology. This hostile takeover is exemplified by the disembodied, electrically transmitted human voice that captures the attention of the telephone operator completely, while captivating his virtually immobile body; the writing hand carries out its twitching action through a mechanical motion that seems no longer directly controlled by the man's brain and appears to be disconnected from his rudimentary speech. What causes the employee's dehumanizing alienation is less the anonymous mechanics of commercial transaction than the radical standstill to which he is being subjected by the man-telephone interface itself. Instead of functioning as a facilitating instrument in the hands of the operator, the telephone transforms the employee into a mere extension of itself.[24] As Wolf Kittler has noted, in this scenario, as in Kafka's "In the Penal Colony" ("In der Strafkolonie," 1914), humans are no longer speaking subjects able to understand and respond to the words coming from the telephone receiver; rather, they are transformed into media themselves, whose task it is merely to transmit and store messages as smoothly as possible.[25] Like the direct telephone conversation between the parlograph in Berlin and the gramophone in Prague, but without that scene's parody of human dialogue, the telegraph and telephone network in the uncle's enterprise seems essentially capable of executing the immense tasks of capitalist industry, commercial traffic, and bureaucratic efficacy without the intervening agency of the human subject. Here too, Kafka does not explicitly offer the traditional moral message of modernity that machines dehumanize people; rather, the text confines itself to a positivistic description of the external facts of telecommunication, of the physical workings of the technological apparatus and its human appendage. In so doing, the novel stages a fictional experiment, exploring the ramifications of media autonomy outside the ethical norms of modern bourgeois society. Therefore, Karl and his uncle do not directly comment on the scene before them; instead, the senator proudly explains the bare chronology of his remarkable business success; and when his nephew naively exclaims: "Well, that's almost miraculous," the senator states coldly that everything in America happens that quickly (*A*, 44).[26]

Whereas Kafka's hypermodern New York is founded on the real-time presence of the electrically dehumanized voice, Virilio's teletopical metacity is structured by the electronic telepresence of a digitized consumer society. Being telepresent means "being here and elsewhere, *at the same time*" in the "no-place of teletopical techniques (the man-machine interface, the modes or packet-switching exchanges of teletransmission" (10). Here the popular conveniences of remote control devices and instantaneous transmission technologies — television, home shopping, working on the computer from home, "online apartments and buildings" — do not necessarily make life easier but lead to a "*growing inertia*." Being even more instrumentalized than Kafka's telephone operator, Virilio's individual turns into a "*citizen-terminal* soon to be decked out to the eyeballs with interactive prostheses based on the pathological model of the 'spastic,' wired to control his/her domestic environment without having physically to stir." Suffering from technologically induced (physical and mental) paralysis, the individual loses his autonomy in actual space, abandoning himself "to the capabilities of captors, sensors and other remote control scanners that turn him into a being controlled by the machine with which, they say, he talks" (20).

In contrast to Kafka's cool suspension of direct moral messages, Virilio's critique of the electronically wired city of today is driven by the sociopolitical critique typical of enlightened humanism. For Virilio the malaise of the teletopical metacity is directly linked to the loss of the individual's capability for seeing material reality directly and authentically. In this context he quotes Kafka repeatedly as saying that "*Cinema means pulling a uniform over our eyes*" (91),[27] leading to a "standardization of vision" (94) that Virilio sees reappearing today in television (97), video, and the "digitized images of computer graphics" (91). For Virilio today's electronically (re-)produced images accelerate early film's tendency to standardize the viewer's perception. In order to combat this typical problem of the teletopical city, Virilio proposes a "gray ecology" analogous to the green ecology of nature protection. He advocates a new "*freedom of perception*" and even a "*right to blindness*" that are meant to combat the "industrialization of vision and of hearing" enforced by the omnipresence of modern media (96). Virilio's proposal stems from his fears that we may "lose our status as *eyewitnesses* of tangible reality once and for all" (91). His phrase evokes the early modernist desire to recover the possibility of an authentic perception of reality, as opposed to the standardization of the "natural" human gaze and voice by technological media industries.

Kafka was all too aware of this problem. On 20 November 1913 he notes in his diary that he has been to the cinema, where he was moved to tears but was also "tremendously entertained." He goes on writing: "Am entirely empty and meaningless (*sinnlos*), the passing trolley has more living meaning" (*D*1, 310; trans. modified).[28] Kafka emphasizes here that the movies trigger emotions that are superficial, evanescent, and illusory, and hence rob the viewer of his meaningful self-identity and self-consciousness as a subject, whereas the real, even when it too rushes by quickly, retains a genuine presence and authenticity that cannot be captured by media technology. The fact that Kafka attributes lively meaning directly to the electric tram, rather than treating that attribute explicitly as a product of the human gaze, is significant here.[29] Apparently the gaze suddenly focusing on the tram is not seen as projecting subjective sentiments onto the object; instead, the gaze ascertains the trolley's essential properties as a spontaneously natural act that Kafka does not have to explicate directly. He wants to be what Virilio identifies as an "eyewitness of tangible reality" at a time when this *flâneur*-like role was increasingly displaced by the modern media of technological reproduction and communication. Here, again, he anticipates Virilio's fear that instead of being authentic eyewitnesses of the real, we are turned into "visually challenged" people "afflicted with a kind of paradoxical blindness caused by overexposure of the visible and the development of *sightless* vision machines" of optoelectronics (91).

The technologically induced acceleration of urban space; desubjectivizing man-machine interfaces; the loss of actual space relations in real-time transmission processes; the disappearance of bodily movement and authentic experience through the static use of communication and remote control devices — these are obsessions that haunt Virilio as much as they did Kafka. This does not mean, however, that Kafka's modernity in any way fulfills itself teleologically in postmodernity; rather, postmodernity recognizes its own historical origins in a modernity that it ultimately tries to escape or supersede in vain — its technological innovations, social changes, and cultural differences notwithstanding. These anticipatory moments require that we do not confine our readings of Kafka's texts to a reconstruction of their meanings in their cultural and historical contexts alone but rather inscribe such philological hermeneutics into reinterpretations within the parameters of our own times.

Yet it is not only continuity in subject matter that warrants such readings but also formal attributes. Virilio's style — eschewing linear and fully developed analysis for brief, often allusive and repetitive fragments that seem as fleeting as the electronic media images and sounds they seek to criticize — mimics the characteristics of its subject matter in order to expose its shortcomings and dangers in the very materiality and movement of the written signifier itself. Although Kafka, too, explicitly evokes the media systems that he criticizes, and simulates some of their stereotypical techniques,[30] he designates his own media descriptions as a defense mechanism against newer, competing media that question the classical position of privilege held by writing as the primary repository of truth, beauty, and moral authority. Films claim to reflect visual phenomena more directly than the most meticulous narrative descriptions could; the gramophone may commonly be seen as recording the human voice more immediately than written transcripts of dialogues; and telephone and telegraph seem to cope with long distances faster and more efficiently than letters sent through the mail. But Kafka's texts compensate for such pragmatic shortcomings by *writing about* other media systems, critiquing the technical apparatus, social functions, and self-preserving ideologies of competing media on its — writing's — own terms, not on the indigenous terms set by technological media for themselves. This is the totalizing strategy that Kafka's writing devises in order to reclaim its endangered hegemony in the flourishing marketplace of accelerated media competition in the early twentieth century.[31] Diagnosing the rising domination of alternative media, Kafka's writing asserts its own role as a self-reflexive meta-discourse that represents other media more authentically and critically than they could or would represent themselves.[32]

Notes

[1] For the role of photography in Kafka's writing, see Carolin Duttlinger, *Kafka and Photography* (New York; Oxford UP, 2007). For Kafka's interest in film, see Hanns Zischler, *Kafka Goes to the Movies* (Chicago and London: U of Chicago P, 2003) and Peter-André Alt, *Kafka und der Film: Über kinematographisches Erzählen* (Munich: C. H. Beck, 2009). For Kafka's preoccupation with gramophone, telephone, and telegraph, see Wolf Kittler and Gerhard Neumann, eds., *Franz Kafka: Schriftverkehr* (Freiburg: Rombach, 1990). Informed by recent media theory following the work of Friedrich A. Kittler and others, the volume provides a wide-ranging discussion of the interrelations between Kafka's writing process and erotic life and the effects of media of technological reproduction and communication. My essay has significantly benefitted from this collection.

[2] Patrick Fortmann, "Driving, Riding, Running, Swimming: On Modalities of Media and Movement in Kafka's Writing," a paper delivered at the Kafka@125 conference, April 2009.

[3] See chapter 10 in this volume.

[4] Paul Virilio, *Open Sky*, trans. Julie Rose (London: Verso, 1997). All page references in the text are to this edition. See also the review by Douglas Kellner: "Virilio on Vision Machines," *Film-Philosophy* 2.30 (October 1998), http://www.film-philosophy.com/vol2-1998/n30kellner.

[5] For a comprehensive account of Kafka's letters to Milena in the context of traveling, writing, and modern technology, see John Zilcosky, *Kafka's Travels: Exoticism, Colonialism, and the Traffic of Writing* (New York: Palgrave-Macmillan, 2003), 153–73.

[6] "Geschriebene Küsse kommen nicht an ihren Ort, sondern werden von den Gespenstern auf dem Wege ausgetrunken" (*BM*, 302).

[7] "Die Geister werden nicht verhungern, aber wir werden zugrundegehn" (*BM*, 302).

[8] On Kafka's relationship with Felice in the context of media systems, see also Friedrich A. Kittler, *Aufschreibesysteme*, 4th ed. (Munich: Fink, 2003), 437–40.

[9] "entwürdigt und ein Fabriksarbeiter der mit seinem Gehirn eine schnurrende Maschine bedienen muss" (*B2*, 31).

[10] See also Gerhard Neumann, "'Nachrichten vom 'Pontus'": Das Problem der Kunst im Werk Franz Kafkas," in Kittler and Neumann, *Franz Kafka: Schriftverkehr*, 164–98; Neumann's comprehensive account situates Kafka's poetics and erotics within the ascendency of technological media.

[11] "Neuigkeiten vom 'Pontus'"; "traurigen mächtigen wortlosen Gesang und das Rauschen des Meeres"; "daß es für Menschenstimmen nicht möglich war, sich durch diese Töne zu drängen" (*B2*, 55).

[12] Neumann, "Nachrichten vom Pontus," 166–67.

[13] Neumann, "Nachrichten vom Pontus," 167.

[14] "weil man ja das Grammophon überhaupt nicht versteht und ein Parlograph nicht um deutliche Aussprache bitten kann" (*B2*, 57).

[15] "Übrigens ist die Vorstellung ganz hübsch, daß in Berlin ein Parlograph zum Telefon geht und in Prag ein Grammophon und diese zwei eine kleine Unterhaltung mit einander führen" (*B2*, 57–58).

[16] Gerhard Neumann, "Franz Kafka: Der Name, die Sprache und die Ordnung der Dinge," in *Franz Kafka: Schriftverkehr*, ed. Kittler and Neumann, 27.

[17] My literal reading differs from Neumann's interpretation of this passage as a poetological/erotic allegory of the writer, where the traditional voice of the Muse telling the poet the tale of love is replaced by the wordless song of media keeping the lovers' bodies apart while making possible the free but one-way distribution of signs, i.e., the writer's words reaching the distant ear of the woman ("Nachrichten vom Pontus," 173).

[18] "Aber Liebste die Verbindung zwischen Parlograph und Telephon muß unbedingt erfunden werden" (*B2*, 58).

[19] See also Mark M. Anderson's reading of *Der Verschollene*, emphasizing themes such as traffic, the destabilization of modern urban life, and cinematographic technique. Anderson, *Kafka's Clothes: Ornament and Aestheticism in the Habsburg* Fin de Siècle (Oxford: Clarendon, 1992), 98–122.

[20] "ganz genaue und unaufhörliche telephonische und telegraphische Verbindungen mit den Klienten" (*V*, 66).

[21] "sprühenden elektrischen Licht"; "eingespannt in ein Stahlband, das ihm die Hörmuscheln an die Ohren drückte. Der rechte Arm lag auf einem Tischchen, als wäre er besonders schwer und nur die Finger, welche den Bleistift hielten, zuckten unmenschlich gleichmäßig und rasch" (*V*, 66).

[22] "In den Worten, die er in den Sprechtrichter sagte, war er sehr sparsam und oft sah man sogar, daß er vielleicht gegen den Sprecher etwas einzuwenden hatte, ihn etwas genauer fragen wollte, aber gewisse Worte, die er hörte zwangen ihn, ehe er seine Absicht ausführen konnte, die Augen zu senken und zu schreiben" (*V*, 66–67).

[23] See also Alt, who reads this scene in the context of Kafka's cinematic way of writing, suggesting that the "sparkling electric light" surrounding the telephone operator is a metaphor of the filmic image flickering across the movie screen (*Kafka und der Film*, 70).

[24] One could make a comparison to Kafka's story "The Neighbor" here, as well, where the telephone, rather than facilitating business for its user, betrays his secrets to his neighbor and rival.

[25] Wolf Kittler, "Schreibmaschinen, Sprechmaschinen.: Effekte technischer Medien im Werk Franz Kafkas," in *Franz Kafka: Schriftverkehr*, ed. Kittler and Neumann, 116.

[26] "Das grenzt ja ans Wunderbare" (*V*, 68).

[27] Virilio here refers to a passage from Gustav Janouch's *Conversations with Kafka*, in which the writer is remembered as arguing that because of the rapid speed of the images, "cinema disturbs one's vision" and its pictures "flood one's consciousness": "The cinema involves putting the eye into uniform, when before it was naked." The authenticity of Janouch's account, of course, remains very much in

question. See Gustav Janouch, *Conversations with Kafka*, trans. Goronwy Rees, 2nd rev. and enlarged ed. (New York: New Directions, 1971), 160.

[28] "Maßlose Unterhaltung"; "Bin ganz leer und sinnlos, die vorüberfahrende Elektrische hat mehr lebendigen Sinn" (*T*, 595).

[29] For further comments on the role of the technologically mediated human gaze, see Beicken's contribution in this volume (chapter 10).

[30] For a theoretical analysis of such strategies of intermedial writing, see Irina O. Rajewsky, *Intermedialität* (Tübingen, Germany: A. Francke/UTB, 2002).

[31] On the historical changes of discursive systems between 1800 and 1900 and the competition between media technologies, see Friedrich A. Kittler, *Aufschreibesysteme*.

[32] Such meta-discursive representation of other media is typical of the intermedial form. It is also a special case of multimediality as a subcategory of intermediality. For a programmatic analysis of these terms, see Karl Prümm, "Intermedialität und Multimedialität: Eine Skizze medienwissenschaftlicher Forschungsfelder," in *Ansichten einer künftigen Medienwissenschaft*, ed. Rainer Bohn, Eggo Müller, and Rainer Ruppert (Berlin: Edition Sigma Bohn, 1988), 195–200.

10: Kafka's Visual Method: The Gaze, the Cinematic, and the Intermedial

Peter Beicken

KAFKA IS REMARKABLE, above all, for the visual density of his writing, a visual prowess that can be linked to his self-image as an "eye-person" (Augenmensch).[1] His extraordinary literary imagination generates an imagery that startles and challenges the reader who expects the recognizable. Kafka's intent, it has been said, is "to make strange the familiar."[2] Like his much admired model, Gustave Flaubert, he radically changed the fictional worlds that European realism had mapped out.[3] The transformative power of his writing, however, unlike Flaubert's, arises from the stark, suggestive force of his images: the resulting dynamics of puzzlement and shock reveal the crafty use of the gaze, cinematic techniques, and intermedial linkages. Many of Kafka's narratives rely on the gaze of the main characters; he employs cinematic means to structure the visual plane of his narratives; and he connects the elements of different media to produce an active exchange of medial domains.

Kafka found new means of representation. Metamorphosing the metaphor, he suspended its literalization.[4] The familiar seems fantastic, while the unfamiliar takes on the appearance of the normal and realistic.[5] Kafka's visuality uses innovative strategies and transformative techniques to create a literary and intermedial imaginary that is both realist and fantastic. He clearly privileges the perception and representation of the visual. Kafka critics have noticed the filmic quality of his texts, commenting also on his love of contemporary cinema, although the extent to which Kafka "goes to the movies" in his writing is in some dispute.[6] While some critics claim that Kafka's writings are not informed by the cinema, others see a significant intermediality.[7] Nonetheless, Kafka's "visual method" uses the main character as a narrative vehicle and center of perception, employing the cinema as a model and structuring principle. This results in a form of cinematic representation that asks the reader to experience a viewer's perception.[8]

Kafka often begins his narratives by inhabiting the position of observer. This is true for his earliest extant narrative, "Description of a

Struggle" ("Beschreibung eines Kampfes," 1936), an unfinished work, parts of which were probably begun in 1902.[9] Remarkable for its structural complexity and intricacy of theme and variations, this narrative strategically places the first-person narrator as passive observer at a Lenten party, making him the agent or focalizer of narrated perception.[10] This form of perception-based narration evolves into a "mono-perspectival" third-person narrative in "Wedding Preparations in the Country" ("Hochzeitsvorbereitungen auf dem Lande," 1907). The observational strategy manifest here for the first time continued in "breakthrough" works, such as "The Judgment" ("Das Urteil," 1912) and *The Metamorphosis* (*Die Verwandlung,* 1915). Subsequently, most of Kafka's narratives open with figures of observation, notably in the late novel *The Castle* (*Das Schloß,* 1926), where the main character approaches the opaque and inaccessible world of the castle by standing on a bridge looking up at the castle mount in the wintry fog (*C,* 1). The observational mode so prevalent in the beginnings of Kafka's narratives attests to his distinct visual inclination.

Kafka's preference for the observational mode starts out in "Description of a Struggle" as a variation of first-person narration. From the opening, there is an emphasis on figural stasis, with the narrator serving as observer and turning into a mobile focalizer, as he strolls the nightly city of Prague in the role of *flâneur.* However, while the narrator/observer is uneasily preoccupied with his companion, an acquaintance, a noticeable sexual tension exists between the two who are "cruising" the city. This anticipates situations of conflicted male-male relationships in Kafka's later works.[11] Insecure and anxious in his role as observer, the first-person narrator fears that his acquaintance will bludgeon him to death. No help seems available in the deserted streets as he watches a nearby policeman who appears totally self-absorbed, gliding on the icy pavement like a skater, hand on his sword and crowing with pleasure while oblivious to his surroundings.[12] Suggestions of a sexual, violent, and deadly nature abound, and the effect on the fearful *flâneur* is instantaneous; he misses a step and falls to the ground. Despite his physical incapacitation, he manages to train his scopophilic gaze on another suggestive scene as he looks at a fat woman who appears in the street only to be dragged back into a tavern by a lusting male.[13] The voyeuristic aspect of this scene is obvious, as is the eroticism that contrasts with the narrator's fear for his life. Both the physical pain of his hurt knee and his state of high anxiety dampen his voyeuristic pleasure. Trying to overcome his pain and anguish, the inebriated narrator fancies himself swimming in the air above ground and circling around one of the statues on the Charles Bridge as he and his acquaintance proceed on their way across the river to the Laurenziberg. In this elevated state, the previously stationary voyeur overcomes his impediment and seemingly achieves anew the status of mobile *flâneur.* He assumes an apparently superior stance until his flight and fantasy end with his being pulled down to earth by his acquaintance.

In addition to the faltering *flâneur*, Kafka conceives of a narrative observer who is in dire need of being looked at in order to feel noticed, accepted, and confirmed in his insecure existence. Take, for example, the supplicant, one of the permutated manifestations of the first-person narrator who craves the gaze of others.[14] Other main characters in Kafka's works are often made insecure by an opposing gaze that presents the threat of challenge, surveillance, and control.[15]

The observational situations involve *flânerie* and voyeurism, albeit in forms that differ from the traditional model of the Baudelairean city stroller who is both one with the crowd and, at the same time, set apart from the throng of humanity in the urban space.[16] Kafka enlists obstacles, inhibitions, and incapacitations that have a disabling effect on the main character as superior *flâneur*, although his status of camera-like observer is maintained.

In "Wedding Preparations in the Country" Kafka changes to a coherent third-person narration and "Einsinnigkeit," the figural perspective that became the hallmark of his writing. He also solidifies the observational mode by making the focalizer a consistent narrative camera that gives clear signals as to the subjective perception of the main character.

Eduard Raban's perspective shapes the presentation of the narrated events. Kafka's opening of this fragmentary novel ingeniously grounds the narrative perspective and creates what in film analysis is termed an "establishing shot." The main figure stands in an open doorway and watches the urban sphere outside, where it is raining, but not much. In a threshold situation between two different spaces, Raban appears like a figure arrested in transition as he takes in a visual field that is filled with moving images, dynamic and dense, detailed and deep, differentiated and delicate, detached and distanced. The wide-angled "establishing shot" has both depth of field and panoramic vision. Then there is the distinct zoom-in quality when the focus changes to detail, such as the tired, small dog on the outstretched arms of the little girl, or the lady's hat that is "heavily laden with ribbons, buckles, and flowers" (*CS*, 52).[17]

Unlike the strolling *flâneur*, Raban is fixed for quite some time in his stationary position, a narrative camera in stasis that records the hustle and bustle of urban life by compiling impression upon impression in the visual field.[18] Serving as camera-eye for narration, Raban's position as observer is not fully secure, as he is also the subject of observation. Watching a lady across the street, he assumes that he has become the object of her scrutinizing look (*CS*, 53; *NS*1, 13). It is remarkable that a woman's alleged gaze unsettles him: his uneasiness during this encounter with a representative of the "opposing world" (Gegenwelt)[19] creates anxiety and reveals his fragile state of being. Subsequently the narrative turns inward and ceases to register Raban's visual intake, instead relating his thoughts and his sense of insecurity, inadequacy, and infirmity. Fatigued and unhappy at the office, Raban sees himself as overworked, unappreciated, and estranged. His sense of alienation has reached crisis proportions and is not alleviated by his present trip to the countryside to join his fiancée, Betty, and his mother. His journey simply adds an unwanted burden.

The depiction of Raban's conflictedness shifts from visual perception to narrated monolog and interior vision. While Raban serves as narrative camera scanning the visual field, the subjectivization of his gaze is intensified by the "intermedialization" of the narrative. This process occurs very strikingly in Raban's daydream, an anticipation of Kafka's most stunning narrative, *The Metamorphosis*. In contrast to this later horrific tale, in this story Raban indulges in a wishful childhood fantasy of being a beetle lying in bed and separated from his body, which he commands as he would a servant to perform his unattractive daily obligations and chores. While this fantasy creates a space that helps Raban escape "matters that were dangerous" (*CS*, 55),[20] the regressive daydream anticipates the more elaborate interior *flânerie* of *The Metamorphosis*.

Kafka's "cinematic narration" (kinematographisches Erzählen)[21] intensifies the role of the main character as focalizer by using filmic means and techniques to visualize interior aspects of the figure. For example, in the scene where Raban is waiting at the train station in the countryside for a bus to take him to his final destination, he engages in small talk about the unfortunate weather with an official who "had put his right hand on his hip, and through the triangle formed by the arm and the body, Raban saw the girl, who had now shut the parasol, on the seat where she sat" (*CS*, 68).[22] The "triangle" described here serves as a means of directing Raban's gaze to fix on the girl. While the triangle resembles a mask frequently used in early cinema, Raban's gaze is guided to focus on an object of desire, the young female. A connection to Raban's psychological state and his erotic investment is suggested when his frustration about his unwanted journey to the countryside makes him realize his mistake: "he could have remained in town and spent an agreeable night at Elvy's" (*CS*, 68).[23] As the triangle focuses Raban's eroticized gaze on the girl as an object of desire, a link is created to the missed opportunity with Elvy, evidently a woman who provides the pleasures of the night.[24] Raban is now an immobilized, if not incapacitated, *flâneur* who longs for diversions in the *demi-monde*.

The eroticized gaze is strikingly evident in "The Passenger" ("Der Fahrgast," 1908). A signature prose piece of Kafka's observational mode of perception, this brief meditation or observation ("Betrachtung")[25] reflects life in the metropolis in the way that Georg Simmel described it in his seminal essay "Die Großstädte und das Geistesleben" (1903). Simmel examines the intensification of nervous stimulation, anonymity, tempo, acceleration, and the rapidity of life and relations, while focusing on aspects of circulation and the impact of the market and money economy on the life of the metropolis.[26] Kafka's man on the tram experiences the city as a place of insecurity and alienation, as this first-person observer is "completely unsure of my footing in this world, in this town, in my family" (*CS,* 388).[27] Uprootedness, anguish and *angst* mark this dispirited urban dweller, who sees himself completely isolated and lost.

The narrator's predicament does not prevent him from taking in the fascinating dynamics of city life in the midst of traffic. Standing on the platform of the tram, holding on to the strap that provides a measure of security for his body, the gazer scans the phenomena of the street scenes changing before his eyes as he is carried through the cityscape: people dodge the tram or walk quietly along or stand looking into shop windows while the tram passenger partakes vicariously in the diversions of consumer culture in the city through his gaze.[28] Then this male observer focuses voyeuristically on "a girl" ready to disembark at the next stop: "She is as distinct to me as if I had run my hands over her" (*CS,* 388–89).[29] The transgressive nature of the eroticized gaze is obvious. The imagined invasive touching of the female's body betrays a possessive, if not lewd, desire. The first-person narrator continues his intrusive examination of the female passenger, noting every detail of her appearance, such as her black clothes, the pleated skirt, the tight blouse, the fine-meshed white lace collar; her brown face, and various body parts, such as the nose that is slightly pinched at the sides and has a broad round tip; her brown hair and the stray little tendrils on the right temple. Then the male gaze focuses on the ear: "Her small ear is close-set, but since I am near her I can see the ridge of the whorl of her right ear and the shadow at the root of it" (*CS,* 389).[30] The visual "touching" of the female figure is charged with both erotic and aesthetic interest and proceeds like a slowly moving camera zooming in to take various close-up shots. As the gaze zeroes in on the ear, it invades an intimate body area and erogenous zone.

Kafka's "The Passenger" evidences a cinematic gaze consisting of the zoom and various close-ups montaged together. The cinematic vision that easily shifts from the observation of city life and the diverse street scenes to a close object of desire has not been previously noted and appreciated as such.[31] In his voyeuristic focus on the female, Kafka's tram passenger reminds us of the look in Baudelaire's famous poem "À une passante" from *Les fleurs du mal* (1861), which records the *flâneur*'s experience of rapture and anxiety in the "ecstasy of the streets" (Straßenrausch).[32] Though far more anxious and unsettled than Baudelaire's *flâneur*, Kafka's gazing city dweller gains some stability from the visual fixation on his object of desire, as his eroticized voyeurism combines with a scrutinizing aesthetic gaze that visually dissects the object of observation. The resulting process of virtual commodification, cinematic in its visual approach, is both possessive and transformative, as the human being is turned into an object for visual (and erotic) pleasure. The speaker's method of collecting individual "shots" like the eye of a camera transforms the visual field into a montaged image that creates a fantasy. In lieu of sexual penetration, it is the gaze that virtually invades the body, as is suggested visibly in the close-up of the ear. Upon fragile forms like the "stray little tendrils on the right temple" (*CS*, 389),[33] Kafka superimposes the compactness of the entire ear's roundness, which fades into the "shadow at the root" (*CS*, 389), an area of dark, secretive openness foreshadowed by the metaphor of the "Ohrmuschel" (literally "earshell"). Kafka's visual process in "The Passenger" resembles a film that takes the reader/viewer right into the mysteries of attraction, eros, and virtual sexuality in a way that is reminiscent of the suggestiveness and thrill of early cinematic spectacles of unusual attractions, exotic travels, melodramatic tales, erotic stimulation, and licentiousness.

Time and again, Kafka creates situations where the reader/viewer is confronted with stark and stunning threshold experiences. In "Absent-minded Window-gazing" ("Zerstreutes Hinausschaun") the reader is presented with a literary imaginary that calls for a mode of perception resembling a viewer's attitude in screening a film when the desires for visual pleasure, entertainment, and diversion amalgamate. The speaker/observer in Kafka's text appeals to the reader/viewer to perceive the visual changes in the cityscape and consider questions of meaning as well. Daylight fades into sunset, and, accordingly, this poetically structured text shifts its main focus from the weather of a spring day and the gray sky of morning to the light of the setting sun on a face, all topped by a visually stark street scene.[34] A little girl ("kindliches Mädchen") is rapidly approached and overtaken by a man who, for a moment, casts a shadow on her face that at the same time is lit up by the light from the setting sun: "at the same time you see her eclipsed by the shadow of the man behind overtaking her. And then the man has passed by and the little girl's face is quite bright" (*CS*, 187).[35] The German phrase "kindliches Mädchen" emphasizes an innocent being, while the brightness of her face adds to this impression, figuratively, a halo-like shine. Strangely enough, the girl is on a stroll by herself, and she looks over her shoulder, as the man, potentially a present danger, approaches rapidly. The nearing of an apparent menace recalls the street encounters of early cinema that often show women subjected to violence.[36] In depicting a cast shadow and the brightening of the girl's face after the passing of the man, Kafka creates a special screen-like event. Unlike the montaged shots in "The Passenger," the viewing by the observer/speaker is continuous and supports the screen effect of the seen/scene events: it is the viewer's perspective, uninterrupted, that perceives the light from the sinking sun on the girl's face, her turning backward to look over her shoulder, while the narrative statement "and at the same time you see the shadow of the man who is approaching more rapidly" makes the continuity of the speaker's viewing fully evident. The "gaze guidance" (Blickführung) allows for no break in perspective, no stitching together or suture of separate "shots." Not for a single moment does the narrative switch to the girl's perspective or the man's point of view.[37]

In "Absent-minded Window-gazing" Kafka brings to light a spectacular moment: the birth of film out of shadowplay. As the gray skies represent a state of undifferentiated light, Kafka proceeds to focus on the gazer, who is surprised by the changing visual field and then relaxes, while leaning on the window handle and holding the classical position of the stationary *flâneur*. Like E. T. A. Hoffmann in "My Cousin's Corner Window" ("Des Vetters Eckfenster"), Kafka privileges the human gaze as a selecting and zooming apparatus of cinematic significance.[38] The reader/viewer takes in the story of the girl, her being eclipsed and overtaken by the passing man, as a shadowplay forming the primal scene of cinema.

Kafka's narrative screen effect often features a window or mirror. In "The Street Window" ("Das Gassenfenster") the speaker is described as a loner and thus solitary. To overcome the predicament of isolation, he envisions stepping to the window but is reluctant to let his gaze roam freely.[39] In the end, horses from the busy street "draw him down into the train of wagons and tumult, and so at last into human harmony" (*CS*, 384).[40] As the speaker hesitates to be integrated, the stationary position at the window is dissolved into a "Straßenrausch" that ensues from the tumultuous life in the street. Seen as a cinematic event, "The Street Window" skirts the "birth of cinema out of shadowplay" pictured in "Absent-minded Window-gazing." Instead Kafka envisions a "tired man" whose exhausted gaze involuntarily pans from the street throng ("Publikum") to the sky ("Himmel," *DL*, 32). The concept of "public" suggests an audience poised to watch a performance that comes in the form of a tumultuous event hardly to be understood in a literal sense. The observer being pulled from his window post by horses symbolically addresses the intense visual identification process germane to film: the rapture at viewing moving images. Here, the visual power of a riotous street scene transports the viewer into film-like action reminiscent of the "stupor and shock" of early cinema that was so appealing to audiences and caused them to experience a powerful identification with the moving pictures; in particular the fascination with motion and melodrama that Kafka frequently surrendered to in a state of intense emotional upheaval.[41]

Cinema, in its origin a shadowplay, deeply impacts the affective domain. Kafka uses mirrors for similar screen effects by staging an intense interior visual fantasy or cinematic event. In "The Tradesman" ("Der Kaufmann") (*DL*, 21–24; *CS*, 385–86), repressed psychic energy and visual release are closely linked when the troubled tradesman returns home from the travails of his small business filled with unending worries. Literally getting a "lift" in the elevator, he fixes his "gaze into the narrow looking glass" (*CS*, 386).[42] Instantly, he addresses the mirror as if conjuring up events before his eyes. Acting as the classical "live narrator" (Kinoerzähler), who was a common narrator/commentor at silent film screenings, the tradesman invokes a stream of moving images with rapid-fire commands and questions. Addressing winged creatures, he seems to summon mythological figures of fantasy that are supposed to enjoy "looking out of the window" (*CS*, 386) as processions converge on squares while "the beautiful lady" (*CS*, 386)[43] drives past. These urgent appeals stimulate the reader's fantasy. Positioned at the window high above the crowds and multiple actions down below, the tradesman scans with voyeuristic pleasure the events that take place. His look into the mirror and interior monolog with exhortations trigger the inner cinema that reels off its film of the city as a place of modernity: the actions, visuals, sights, movements, rhythms, dynamics, and thrills of the urban sphere are sutured into a magnificent spectacle. This breathtaking show of moving pictures ends abruptly as the lift stops and the tradesman enters his apartment. But the grand effect of this "pictorial rush" (Bilderrausch) lingers in the reader's imagination.

The tradesman's view into the mirror reveals the screen event as a self-encounter that is similarly played out in an even more stunning enactment in "Unhappiness" ("Unglücklichsein"; *DL*, 33–40; *CS*, 390–94). Here the look into the mirror produces not an inner film of flowing images but the emergence of a child "like a small ghost" (*CS*, 391).[44] As the cinema of self-encounter unfolds, the theatricality of meeting the "apparition" (Erscheinung) (*DL*, 39) turns this scene into a comedy of errors. The verbal back and forth between the self and the apparition reveals a miscommunication that remains unresolved in the conversation with the neighbor whom the first-person narrator meets in the stairwell. The cinematic melodrama ceases as the ghostlike appearance fades out of sight and the screen darkens: the self goes to sleep. A sense of loneliness remains. No dreams or nightmares are recollected and no images like rushes of film pictures are conjured up.

The visually ravishing opening paragraph of "The Stoker" ("Der Heizer," 1913), the only part of the novel fragment *Amerika: The Missing Person* (*Der Verschollene*, 1927) that Kafka published, is equally film-like. The first part of the introductory sentence telescopes the pre-history of the protagonist's misfortune, his having been seduced by a servant into fathering a child and his subsequent banishment by his parents. The continuation depicts how Karl Roßmann sails into the harbor of New York and sees the "statue of the Deity of Liberty" (Statue der Freiheitsgöttin) as a sudden burst of sunlight lights up her arm with the "sword" (Schwert, *DL*, 65) reaching aloft, and the free winds blow around her figure. Though traumatized by his exile, Karl serves as narrative camera stationed on deck, and the slowing ship provides a steady movement for this camera eye that takes in a panoramic view of the harbor before zooming in on the re-mythologized Statue of Liberty. Kafka's imaginatively refigured "Deity of Liberty" displays the attributes of a vengeful justice that remind the youngster of the transgression and defeat he suffered at the hands of the female cook. Kafka employs a kind of breathtaking cinematic zoom to engage the reader/viewer in focusing on the glistening sword that soars into the skies as a token of nemesis.[45]

Kafka's remarkable affinity to the cinema, which predates his actual familiarity with films, is already evident in his early development of cinematic narration. In his depiction of the visual, he used elements like the gaze, gaze guidance, camera eye, moving camera, changing camera angles, zoom, sequencing, interior film and the positioning of a figure as narrative camera in portals and windows as well as stationing the character on moving objects such as a tram, train, a boat, etc. As Kafka subsequently "went to the movies," he learned how to incorporate additional film elements and structures into his narratives beyond the cinematic culture of the gaze in his early works.

In *The Trial* (*Der Process*, 1925), the culture of the gaze and Kafka's camera eye do not go unchallenged. The "opposing world" is a powerful agent representing a watchful society and mostly invisible court, both transcending the ordinary. When Josef K. awakens, he immediately notices being observed by an old woman across the street from his room. Very soon an old man appears, and the couple is joined by a younger male figure, a bearded fellow who seems to be a son figure. To K. the threesome appears as a family icon of the heterosexual society or "Gesellschaft," as the three are called. Their intense observation irritates him severely. He senses it to be a form of obtrusive surveillance that increases as the party "over there" follows, in the way of cinematic parallel action, his every step from his room through the room next door to Fräulein Bürstner's room, where K. is interrogated by the "overseer" (Aufseher).[46] Clearly, K. is exposed to the hostile social gaze of the "opposing world" that disapproves of his being and life style. When the trial wears K. down in the unfinished chapter "The Building" ("Das Haus"), he feels confronted by "two totally unknown eyes" (*T*, 261–62)[47] that make him seek refuge in the antichamber of the court building, where he observes a dancer-like "bullfighter" (Stierfechter) whose exotic clothes, particularly the laced "little jacket" (*T*, 262; Röckchen, *P*, 350) and androgynous appearance, fascinate him. The suggestive masquerade leaves him aghast. Infatuated with the eroticized object of his desiring gaze, he seeks comfort in a daydream in which he encounters the court painter Titorelli, to whom he makes advances. The unfolding interior *flânerie* leads to a cinematic revelry with a remarkable "gaze guidance" and "lighting" (Lichtführung) as K. experiences the epiphany-like moment of his "transformation" that changes his gender identity, a change visibly indicated by the new clothes he wears.[48]

Kafka's visual method, striking in its spectacular form and impact, developed before his encounter with the cinema that began around 1907–8. The experience of the movies, however, was exhilarating and had a profound impact on his imagination and writing. Film's amazing intermediality confirmed his affinity to visual perception and cinematic representation. Kafka created a culture of seeing that enabled him to transform narration through the incorporation of cinema's intermediality into his narratives. Using his main characters as visual focalizers, he turned them into special perceivers that function as camera eyes. The mono-perspectival narrative perspective is unique to Kafka's work, and the intermediality of the visual method in his works exhibits a truly remarkable cinematic quality throughout.[49]

Notes

[1] Gustav Janouch, *Gespräche mit Franz Kafka* (Frankfurt am Main: Fischer, 1961), 105. "Eye-Person" is my replacement for "Eye-Man" in Gustav Janouch, *Conversations with Kafka*, trans. Goronwy Rees, 2nd, enl. ed. (New York: New Directions, 1971), 160.

[2] Stanley Corngold, "Kafka's *The Metamorphosis*: Metamorphosis of the Metaphor," in *Franz Kafka, The Metamorphosis*, trans. and ed. Stanley Corngold (New York: Norton, 1996), 88. For Kafka's "estrangement," see Walter Benjamin, "Franz Kafka: On the Tenth Anniversary of His Death," in *Illuminations: Essays and Reflections*, ed. Hannah Arendt (New York: Schocken, 1968), 111–40.

[3] Charles Bernheimer, *Flaubert and Kafka: Studies in Psychopoetic Structure* (New Haven, CT: Yale UP, 1982).

[4] See Corngold, "Kafka's *The Metamorphosis,*" and the works of Walter H. Sokel he quotes.

[5] Cf. TzvetanTodorov, *The Fantastic: A Structural Approach to a Literary Genre*, trans. Richard Howard, with a new foreword by Robert Scholes (Ithaca, NY: Cornell UP, 1975).

[6] Regarding Kafka's visual inclination and interest in the cinema, see Wolfgang Jahn, *Kafkas Roman "Der Verschollene" ("Amerika")* (Stuttgart: Metzler, 1965), 32–67. Bettina Augustin, "Raban im Kino.: Kafka und die zeitgenössische Kinematographie," *Schriftenreihe der Franz-Kafka-Gesellschaft* 2 (Wien: Braumüller, 1987), 38–69. Peter Beicken, "Kafkas visuelle Methode," in *Franz Kafka: Der Process*, 2nd rev. ed. (1999; repr., Munich: Oldenbourg, 2005), 162–71. Hanns Zischler, *Kafka Goes to the Movies*, trans. Susan H. Gillespie (Chicago, London: U of Chicago P, 2003). Contrary to Jahn's observations of Kafka's use of cinematic means such as visual continuity and gestures, "intercut images" (Zwischenbilder), "dynamic montage" (Bewegungsmontage), and "parallel action" (Parallelmontage), Zischler claims: "In the prose, cinematography is not thematized either as a technique or as an image; it remains oddly excluded, as if Kafka, in distinct contrast to

many writers of his generation, doubted its ability to be turned into literature. That cinematic images, artfully camouflaged, have entered into the slapsticklike despair of Karl Rossmann, for example, cannot be automatically excluded, but the evidence for this fact, which has meanwhile assumed the status of near-certainty, is nowhere to be found" (107). For Kafka's preference for photographs and pictorial representation see Carolin Duttlinger, *Kafka and Photography* (Oxford: Oxford UP, 2007).

[7] For additional studies see Dietmar Schings, *Franz Kafka und der Mann ohne Schatten: "Eiserne Fensterläden"— Kafka und das Kino* (Berlin: Vorwerk 8, 2004); and Peter-André Alt, "Im Kino," in *Franz Kafka: Der ewige Sohn; Eine Biographie* (Munich: Beck, 2005), 214–19. Following Zischler, Oliver Jahraus claims: "Neither film nor cinema — whether as theme or medial means of representation or institution — is of obvious significance for his [Kafka's] literature." Oliver Jahraus, "Kafka und der Film," in *Kafka Handbuch*, ed. Bettina von Jagow and Oliver Jahraus (Göttingen: Vandenhoeck & Ruprecht, 2008), 224. Most recently, Peter-André Alt, *Kafka und der Film: Über kinematographisches Erzählen* (Munich: C. H. Beck, 2009); and Anne Brabandt, *Franz Kafka und der Stummfilm: Eine intermediale Studie* (Munich: Meidenbauer, 2009). Regarding *Der Verschollene*, see Johannes Roskothen, *Verkehr; Zu einer poetischen Theorie der Moderne* (Munich: Fink, 2003), 239–45. On Kafka's "filmic writing" (filmische Schreibweisen) see Carolin Duttlinger, "Film und Fotografie," in *Kafka-Handbuch: Leben, Werk, Wirkung*, ed. Manfred Engel and Bernd Auerochs (Stuttgart: J. B. Metzler, 2010), 72–79.

[8] For elaborations on Kafka's visuality, his cinematic gaze and imaginary, and the cinematic *flânerie* in his works, see Peter Beicken, "Kafka's Gaze/Gays," *Journal of the Kafka Society of America* 23. 1+2 (Jun./Dec. 1999 [2002]): 3–22; "Kafka's Mise-en-Scène: Literary and Cinematic Imaginary," *Journal of the Kafka Society of America* 24.1–2 (Jun/Dec. 2000 [2003]): 4–11; and "Le flâneur de Kafka: Regard, image, vision cinématographique," *Europe* 84.923 (Mar. 2006): 160–83.

[9] See "Fassung A" (1907–8) and "Fassung B" (1909–10) respectively (*NS*1, 54–171). "Description of a Struggle" (*CS*, 9–51) is based on Max Brod's edition, which alters both versions to create one unreliable text.

[10] On Kafka's narrative perspective see Peter Beicken, "Perspektive und Sehweise bei Kafka," (PhD diss., Stanford U, 1971); and Dirk Oschmann, "Kafka als Erzähler," in Engel and Auerochs, *Kafka-Handbuch*, 438–49. On perspectivization see Franz K. Stanzel, *A Theory of Narrative*, trans. Charlotte Goedsche, preface Paul Hernadi (Cambridge: Cambridge UP, 1984), 123. For focalizer, focalizing see Mieke Bal, *Narratology: Introduction to the Theory of Narrative*, 3rd ed. (1985; repr., Toronto: U of Toronto P, 2009); and Luc Herman and Bart Vervaeck, *Handbook of Narrative Analysis* (Lincoln: U of Nebraska P, 2005).

[11] Gregory Woods observes "sudden, unpremeditated outbursts of intimacy and/or aggression between men." Gregory Woods, *A History of Gay Literature: The Male Tradition* (New Haven, CT: Yale UP, 1998), 227.

[12] For the scene with the policeman see "Fassung A" of "Description of a Struggle" ("Beschreibung eines Kampfes"; *NS*1, 66; *CS*, 17).
[13] See *NS*1, 67 and *CS*, 18.
[14] See "Beginning of a Conversation with the Supplicant" ("Begonnenes Gespräch mit dem Beter") where the supplicant states: "The purpose of my praying is to be looked at by people" (passage omitted in *CS*, 33). ("Der Zweck meines Betens ist von den Leuten angeschaut zu werden"; *NS*1, 89).
[15] On the controlling gaze see Beicken, "Kafka's Gaze/Gays"; "Kafka's Mise-en-Scène"; and "Le flâneur de Kafka."
[16] Charles Baudelaire, *The Painter of Modern Life and Other Essays*, trans. and ed. Jonathan Mayne, 2nd ed. (New York: Phaidon, 1995).
[17] "Da erblickte man eine Dame, deren Hut viel beladen war mit Bändern, Spangen und Blumen" (*NS*1, 12).
[18] For a precursor see E. T. A. Hoffmann, "My Cousin's Corner Window," in *The Golden Pot and Other Tales*, new trans. Ritchie Robertson (Oxford: Oxford UP, 1992), 377–401. See also Beicken, "Kafkas visuelle Methode," 164. For a study of the camera eye in the modern novel, see Alan Spiegel, *Fiction and the Camera Eye: Visual Consciousness in Film and the Modern Novel* (Charlottesville: U of Virginia P, 1976).
[19] For the concept of "Gegenwelt" see Martin Walser, *Beschreibung einer Form. Versuch über Franz Kafka* (Munich: Hanser, 1961).
[20] "bei gefährlichen Geschäften" (*NS*1, 17).
[21] Alt, *Kafka und der Film*. Alt overlooks Beicken's case for Kafka's "filmische Sehweise," "Erzählkamera," and "filmisches Inszenieren." Beicken, "Kafkas visuelle Methode," 162–71.
[22] "Der Beamte hatte die rechte Hand an die Hüfte gelegt und durch das Dreieck, das zwischen dem Arm und dem Körper entstand, sah Raban das Mädchen, das den Schirm schon geschlossen hatte, auf ihrer Bank" (*NS*1, 37).
[23] "hätte recht gut also noch in der Stadt bleiben und bei Elvy eine angenehme Nacht verbringen können" (*NS*1, 38).
[24] For the eroticized, privileged male gaze see Laura Mulvey, "Visual Pleasure and Narrative Cinema," *Screen* 16.3 (Autumn 1975): 6–18.
[25] *The Complete Stories* (*CS*) renders Kafka's title "Betrachtung" as "Meditation" (*CS*, 473). Edward Timms suggests that "the prose sketches of *Betrachtung* are so sharply observed that the English title might well be 'Observation' rather than 'Meditation.'" Edward Timms, "Musil's Vienna and Kafka's Prague: The Quest for a Spiritual City," in *Urban Experience in Modern European Literature and Art*, ed. Edward Timms and David Kelly (New York: St. Martin's, 1985), 260–61.
[26] Georg Simmel, "Die Großstädte und das Geistesleben," in *Aufsätze und Abhandlungen, 1901–1908*, ed. Rüdiger Kramme, Angela Rammstedt, and Otthein Rammstedt, vol. 1, vol. 7 of *Georg Simmel Gesamtausgabe*, ed. Otthein Rammstedt (Frankfurt am Main: Suhrkamp, 1995), 116–31; "The Metropolis and Mental Life," in *Simmel on Culture*, ed. David Frisby and Mike Featherstone (London: Sage Publications, 1997), 174–85.

[27] "vollständig unsicher in Rücksicht meiner Stellung in dieser Welt, in dieser Stadt, in meiner Familie" (*DL*, 27).

[28] See Charles Baudelaire, *The Painter of Modern Life*; and Walter Benjamin, "The Flâneur," in *The Arcades Project*, trans. Howard Eiland and Kevin McLaughlin (Cambridge, MA: Harvard UP, 1999), 416–55. For a feminist view see Anne Friedberg, *Window Shopping: Cinema and the Postmodern* (Berkeley: U of California P, 1993).

[29] "Sie erscheint mir so deutlich, als ob ich sie betastet hätte" (*DL*, 27).

[30] "Ihr kleines Ohr liegt eng an, doch sehe ich, da ich nahe stehe, den ganzen Rücken der rechten Ohrmuschel und den Schatten an der Wurzel" (*DL*, 28).

[31] Erward Timms states: "Under Kafka's gaze, the routine experience of the city commuter becomes an existential challenge." Timms, "Musil's Vienna and Kafka's Prague," 261. Robert Alter observes a suggestion of erotic violence. Robert Alter, "Kafka: Suspicion and the City," in *Imagined Cities: Urban Experience and the Language of the Novel* (New Haven, CT: Yale UP, 2005), 144. Alt speaks of a "an uncut camera movement as it were" (gleichsam ungeschnittenen Kamerafahrt) when, in fact, closely related "shots" are montaged together (Alt, *Kafka und der Film*, 40).

[32] See Eckhardt Köhn, *Straßenrausch: Flanerie und kleine Form; Versuch zur Literaturgeschichte des Flaneurs bis 1933* (Berlin: Das Arsenal, 1989).

[33] "verwehte Härchen an der rechten Schläfe . . ." (*DL*, 29).

[34] "Frühlingstage"; "früh war der Himmel grau"; "das Licht der freilich schon sinkenden Sonne auf dem Gesicht" (*DL*, 24–25).

[35] "kindliches Mädchen"; "zugleich sieht man den Schatten des Mannes darauf, der hinter ihm rascher kommt. Dann ist der Mann schon vorübergegangen und das Gesicht des Kindes ist ganz hell" (*DL*, 24–25).

[36] Kafka saw male violence against a female in the Danish film *Die weiße Sklavin* (*Den hvide slavehandel sidste offer*), *The White Slave Girl*, in Prague in 1911. The heroine is being forced into service at a bordello. See Zischler, *Kafka Goes to the Movies*, 33–34.

[37] Erroneously, Alt sees a change in perspective and thinks the filmic sequence stitched together from successive images/shots. Alt, *Kafka und der Film*, 38.

[38] For "My Cousin's Corner Window" see Beicken, "Kafkas visuelle Methode," 164.

[39] Reluctant to pursue visual pleasures, this window-*flâneur* is not a voyeur, as Alt claims (*Kafka und der Film*, 43).

[40] "reißen ihn doch unten die Pferde mit in ihr Gefolge von Wagen und Lärm und damit endlich der menschlichen Eintracht zu" (*DL*, 32).

[41] Zischler, *Kafka Goes to the Movies*, 9.

[42] "schaue . . . in den schmalen Spiegel" (*DL*, 23).

[43] "die Aussicht des Fensters" . . . "die schöne Dame" (*DL*, 23).

[44] "als kleines Gespenst" (*DL*, 34).

[45] Alt discusses the "camera eye" but ignores the distinct camera zoom (*Kafka und der Film*, 94).

[46] For linking cinematic parallel action and the social gaze see Beicken, "Kafkas visuelle Methode," 166–71. For surveillance see Michel Foucault, *Discipline and Punish: The Birth of the Prison*, trans. Alan Sheridan (New York: Vintage Books, 1995). For the "Stierfechter" episode see Beicken, "Le flâneur de Kafka."

[47] "ihm zwei gänzlich fremde Augen" (*P*, 349).

[48] "Verwandlung," in Kafka, *Der Proceß: Apparatband*, ed. Malcolm Pasley (Frankfurt am Main: S. Fischer, 1990), 346.

[49] Alt's *Kafka und der Film*, though problematic at times in its analyses, confirms that Kafka thoroughly incorporated intermediality into his narratives and literary imaginary.

11: "Samsa war Reisender": Trains, Trauma, and the Unreadable Body

John Zilcosky

FRANZ KAFKA ONCE CLAIMED that all human beings were caught between two competing technological systems: one sponsoring "ghostly" absence (the postal system, telegraph, and telephone) and one encouraging "natural" presence (trains, planes, and automobiles). To humanity's woe, the ghostly side was winning: "To attain a natural intercourse, a tranquility of souls, [humanity] has invented the railway, the motor car, the aeroplane — but nothing helps anymore: These are evidently inventions devised at the moment of crashing" (*LM*, 223; *BM*, 302).[1] Kafka famously spent most of his life on the side of the ghosts, sending Felice Bauer up to three letters per day for weeks on end, yet never boarding a train that would have brought him to Berlin in a few hours. This question — Why does Kafka not get on a train? — recurs for media theoreticians, and their answer is clear: Kafka, the techno-wizard, wants to create a literary "feedback loop" (Endlosschleife) rivaling those produced by films, gramophones, and parlographs.[2] But this argument fails to acknowledge the quiet irony in Kafka's claim that the "natural" technologies transport humans at decidedly unnatural speeds; they are invented precisely "at the moment of crashing."[3] If traditional critics have fatefully forgotten the medial "other" of Kafka's literature,[4] then media theorists have equally forgotten that other's other: Kafka's counter-alliance of modern transportation technologies, which allow faraway lovers to engage in "natural intercourse [natürlichen Verkehr]" yet unnaturally alter these lovers through mechanization and speed. Kafka's trepidation regarding such technologies extends back to his early years as a tourist and business traveler, when racing automobiles appear, as in the 1911 accident Kafka witnesses on the Parisian boulevard, the lines of cars bumping into each other in *Amerika: The Missing Person* (*Der Verschollene*, 1927), the rumbling omnibus in *The Judgment* (*Das Urteil*, 1913), and the daredevil Munich sightseeing trip in the 1911 novel fragment, *Richard and Samuel* (*Richard und Samuel*). Even more than automobiles, trains are for Kafka constitutionally "violen[t]," not least because they almost doubled their speeds in his lifetime alone (*D*1, 69; *Ta*, 43, entry of 29 Sept. 1911).[5] As Karl

Rossmann notes in *The Missing Person*, trains ferociously "thunder" across rails and over "vibrating" — *sich schwingenden* — viaducts (*A*, 101; *V*, 151, trans. rev.). This railway turbulence transforms Kafka's protagonists into unnatural bundles of symptoms as ghostly as the letters themselves.

Kafka's interest in train-transported bodies is already in evidence in his novel fragment, *Wedding Preparations in the Country* (*Hochzeitsvorbereitungen auf dem Lande*, 1907), where the hero, Eduard Raban, boards a train that "beat[s] on the rails like a hammer" and even keeps "shaking" (zitter[n]) after it stops (*CS*, 64, 66; *NS*1, 31, 35). Across from Raban sits a commercial traveler who bears the marks of this turbulence: he can find no place to rest his vibrating arm, and his notebook "trembles" (zittert; *CS*, 64; *NS*1, 31). This traveler then mentions some worries about his profession and, for no clear reason, begins to shake and cry: "not ashamed of the tears in his eyes," he looks at Raban and presses his knuckles into his "quivering" lips (seine Lippen zitterten; *CS*, 65; *NS*1, 34). This shaking and sobbing man prefigures the post–First World War "war tremblers" — *Kriegszitterer* — and echoes an earlier traveler from *Wedding Preparations*: the "clothed body" that Raban had always sent on journeys in his stead; this body now appears as "sobbing," "stumbling," and "staggering" (*CS*, 55; *NS*1, 17–18).[6] Yet another early Kafkan train traveler — Samuel from *Richard and Samuel* — is likewise exposed to the initially soothing "action of the [train's] carriage springs," "friction of the wheels," "collision of the rail points," and "vibration [Zittern] of the whole wooden, glass, and iron structure," until the accelerations, jerks, and stops eventually startle him awake and render his body one with the train's vibration: a change in speed "transmits itself through the whole of my sleep just as through the whole body of the train." Like the commercial traveler and the "clothed body" before him, Samuel, now covered in "railway grit," ultimately finds himself inexplicably at the point of "tears" (*MP*, 293, 294, 296; *DL*, 436, 437, 438, 440).

Although these characters' symptoms are overdetermined — the commercial traveler also has work worries; the clothed body must meet with the dreaded fiancée; Samuel is sexually frustrated — the very fact that they appear repeatedly during or after turbulent train travel suggests the influence of contemporaneous medical discourse. "Railway doctors" (Eisenbahnärzte) specializing in "railway illnesses" (Eisenbahnkrankheiten) and "railway health" (Eisenbahnhygiene) regularly saw similar bodies that quivered, shook, and trembled without apparent cause. Beginning as early as the 1860s, British, French, and German researchers had reported that railway personnel and passengers experienced "contract[ing]" muscles throughout the entire journey and "continuous tremors [Erzittern] of all the joints" long after deboarding.[7] After the legal debate heated up in the 1890s about whether train-induced neuroses were physio- or psychogenic, researchers still insisted on the pathogenic importance of material vibrations; the train's shaking seemed to transfer directly to the body. Many doctors cited passengers who even continued to tremble in their sleep.[8] One German researcher argued in 1908 that railway neurosis was — like seasickness — a "kinetosis," an illness brought on by "abnormal motion" that led, in severe cases, to "traumatic shock."[9] In these birth years of modern trauma theory, Freud similarly speculated that the railway's mechanical "*Erschütterung*" — meaning both "shaking" and "shock" — combined with fright to produce a "traumatic neurosis."[10] The British *Book of Health* had already insisted on these neuroses' material substratum twenty years earlier: "Man, for the time being, becomes a part of the machine in which he has placed himself, being jarred by the self-same movement, and receiving impressions upon nerves of skin and muscle."[11] Whereas horse-drawn carriages put wooden wheels on dirt, trains set steel upon steel, and this rigidity — for Kafka, "the collision of the rail points" — sent a series of "small and rapid concussions" through the traveler's body.[12] The "nervous-making shaking" nestled into the passenger's nervous system and left him quivering long afterwards.[13] In Kafka's words, the turbulence transmits itself "through the whole body of the train" into the physiognomy of the traveler. To steel travelers against such damage, one German expert recommended sitting in a vibrating chair — a *Vibrationsstuhl* — before a journey; but even this could not ultimately protect passengers, who still mirrored uncannily the vehicles that had transported them.[14] In his bestselling 1892 book, *Degeneration*, Max Nordau, like many cultural commentators of his day, came to the same conclusion as the doctors: modern nervous diseases issued from civilization itself, and often from the "shaking" (Erschütterung) that travelers "constantly suffer in railway trains."[15]

Kafka's awareness of this popular discourse is clear in the technological diction of his early heroes — the "action of the carriage springs," the "friction of the wheels," and the "vibration of the entire wooden, glass and iron structure" — but also in his later story, *The Metamorphosis* (*Die Verwandlung*, 1915), which borrows heavily from *Wedding Preparations*. When Raban sent his "clothed body" traveling in 1907, he famously wanted to remain in bed and metamorphose into a "beetle" (*CS*, 56; *NS*1, 18). The widespread critical assumption that Raban prefigures the 1912 Gregor Samsa forgets, however, an important distinction: whereas Samsa is explicitly a traveler — "Samsa war Reisender" — Raban unequivocally is not: "I have never traveled" (Ich bin nie gereist; *CS*, 89, 45; *DL*, 115; *NS*1, 15; see fig. 11.1).[16] From this perspective, Samsa has more in common with the sobbing commercial traveler — also a "*Reisender*" — than he does with Raban. If we imagine, as Kafka often did, that his stories conversed internally with one another,[17] it is even possible that this early "Reisender" *becomes* Samsa, playfully reconfigured by Kafka five years later. We learn in the opening paragraphs of *The Metamorphosis* that Samsa has

I.

ALS Gregor Samsa eines Morgens aus unruhigen Träumen erwachte, fand er sich in seinem Bett zu einem ungeheueren Ungeziefer verwandelt. Er lag auf seinem panzerartig harten Rücken und sah, wenn er den Kopf ein wenig hob, seinen gewölbten, braunen, von bogenförmigen Versteifungen geteilten Bauch, auf dessen Höhe sich die Bettdecke, zum gänzlichen Niedergleiten bereit, kaum noch erhalten konnte. Seine vielen, im Vergleich zu seinem sonstigen Umfang kläglich dünnen Beine flimmerten ihm hilflos vor den Augen.

»Was ist mit mir geschehen?«, dachte er. Es war kein Traum. Sein Zimmer, ein richtiges, nur etwas zu kleines Menschenzimmer, lag ruhig zwischen den vier wohlbekannten Wänden. Über dem Tisch, auf dem eine auseinandergepackte Musterkollektion von Tuchwaren ausgebreitet war — Samsa war Reisender —, hing das Bild, das er vor kurzem aus einer illustrierten Zeitschrift ausgeschnitten und in einem hübschen, vergoldeten Rahmen untergebracht hatte. Es stellte eine Dame dar, die, mit einem Pelzhut und einer Pelzboa versehen, aufrecht dasaß und einen schweren Pelzmuff, in dem ihr ganzer Unterarm verschwunden war, dem Beschauer entgegenhob.

Gregors Blick richtete sich dann zum Fenster, und das trübe Wetter — man hörte Regentropfen auf das Fensterblech aufschlagen — machte ihn ganz melancholisch. »Wie wäre es, wenn ich noch ein wenig weiter-

3

Fig. 11.1. The first page of the first edition of Die Verwandlung.

worked as a commercial traveler for exactly five years: from precisely the time Kafka wrote most of *Wedding Preparations*, in 1907, to the year he began *The Metamorphosis* (1912; *CS*, 91; *DL*, 118). That Kafka was more than passingly interested in this traveler from *Wedding Preparations* is evident in the traveler's unusually intimate relation to Raban. This commercial traveler looks intently at Raban the entire time, never once "turn[ing] his face away from Raban," until Raban feels compelled to engage him in small talk. But then this traveler, like the clothed body before him, begins to shake and cry (*CS*, 63, 65; *NS*1, 30–31, 32–33, 34). If Samsa has a cameo in *Wedding Preparations*, then, it is not as Raban's happily lounging, stay-at-home "beetle" but as this proto-hysterical traveler tossed about in a train that "beats on the rails like a hammer."

This supposition gains force when we learn that Raban — long seen as a cipher for "Kafka"[18] — can not understand the business talk of this commercial traveler, claiming that "much preparation [Vorbereitung] would first be required" (*CS*, 64; *NS*1, 31). The "preparations" for *The Metamorphosis* begin precisely here, on this 1907 train, with Kafka/Raban declaring his need to gain more knowledge of professional travel, which Kafka notoriously does during his five subsequent years of "maddening" business journeys (*LF*, 64; *BF*, 125).[19] While writing *The Metamorphosis*, Kafka uses the same word that Samsa does — "agitations" (Aufregungen) — to describe his workaday woes, and Kafka's recurring complaints about professional travel mirror Samsa's (*LF*, 48; *BF*, 102; *CS*, 92; *DL*, 121, trans. rev.). Kafka, too, must repeatedly catch early trains — "Tomorrow I have to get up at 4:30 AM again" — and Kafka, too, suffers what Samsa calls the "trouble of constant traveling": the "irregular, bad meals," the lack of sleep, and the general loneliness (*LF*, 229; *BF*, 346; *CS*, 90; *DL*, 116, trans. rev.). Consider, for example, Kafka's departure for a business trip to Leitmeritz just two days after completing *The Metamorphosis*: "Off I march while it's still almost night, wander through the streets in the piercing cold — past the breakfast room at the 'Blaue Stern,' its lights already on but curtains still drawn" (*LF*, 97; *BF*, 170). A couple of months later, before a trip to Aussig, Kafka cannot sleep despite great weariness, because he is haunted by visions of the very trains that will transport him: "Trains came, one after another they ran over my body, outstretched on the tracks, deepening and widening the two cuts in my neck and legs." The trains of course do not actually slice him up, but they do exhaust him, to the point that he, like the "clothed body," sits soullessly at his hotel table "like a puppet" (*LF*, 230; *BF*, 347). Beside himself for days with "sleepiness, exhaustion, and anxiety [Unruhe]," Kafka eventually even transforms into an animal, like Samsa: "What I bore on my body was no longer a human head" (*LF*, 229, 230; *BF*, 346, 347).

Business travel repeatedly gives Kafka this same anxiety (Unruhe). Consider again his trip to Leitmeritz, when he feels "all the time uneasy, all the time uneasy [unruhig]," and his journey to Kratzau, in the midst of writing *The Metamorphosis*: "There wasn't a single moment on the trip when I didn't feel at least a tiny bit unhappy," most notably during the train ride itself, when "[I] felt restless [unruhig]" from very beginning of the journey (*LF*, 97, 67; *BF*, 171, 130). Worrying "that the trip may have harmed my story," Kafka concludes bluntly to Bauer: "One shouldn't ever go away," should not ever travel (wegfahren; 67; 130). Yet he soon finds himself "threatened" again by an impending journey.[20] It is however precisely these journeys that "prepare" Kafka — as Samsa later insists, *am eigenen Leibe* — for *The Metamorphosis* (*CS*, 101; *DL*, 136–37). Kafka awakens one morning five years after writing *Wedding Preparations*, in misery, dreading another "beastly" professional journey, only to invent a new story (*LF*, 47, 66; *BF*, 102, 127). The "incubation period" typical for traumatic neuroses had begun five years earlier, in 1907, and ends now, with a young traveler waking from "uneasy dreams" (unruhigen Träumen) to find himself pathologically transformed (*CS*, 89; *DL*, 115).[21]

The Metamorphosis begins precisely with the assumption that Gregor is "ill" from the same beastly rigors of professional travel that afflicted his author. Mrs. Samsa says, "Gregor is ill"; Grete asks, "Aren't you well?"; and Gregor himself concludes that he has contracted a "standing ailment of commercial travelers" (Berufskrankheit der Reisenden; *CS*, 98, 92; *DL*, 131, 120, 121). Gregor's symptoms tally with the findings of train-illness research from the earliest years onward, which claimed that five years of regular train travel would be dangerous to anyone — especially to commercial travelers, who were more susceptible to everything from "overexcitement" to premature aging.[22] Gregor's symptoms echo the railway doctors' descriptions, which included the same melancholia, anxiety, and involuntary muscle movements present in travelers in *Wedding Preparations*: Gregor, anxious and dejected, can suddenly "not control" his limbs, which wave "wildly in a high degree of unpleasant agitation" (Aufregung; 92; 121). Researchers furthermore cited chronic fatigue as a symptom of railway illness, and Gregor, like his author, complains repeatedly of "exhausti[on]," "drowsiness," and "general fatigue" (allgemeiner Müdigkeit; *CS*, 89, 91, 101, 111, 123; *DL*, 116, 119, 136, 153, 173, trans. rev.).[23] Doctors also discovered that victims of railway crashes and those simply afraid of crashes had "distressing and horrible" dreams; they woke up "suddenly with a vague sense of alarm" and were "unusually talkative" and "excited."[24] Such premonitions of modern trauma theory apply to Gregor, who suffers first from "unruhigen Träumen" and then, after remaining silent at first, explodes in nervous "twittering squeak[s]" that tumble out of him "pell-mell" (91, 98; 119, 130).

Another regularly-reported symptom of train travelers was failing vision caused by eye fatigue and blurring landscapes. Observers claimed that the human eye, accustomed to the leisurely pace of horse carriages

— eight kilometers per hour — could not focus at the subsequent fifty (1840), sixty-five (1860), and 100 kilometers per hour (1910) of trains.[25] The "incessant shifting of the adaptive apparatus by which [objects] are focused upon the retina" was particularly harmful to commercial travelers who "in the course of one day have to cast their eyes upon the panoramas of several hundreds of places."[26] Nordau made similar claims in 1892: "Every image that we perceive from the compartment-window of an express train sets our sensory nerves and brain centers in action."[27] When Raban looks out of his "racing" train window in 1907, he likewise sees only "lights flitting past," villages "com[ing] toward us and flash[ing] past," and bridges that appear to be moving: "torn apart and pressed together," or so "it seemed" (*CS*, 64, 65; *NS*1, 31, 33). These high-speed apparitions tire Raban's eyes and those of his fellow travelers. When Raban gets off the train, the others see him blurrily from the train window, "as though the train were [still] in motion" (67; 36). The 1912 professional traveler, Gregor Samsa, similarly discovers his vision abruptly weakened: "Day by day things that were even a little way off were growing dimmer to his sight." Even the hospital across the street, which might have been the ill traveler's only hope, is now "beyond his range of vision." If Gregor hadn't known that he lived on a city street, he would have thought he was still looking out of a train window onto a blur, where "gray sky and gray land blended indistinguishably into each other" (112–13; 155–56).

Like Gregor's failing eyesight, his "worrying about train connections" jibes with medical claims that the railway's ruthless punctuality caused debilitating psychological stress, especially because of travelers' lingering confusions about standardized time (*CS*, 90; *DL*, 116). Before the railway, every town had a slightly different time: Reading, for example, was four minutes later than London, but ten minutes ahead of Bridgewater. Because these differences did not allow for interregional timetabling and often caused crashes, railway companies eventually introduced "railway time" — *Bahnzeit* — which at first meant only that each company kept its own time, enforced by the originating conductor passing his watch to a new conductor at the next station. Not surprisingly, mix-ups between "railway" and "local" time persisted long after the introduction of international standard time (in 1893 in Germany and Austria-Hungary). Arthur Schnitzler's 1900 protagonist of *Lieutenant Gustl*, for example, comically can't decide whether he should commit suicide at 7 AM "Vienna time" or "railway time."[28] More seriously, researchers from the mid-nineteenth through to the early-twentieth century claimed that many railway illnesses issued not primarily from industrial mechanics but rather from time's mechanization: from the "excitement, anxiety, and nervous shock" caused by the "fearfully punctual train."[29] This anxiety about missing trains runs through Kafka's fiction from *Wedding Preparations* all the way to the 1922 parable, "Give it Up!" (Ein Kommentar, 1922, sometimes translated as "A Comment"): "I was on my way to the station. As I compared the tower clock with my watch I realized it was much later than I had thought and that I had to hurry; the shock [Schrekken (*sic*)] of this discovery made me feel uncertain of the way" (*CS*, 456; *NS2*, 530). Raban had already experienced this same time-*Schrekken* during his 1907 walk to the station: a clock suddenly strikes a quarter to five, which should give him "plenty of time," but he is nonetheless certain he'll "miss the train"; a friend tells Raban that it's now a quarter to six, but the station clock only strikes this time later, when Raban arrives. When the porter finally rushes Raban onto the train, Raban experiences the same excitement and heart "palpitations" (Herzklopfen) that in 1908 railway doctors still attributed to punctuality fears, as already detailed by Dr. Alfred Haviland in his 1868 medical monograph about the railway, *Hurried to Death* (*CS*, 55, 59, 60, 61, 62; *NS1*, 17, 23, 25, 26, 28).

Gregor suffers likewise from anxieties about missing trains, to the point that he spends his evenings obsessively perusing railway timetables (*CS*, 96; *DL*, 126). He recalls here his author, who speaks to Felice Bauer of "train hours" (Eisenbahnstunden) and of his debilitating personal timetabling (sonderbare Zeiteinteilung): "I have to leave at 6 tomorrow evening; I get to Reichenberg at 10, and go on to Kratzau at 7 the next morning"; "[I can write] until 5 in the morning; no later, because my train leaves at 5:45"; and "before my trip to Aussig, I did not get to bed until 11:30 . . .; I still heard 1 o'clock strike, and yet had to be up again [to catch a train] at 4:30" (*LF*, 62, 95, 230; *BF*, 122, 168, 347). On the morning of his transformation, Gregor Samsa similarly thinks comically only about the railway's pitiless punctuality, not about his physical state: "I'd better get up, since my train goes at five" (*CS*, 90; *DL*, 118). Railway time oppresses Gregor partially because it moves irrationally fast, as it did for Raban. After realizing that he has overslept and that it is already half-past six, Samsa watches as the clock hands move on uncannily quickly, continuing "past the half-hour," with Gregor now watching as the hands move, before his eyes, toward a quarter to seven (*CS*, 90; *DL*, 118). Like the clock in Fritz Lang's *Metropolis*, these accelerated hands parody global modern mechanized time. Gregor's clock continues to torment him for the next forty-five minutes, the entire duration of the first third of the story. To cite just a few examples: "the alarm clock had just struck a quarter to seven"; "'Seven o'clock already,' [Gregor] said to himself when the alarm clock chimed again"; and "before it strikes a quarter past seven I must be quite out of this bed" (*CS*, 91, 93; *DL*, 119, 123). Gregor attributes this unforgiving timekeeping to the punctuality of trains: "The next train went at seven o'clock; to catch that he would need to hurry like mad," and "even if he did catch the train he wouldn't avoid a row with the boss, since the firm's porter would have been waiting for the five o'clock train" (*CS*, 91; *DL*, 118; trans. rev.). Gregor's family, too, is obsessed with railway time: "Gregor, it's a quarter to seven," Mrs. Samsa asks, "Hadn't you a train to catch?"; Mr. Samsa yells, "Gregor, the chief clerk has come and wants to know why you didn't catch the early train"; and Mrs. Samsa adds, "[Gregor's] not well, sir, believe me. What else would make him miss a train!" (*CS*, 91, 95; *DL*, 119, 126). Time slips by with each missed departure, and, as if Gregor didn't already know it, the chief clerk reminds him that time is money: "You are wasting my time" (97; 129). Out of joint with time, Kafka's always-prompt traveler loses his bearings: tormented by conscience for "wast[ing] only an hour or so of the firm's time," Gregor is "driven out of his mind" and becomes "actually incapable of leaving his bed" (94–95; 125). When Gregor finally dies at the end of the story, he does even this according to the timepiece: "In this state of vacant and peaceful meditation he remained until the tower clock struck three in the morning" (135; 193).

Driven mad by railway time, Gregor is, as critics have noted, an alienated worker: a subject transformed into a Marxian object.[30] But it is vital to add that Gregor's objectification is amplified because of his job as a professional traveler. As Marx insists, transportation is the only industry where production and consumption occur "simultaneously"; that is, where the product — change of place — is consumed at the same time it is produced, resulting in a commingling of labor and consumption.[31] Even though the traveler — unlike the conductors, stokers, and personnel — is not explicitly working, the machinery works on him. The train's vibrations and noise give the modern bourgeois his only direct experience of industry: in Samsa's words, "on his own body" (am eigenen Leibe).[32] It is as if consumers of industrial goods were to consume them *inside* the factory. This comparison cannot ultimately be nullified by the upholstered train compartments of the first and second classes, and certainly not by the third-class wooden benches on which Kafka and probably Gregor Samsa traveled.[33] With production and consumption so unusually intertwined, the transport industry unmasked any last delusions about a bourgeois subject that could remain autonomous and non-commodified. As Marx writes, "humans and commodities" travel with the same "means of transport"; more explicitly than in other industries, consumers become here "living appendages" to machinery.[34] Early train travelers from all political stripes agreed: unlike the passenger in a horse carriage, who could see the natural sources of horse power and of the bumps and jerks, the industrial passenger knew neither how his vehicle functioned nor why it shook and clattered. The traveler was alienated and unaware, ultimately nothing more than a "package," a "bale of commodities," or, in the words of Joseph Maria von Radowitz, a "piece of freight."[35] Gregor Samsa becomes precisely such a commodity, a body transported from place to place for the profit of both his firm and his family.[36]

Given Gregor's symptoms — fatigue, twitching muscles, uneasy dreams, nervous volubility, blurred vision, and psychological stress from timetables and alienation — it is not surprising that he minces no words about his diagnosis: "traveling about day in, day out," "the trouble of constant traveling," and "worrying about train connections" have caused these traumatic agitations (Aufregungen; *CS*, 89–90; *DL*, 116). Gregor does not have "the least possible doubt" that he is suffering from this common "standing ailment of commercial travelers" (92; 121).[37] But as with so many other possible interpretations of *The Metamorphosis*, this one is challenged by Kafka, from as early as the pre-story — *Wedding Preparations* — when Raban explicitly denies that his clothed body is diagnosable in any way. According to Raban, his body's first symptom ("staggering") "indicate[s] not fear but its nothingness." Raban does not simply refute the reading, "My 'clothed body' is pathologically scarred by train travel"; he refutes *any* such direct relation of a signifier ("staggering") to a signified ("fear"). The body points only to "nothingness." Its "stumbling," Raban continues, is furthermore *not* "a sign of agitation [Aufregung]." Like Gregor's hermeneutically resistant shell, Raban's "clothed body" is vehemently *not* a "sign"; it "zeigt . . . nicht" (*CS*, 55; *NS*1, 17–18). Indeed, as critics have pointed out, Kafka's bodies resist metaphorical — and diagnostic — readings, because Kafka's human tenors and material vehicles are labile: the metaphor is always in motion.[38] Samsa's transformation is unfinished — Is he an animal or is he our son? — and all readings remain unstable. Because Samsa's body, like the clothed body, cannot function reliably as a "sign," the reader is at an interpretative impasse: Why does the traveler stagger and stumble? Why does he cry? Why, in its most extreme form, does he metamorphose? Kafka's bodies deny our answers before we can formulate them.

But precisely this problem of the opaque sign lies at the heart of fin de siècle trauma discourse, especially its legal branch. For Gregor, the confusion about his bodily symptoms leads him to fear the "health-insurance doctor" (Kassenarzt), whose job resembles that of the deconstructivist critic: he must prove that the body is *not* a functioning sign, that it points to *nothing*. According to the feared *Kassenarzt*, nothing at all is causing Gregor's symptoms; he simply doesn't want to go to work, is "work-shy" (arbeitsscheu; *CS*, 91; *DL*, 119).[39] Gregor's dread of the *Kassenarzt* lends a legal-technological context to the long-standing literary problem of Gregor's apparently unreadable body. As Kafka certainly knew, severe railway turbulence and crashes had already created many people who presented no physical injuries but nonetheless suffered breakdowns and were, like Gregor, unable to work (unfähig zu arbeiten) (*CS*, 101; *DL*, 135). Because the German railways became legally liable for injuries after 1871 — almost single-handedly creating Kafka's profession of accident insurance in 1884 (1887 in Austria-Hungary) — the legal-medical debate about traumatic neuroses exploded by the fin de siècle.[40] Doctors now had to distinguish between the truly injured and what Samsa's *Kassenarzt* calls the "perfectly healthy" simulators (*CS*, 91; *DL*, 119).

The debate had begun after railways became liable in England in 1864, with medico-legal doctrine generally following John Erichsen's 1866 claim that victims of crashes or of severe shaking in trains were anatomically damaged: they had received lesions on their spinal column, known as "railway spine."[41] From the early 1880s, often after autopsies of spines proved negative, researchers argued that there was no spinal damage. They shifted the focus to the brain — "railway brain" — and to what Hermann Oppenheim in 1889 influentially termed a "traumatic neurosis" of the cerebral cortex. This move from spine to brain simultaneously replaced Erichsen's theory of pathological anatomy with chemistry: "molecular displacements" or "functional disturbances" in the cerebral cortex affected "the psyche as well as the centers for motility, sensitiveness, and sensate functions."[42] Oppenheim's book led to immediate changes in German insurance law: the Imperial Insurance Office now rendered "traumatic neuroses" eligible for compensation.[43] But because Oppenheim's "molecular" or "functional" damage remained submicroscopic, doctors had difficulty distinguishing between the work-shy simulators and the truly ill, leading to an explosion of the already simmering battle around simulation: the *Simulationsstreit*, which culminated in the 1890 Medical Congress in Berlin.[44] Opponents of Oppenheim argued that neuroses could be too easily simulated, claiming that more than 25 percent of all "traumatic neuroses" were faked.[45] Oppenheim argued that most of his opponents were *Kassenärzte* who, just as Samsa had feared, were in the pockets of the insurance industry and "saw simulation everywhere they looked [erblickte[n] überall Simulation]."[46]

Enough doubt was shed here on Oppenheim's "molecular" argument that the 1880s psychogenic theories of Herbert Page, Jean Martin Charcot, Pierre Janet, and Paul Julius Möbius gained new momentum.[47] Although all of these still held, more or less, to the likelihood of accompanying somatic traumas, they argued that Oppenheim's "traumatic neuroses" — which Charcot had termed "traumatic hysterias" as early as 1876 — could also be caused by ideas, suggestions, or fantasies.[48] Even before Freud deemphasized his seduction theory in 1897, he stressed the etiological importance of psychic predisposition: each patient's life story determined whether they could endure shock — psychic or mechanical — without suffering the profound disruption of the "sexual mechanism" that caused hysteria (*SE*, 7:201–2; *GW*, 5:103).[49] Despite Freud's hope of improving his patients' lives, his insistence on psychogenesis did not help the victims of the railway or of the First World War financially, leaving Freud with strange bed partners: the nationalist simulator-hunters ("Simulantenjäger") used psychoanalysis during the war to buffer their theory that traumatic neuroses were all in the soldiers' heads.[50] And the legal principle remained that only primarily physical injuries could be compensated, with European tort law not altering this position until after the Second World War.[51]

During this period after the theorization of psychogenic trauma but before its legal acceptance, Kafka, a legal clerk at Prague's Imperial Accident Insurance Institute, created a damaged body that had to submit itself to a *Kassenarzt* for interpretation. This *Kassenarzt*, even if he were benevolently inclined, could never find the somatic source necessary for legal compensation. Samsa has the typically hysterical body of his day: symptomatic but with an "undetectable pathological-anatomical substrate." This "submicroscopic" cause of his suffering is at once also the missing origin; molecular damage could not be proven. In this way, the "ultramodern" medical language of hermeneutic undetectability mirrors the "postmodern" assertion of Samsa's "unreadability."[52] But this interpretative language now develops significance beyond literary criticism's games of semiotic self-reference; opaqueness points instead toward the traumatized body itself. Like the slanderous rumors swirling around about commercial travelers, Samsa's symptoms are only felt subjectively, on his own body — *am eigenen Leibe* — and can therefore never be "trace[d] back to their original causes [auf ihre Ursachen hin]" (*CS*, 101; *DL*, 136). His injured body is left only to make mute or garbled entreaties that are not even understood (*CS*, 103; *DL*, 140). By the end of Gregor's story, the three boarders threaten to use his body as legal proof in a suit against the Samsa family, but the tragedy is that this same body cannot be used to supply evidence for itself: it cannot help doctors to uncover an "original cause" and therefore, perhaps, a cure (132; 188). Even Gregor admits, despite his telltale symptoms, that his job-related diagnosis will not convince the authorities: the *Kassenarzt* would not be so wrong in assuming that he is simulating (91; 119). Gregor's statement here prefigures Freud's of 1920, "All neurotics are malingerers; they simulate without knowing it, and this is their sickness."[53] To rephrase this in terms of my reading: we can not know whether Gregor is suffering from a train-induced trauma, but we do know that he suffers from that same illness of suspected simulation that haunted traveling bodies at the fin de siècle.

Even if railway trauma inheres precisely in diagnostic doubt, one could still object to my reading on the basis of Gregor's radical transformation, which parodies any imaginable case history of traumatic neurosis. Gregor does not simply quiver, blather, and sleep badly; he becomes a giant insect. But if we look at Kafka's story in the context of his general interest in mechanized bodies from 1907 through 1914, we see a steady progression toward hyperbole that could explain such an overstatement. On the heels of the lightly damaged travelers from *Wedding Preparations* and *Richard and Samuel*, Kafka now creates a commercial traveler who explodes medical orthodoxy: travel "agitations" lead not only to uneasy dreams, fatigue, twitching muscles, and blurred vision but to a complete metamorphosis. The way is now clear for Kafka's exaggerated victim-bodies, as foreshadowed in the abovementioned 1913 dream, where "trains came, one after another they ran over my body, . . . deepening and widening the two cuts in my neck and legs" (*LF*, 230; *BF*, 347). The 1914 "In the Penal Colony" ("In der Strafkolonie," 1914) creates such a body by reconfiguring the steam locomotives from *Wedding Preparations* and *Richard and Samuel*. The new machine has "screeching" [kreischende] "wheels" that cause a thoroughgoing trembling (Zittern)": "It quivers [zittert] in minute, very rapid vibrations, both from side to side and up and down" (*CS*, 143; *DL*, 209). As in contemporary medical discourse, this vibrating machinery reproduces itself on the vibrating [zitternd] body, which, in Kafka's hyperbole, now becomes either wholly "transfigur[ed]" or "murder[ed]" (*CS*, 147, 165, 154, 165; *DL*, 215, 244, 226, 245).

Kafka's 1914 penal apparatus is not simply a train in disguise, but neither is it, as scholars have asserted, a planing machine, a phonograph, or even a new weapon from the First World War.[54] As a symbol of mechanized violence, however, the machine's screeching wheels and vibrating frame connect it to an over-determined atmosphere of technological brutality that culminated in the Great War — also known as the "war by timetable."[55] In the prewar years the German General Staff concentrated more on improving railway effectiveness than on developing new weapons systems, and officers gained prestige for saving minutes off timetables.[56] By the time tensions boiled over in July 1914, a sense of railway inevitability had set in. The German military scheduled the nine railway directorates nearest the French and Russian borders to receive 530 locomotives and 8650 freight cars in just four days, and envisaged sending 650 trains to France through the city of Cologne alone.[57] Because it would take weeks for each side to transport their soldiers and weaponry to the fronts, mobilization took on the severity of a declaration of war, thus explaining Tsar Nicholas II's comical signing, then revoking, then re-signing of a general mobilization in the space of one day.[58] His final mobilization did mean counter-mobilization and war, as illustrated by Kafka, who generally ignored the saber rattling of summer 1914, yet remarked on July 31st: "General mobilization. K[arl] and P[epa] [Kafka's brothers in law] called up." Kafka understood first-hand that the war was a massive transportation effort when he walked the next day "to the train to see K[arl] off." The eventual declaration of war was comparably anticlimactic, a *fait accompli* that earned only Kafka's apathy: "Germany has declared war on Russia — Swimming lessons in the afternoon" (*D2*, 75; *Ta*, 543). Although military historians debate whether the intricate prewar timetabling really made war inevitable, it is clear that decades of railway-planning created a material logic that overwhelmed even the General Staff.[59] Consider when Wilhelm II, encouraged by illusory hopes of British and French neutrality, told

Chief of Staff von Moltke that Germany could now concentrate its full fighting force on Russia and so stop train movements to the West. Instead of feeling relief, Moltke insisted that structural mayhem would ensue, and he suffered a nervous breakdown.[60] Timetables rendered Moltke mad just as they had Samsa two years earlier. Both Moltke and Samsa — likewise a military officer — know that changed plans never mean just "wasting an hour or so"; rather, they catalyze a series of missed connections and possible crashes. The thought of this drives Moltke, too, "out of his mind," leaving him, like Samsa, "actually incapable of leaving his bed" (*CS*, 101, 94–95; *DL*, 135, 125).

War timetabling also provoked unheard-of rail traffic and exponentially more crashes, including the most lethal in British and French history,[61] encouraging Freud to cite the railway again in his 1920 revision of his traumatic-neurosis theory.[62] Because of "railway disasters" and "the terrible war that has just ended," Freud sees bodies that refuse to signify anything beyond themselves (*SE*, 18:12; *GW*, 13:9). They repeatedly dream of their original traumas, thereby troubling Freud's belief in the pleasure principle and also causing him to modify his claim that neuroses always spring from sexual sources.[63] Unable to uncover an origin, Freud argues that these dreams might refer back to a submicroscopic physical injury of the "cerebral cortex" or the "organ of the mind," a speculation that, he realizes, embarrassingly resembles that long-discredited, somaticist "old, naïve theory of shock" championed by the 1880s American "railway brain" theorists and by Oppenheim (*SE*, 18:24, 31; *GW*, 13:23, 31). But Freud ventures beyond Oppenheim, toward Georg Simmel's cultural criticism, when arguing that the cerebral cortex develops a "protective shield" against nervous stimulation; trauma results only when this shield is unexpectedly breached, causing "fright" and "shock."[64] As questionable as Freud's cerebral cartography is, Walter Benjamin was right to view the "protective shield" as a powerful material metaphor for modernity.[65] The shocks of modern technology increase, as does the thickness of our "shields." Like Samsa, we develop "armor," but, in so doing, become dialectically intertwined with the technology we had wanted to ward off. Samsa is "armor-like" (panzerartig), redolent of the body of the medieval knight but also of the armored trains and tanks that first appeared on battlefields in 1916, as well as of Kafka's own body: "For a moment I felt myself clad in steel [umpanzert]" (*CS*, 89; *DL*, 115; *D*, 39; *Ta*, 31, trans. rev.). Because Samsa is a frequent train traveler, his "armor" has been hardening long before his ultimate metamorphosis, but no armor is solid enough; it can always be ruptured. Although Freud insists that psychic causes for trauma remain primary, he admits that, in the cases of the railway and war, these can become less relevant: where the "strength of a trauma exceeds a certain limit," the patient's psychological preparedness "will no doubt cease to carry weight." When there is "no doubt" of biology's primacy, Freud's patients end up not so much beyond the pleasure principle as beyond analysis (*SE*, 18:32; *GW*, 13:32). Perhaps for this reason, Freud loses interest in the traumatic neuroses after 1920, only returning to them at the end of his life. As he admits in his final work, *Outline of Psychoanalysis*, traumatic neuroses caused by "railway collisions and war" seem to repudiate the general rule of analysis: "their relations to determinants in childhood have hitherto eluded investigation" (*SE*, 23:184; *GW*, 17:111).

After Kafka finished "In the Penal Colony" and another chapter of *The Trial* (*Der Proceß*, 1925), he wrote almost no fiction for two years; after recommencing in 1916, he stopped writing about mechanized bodies.[66] Trains and machines rarely appear, and Kafka turns almost exclusively to rural technologies. To name just a few examples relating to travel: the horses in "A Country Doctor"; the ancient "bark" of the hunter Gracchus; and Klamm's sleigh in *The Castle* (*Das Schloß*, 1926). It is as if, in his later years, Kafka returns to the rural traffic of Raban's home neighborhood, safely distanced from the train station.[67] Why? Perhaps because Kafka's literary premonitions have come true. The streets of Prague, Vienna, and Berlin are now shot through with bodies that twitch nervously, as depicted in the work of Otto Dix and others.[68] With the mechanically damaged body now in public view, it no longer belongs to Kafka's nighttime fiction but rather to the daylight of political action. Just ten days before Kafka read "In the Penal Colony" aloud in war-torn Munich, he completed a newspaper appeal calling attention to the injured soldiers who now "twitch and jump with nerves in the streets of our cities." Like Raban's staggering "clothed body," these men signify only their own damage, simulated or not, and they require scientific — not literary — help. Kafka continues that the Great War is primarily a "war on the nervous system" and demands that German Bohemia construct its first hospital for the treatment of nervous diseases. Kafka, like Freud, views these victims as successors to the "peacetime neurasthenics" who suffered from the "intensive industrialization of the past decades." With these prewar victims in mind, Kafka asks for donations from the likely culprits: the railroad management as well as the entire accident industry that springs from it, specifically private insurance companies and social insurance institutes like the one that employed him (*LF*, 580; *BF* 764–65).

Even though Kafka's mechanically damaged bodies eventually disappeared from his fiction, he did not lose interest in them, at least not as a warning to himself. Six years after completing this call to action, Kafka contracted a mysterious anxiety before a twelve-hour train trip to visit Oskar Baum in Georgental. Vehemently denying that he had the widespread pathology known as "travel phobia" — *Reiseangst* — Kafka insisted instead that his fear was existential and spiritual or psychic (geistig): a fear of change, a fear of not writing, even a fear of death (*L*, 336, 333–35; *Br*, 388, 384–86). His sister Ottla disagreed, claiming that his fear's source was physical; Kafka resisted her but had to sense, despite his protests, that his psychic source was ultimately as elusive as Ottla's physical one (336; 388). As researchers on train and war traumas — including Freud — discovered, there are symptomatic bodies that have *neither* a detectable physical injury nor a hidden psychic one: molecular damage cannot be proved and psychic explanations "cease to carry weight." Just as Samsa's mechanized body becomes a pure sign — lacking either a clear physical injury or a psychic source from his childhood — Kafka's body might also end up referring only to itself: "twitching and jumping" on the streets of Prague. A hospital for nervous diseases could symbolize hope, but this hope is as blurry as the hospital outside Gregor's window: neurology and psychiatry, too, have failed to discover an "original cause," only a *mise en abyme* of submicroscopic substrata and pathological simulations. Kafka fears precisely this undiagnosability, this etiology vaguer than tissue damage, childhood trauma, or even the "fear of death": an unnameable injury whose only source, as with Nordau's "degeneration," is modernity itself, and whose victims are primarily "feminine" men.[69] Kafka knows that what happened to Samsa could happen to anyone, especially to a weakened company proxy (Prokurist) such as Franz Kafka, who, like Samsa, has been stuck riding the rails for years: "What had happened to [Samsa] today might someday happen to the company proxy [Prokurist]; one really could not deny that it was possible" (*CS*, 95; *DL*, 125–26, trans. rev.).[70]

This fear of an undiagnosable injury brought on by the mysteries of modernity puts a fine point on my argument. To be clear: I am not claiming that Samsa's transformation is a direct result of train trauma. Such trauma cannot cause a man to turn into a giant bug. Nor am I arguing that Samsa is a malingerer, at least not in the sense suspected by the *Kassenarzt*. Rather, I see Samsa as embodying the modern technological anxiety of indeterminacy, in which even the victims do not know whether they are ill and in which simulation itself becomes the illness. Samsa's body is modernity's prototypical broken sign: a conglomeration of symptoms that does not refer to a physical cause. Vital here is Kafka's decision to transform Samsa into an *Ungeziefer*, a creature "not suited for sacrifice": an un-animal existing somewhere between beast and man.[71] This uncategorizability marries Kafka's interest in medico-legal trauma to his famous "*Schriftstellersein*" (being-as-a-writer). For Kafka would never have been interested in trains and trauma on their own; he was not a Zolaesque realist, even on this more sophisticated level of presenting modern bodies' tragic undiagnosability. Rather, Kafka sees in trauma's semiotic dubiousness the social-political verification of his poetics. As critics have demonstrated for decades, Kafka's writing sprang out of his "despair" regarding metaphor and metaphoric language: vehicles did not refer back to tenors just as signifiers did not point to signifieds (*D*, 398; *T*, 875).[72] Like language itself, Samsa's body emphasizes this unreadability: it is an accumulation of symptoms without causes and, as such, *the* cipher for Kafka's original combining of literary and medico-legal discourses. Kafka's figuration of the fin-de-siècle "language crisis" (Sprachkrise) does not ring hollow, as it does with some of his peers, because he places this linguistic trauma within its analogous social one, creating an aesthetic that truly investigates the suffering of indeterminacy.

In a letter written ten days after his debate about diagnosability with Ottla, Kafka tells Oskar Baum, too, of his travel phobia, now suggesting that he, like Freud, might be suffering from the more specific "railway phobia" (Eisenbahnangst). He playfully tells Baum that he will travel to Georgental only if he doesn't have to take the train: "[I] try to wheedle out of you the most favorable railroad connections in the secret hope that if I only I ask often enough it will turn out that Georgental can be reached only by streetcar (nur mit der Elektrischen)" (*L*, 342; *Br*, 395, trans. rev.). Kafka wants a long-distance streetcar, something slower and more placid than the "rumbling and rattling," "jolting and jouncing" train denounced by Gerhart Hauptmann in "In the Night Train" ("Im Nachtzug," 1888). And Kafka had already reported his joy at jumping on and off Prague's streetcars as a grown man, even though he prohibited this same pleasure to Felice Bauer (*LF*, 36, 31; *BF*, 87, 80). Consider a story Kafka wrote in the same year as *Wedding Preparations*, "The Passenger" ("Der Fahrgast," 1908), where a streetcar transforms an unsure, depressive protagonist into a virile voyeur: staring at a woman next to him in the tram, he confidently remarks that "she is as distinct to me as if I had run my hands over her" (*CS*, 388–89; *DL*, 27). Fourteen years later, in a letter to Milena Jesenská, Kafka praises the streetcar as a catalyst for gregariousness and desire. He would like to become a streetcar conductor, because such men thrive in social traffic, and, moreover, Milena is attracted to them: "You [Milena] also like conductors, don't you?" (*LM*, 174).[73]

Kafka's enduring love of the streetcar brings us back to the ending of *The Metamorphosis*, which is often interpreted as an ironic opposition between authentic death and cheapened life, between artistic suffering and dull-witted sexuality. While Gregor's decrepit corpse is taken out with the garbage, his petit bourgeois family heads to the flourishing countryside, naively feeling reborn and radiant. But what readers have failed to notice is the story's technological frame: after opening with an infirm protagonist complaining about excessive train travel, *The Metamorphosis* closes with his family coming to life in a streetcar. Trains make Gregor ill, at least in his opinion, and the streetcar awakens his family's sexual awareness.[74] After Grete and Mrs. Samsa caress the victorious father, the three of them leave the apartment together, which they had not done for months, and go "by tram into the open countryside [ins Freie]." Once inside the streetcar, the parents notice their daughter's pretty face and "voluptuous" (üppig) figure. She stretches her young body before them, and they realize that it is high time to find her a man (*CS*, 139; *DL*, 199–200, trans. rev.).

Given this image of health and sexuality, we are reminded of Kafka's fantasy of a "natural traffic/intercourse" (natürlichen Verkehr) — and see here a relation of travel and epistolarity directly opposed to the one governing most of Kafka's career. Kafka generally views letters as "ghostly" defenses against physical presence and travel technologies as paradoxically unnatural sponsors of natural traffic/intercourse. But here letters and trains together encourage a "natural intercourse" without apparent side effects. The streetcar brings Grete's body to the site of freedom and sexuality, now with the *assistance* of letters. Grete and her parents use missives to stave off undesired presence, writing to their employers and thereby gaining what Gregor could attain only by becoming an *Ungeziefer*: a day off work.[75] But the Samsas, unlike Kafka with Felice Bauer, ultimately use this epistolary distance to get closer to their intimates and even to plan a procreative "natural" intercourse for their daughter. Critics have pointed to the irony in this ending and viewed it almost unanimously as a parodic stab at philistinism.[76] But this finale also speaks to a more serious utopian possibility. Kafka changed the Samsas' destination from a "city park" to "ins Freie" in his manuscript, meaning "into the countryside" but hinting also at "freedom," suggesting that Kafka wants this streetcar to continue on past Georgental, past Berlin, as a streetcar named desire that will, as Freud argues for slow-moving vehicles, produce pleasurable sensations and even "an exquisite sexual symbolism" (*SE*, 7:201; *GW*, 5:103). For Kafka, this symbolism appears full-bore when Bauer writes a letter to him from a streetcar in 1912, just five days after he had completed the conclusion to *The Metamorphosis*: "Your letter from the tram makes me feel almost insanely close to you (bringt mich in eine fast irrsinnige Nähe zu Dir). How do you manage to write in a tram? With the paper on your knees, your head bent that far down while writing?" (*LF*, 101; *BF*, 176). Whereas Samsa's job on trains drives him "out of his mind" with anxiety, Bauer's writing from trams makes Kafka insane with desire (*CS*, 94–95; *DL*, 125). Writing cooperates with transportation machinery here to create a contradictory techno-natural intercourse, as in *The Metamorphosis*: letters bring people together erotically, the streetcar stimulates bodies, and these bodies remain uninjured, unmarked, and unsymptomatic.[77] They resemble Kafka's own body in his 1920 fantasy with Milena Jesenská, where he promises to crawl into every parcel he sends to her "just in order to travel inside [them] to Vienna." "Please," he continues, "give me as many opportunities to travel as possible" (*LM*, 141; *BM*, 189).[78] But Kafka also warned against such postal utopias — later calling them the "most dangerous" fantasies of all — and his Samsas are right at the edge of this, boarding a technology that promises them a "natural," insane closeness beyond the realm of the ghosts (*LM*, 224; *BM*, 303).

Notes

[1] When necessary, I have emended the standard English translations of Kafka, marking them as "trans. rev."; the original German page numbers for Kafka's texts are always supplied. For the other German texts, the translations are my own, unless specified otherwise. I thank Lara Pehar for her bibliographic assistance.

[2] Friedrich Kittler, *Grammophon, Film, Typewriter* (Berlin, Brinkmann & Bose, 1986), 327. Bernhard Siegert builds on Kittler's *Endlosschleife* argument (227–46), claiming that the "ghostly" media have transported us, via Kafka, into an interminable loop of post-humanism and post-hermeneutics (247–64), in *Relays: Literature as an Epoch of the Postal System*, trans. Kevin Repp (Stanford, CA: Stanford UP, 1999).

[3] Michel Cournot notes with astonishment that Kafka writes Bauer up to three letters per day for twenty-four weeks yet "doesn't get on a train that would have brought him to Berlin in a few hours," in "Toi qui as de si grande dentes. . . .," *Le Nouvel Observateur*, 17 April 1972, 59–61; F. Kittler cites Cournot, noting that "time and again," Kafka "avoided traveling to Berlin" — not because of the dangers of "natural" travel but because of his desire to create a "feedback loop" that could compete with modern media (*Grammophon, Film, Typewriter*, 323, 327); Gilles Deleuze and Félix Guattari miss Kafka's irony completely, referring to travel technologies as his "nice series of beneficial innovations," in *Kafka: Towards a Minor Literature* (Minneapolis: U of Minnesota P, 1986), 94–95n5; Klaus Theweleit argues that Kafka eventually leaves the medial alliance to join the benevolent "counter-alliance" that "transports bodies instead of ghosts," in *buch der könige*, vol. 1, 976–1055 (Basel: Stroemfeld, 1988), 1026.

[4] Siegert, *Relays*, 246 (see also 231).

[5] Fritz Voigt, *Die Entwicklung des Verkehrssystems,* vol. 2 of *Verkehr* (Berlin: Duncker & Humblot, 1965), 598, and *Die Theorie der Verkehrswirtschaft*, vol. 1 of *Verkehr* (Berlin: Duncker & Humblot, 1973), 865. See also Joachim Radkau, *Das Zeitalter der Nervosität: Deutschland zwischen Bismarck und Hitler* (Munich: Carl Hanser, 1998), 193, and Wolfgang Kaschuba, *Die Überwindung der Distanz: Zeit und Raum in der europäischen Moderne* (Frankfurt am Main: Fischer, 2004), 174.

[6] For more on shaking as the paradigmatic symptom of traumatic neuroses, see Esther Fischer-Homberger, *Die traumatische Neurose: Vom somatischen zum sozialen Leiden* (Bern: Verlag Hans Huber, 1975), 86–87, and Paul Lerner, *Hysterical Men: War, Psychiatry, and the Politics of Trauma in Germany, 1890–1930* (Ithaca, NY: Cornell UP, 2003), 61–62, 167, 226–28.

[7] *The Influence of Railway Travelling on Public Health* (published by the leading British medical journal, *The Lancet*; London, 1862), 40; Max Maria von Weber, "Die Abnutzung des physischen Organismus beim Fahrpersonal der Eisenbahnen," *Wieck Deutsche Illustrirte Gewerbezeitung* 25 (1860): 228. For an overview of the early research on the debilitating effects of the railway's shaking and its essential inelasticity, see Wolfgang Schivelbusch, *Geschichte der Eisenbahnreise: Zur*

Industrialisierung von Raum und Zeit im 19. Jahrhundert (Munich: Hanser, 1977), 106–13.

[8] Rudolf Wagner, "Simulation im Bahnbetriebe mit besonderer Berücksichtigung der sogenannten 'traumatischen Neurose,'" *Aerztliche Sachverständigen Zeitung* 6 (1900): 52.

[9] Max Hirsch, "Reisekrankheiten," *Therapeutische Rundschau* (Halle), 2nd series 19 (10 May 1908): 302. Hirsch attributes the roughness of the train ride to the "poor track-construction for the rails" (schlechtem Oberbau der Schienen), especially when the "rails form severe curves," and notes that, as with extreme seasickness, railway "shaking" (zitter(n)) often culminates in severe anxieties, even the "fear of death" (301).

[10] Sigmund Freud, "Three Essays on the Theory of Sexuality [1905]," in *The Standard Edition of the Complete Psychological Works*, trans. James Strachey, ed. Anna Freud (London: Hogarth & the Institute of Psycho-analysis, 1953–74), 7: 201–2); "Drei Abhandlungen zur Sexualtheorie," in *Gesammelte Werke,* ed. Anna Freud (London: Imago), 1940–52, 5:103). Subsequent references to Freud's corpus are cited hereafter as *SE* and *GW* respectively.

[11] J. Russell Reynolds, "Travelling: Its Influence on Health," in *The Book of Health*, ed. Malcolm Morris (London: Castle, 1884), 581.

[12] *The Influence of Railway Travelling on Public Health*, 41.

[13] Otto Gotthilf, "Wie schützt man sich beim Eisenbahnfahren gegen Gesundheitsschädigungen," *Deutsche Alpenzeitung*, vol 9, 1901/2, 17. Gotthilf claims that one can travel healthily in trains if one takes the right precautions. "Nervously predisposed" people, for example, should never sit in the last, "especially swaying" car of an express train (18).

[14] See Hirsch, who cites Ernst Peters's *Vibrationsstuhl* as one of several possible cures for the two main kinetoses of his day: seasickness and railway neuroses ("Reisekrankheiten," 303).

[15] Max Nordau, *Entartung* (Berlin: Duncker, 1892), 1:66. Other late-nineteenth- and early twentieth-century commentators similarly viewed neuroses as *Zivilisationskrankheiten* caused by, among other factors, railway travel. See George Beard's *American Nervousness: Its Causes and Consequences* (New York: G. P. Putnam's Sons, 1881), 112–13, and Sir Clifford Allbutt's "Nervous Disease and Modern Life," *Contemporary Review* 67 (1895): 214–15; for a summary of the early railway's effect on nervous diseases, see Schivelbusch, *Geschichte der Eisenbahnreise*, 51–66 and 106–51, and George Frederick Drinka, *The Birth of Neurosis: Myth, Malady, and the Victorians* (New York: Simon & Schuster, 1984), 108–22. Contemporaneous German texts that broadly diagnosed the fin de siècle as the "age of nervousness" were Karl Lamprecht's *Zur jüngsten deutschen Vergangenheit* (1902), Willy Hellpach's *Nervosität und Kultur* (1902), Georg Simmel's "Die Großstädte und das Geistesleben" (1903), and Johannes Marcinowski's *Nervosität und Weltanschauung* (1910). For overviews, see Andreas Steiner, *Das nervöse Zeitalter: Der Begriff der Nervosität bei Laien und Ärzten in Deutschland und Österreich um 1900* (Zurich: Juris-Verlag, 1964); Radkau, *Das Zeitalter der*

Nervosität (1998); Andreas Killen, *Berlin Electropolis: Shocks, Nerves, and German Modernity* (Berkeley: U of California P, 2005); and Michael Cowan, *Cult of the Will: Nervousness and German Modernity* (University Park: Pennsylvania State UP, 2008).

[16] The importance of this assertion ("— Samsa war Reisender —") is emphasized by its ostentatious typographical position, between long curved dashes, in the middle of the first page of the first edition of *Die Verwandlung* (see fig. 11.1). I thank Thorsten Bothe for calling my attention to this.

[17] For example, Kafka once imagined that one story could "mediate" between two other stories: without *The Metamorphosis*, "The Judgment" and "In the Penal Colony" would be "foreign heads [fremde Köpfe] banging violently against each other" (*L*, 126; *Br*, 149). For more on the internal dialogues between specific Kafka texts, see Stanley Corngold, *Kafka: The Necessity of Form* (Ithaca, NY: Cornell UP, 1988), 228–49, and Mark M. Anderson, *Kafka's Clothes: Ornament and Aestheticism in the Habsburg Fin de Siècle* (Oxford: Clarendon, 1992), 185–86. On Kafka's general intra-oeuvre communications, see Malcolm Pasley, "Kafka's Semi-Private Games," *Oxford German Studies* 6 (1971/72): 112–32.

[18] Wilhelm Emrich, *Franz Kafka* (Bonn: Athenäum, 1958), 127; Hartmut Binder, *Kafka-Kommentar zu sämtlichen Erzählungen* (Munich: Winkler, 1975), 64.

[19] Most of Kafka's business journeys (primarily to northern Bohemia) occur from 1908, when he was still working on *Wedding Preparations*, through to 1916. See *AS*, 981–90.

[20] "Gott, mir droht schon wieder eine Reise" (*LF*, 89; *BF*, 160).

[21] In line with mainstream medical thought about traumatic neuroses and traumatic hysterias, Charcot and Freud insisted that railway-induced symptoms appeared only after a period of incubation (Inkubationszeit), albeit a shorter one than Samsa's. See John Eric Erichsen, *On Railway and other Injuries of the Nervous System* (1866; repr., Philadelphia: Henry C. Lea, 1867), 74–75; Jean-Martin Charcot, *Poliklinische Vorträge (Leçons du mardi)*, vol. 1, trans. Sigmund Freud (Leipzig: Deutike, 1892), 99–100; and Sigmund Freud, *SE*, 1:52–53; *GW*, Nachtragsband, 85, *SE*, 23:67; *GW*, 16:171. For more on incubation time, see Schivelbusch, *Geschichte der Eisenbahnreise*, 123–26; Fischer-Homberger, *Die traumatische Neurose*, 110–11; Cathy Caruth, *Trauma: Explorations in Memory* (Baltimore: Johns Hopkins UP), 7; and Ruth Leys, *Trauma: A Genealogy* (Chicago: U of Chicago P, 2000), 19–20, 277–78.

[22] Gustave Claudin, *Paris* (Paris: Faure, 1867), 73. A doctor studying travelers who rode frequently from London to Brighton claims never to have "seen any set of men so rapidly aged as these [professional travelers]" (Claudin, *The Influence of Railway Travel on Public Health*, 53). Cf. Schivelbusch, *Geschichte der Eisenbahnreise*, 57, 110.

[23] *The Influence of Railway Travel on Public Health*, 40, 41, 53. On the general topic of "fatigue" in railway travelers, see Schivelbush, *Geschichte der Eisenbahnreise*, 109–10 and 113–16.

[24] Erichsen, *On Railway and other Injuries of the Nervous System*, 76, 74. Not only crash victims but also people who simply "catch sight of a locomotive" or continually think of "the possibility of collision" can develop railway neuroses. F. K. A. Schulze, *Die ersten deutschen Eisenbahnen*, 2nd ed. (Leipzig: Voigtländer, 1917), 24; *The Influence of Railway Travel on Public Health*, 43. Cf. Fischer-Homberger, *Die traumatische Neurose*, 40, and Schivelbusch, *Geschichte der Eisenbahnreise*, 198n1.

[25] Voigt, *Die Theorie der Verkehrswirtschaft*, 865, and *Die Entwicklung des Verkehrssystems*, 857.

[26] *The Influence of Railway Travel on Public Health*, 44; Claudin, *Paris*, 72. Many doctors in Kafka's day built on the influential 1889 theory of Hermann Oppenheim, which claimed that severe railway vibrations or crashes caused a shrinking of the field of vision (Wagner, "Simulation im Bahnbetriebe," 70). For more on the effects of railway travel upon vision, see Schivelbusch, *Geschichte der Eisenbahnreise*, 54–57.

[27] Nordau, *Entartung*, 1:63.

[28] Arthur Schnitzler, *Gesammelte Werke* (Frankfurt am Main: Fischer, 1961), 1:228.

[29] Winn, J. M., "Railway Traveling, and Its Effects on Health," *The Journal of Public Health* 4 (Dec. 1855): 425. The fear that the railway's punctuality caused pathologies did not disappear in the decades following this British study. A German doctor reported in 1901 that many people rush to the station distressed and sweating, leading to "tooth or even facial pain, throat and lung catarrh"; another warned in 1908 that eating "in haste," combined with the "rush and excitement before departure" can lead to "revolution-motions in the stomach" (Gotthilf, "Wie schützt man sich beim Eisenbahnfahren gegen Gesundheitsschädigungen," 17–18; Hirsch, "Reisekrankheiten," 302). For an overview of the railway's effects on the perception of time in the second half of the nineteenth century, see Ralph Harrington, "Trains, Technology and Time-Travellers: How the Victorians Re-invented Time" (2003), http://harringtonmiscellany.wordpress.com/essays/time-travellers/ (retrieved 24 Oct. 2010).

[30] Peter Beicken summarizes early socio-critical interpretations of *The Metamorphosis* in *Franz Kafka: Eine kritische Einführung in die Forschung* (Frankfurt am Main: Athenaion, 1974), 265–66. See also Eduard Goldstücker, ed., *Franz Kafka aus Prager Sicht* (Berlin: Voltaire Verlag, 1966), and Kenneth Hughes, ed., *Franz Kafka: An Anthology of Marxist Criticism* (Hanover, NH: UP of New England, 1981).

[31] Karl Marx, *Das Kapital* (vol. 2), in *Marx Engels Werke* (Berlin: Dietz, 1956–90), 24:60; hereafter cited as *MEW*. My argument for the remainder of this paragraph concerning Marx's comments on the transportation industry follows Schivelbusch's (Schivelbusch, *Geschichte der Eisenbahnreise*, 110–12).

[32] *CS*, 101; *DL*, 136–37. Although Schivelbusch does not mention Kafka, he uses Samsa's phrase — ***am eigenen Leibe*** — to describe the powerful effect of train travel on the human body (Schivelbusch, *Geschichte der Eisenbahnreise*, 112).

[33] In a letter to Bauer, Kafka reports that he only travels "third class" (*LF*, 530; *BF*, 736; cf. *LF*, 186; *BF*, 290); cf. also Max Brod and Franz Kafka, *Eine Freundschaft*, vol. 1 (Reiseaufzeichnungen), ed. Malcolm Pasley (Frankfurt am Main: Fischer, 1987), 191. See also Rainer Stach, *Kafka: die Jahre der Erkenntnis* (Frankfurt am Main: Fischer, 2008), 110. Although we don't get a description of Samsa's actual train journeys, we can assume that he, like his fellow traveler from *Wedding Preparations*, travels in a third-class carriage crowded with other traveling salesmen. On the attempt to increase corporeal "elasticity" through upholstery, see Schivelbusch, *Geschichte der Eisenbahnreise*, 112.

[34] Marx, *MEW*, 24:60; 23:445.

[35] Cited in Schivelbusch, *Geschichte der Eisenbahnreise*, 187n8.

[36] Gregor's father has secretly been keeping part of Gregor's wages instead of using this to pay off his debts, thereby increasing the time that Gregor must spend at his onerous job (*CS*, 112; *DL*, 154).

[37] Scholars have generally ignored Gregor's claim that he is suffering from a "standing ailment of civilization" (Zivilisationskrankheit), instead viewing Samsa's transformation as an externalization of an internal conflict: his desire to punish himself (for having usurped his father's dominant role), his masochistic "self-hatred," or his latent "death drive." This "externalization" reading extends even to contemporary post-structuralist readings, which interpret Gregor's transformation as a "becoming-visible" of the "lack" of a "consistent and dependable Other" (Eric Santner, "Kafka's *Metamorphosis* and the Writing of Abjection," in *M*, 199n8). For an overview of the early criticism of *The Metamorphosis*, see Beicken, *Franz Kafka*, 261–72, and Stanley Corngold, *The Commentators' Despair: The Interpretation of Kafka's "Metamorphosis"* (Port Washington, NY: Kennikat, 1973). Sander Gilman emphasizes the diagnosis of "illness," but he never relates this to the railway or Gregor's claim of "*Berufskrankheit*" (*Franz Kafka: The Jewish Patient*, 65, 80–81).

[38] In his seminal 1970 essay, "Metamorphosis of the Metaphor" (revised and republished in 1988 and 1996), Stanley Corngold argues that "the indeterminate, fluid crossing of a human tenor and a material vehicle is itself unsettling"; Gregor is an "opaque sign," a "mutilated metaphor, uprooted from familiar language" (*M*, 86, 87, 89). Although arguing (contra Corngold) for the creative aspect of this opaqueness, Clayton Koelb makes a similar point in 1989: the text's "indeterminacy" results from the possibility that "signifiers" — such as "*Ungeziefer*" — "might detach themselves from their immediate contextual limits" and become "free-floating." Koelb, *Kafka's Rhetoric: The Passion of Reading* (Ithaca: Cornell UP, 1989), 15, 16.

[39] Psychiatrists and neurologists devoted to unmasking simulators (Simulantenjäger) often used this term, "work-shy" (arbeitsscheu or arbeitsunlustig), to describe apparent malingerers. See Max Nonne's report on Walter Cimbal's 1915 lecture, "Die seelischen und nervösen Erkrankungen seit der Mobilmachung," in "Ärztlicher Verein in Hamburg: Sitzung vom 23. Februar 1915," *Neurologisches Zentralblatt* 34 (1915): 414. For an overview of the debates about simulation and

malingering, see Lerner, *Hysterical Men*, 62–67, 137–39, 202–4, and Fischer-Homberger, *Die traumatische Neurose*, 56–73.

[40] For the German and Austro-Hungarian context, see Wolfgang Schäffner, "Event, Series, Trauma: The Probabilistic Revolution of the Mind in the Late Nineteenth and Early Twentieth Centuries," in *Traumatic Pasts: History, Psychiatry, and Trauma in the Modern Age, 1870–1930*, ed. Mark S. Micale and Paul Lerner (Cambridge: Cambridge UP, 2001), 81; Greg A. Eghigian, "The German Welfare State as a Discourse of Trauma," in Micale and Lerner, *Traumatic Pasts*, 99; and Lerner, *Hysterical Men*, 32–33. For the European-wide context of trauma and accident insurance legislation, see Mark S. Micale, *Hysterical Men: The Hidden History of Male Nervous Illness* (Cambridge, MA: Harvard UP, 2008), 140, 317n67.

[41] Erichsen tried to distance himself from this specific term, calling it "absurd," but it stuck to him nonetheless (Erichsen, *On Railway and other Injuries of the Nervous System*, 23). See Fischer-Homberger's *Die traumatische Neurose*, 16–17, and her "Railway Spine und traumatische Neurose — Seele und Rückenmark," *Gesnerus* 27 (1970): 96–111.

[42] Hermann Oppenheim, *Die traumatischen Neurosen nach den in der Nervenklinik der Charité in den letzten 5 Jahren gesammelten Beobachtungen* (Berlin: Hirschwald, 1889), 125, 127. See Fischer-Homberger, *Die traumatische Neurose*, 32–34, and Schivelbusch, *Geschichte der Eisenbahn*, 130–31.

[43] See Lerner, *Hysterical Men*, 32–33.

[44] See Fischer-Homberger, *Die traumatische Neurose*, 56–73, and Lerner, *Hysterical Men*, 32–36.

[45] Fischer-Homberger, *Die traumatische Neurose*, 71.

[46] Hermann Oppenheim, "Der Krieg und die traumatischen Neurosen," *Berliner klinische Wochenschrift* 52 (15 Mar. 1915): 257. See Lerner, *Hysterical Men*, 35–36.

[47] Möbius argued that he would rather have relatively reliable and testable psychological theories than Oppenheim's "labile molecules," for which there were no "demonstrable data." Cited in Fischer-Homberger, *Die traumatische Neurosen*, 116.

[48] See Fischer-Homberger, *Die traumatische Neurose*, 73–83, 30.

[49] Freud insists on the importance of psychic predisposition throughout his work, beginning as early as 1895 in his "Reply to Criticisms of My Paper on Anxiety Neurosis" and carrying through to the 1905 *Three Essays on the Theory of Sexuality*, the 1917 *Introductory Lectures on Psychoanalysis*, and the 1920 *Beyond the Pleasure Principle* (*SE*, 3:130–31; *GW*, 1:366, *SE*, 16:362; *GW*, 11:376, *SE*, 7:201; *GW*, 5:103, *SE*, 18:31–32, *GW*, 13:31–32).

[50] Psychoanalysis enjoyed unusual acceptance by established medicine toward the end of the First World War. Freud was proud that the wartime governments now employed some of his terms ("flight into illness," "gain from illness") and were even prepared to build "psychoanalytic centers" behind the front lines (*SE*, 17:209; *GW*, 12: 321–22).

[51] See Eghighian, "The German Welfare State as a Discourse of Trauma" (on West German legal changes in 1962), 110, and Schivelbusch, *Geschichte der Eisenbahnreise* (on British legal changes in 1963), 132.
[52] Fischer-Homberger, *Die traumatische Neurose*, 73, 23, 24.
[53] Cited in K. R. Eissler, *Freud as Expert Witness: The Discussion of War Neuroses between Freud and Wagner-Jauregg*, trans. Christine Trollope (Madison, CT: International UP, 1986), 62. With this statement, we see how Freud distanced himself after the war from *Simulantenjäger* like Wagner-Jauregg, as well as from Freud's own wartime enthusiasm for working together with the "highest quarters of the Central European Powers" (*SE*, 17:209; *GW*, 12:321).
[54] For planing machines, new weaponry, and other possible mechanical sources, see Klaus Wagenbach, ed., *In der Strafkolonie: Eine Geschichte aus dem Jahre 1914*, expanded edition (Berlin: Wagenbach, 1995), 77–79, 113–15. For the phonograph, see Wolf Kittler's discussion in "Schreibmaschinen, Sprechmaschinen: Effekte technischer Medien im Werk Franz Kafkas," in *Franz Kafka: Schriftverkehr*, ed. Wolf Kittler and Gerhard Neumann (Freiburg: Rombach, 1990), 116–41.
[55] A. J. P. Taylor, *War by Timetable: How the First World War Began* (London: MacDonald, 1969). Cf. John Westwood, *Railways at War* (San Diego, CA: Howell-North, 1980), 129, and Dennis E. Showalter, "Railroads, the Prussian Army, and the German Way of War in the Nineteenth Century," in *Railways and International Politics: Paths of Empire, 1848–1945*, ed. T. G. Otte and Keith Neilson (New York: Routledge, 2006), 40.
[56] Showalter, "Railroads, the Prussian Army, and the German Way of War," 21, 40.
[57] Westwood, *Railways at War*, 122, 125.
[58] Westwood, *Railways at War*, 129.
[59] On August 1st, before hostilities began, Chief of Staff von Moltke claimed that "the deployment in the West could no longer be stopped." Annika Mombauer, *Helmuth von Moltke and the Origins of the First World War* (Cambridge UP, 2001), 219. See also Showalter, "Railroads, the Prussian Army, and the German Way of War," 40, and Westwood, *Railways at War*, 131.
[60] After Moltke's meeting with the Kaiser, Moltke's wife found his pulse "hardly countable" and claimed that he had suffered a "light stroke." Although Moltke's final collapse did not occur until 22 October, after the Battle of the Marne, he never regained his health after this first breakdown on 1 August: his wife asked as early as 9 August if she could accompany him to the front because of his health (Mombauer, *Helmuth von Moltke*, 222, 234)
[61] On 22 May 1915 a British troop train collided with a stationary passenger train, leaving at least 200 dead. On 12 December 1917 a French military train derailed, and 543 soldiers were killed. Nicholas Faith, *Derail: Why Trains Crash* (London: Macmillan, 2000), 78–79.
[62] The railway is, for Freud, the primary non-military cause of the traumatic neuroses throughout his career, especially at three points in time: the late 1880s and early 1890s, while he was reworking Charcot's theories of traumatic hysteria and

developing his own; in 1919–20, when he was comparing the railways to the war; and at the very end of his life, in *Moses and Monotheism* and *Outline of Psychoanalysis*. *SE*, 1:12 (1886); *GW*, Nachtragsband, 42–44, *SE*, 1:51–52 (1888); *GW*, Nachtragsband, 84, *SE*, 1:152 (1892); *GW*, 17:10–11, *SE*, 7:201–2 (1905); *GW*, 5:103, *SE*, 16:274–76 (1917); *GW*, 11:283, *SE*, 17:211 (1920); *GW*, Nachtragsband, 706, *SE*, 20:127–28 (1925); *GW*, 14:157–58, *SE*, 23:67 (1934–38); *GW*, 16:171, *SE*, 23:184 (1938); *GW*, 17:111.

[63] As late as his introduction to the volume on war neuroses from the 1918 Psychoanalytic Conference, Freud still insisted on the "sexual etiology" of all neuroses. Freud's colleague, Karl Abraham, did so even more vehemently, linking shell shock to latent homosexuality (*SE*, 17:209; *GW*, 12:323) See also Karl Abraham, "Erstes Korreferat," in *Zur Psychoanalyse der Kriegsneurosen* (Leipzig: Internationaler Psychoanalytischer Verlag, 1919), 31–41.

[64] Freud, *SE*, 18:27, 31; *GW*, 13:26, 31. Especially the first part of Freud's biosociological theory is remarkably similar to Simmel's, who claims that that modern man "develops an organ protecting him against the threatening currents and discrepancies of his external environment": against "nervous stimulation." For Simmel, however, this organ is "the intellect" itself, which he sees as relatively resistant to shock; the tragedy for Simmel is not that this organ is eventually penetrated but rather that it dominates modern man, leading him always to "react with his head instead of his heart." Georg Simmel, "The Metropolis and Mental Life" (1903), in *The Sociology of Georg Simmel*, ed. Kurt H. Wolff (London: Free Press of Glencoe, 1950), 410.

[65] Walter Benjamin, *Charles Baudelaire: Ein Lyriker im Zeitalter des Hochkapitalismus* (Frankfurt am Main: Surhkamp, 1955).

[66] On 7 December 1916 Kafka speaks of "2 years of not writing" (*LF*, 536; *BF*, 744). The meager post–December 1914 exceptions prove the rule: the "Blumfeld" fragment; a couple of pages on "The Village Schoolmaster" and "The Assistant District Attorney"; and seven lines of *Der Verschollene* (*NS*1, 447–48) See also Binder, *Kafka-Kommentar zu sämtlichen Erzählungen*, 186–92; and Bezzel, *Kafka Chronik zusammengestellt von Chris Bezzel* (Munich: Hanser, 1975), 103–21.

[67] Again, the exception proves the rule. After 1914, only the 1922 short stories "First Sorrow" and "Give it Up!" describe modern traffic. Not surprisingly, these travelers, like their predecessors, experience destroyed nerves and shock (*CS*, 447, 456; *DL*, 319; *NS*2, 530). For the horse-drawn carts of Raban's home neighborhood — before he gets to the illuminated square filled with street cars — see *CS*, 52–56; *NS*1, 12–18.

[68] The wartime shakers (Kriegszitterer) were followed in 1919 by the uniformed panhandling *Zitterer*, many of whom had not even been in the war but discovered that borrowed uniforms increased their income (Lerner, *Hysterical Men*, 226–27).

[69] Because of the stereotype of hysteria as a "feminine" disorder, Charcot insisted that his male hysterics were unquestionably virile, including one "manly artisan, solid, unemotional, a railway engineer." Charcot, "A propos de six cas d'hystère

chez l'homme," in *J. M. Charcot: L'Hystérie*, ed. E. Trillat (Toulouse: Privat, 1971), 157–58. See also Elaine Showalter, "Hysteria, Feminism, Gender," in Sander Gilman et al., *Hysteria Beyond Freud* (Berkeley: U of California P, 1993), 308–9. This fear of being labeled "feminine" may explain why Kafka insisted that he was suffering neither from the hysteric disorder of fear of travel (Reiseangst) nor from "weakness of the will" (Willenschwäche; *L*, 333; *Br*, 384). For the male tendency to deny *Reiseangst*, see Fischer-Homberger, *Die traumatische Neurose*, 41–42; for the relation of *Willenschwäche* to hysteria and femininity, see Cowan, *Cult of the Will*, 10–15, 104–10, 269n61. Sander Gilman argues that Jewish men were seen to be especially predisposed to hysteria — including railway hysteria — especially because they were stigmatized as "feminized" (Gilman, "The Image of the Hysteric," in *Hysteria Beyond Freud*, 416–18, 405–6).

[70] By the time Kafka wrote *The Metamorphosis*, his official title was "Konzipist" (project manager) not "Prokurist," but he did hold the important institutional "Prokura" (proxy power), granted to him on 10 February 1911. Kafka would never have officially been called "Prokurist," simply because governmental or partly-governmental institutions like Kafka's did not use this term, even for someone who, like Kafka, had "Prokura" powers (*AS*, 984). I thank Benno Wagner for the reference to *AS*.

[71] On the etymology of "Ungeziefer," see Corngold, "Metamorphosis of the Metaphor," *M*, 87.

[72] See Corngold, "Metamorphosis of the Metaphor," in *M*, 84–85.

[73] "Du [Milena] hast auch Kondukteure gern, nicht wahr?" (*BM*, 236).

[74] If, as Nina Pelikan Straus claims, Kafka transforms "Gregor" into "Grete," then this happens only with the help of the streetcar, which encourages Grete to metamorphose Gregor's "trouble with travel" (Plage des Reisens) into an ultimately positive "sorrow" (Plage), out of which she can rejuvenate herself (*CS*, 90, 139; *DL*, 116, 200). See Straus, "Transforming Franz Kafka's *Metamorphosis*," in *M*, 129).

[75] Cf. W. Kittler, "Schreibmaschinen, Sprechmaschinen," 100.

[76] For Herbert Kraft, the "exaggeration of the parody" is precisely what caused Kafka to label the ending of *The Metamorphosis* "unreadable"; Kraft, *Kafka: Wirklichkeit und Perspektive* (Bebenhausen: Lothar Rotsch, 1972), 49. Peter Beicken concurs, claiming that this parodic "sentimental, petty bourgeois" ending leads too easily to "moralistic partiality." Beicken, *Franz Kafka*, 271–72. Carsten Schlingmann reads the "banal ending," with its "depressing bourgeois-ness," as "undoubtedly cynical." Schlingmann, "Die Verwandlung," in *Interpretationen zu Franz Kafka: Das Urteil, Die Verwandlung, Ein Landartzt, Kleine Prosastücke* (Munich: Oldenbourg, 1968), 89, 88. For more recent interpretations, see Straus ("In the finale of *Metamorphosis* a return to normal sex roles is parodically celebrated"; Straus, "Transforming Franz Kafka's *Metamorphosis*," 139); Corngold (Kafka changes a phrase because the original was "too kitschy," "even" for the Samsa family; *M* 56); and Kevin W. Sweeney (the "smug" family produces a "false

sense of closure"; Sweeney, "Competing Theories of Identity in Kafka's *The Metamorphosis*," in *M*, 152).

[77] Given the futurists' antagonism toward "nature," Kafka's ending represents an unusually naturalist futurism, but it nonetheless has futurist tendencies, thereby connecting Kafka to the techno-vitalist avant-garde. Kafka's inclusion in this modernist stream — against the "unconscious"-oriented "surrealist" stream — troubles Michael Cowan's attempt to ally futurism/vitalism with proto-fascism (Cowan, *Cult of the Will*, 257–64, and 315n29).

[78] See John Zilcosky, *Kafka's Travels: Exoticism, Colonialism, and the Traffic of Writing* (New York: Palgrave, 2003), 171. Kafka had a version of this same fantasy as early as 1903, when he imagined mailing to Oskar Pollak "a piece of my heart," packed "neatly in a few sheets of inscribed paper" (*L*, 9; *Br*, 19). I thank Mark Harman for the reference to Pollak.

12: The Comfort of Strangeness: Correlating the Kafkaesque and the Kafkan in Kazuo Ishiguro's *The Unconsoled*

Robert Lemon

ALTHOUGH AN AUTHOR'S NAME rarely becomes famous enough to give rise to its own adjective, this honor comes with a price. The phrase is now subject to vague and broad usage that sheds light on neither its object nor its origin. The expression "Kafkaesque" is a case in point. As Rainer Nägele observes, Duden's definition ("in the manner of Kafka's description; uncanny and threatening in an enigmatic fashion") manages to combine tautology with awkwardness.[1] In the English-speaking world the term also denotes the mysterious and unsettling qualities associated with Kafka's texts, whether manifested in Gregor Samsa's transformation in *The Metamorphosis* (*Die Verwandlung*, 1915) or the arcane bureaucracies of *The Trial* (*Der Process*, 1925) or *The Castle* (*Das Schloss*, 1926). As such, the term "Kafkaesque" gestures toward both the content and the form of his narratives, their creation of enigmas and refusal to resolve them. The term can be usefully compared to the more rigorous and restrictive adjective "Kafkan,"[2] which implies a greater degree of similarity with, and/or the direct, attributable influence of, Kafka's actual works. My purpose here is to use this distinction between the Kafkaesque and Kafkan to consider the thematic and narrative correlations between Kafka's works and Kazuo Ishiguro's 1995 novel *The Unconsoled*. While critics agree that Ishiguro's novel possesses broadly Kafkaesque characteristics, such as an indeterminate setting, a dream-like tone, and the absence of a conventional narrative resolution,[3] this study will consider the work as more narrowly Kafkan in its themes of music, ethnology, and familial conflict and in its references to extra-diegetic reality. Moreover, I will argue that Ishiguro's novel combines two modes of narration associated with Kafka — the circumscribed perspective of the first-person narratives found in his shorter fiction and the endless detours and diversions experienced by the third-person protagonists of the novels — to produce a hybrid Kafkan text. Finally, we will examine how Ishiguro's text departs from Kafka's modes of narration in its violation of diegetic convention. In particular, we will consider how Ishiguro grants his protagonist, Ryder, direct access to people, places, and objects from Ryder's distant past and moments of superhuman, omniscient insight in order to provide the reader with the comforting prospect of a comprehensible, if thoroughly unconventional, resolution to the novel's themes and plot. Comparing Kafka's oeuvre to *The Unconsoled* will thus provide an insight into the different modes of narrative alienation and consolation offered by modernist and postmodernist fiction.

A brief synopsis of *The Unconsoled* indicates the novel's eschewal of conventional narrative development and resolution. Ryder, a famous English pianist, travels to an unspecified town in Central Europe to give a lecture and perform a concert, neither of which ultimately takes place. Although the townspeople fervently hope that Ryder's lecture and performance will cure their profound cultural malaise, they involve him in a series of bewildering errands that thwart his mission. Ryder's chronic disarray extends to his own biography: he greets Sophie and her son Boris as strangers, yet gradually acknowledges them as his wife and child. To compound the protagonist and reader's confusion, Ryder encounters people, places, and objects from his past in England whose appearance in this foreign setting remains unexplained. Finally, the novel's conclusion resists resolving these issues: the townspeople remain uncannily unperturbed by Ryder's failure to perform, and although he is confronted with both his long-standing estrangement from his parents and the breakdown of his relationship with Sophie and Boris, Ryder also stays sanguine about the chances of his next mission in Helsinki. While many initial reviews of *The Unconsoled* responded to its lack of a traditional resolution with "lukewarm perplexity,"[4] most critics were certain of Ishiguro's stylistic and thematic debt to Kafka,[5] as was Ishiguro himself.[6]

Yet although critics repeatedly link *The Unconsoled* with Kafka's novels, I contend that Ishiguro's novel also reveals the thematic influence of Kafka's shorter prose fiction.[7] For the purposes of comparison I will focus on three thematic progressions in Kafka's stories. The first phase addresses the domestic and familial sphere, particularly conflicts with parents, as in "The Judgment" ("Das Urteil," 1913) and *The Metamorphosis* (*Die Verwandlung*, 1915). The second opens out onto broader geographical and historical vistas and often features an ethnographically minded protagonist investigating native or foreign cultures, as in "Building the Great Wall of China" ("Beim Bau der chinesischen Mauer," 1917) or "In the Penal Colony" ("In der Strafkolonie," 1914).[8] In the final phase Kafka turns to a theme that recurs throughout his career: the role of aesthetics, but in particular to the relation between art and the broader community, as in his final story, "Josephine, the Singer, or the Mouse People" ("Josefine, die Sängerin, oder das Volk der Mäuse," 1924).[9] Ishiguro reshuffles these themes in *The Unconsoled*, presenting a cast of characters obsessed with the relationship between the community and aesthetics, as represented by music, a protagonist with an ethnographic curiosity about the town he is visiting, and the final revelation of the conflict between Ryder and his parents.

The theme of music in Kafka's works and Ishiguro's novel is too extensive for a thorough analysis here. However, a comparison of a few key passages addressing this theme will show how Ishiguro's novel merits the adjective "Kafkan" by recalling aspects of Kafka's depictions of music and musicality that often go unheard. In particular, *The Unconsoled* suggests Kafka's influence in its reinterpretation of the German Romantic notion of music as sublime and transcendent, as a source of both elevation and revelation. While this transcendent vision of music holds sway over many of the critics who address Kafka and/or Ishiguro's treatment of the topic, it requires reevaluation. For example, in his study of music in *The Unconsoled* and Kafka, Stephen Benson posits a form of musical transcendence, whereby its absence from a musically inclined literary text "only serves . . . to make it more palpably present."[10] Benson cites the passage in the early text "Description of a Struggle" ("Beschreibung eines Kampfes," 1904–8, published 1936) in which the character identified as the Supplicant announces his intention to play the piano, despite the fact that he does not know how, but is thwarted by two men who lift him up and carry him from the piano to the dining table (*CS*, 38–39; *NS*1, 98–100). For Benson, this Cageian episode distills the movement of *The Unconsoled* "towards a public pianistic catharsis, music *as* catharsis, predestined to silence."[11] However, both this episode with the Supplicant and *The Unconsoled* as a whole present the non-appearance of music as comedic farce, rather than dramatic catharsis. This thrust is apparent in the humorous musical accompaniment to the Supplicant's non-performance provided by the two gentlemen who spirit him away while "whistling a song and rocking [him] to and fro" (*CS*, 39; *NS*1, 100). Indeed, their intervention amounts to an ironic, slapstick literalization of the notion that music elevates and transports the listener.

The Unconsoled expands this process of using farce to prevent music *ad infinitum* by providing a complex concatenation of errands and obstacles to thwart Ryder's concert. At one point Ishiguro even goes so far as to place a brick wall across a street to stop his protagonist from reaching the concert hall (388).[12] Kafka and Ishiguro's obstruction of musical performance suggests both a self-referential acknowledgement of the incommensurability of literature and music and a shared awareness that the insuperable gap between text and score can be played for laughs.

This is not to say, however, that the notion of transcendence is entirely absent from Kafka's depictions of music. For Kafka, music's transcendent qualities consist not merely in its elevation of the listener but rather in its ability to surpass the boundaries between dichotomous experiences, to express both the ethereal *and* the earthy, the spiritual *and* the corporeal, and thus convey the totality of existence. Curiously, even critics who subscribe to the more traditional notion of music as ennobling and uplifting are also drawn to this broader vision of the form's expressive capability. Alison Turner sees Kafka's imagined depictions of music as symbolizing the "creative ecstasy of the writer, who . . . succeeds momentarily in transcending the normal limitations of his existence"; at the same time she also presents music not as an escape from reality but rather as "a vision of the truth in its entirety," which, like the music that assails the canine narrator of "Researches of a Dog ("Forschungen eines Hundes," 1922), consists of the terrible as well as the sublime.[13] Five decades later, Stanley Corngold engages with the same conundrum. On the one hand, he presents music as a lofty source of plenitude, connecting the narrator's decision to abandon his investigation of music in "Researches of a Dog" with Kafka's own awareness that his writing could never attain the purity of which he dreamt as young man.[14] On the other hand, in his discussion of Kafka's music and the organic, he invokes "a consciousness that is close to the body" and the idea that music stands "for the person as the subject of psychology" (9–10).[15] Turner and Corngold thus negotiate via Kafka the historical transition in musical theory from the Romantic insistence on transcendence to Schopenhauer's vision of music as an all-encompassing medium, which, alone among art forms, can represent the Will directly.[16] This idea that music can reflect the contradictory and multifarious nature of life itself is vital for an understanding of Kafka's and Ishiguro's representations of the medium.

Both Kafka and Ishiguro depict the production and reception of music as arising not only from sublime aspirations but also from psychological and even pathological impulses. For example, in *The Metamorphosis* Gregor Samsa's response to his sister Grete's violin-playing initially indicates a desire for transcendence that appears to demonstrate his continued humanity: "Was he an animal that music could move him so? He felt as if the way to the unknown nourishment he craved were coming to light" (*M,* 36).[17] Yet this yearning for spiritual sustenance gives way to Gregor's incestuous and bestial desire to imprison Grete in his room and kiss her bare throat (*M,* 36; *DL,* 186). Similarly, in "Researches of a Dog" the canine troupe that provides the narrator with his first experience of the sublimity of music nevertheless flout conventions of decency by standing on their hind legs and exposing themselves (*NS2,* 432; *KSS,* 136). Kafka's stories thus combine through music a transcendental aesthetic experience and unsavory and taboo corporeal desires. In *The Unconsoled,* Ishiguro has the figure of Brodsky, the washed-up conductor and recovering alcoholic, convey this Kafkan concept of music as paradox. Brodsky repeatedly identifies the source of his inspiration in his own body, in an unhealed wound whose pain can only be assuaged by music (309). However, during the concert in which Ryder fails to perform, Brodsky overcomes a far graver injury, staggering on stage after a bicycle accident with one leg missing (488–90). (Here Ishiguro again indulges in farcical, physical comedy in the attempt to prevent the entry of music into the text.) Through Brodsky the author literalizes the notion of transcendence by having the conductor rise momentarily into the air before his final collapse (496). Nevertheless, as Ryder's response makes clear, Brodsky's achievement consists not in raising the listener to sublime heights, but rather in probing what lies below:

> He was almost perversely ignoring the outer structure of the music . . . to focus instead on the peculiar life-forms hiding just under the shell. There was a slightly sordid quality about it all, something close to exhibitionism, that suggested that Brodsky was himself profoundly embarrassed by the nature of what he was uncovering, but could not resist the compulsion to go yet further. The effect was unnerving, but compelling. (492)

Like the musical canines in "Researches of a Dog," Brodsky gives a performance that is simultaneously indecent and irresistible. And in a manner that recalls the response of that peculiar life-form, Gregor Samsa, to Grete's playing, Brodsky's performance makes the task of distinguishing the transcendental from the transgressive unexpectedly difficult. Given the Kafkan conception of music in *The Unconsoled*, it is fitting that Ishiguro should pay what appears to be a homage to "Researches of a Dog" by having Ryder's one and only piano performance take place at the funeral of Brodksy's late lamented canine (356–58).

Ishiguro's depiction of music reveals other Kafkan traits in its irreverent attitude toward musicology and its privileging of communal over critical aesthetic standards. Although the canine scientist in Kafka's "Researches of a Dog" is fascinated by the mysterious origins of music, he himself dismisses music theory as an "especially difficult" branch of science "that becomes aristocratically impenetrable to the crowd" (*KSS*, 160).[18] Ishiguro's disdain for this field is apparent when he satirizes the melocentric locals' discussions of modern music by employing terminology and references that remain comically opaque to the reader. He has particular fun with invented musical terms such as "crushed cadence," "struck motif" (186) and "pigmented triad" (197), as well as with the archly highbrow titles for fictitious pieces, such as Mullery's *Verticality*.[19] In his final story, "Josephine, the Singer, or the Mouse People," Kafka rejects the narrator's academic musical criteria in favor of communitarian standards. Indeed, even the critics of Josephine, among whom the narrator belongs, cannot maintain their opposition to her work, because they yearn for the feeling of solidarity that can be obtained only from participating in the audience's communal response to her song: "Soon we, too, are plunged into the sensation of the crowd as, body warmly pressed on body, breathing with awe, it listens" (*KSS*, 98).[20] In a similar fashion, the bizarre, anti-climactic concert at the end of *The Unconsoled* brings a shared sense of solace to the audience:

> All around me voices were greeting one another in delight, and it struck me the whole atmosphere resembled that of a reunion. And yet these were people who saw each other constantly. Clearly, the evening's events had made them re-assess themselves and their community in some profound way, and the resulting mood, for whatever reason, appeared to be one of mutual celebration. (523)

Here Ishiguro replaces the aesthetic reception of the concert, which the novel repeatedly posits as its climax, with another kind of reception: a formal, social gathering. Perhaps the festive atmosphere derives from the townspeople's belated recognition that they, as the audience, can determine the concert's success without recourse to arcane aesthetic criteria, that they can liberate themselves from their self-imposed tyranny of taste. Ishiguro's novel thus draws our attention to an aspect of Kafka's aesthetic sensibility that is often overlooked. Instead of the rigorously ascetic aestheticism commonly associated with the author, this comparison reveals a writer who, in the manner of his 1911 diary entry on minor literatures (*D*1, 191–95; *Ta*, 312–15), celebrates the ability of art to foster a communal sense of identity.

The cultural crisis afflicting the town, which dissolves so unexpectedly at the end of the novel, brings us to the second Kafkan theme of ethnographic enquiry, as represented in Ryder's other task: his speech on "local conditions." In this regard he recalls the Westerner traveling in the North African desert in Kafka's story "Jackals and Arabs" ("Schakale und Araber," 1917). Here the narrator-protagonist finds himself hailed by a pack of talking jackals as their Messiah, come to rid them of the Arab scourge. He responds initially by asserting his independent, impartial, and distanced perspective: "I do not presume to judge matters so remote from me" (*KSS*, 70).[21] However, the narrator's rhetorical claims to a distanced and uninvolved view are undermined by the jackals' literal encroachment on his personal space (*KSS*, 69; *DL*, 270) and by his own susceptibility to the jackals' blandishments, both of which invoke the supposed superiority of his European powers of reason (*KSS*, 69; *DL*, 271). In the end the traveler contravenes his own precept of impartiality by holding back the whip hand of the Arab caravan leader, as the latter reasserts his authority over his unruly "dogs" (*KSS*, 72; *DL*, 275). Moreover, any pretensions to objectivity on the part of the traveler are revealed as misplaced from the outset when the caravan leader discloses that the jackals greet *every* European as the savior who will rid them of the Arabs (*KSS*, 71; *DL*, 274). In other words, the narrator's very presence precipitates the crisis from which he tries to distance himself.

Much the same could be said of Ryder's ethnographic mission in *The Unconsoled.* The townspeople greet his arrival and planned performance with such fervent enthusiasm that it becomes impossible for Ryder to obtain an objective viewpoint on the local situation without the distorting effect of his own presence. Furthermore, as a potential savior he displays the diffidence, interference, and Messianic delusions found in "Jackals and Arabs." Here, familial rather than physical entanglements undermine Ryder's pretensions to independence. As his ties to the town become apparent, his claims to be unqualified to comment on local matters are revealed as evasions. For example, when Sophie's father Gustav asks for help in restoring his relationship with his daughter, Ryder's exasperated response does not indicate that he is Gustav's son-in-law or Sophie's husband: "'As I keep saying, these are family matters . . . I'm merely an outsider, how can I judge?'" (86). Yet it is precisely his perspective as an outsider that is coveted by the townspeople, who expect him to diagnose and cure their cultural malaise. Paradoxically, Ryder shows no qualms about interfering in this matter, where he should be most circumspect. While arguing with Christhoff, an out-of-favor conductor whose name suggests the Messianic expectations that he once inspired,[22] Ryder stoops to personal invective, accusing him of "'megalomania masquerading behind a modest and kindly manner'" (202). One might well level this charge at the accuser, since Ryder explains his incessant travel by claiming that his next assignment might be "'the very special one, . . ., the one that's very, very important, not just for me but for the whole world'" (217). Ryder thus not only shares the townspeople's vision of him as a savior but also harbors global ambitions. Like Kafka, Ishiguro undermines the notion of ethnographic objectivity by stressing the intrusion and interference caused by the foreign observer's presence and personal biases.

However, this characteristically Kafkan skepticism toward ethnographic encounters between cultures also extends to the task of objectively assessing one's own. For if we consider his long-term ties to the town as proof of his insider status, Ryder comes to resemble Kafka's native ethnographer/narrators, such as the canine scientist of "Researches of a Dog" or the Chinese anthropologist in "Building the Great Wall of China." Both these cultural investigators reach an impasse. The canine researcher is unable to complete his investigation into the origins of food and music since he, like all other dogs, cannot perceive humans. The Chinese anthropologist feels compelled to halt his research on the wall and the institution of empire, lest he undermine the foundations of Chinese self-identity (*KSS*, 123; *NS*1, 356). Like the dog investigator, Ryder remains oblivious to debilitating gaps in knowledge, especially regarding his recent family life with Sophie and Boris, in the town that he now seeks to observe. And like his Chinese counterpart, Ryder must repress his findings, in this case his traumatic relationship with his parents, in order to preserve his fragile self.

Far from providing greater insight, Ryder's simultaneous occupation of the roles of insider and outsider doubly delimits his perspective.

Although the third Kafkan theme of familial conflict may seem too broad, here again the two authors reveal striking similarities. Both depict dutiful sons who are driven by a desire to please their parents that is so overwhelming that the failure to do so annihilates the sons' sense of self. In Kafka's breakthrough story "The Judgment," the protagonist Georg Bendemann complies with the death sentence imposed by his father by throwing himself into a river while still professing his abiding filial love (*KSS*, 12; *DL*, 61). At the end of *The Unconsoled*, we learn that although Ryder's peripatetic pursuit of pianistic perfection is undertaken to please his parents, they are not coming to the concert and, moreover, have never heard him play (511–12). Both Georg and Ryder consign their knowledge of their filial failure to oblivion. Georg drops into the Lethean waters, and Ryder reverts to repression and the repetition compulsion, setting off in the hope that his next foreign performance will be the one that changes everything and thereby condemning himself to an endless circuit away from and toward his parents.[23]

Here, however, we need to draw an important distinction between the two authors' representations of familial trauma. Since "The Judgment" is narrated from a perspective close to that of the third-person protagonist, and Georg cannot consciously confront his father's accusations, the reader is not vouchsafed any further insight into the motive behind his suicide. In contrast, the revelation of Ryder's estrangement from his parents brings to light an original trauma that is paradoxically reassuring in its explicability. Indeed, this disclosure encourages the reader to look for previous motifs of familial discord, such as the very room that he played in while listening to his parents argue (16), an actual childhood friend who tried to explain their quarrelling (171), and the wreck of the car in which he tried to play during another parental argument (264–65). While the appearance in Central Europe of these places, people, and objects from Ryder's English past breaks with conventional realism, it offers the consolation that the reader can connect these motifs to form a comprehensible chronology. Ishiguro's oblique account of Ryder's familial trauma thus contrasts with Kafka's terse and, for the reader, all the more traumatizing, depiction of a fatally fractured and uncomprehending consciousness.

Thus far we have focused on the themes, such as music, ethnography, and familial conflict, that link Kafka's short stories to Ishiguro's novel and which, in my view, merit the adjective "Kafkan." Now we turn to those aspects of narrative technique that critics often cite when linking Kafka's novels to *The Unconsoled*: an indeterminate setting and more generally an unclear relationship to extra-diegetic reality, a dream-like narrative tone, and the absence of a traditional narrative resolution. As we shall see, these similarities in narrative technique may be termed *Kafkaesque*, rather than

Kafkan, because there are important distinctions to be made between the authors' use of these features.

For example, while critics have pointed out that *The Unconsoled* shares an indeterminate geographical setting with *The Trial* and *The Castle*,[24] the two authors use different techniques to avoid mooring their visions to a particular locale. On the one hand, *The Trial* and *The Castle* are almost entirely devoid of geographical and national markers. On the other, Ishiguro's novel provides a profusion of references to where the town is *not*, as for example when characters mention Switzerland (5) and Germany (65) or visit a Hungarian café (393–414).[25]

However, the fact that both Kafka and Ishiguro occasionally abandon their indeterminate settings to make explicit references to the reality beyond the texts has escaped critical notice. Indeed, both authors use the same technique of invoking a real work of art that they nevertheless alter for symbolic purposes. At the opening of Kafka's novel *Amerika: The Missing Person* (*Der Verschollene*, 1927), the protagonist Karl Rossmann catches his first glimpse of the New World in the figure of the Statue of Liberty, which has sprouted a new appendage: "The arm with the sword now reached aloft and about her figure blew the free winds" (*A*, 3).[26] In *The Unconsoled* Ryder goes to the movies to watch a film entitled *2001: A Space Odyssey* (93) that inexplicably features Clint Eastwood, Yul Brynner, and an entirely unfamiliar plot (94, 98, 100, 108). Thus the technique of ekphrasis, which for realist novelists represents a means of anchoring their fictions to reality, becomes for Kafka and Ishiguro a means of creating an alienation effect, as the reader realizes that the statue and film in question do not correspond to the real and iconic works of art.

Kafka uses the differences between the real Statue of Liberty and his fictionalized version to convey symbolic meaning and to provide a metaliterary commentary on the subsequent narrative. As Carolin Duttlinger explains, Kafka's transformation of the statue's torch into a sword in *Amerika: The Missing Person* invests "this supposedly liberating sight with a castrating authoritarian power," and the resulting tableau "has a retrospective and anticipatory function" in that it suggests both Karl's past banishment by his parents and his future fate in the New World.[27] However, I take issue with Duttlinger's claim that the stark image of the State of Liberty prefigures the novel's overall narrative strategy in which "the textual flow is [repeatedly] interrupted by photographically detailed static tableaux which are thrown into sharp relief."[28] It seems to me rather that a more dynamic photographic technique, that of superimposition or double exposure, is at play here. Kafka's vivid image jostles for attention with our preexisting knowledge of the real statue. In the mind's eye, the images of the sword and torch become conflated to become the flaming sword of the cherubim barring Adam and Eve's return to Paradise (Gen. 3:24). The invocation of these images signals in various ways a decisive break with the past. For not only do they indicate Karl Rossmann's irrevocable expulsion from the "Paradise" of the Old World, but also, in Kafka's surreal modification of the famous icon, the author's own modernist disavowal of conventional realism.

In contrast, Ishiguro's postmodern appropriation of *2001: A Space Odyssey* combines the "alienation effect" of radically reconfiguring a known work of art with the consolation of conventional narrative. While it is initially puzzling to find that the film now stars Clint Eastwood and Yul Brynner, the account of the film that Ishiguro provides suggests a much more traditional Hollywood storyline than Stanley Kubrick's ambiguous and abstract opus. Ishiguro refers to the following scenes: Eastwood stalks the ship's corridors with "a long-barrelled gun" (98), has a tearful conversation with his wife back home (100), has his speed on the draw tested by Yul Brynner (100), and finally prepares to dismantle the malevolent computer HAL with a giant screwdriver (108). Thus Ishiguro replaces Kubrick's famously enigmatic narrative with the staples of conventional cinema: heroism, romance, machismo, gadgets, and, of course, guns. This fictionalized ekphrasis offers an ironic commentary on *The Unconsoled* itself. A film celebrating the triumph of men of action could not be further removed from Ishiguro's own text, which features a protagonist who conspicuously fails to achieve any of his stated goals and refuses to offer a conventionally satisfying thematic or narrative resolution. Nevertheless, readers and critics have remained baffled by these extra-diegetic references to an alternative *2001*, with one nonplussed reviewer ascribing them to an editorial oversight.[29] In this way Ishiguro's heterodiegetic disruption of the narrative enables him to reflect not only on his protagonist's predicament but also on his own novelistic practice. The implicit nostalgia for the comfort of traditional form found in the fictionalized account of the film contrasts starkly with Kafka's brazen assertion of his own vision of a reimagined America.

Kafka's and Ishiguro's surreal alterations of the Statue of Liberty and *2001* bring us to a feature that critics have discerned in both writers' works: a dream-like narrative tone. However, in my view the notion of an oneiric narrative serves as a point of distinction between the two authors and between the Kafkan and Kafkaesque. Aside from the surreal antics of the early text "Description of a Struggle" and Gregor Samsa's fantastic transformation, Kafka's texts generally show more restraint in their use of such narrative devices than does Ishiguro's novel. Even an avowedly dream-like narrative such as "A Country Doctor" ("Ein Landarzt," 1919) presents the telescoping of space and time experienced by its narrator/protagonist in the subjunctive ("as if my patient's yard opened up right in front of my own gate, I have already arrived" [*KSS*, 62][30]) and thus renders the prospect of spatial and temporal instability as hypothetical rather than actual. Contrast this sentence with the episode in which Ryder leaves Boris in a café, travels miles to be photographed in front of a historically significant monument, and then visits another nearby café only to find that it is in the same building in which he left Boris (203). Here time and space have become entirely subject to the desire to continue to dream and to the secondary revision ("sekundäre Bearbeitung"). Yet the fact that we as readers of his first-person narrative are trapped in Ryder's consciousness does not necessarily mean that our reading of the novel is a "nightmarish," frustrating experience.[31] Unlike Kafka's liminal, third-person narratives that hover between waking and sleeping, Ishiguro's thoroughly oneiric first-person novel offers the consolatory prospect of dismissing the text as "only a dream."

However, there is one facet of Ishiguro's narrative style that does not conform to oneiric experience and undermines the notion that the fragments of Ryder's psyche represented by the people, places, and objects around him can be pieced together to form a coherent whole. Shortly after arriving at his hotel, Ryder makes the following unlikely surmise about the issue that is troubling Gustav, the porter: "it occurred to me that . . . a certain matter than had been preoccupying him throughout the day had pushed its way to the front of his mind. He was, in other words, worrying once more about his daughter and her little boy" (13). Here I should stress that at this stage the reader is unaware of any familial connection between Gustav and Ryder; but even bearing in mind the father-in-law/son-in-law relation, the confidence and precision with which Ryder reads Gustav's thoughts is startling. Time and again Ryder demonstrates this uncanny ability to eavesdrop on the internal thought processes and private recollections of other characters. Furthermore, he repeatedly demonstrates a god-like omniscience regarding events and exchanges that take place out of sight and earshot.[32] The question is, Why does Ishiguro have such frequent recourse to this heterodiegetic maneuver, which obliges Ryder to straddle the gulf between an unreliable narrator/protagonist and an omniscient narratorial voice?

In my view, the answer lies in the particular combination of Kafkan narrative techniques that Ishiguro employs in composing *The Unconsoled*. As we have seen, the plot frustrates the protagonist's central aim — to perform at the concert — in a manner that recalls the diversions and detours experienced by K. and Josef K. in Kafka's novels. To this we might add the use of interpolated narratives: as in *The Castle,* the protagonist of *The Unconsoled* is frequently importuned by garrulous and long-winded interlocutors, whose own narratives not only retard the hero's progress but also that of the narrative as whole.[33] Conversely, as we have seen, the first-person narration and the themes of ethnological and aesthetic inquiry invoke many of Kafka's short stories. It is therefore possible to view *The Unconsoled* as a text that combines Kafka's two main narrative modes. Ryder, a narrator/protagonist with a severely occluded perspective and a penchant for anthropological and aesthetic enquiry, recalls the narrators of such works as "Building the Great Wall of China," "Researches of a Dog", and "Josephine, The Singer, or The Mouse People." Yet he finds his attempts at ratiocination constantly frustrated by a plot that recalls Kafka's novels in its proliferation of plot complications. This combination of narrative modes explains why Ishiguro has Ryder engage in heterodiegetic mind-reading so often: without this device, a narrator with a perspective as occluded as Ryder's is simply not in a position to provide a coherent narration for the alienating and bewildering world in which he finds himself. Thus what the reader loses in terms of verisimilitude and diegetic coherence, she gains in terms of a narrative mechanism that, in contrast to Kafka's narratives, has the power to propel the novel to a conclusion.

In conclusion, we can see that the attempt to distinguish the Kafkan from the Kafkaesque elements in Ishiguro's novel offers new insights not only into both authors' oeuvres but also into their respective eras. By comparing the narrative consolations offered by Ishiguro and Kafka, we can gain a fresh perspective on the differences between modernist and postmodernist fiction. For Jean-François Lyotard, modern aesthetics provides greater consolation to the reader than the postmodern variety, by virtue of its adherence to a recognizable form: "Modern aesthetics is an aesthetic of the sublime, though a nostalgic one. It allows the unpresentable to be put forward only as the missing contents; but the form, because of its recognizable consistency, continues to offer the reader or viewer matter for solace and pleasure."[34] Lyotard contrasts the relatively traditional formal aspects of modernism with postmodernism's more radical interrogation of form:

> The postmodern would be that, which, in the modern, puts forward the unpresentable in presentation itself, that which denies itself the solace of good forms, the consensus of a taste which would make it possible to share collectively the nostalgia for the unattainable, that which searches for new presentations, not in order to enjoy them, but in order to impart a stronger sense of the unpresentable.[35]

Lyotard is saying that while the modern addresses the unpresentable, or what cannot be said or written, on a thematic level, modern aesthetics retains the solace provided by consistent or good forms. In contrast, the postmodern extends this notion of the unpresentable to the form of the work itself, forsaking this source of pleasure and comfort. However, comparing Ishiguro's novel to Kafka's work produces a counter-argument to Lyotard's account of modern and postmodern aesthetics. For while the postmodern Ishiguro denies himself "the solace of good forms" in his violation of diegetic convention, Ryder's sporadic omniscience serves a larger formal goal by enabling the narration of the story to the end. Conversely, Kafka's narratives, whether short stories or novels, first or third-person, conform strictly to diegetic convention and yet enact the problematic of "missing contents" in their own refusal, whether deliberate or unintentional, to offer a thematic or narrative resolution. In contrast to the solace proffered by Ishiguro's diegetic violations, Kafka leaves his texts unresolved and his readers unconsoled.

Notes

I am indebted to Ruth Gross for her helpful suggestions regarding this article.

[1] Rainer Nägele, "Kafkaesk," in *Odradeks Lachen: Fremdheit bei Kafka*, ed. Hansjörg Bay and Christof Hamann (Freiburg i. Br.: Rombach Verlag, 2006), 21 (my translation).

[2] Richard Robinson also draws on the distinction between "Kafkan" and "Kafkaesque" as one of degree, but without elaboration. Richard Robinson, *Narratives of the European Border: A History of Nowhere* (Basingstoke, UK: Palgrave Macmillan, 2007), 168.

[3] Although most of the critical responses to *The Unconsoled* at least mention Kafka, the following raise the specific points of comparison listed here. Wai-Chew Sim refers to the "indeterminate spatial coordinates" that link the authors (61), Ishiguro himself cites Kafka's dream-like quality and its influence in an interview with Maya Jaggi (114), and Stephen Benson refers to the shared lack of resolution in Kafka's works and the *The Unconsoled* (155). See Wai-Chew Sim, *Globalization and Dislocation in the Novels of Kazuo Ishiguro* (Lewiston, NY: Edwin Mellen, 2006); Maya Jaggi, "Kazuo Ishiguro with Maya Jaggi," in *Conversations with Kazuo Ishiguro,* ed. Brian W. Schaffer and Cythia F. Wong (Oxford, MS: UP Mississippi, 2008), 110–19; and Stephen Benson, "Words without Song: Kafka and *The Unconsoled*," in *Literary Music: Writing Music in Contemporary Fiction* (Burlington, VT: Ashgate, 2006), 141–60.

[4] Natalie Reitano, "The Good Wound: Memory and Community in *The Unconsoled*," *Texas Studies in Language and Literature* 49.4 (Winter 2007): 361. For further discussion of the critical reception of *The Unconsoled,* see Brian W. Schaffer, *Understanding Kazuo Ishiguro* (Columbia: U of South Carolina P, 1998), 119–20 and 143–46.

[5] For critical responses that discuss Ishiguro's stylistic debt to Kafka in detail, see Benson, "Words without Song," Robinson, *Narratives of the European Border,* and Gary Adelman, "Double on the Rocks: Ishiguro's *The Unconsoled*," *Critique* 42.2 (Winter 2001): 166–79.

[6] Jaggi, "Kazuo Ishiguro with Maya Jaggi," 113. Ishiguro describes Kafka's influence on *The Unconsoled* thus: "Kafka is an obvious model once you move away from straight social or psychological realism" (113). However, the influence of Kafka on Ishiguro's text in terms of both themes and narrative technique represents more than a "default mode" that is inevitably entered once an author abandons verisimilitude.

[7] Adelman is one of the few critics to link *The Unconsoled* to Kafka's shorter fiction, including "The [*sic*] Country Doctor" ("Double on the Rocks,"169), "In the Penal Colony" (169, 173), and "Description of a Struggle" (177). However, Adelman undermines his case through unsupported claims that Ryder's art "would serve the Third Reich" (174) and that the character is "a potential pedophile" (178).
[8] My initial distinction between the "domestic" and "global" phases of Kafka's career draws upon Gerhard Neumann's observation that one of the key problems in Kafka's poetics is the "antithesis between world history and a family squabble, between *grande* and *petite histoire*." Gerhard Neumann, "Literature as Historiography: Franz Kafka's Concept of the 'Diary-Keeping of a People,'" *Journal of the Kafka Society of America* 26.1–2 (2002): 35.
[9] Mark M. Anderson argues for the importance of aestheticism as an influence throughout Kafka's career in *Kafka's Clothes: Ornament and Aestheticism in the Habsburg* Fin-de-Siècle (Oxford: Clarendon, 1992).
[10] Benson, "Words without Song," 142.
[11] Benson, "Words without Song," 152.
[12] All references to *The Unconsoled* are to the following edition: Kazuo Ishiguro, *The Unconsoled* (New York: Vintage Books, 1995), which will henceforth be cited in the text.
[13] Alison Turner, "Kafka's Two Worlds of Music," *Monatshefte* 55.5 (Oct. 1963): 275.
[14] Stanley Corngold, "Kafka and the Philosophy of Music; or, des Kommas Fehl hilft" (unpublished manuscript sent as an electronic document to the author, 22 May 2010), 27–28. This is an updated version of an article that appeared in 2008, and I would like to thank the author and Ruth Gross for generously furnishing me with a copy. See Stanley Corngold, "Kafka and the Philosophy of Music; or, des Kommas Fehl hilft," *JKSA* 28.1–2 (2004): 4–16.
[15] Corngold, "Kafka and the Philosophy of Music," 9–10.
[16] Arthur Schopenhauer, *Die Welt als Wille und Vorstellung*, vol. 2/2, ed. Rolf Toman (Dortmund: Könemann, 1997), 597.
[17] "War er ein Tier, da ihn Musik so ergriff? Ihm war, als zeige sich der Weg zu der ersehnten unbekannten Nahrung" (*DL*, 185).
[18] "Sie [die Musikwissenschaft] gilt als besonders schwierig und schließt sich vornehm gegen die Menge ab" (*NS2*, 480–81).
[19] The synaesthetic and concrete qualities of these terms are, however, not far removed from those used in actual musical theory. Terms related to pigmentation, such as "bright," "dark," and "colored," are routinely employed to describe chords. Moreover, Shostakovich studies have given the world the phrase "brutalized motif," a term whose violence is echoed in Ishiguro's "crushed cadence" and "struck motif." I am indebted to Dr. Sarah J. Reichardt of the School of Music at the University of Oklahoma for these insights into musical terminology.
[20] "Schon tauchen auch wir in das Gefühl der Menge, die warm, Leib an Leib, scheu atmend horcht" (*DL*, 356).

[21] "Ich maße mir kein Urteil an in Dingen, die mir so fern liegen" (*DL*, 271).
[22] "Christhoff" suggests "Christ" and "to hope" (hoffen) in German.
[23] Natalie Reitano ("The Good Wound") links Ryder's repetitive compulsive behavior as an adult with the childhood "training sessions," in which he resisted the urge while playing outside to run home to his parents. For Reitano, Ryder's equation of home with a distant destination, of origin with telos, precludes the "complicated detours" that lead to difference in Freud's scheme. I would argue that Ryder does engage in a series of "complicated detours" in the course of the novel as he tries to carry out a series of haphazard errands, and that these apparent frustrations represent a unconscious strategy for delaying the inevitable trauma of his estrangement from his parents.
[24] See Sim, *Globalization and Dislocation*, 162, and Robinson, *Narratives of the European Border*, 158.
[25] Cf. Robinson, *Narratives of the European Border*, 158.
[26] "Ihr Arm mit dem Schwert ragte wie neuerdings empor, und um ihre Gestalt wehten die freien Lüfte" (*V*, 7).
[27] Carolin Duttlinger, *Kafka and Photography* (Oxford: Oxford U P, 2007), 68.
[28] Duttlinger, *Kafka and Photography*, 67.
[29] Ned Rorem, "Fiction in Review," *Yale Review* 84.2 (1996): 157. Quoted in Barry Lewis, *Kazuo Ishiguro* (Manchester: Manchester UP, 2000), 126.
[30] "als öffne sich unmittelbar vor meinem Hoftor der Hof meines Kranken, bin ich schon dort" (*DL*, 255).
[31] Robinson, *Narratives of the European Border*, 174.
[32] For example, from his vantage point in a car parked in the street, Ryder can hear perfectly every word of a conversation between two characters who are in a nearby house (56–61) and is magically aware of what has happened at a reception held in his honor before his arrival (129).
[33] Cf. Robinson, *Narratives of the European Border*, 174.
[34] Jean-François Lyotard, "Answering the Question: What is Postmodernism?" in *The Postmodern Condition: A Report on Knowledge*, trans. Geoff Bennington and Brian Massumi (Minneapolis, MN: U of Minnesota P, 1979), 81.
[35] Lyotard, "Answering the Question," 81.

13: Kafka's Journey into the Future: Crossing Borders into Israeli/ Palestinian Worlds

Iris Bruce

and do not forget, even a fist was once an open palm and fingers.
— Yehuda Amichai, "Anniversaries of War"

FRANZ KAFKA'S WRITINGS have crossed many ideological and cultural borders, yet the country to which he wanted to emigrate — Palestine then, Israel now — named a street after every important Jewish figure and virtually every Zionist except Kafka. Even his friend Max Brod, a writer of much lesser renown, is now receiving this posthumous honor in Tel Aviv.[1] The reasons for ignoring Kafka were largely ideological: Kafka's generation of German-speaking Jews presented a challenge to the militant and chauvinistic ideology of political Zionism that became prominent after the Second World War. Kafka was also regarded as a Diaspora writer, whose social critique exemplified the political defeatism and passivity that postwar Zionists vehemently rejected. However, precisely the intellectual debates and self-criticism that Kafka was exposed to — the critiques of Zionist prejudice and political dogmatism, combined with a firm belief in a humanist, spiritual, cultural Zionism — represent a path that Zionism did not follow but could have taken after the war and offer an alternative vision for contemporary political Zionism, even today.

Many Israeli writers and intellectuals have long been critical of their society. It therefore comes as no surprise that Kafka's individualistic, dialogical, ambiguous prose, which invites commentary and debate, has inspired many Israeli artists[2] and that in their works we encounter familiar *Kafkaesque* themes, such as metamorphosis, existential absurdity, bureaucratic nightmares, marginality, power, and identity. However, there is little scholarship on the topic of Kafka and Israeli literature and none, to my knowledge, that involves the history of Zionism.[3] Yet Kafka has had an important influence on the Israeli and Palestinian literatures that criticize the Zionist state: we will see how two writers, one from each side, have utilized Kafka in their social satires.

Given the fact that Kafka was never able to visit or migrate to Israel/ Palestine, I will ask for the reader's "willing suspension of disbelief" and invite Kafka to continue his journey — which began with "Jackals and Arabs" ("Schakale und Araber") in 1917 — in order to witness his legacy in the contemporary literary landscape. Our travels take us to *The Secret Life of Saeed: The Pessoptimist* (1974; trans. 1985) by Palestinian-Israeli novelist Emile Habiby (1919–96) and end with *A Woman in Jerusalem* (2004; trans. 2006) by A. B. Yehoshua (1936–). We will encounter fanatics who refuse to cross borders, individuals who cross over but belong nowhere, and others who attempt to create new possible worlds. Kafka is the obvious intertext for both Habiby and Yehoshua in their critiques of Israeli society, which they depict as a claustrophobic space for Palestinians and Jews alike.

Kafka's "Jackals and Arabs" highlights Arab and Jewish prejudice in Palestine at the beginning of the British Mandate (1917–48). Zionism, for Kafka, offered a very real alternative to the anti-Semitism around him. In 1916 he saw it as "positively the only path . . . that can lead to spiritual liberation" (*LF,* 500–501).[4] Though he never engaged in an activist political Zionism, Kafka understood the "universal Zionist yearning" (*LF,* 421).[5] Several of his friends visited or emigrated to Palestine during the second *aliya* or immigration wave (1904–14), and he himself planned to visit in 1923, during the third *aliya* (1919–23). In October 1917 contemporary Jewish-Arab conflicts in Palestine became the subject matter of Kafka's "Jackals and Arabs."

During the First World War many negotiations between Zionist and world leaders took place concerning the realization of Theodor Herzl's political dream, and Britain increasingly supported a national homeland for the Jewish people in Palestine. The Balfour Declaration symbolizes the first political recognition of Zionist goals by a major world power. "Jackals and Arabs" was written during these negotiations and published a month before the decisive Balfour Declaration was issued (2 November 1917). Here Kafka is drawing on the history of the first (1882–1903) and second (1904–14) *aliyot.* The first Jews to immigrate in the nineteenth century were religious Jews from Russia, who arrived even before 1882. They were not political and not interested in founding a new state. The Zionist immigrants during the first *aliya,* young Russian intellectuals, regarded these religious Jews "as the most abject, parasitic aspect of Jewish Diaspora life."[6] Similiarly, many Jews of the second *aliya* — who were still arriving when Kafka's protagonist, in "Jackals and Arabs," was visiting the desert — were Westerners and secular, enlightened socialists and labor Zionists. The jackals' religious fanaticism was foreign to them, too, and no different from the diaspora mentality that the Zionists rejected.

The Northern traveler with his western mindset (possibly an allusion to the famous Zionist Max Nordau)[7] finds it hard to take the jackals seriously. Unwilling to compromise their beliefs, backward rather than forward looking, and waiting for help and redemption from the outside, the jackals seek a solution to their plight. The Northern traveler learns how they are continually abused by the Arabs. During the First World War and especially after the Balfour Declaration, racist sentiments grew, and the militant slogan — "Palestine is our land, and the Jews our dogs"[8] — could be heard in the towns. The Arab in Kafka's story repeats this sentiment: "They are our dogs; more beautiful than yours" (*KSS,* 71).[9] Since the jackals in this text are represented as anything but beautiful, the Arab's ironic comment makes the racial slur even more offensive. Yet the religious jackals are no more tolerant of Arab culture than the Arabs are of them. They refuse to talk to the Arabs, insisting that communication is impossible, and run away to their home in the desert (*KSS,* 69–70). Racial prejudice exists on both sides, and the political reality seems like a continuation of the old in a new guise. The jackals are constantly whipped by the Arabs, who feel scorn and resentment; it seems as if the Jews are trapped in a continual exile. The Arab's last comment is: "'Wonderful animals, aren't they? And how they hate us!'" (*KSS,* 72).[10] Ironically, Theodor Herzl's great utopian novel *Old New-Land* does not point to a new beginning. Both Arabs and Jews here continue to fuel the racial conflict.

Kafka's critical representation of Jewish racial prejudice was not commonly shared by European Zionists; however, the cultural Zionism Kafka was exposed to "held that the transformation of Judaism into a national and secular culture would allow Jewry to enter into a free and creative discourse with other cultures."[11] The jackals' problem is that for them no transformation of Judaism has yet taken place. Moreover, many Zionists did not pay much attention to the presence of Arabs: an (in)famous Zionist slogan was "A land without a people for a people without a land."[12]

Like the jackals, Zionists frequently thought they were culturally superior: Arthur Holitscher, in 1921, for instance, calls the Arabs "a primitive monster, separated from Western man by an abyss a thousand years wide."[13] Kafka has reversed this common prejudiced representation. The Arab in his story appears cultured and in control of himself, whereas the jackals behave in an uncivilized manner, like the animals they are.

The cultural Zionists around Kafka, on the other hand, did not think of Arabs as inferior; Hugo Bergmann especially stressed the process of civilization that Arab culture was undergoing at the time.[14] For Bergmann, an Arab was "exposed to modern life, wandering about the Middle East and even the wide world in search of fresh economic opportunities"; "in his outward appearance he closely resembl[ed] a citizen of a modern European nation in the making."[15] The nationalism of the Prague Zionists was thus no dogmatic assertion of cultural superiority and, as we can see in Kafka's "Jackals," it involved Jewish self-criticism.

Like many of his generation, Kafka was influenced not only by Herzl and Ahad Haam but especially also by Micha Berdyczewski, whose slogan — "We are Jews only because we are human beings who are part of the Jewish people and our humanity is our Judaism"[16] — was echoed in many Zionist publications of the time. Kafka himself repeatedly stressed that the "main thing is the human element, only the human element"; Zionism "is not something that separates well-meaning people" (*LF*, 498 and 501).[17] However, as our story shows, Kafka realized that this kind of humanism was a Zionist dream, for he was too much the realist to transpose this philosophy — in which he wanted to believe — into the Arab-Jewish conflict of the time. In "Jackals" neither the civilized Arab nor the fanatic, religious jackals are "well-meaning" with regard to the other. It is deeply ironic that — civilized or not — the Arab immediately reaches for the whip and resorts to brutality; he lets up only when the visitor "takes him by the arm" (*KSS*, 72).[18] All the Northern mediator achieves is a brief moment of peace for the jackals: otherwise, the future looks bleak indeed in Herzl's promised land.

During Kafka's lifetime Arab violence increased, and both he and Brod followed newspaper accounts of the racial conflicts from 1919 to 1921.[19] After Kafka's death in 1924 the situation did not get better; yet the vision of the cultural Zionists found expression in "Brit Shalom" ("A Peace Treaty"), a Jewish peace group founded in 1925 and supported by Martin Buber, Arthur Ruppin, Hugo Bergmann, Gershom Scholem, Walter Benjamin, and Albert Einstein. A forerunner of today's *Peace Now*, Brit Shalom advocated peaceful coexistence between Jews and Arabs; Buber especially stressed that "the altogether desirable immigration of steadily increasing numbers of Jews into Palestine should take place without any violation of the rights of the country's Arab inhabitants."[20] Buber and others already envisioned a multinational or bi-national state, and when Ben-Gurion created the State of Israel, Buber held fast to his belief that "it should not be the state of the Jews alone."[21] Political circumstances, however, dictated otherwise. Obviously, different Zionist realities determined the direction Zionism would take after the Second World War. Faced with the task of creating an instant state, political Zionism naturally won out over spiritual, cultural Zionism. Given the necessity for national security and self-defense, "The Zionist culture that emerged in Jewish Palestine idealized the New Muscle Jew" and was also "unmistakably gendered; for it was largely the men who claimed the additional mission of national defense."[22]

Jumping ahead in time, we find ourselves in a different and yet strangely familiar world. The Arab protagonist in Emile Habiby's novel, *The Secret Life of Saeed: The Pessoptimist*, is a downtrodden *shlemiel*. His name, Saeed, ironically means lucky and happy — he is a survivor like Voltaire's Candide (1759) or the Czech writer Jaroslav Hašek's good soldier Schweik (1923). In 1948, when Saeed is twenty-four, he and his family emigrate to Lebanon, where his father (a former collaborator for Israel) is shot. Saeed alone crosses the border again and returns to Israel to thirty years of occupation. Habiby himself was an Israeli Palestinian, a member of the knesset representing the communist party, one of Israel's most prominent Arab journalists and writers and winner of Israel's prestigious Prize for Literature (1992). His novel depicts the secular Zionist state until just before the Yom Kippur War (1973).

Like the ape Rotpeter in Kafka's "A Report to an Academy" ("Ein Bericht für eine Akademie," 1919), Saeed is a tragicomic anti-hero, who is doing everything he can to survive. In the end he loses not only his family but also his (Palestinian) identity. Kafka's Rotpeter claims that his evolution into a "human" was never based on a free decision. Caught in Africa and brought to Europe, he finds himself in a new and alien world where, he says, "I had no way out but had to provide myself with one. . . . Just a way out; to the right, to the left, wherever; . . ." (*KSS*, 79–80).[23] Rotpeter decides to assimilate into the dominant culture. Similarly, Saeed sees "no way out" and does his utmost to adapt to the new world by becoming a collaborator like his father before him, an informer for the Zionist state.

Habiby's critique of Saeed is as devastating as many prewar Zionist critiques of assimilation: "I see what other people do and the price they pay, . . . and then I become furious with you. What is it you lack? Is any one of you lacking a life he can offer, or lacking a death to make him fear for his life?" (39). Like the Zionists of Kafka's generation, Saeed's son Walaa (loyalty) rebels against his parents: "I'm sick of your submissiveness!" (111), he exclaims, and states he has "taken up arms only because I'm sick and tired of your hiding" (110). Walaa feels as if his "whole life has been inside a cellar" (111); he cannot wait and becomes a guerilla fighter. Pushed into a corner when Walaa is arrested, he and his mother choose death: she stands by her son and dies with him.

Saeed continues his life alone. By necessity, he must learn Hebrew, but it takes him ten years until his "first welcome address in Hebrew, which [he] did in the presence of Haifa's mayor, who registered it as a precedent" (49). Reminiscent of Kafka's Rotpeter, he receives some recognition from the Israeli "Academy," but this acknowledgment is ironic and seems rather pathetic when we hear how quickly others after him advance in Israeli society by playing the political game. Saeed is not smart enough to play it right and not insensitive enough to step on other people. This is what makes him likeable: he does not hurt anyone except himself.

Saeed is caught in a grotesque, kafkaesque bureaucracy, where everyone enriches himself by taking from the "evacuated Arab homes in Haifa" (45). He understands that his boss Jacob is just a pawn in the big machine: he is only a little Sephardic Jew who "hates the Ashkenazi or 'Western' Jews" (80). Above Jacob is the BIG MAN with dark glasses, the Ashkenazi who calls Saeed in and beats him (51). The Sephardic Jacob, on the other hand, sympathizes with Saeed. The difference between these two Jews (Jacob and the BIG MAN) is much greater than the difference between Jacob and Saeed. There is no "ethnic," essentialist Jewishness for Habiby: class and hierarchy are the determining factors. Eventually Saeed understands that his collaboration is wrong but not before he feels the brutality of the Zionist security state and has to go into hiding. Book 2 already is composed in the catacombs of Acre, in the tunnels underground, where Saeed is "safe but not secure": he has not written "for some time for reasons of security — this time mine and not the state's . . ." (69).

Habiby shows much sympathy for Saeed, the little man who is caught in the wheels of history and bureaucracy. Saeed simply cannot stand up to anyone: he is not that kind of a brave person. In contrast, Kafka, in his ape story, is relentless in his satire of the assimilated Jew. However, for the young Zionists in Prague, assimilation and its consequences were a disease that could be cured by embracing Zionism and moving to Palestine. Habiby's protagonist sees no way out and imagines the existence of possible worlds in outer space from where help might come in the future:

> There must certainly be worlds other than ours, and better too. No doubt they'll find us before we them. Well, the Turks left and the British came to us . . . so how can I doubt them — I, a young man whose whole life is still before him, the British having left and Israel come in? Yes, ever since that time I began looking upward and awaiting their arrival. Either they will transform my monotonous and boring life completely, or they can take me away with them. Is there an alternative? (30–31)

Upon completing his life's story (like Kafka's ape, though uninvited), Saeed finds himself holding onto a blunt stake high up in the air — he is a *luftmensch* if ever there was one — holding on for dear life, waiting to be rescued. Another variation of the ending suggests that he was in an insane asylum all along, having only invented the story about the aliens who carried him off, and now is dead. Then again, a mysterious gentleman will continue looking for him, and readers are invited to do the same, but the search seems futile, because the novel ends with a question: "The point is, gentlemen, how will you ever find him unless you happen to trip right over him?" (163) In other words, Saeed will always remain invisible, a complete antihero. Habiby's novel is a pessoptimistic perversion of the humanist quest for the best of all possible worlds.

Like Kafka in his humanist satires, Habiby depicts no essentialist (Jewish or Palestinian) identity. Moreover, the fact that a Palestinian writer can critique the Zionist state by drawing on a Kafka text that was a prewar Zionist satire of Jewish assimilation is not ironic but underscores commonalities rather than differences in Jewish and Arab "diaspora" experiences. In our next novel the protagonist will transcend the ethnic divide altogether, cross physical and mental borders into the global world, and return home with a newly discovered identity that resembles the spiritual, humanist Zionist ideals of the early Zionist founders.

A. B. Yehoshua's *A Woman in Jerusalem* (2004) takes us into the period of the Second Palestinian uprising or Al Aqsa Intifada (2000–2003), with its wave of terrorist attacks and suicide bombings, "a time when pedestrians were routinely exploding in the streets" (4). The English title refers to a forty-eight-year-old woman engineer from Russia, Yulia Ragayev, a recent non-Jewish immigrant, who dies after "being critically wounded after a bombing in the Jerusalem market" (5). Yulia is one of over a hundred thousand immigrants from Russia after the fall of the Soviet Union, most of them professionals — engineers, architects, doctors, nurses — and many of them (Jewish or not) struggling like her to integrate into Israeli society.

At the same time, the original title, *Shlichuto shel hamemuneh al meshave enosh* (The Mission of the Human Resources Manager), identifies a nameless thirty-nine-year-old protagonist as the central character; "a natural leader" in the army (201), he ultimately leaves it because he is "too much of an individualist" (184) and believes "that there was nothing in the world he thought worth being killed for in battle" (201). The novel depicts a vicious circle in a country that is literally and figuratively breeding and feeding its military and keeps returning psychologically damaged individuals to society. The protagonist is one such individual, who embarks on a quest for his humanity.

The two separate narratives connect when the protagonist's quest becomes intertwined with his "mission" to return Yulia, the victim of the "suicide bombing" (23), to her "family" in Russia. What unites these characters further is that they are both kafkaesque: Yulia's fate contains echoes of several Kafka stories, and the male protagonist changes from the guise of one Kafka character to another. At times, both protagonists embody several Kafka personas at once.

Yulia's death represents an "awakening" for the protagonist from his monotonous life and "cut-and-dried job" (38). Reminiscent of Gregor Samsa, he works as a "traveling salesman" (85, 122, 139) for a large bakery after leaving the army. All these years he carries the army with him, as is shown by his "military crew cut" (11, 39) and the fact that he "still carr[ies] a shell on [his] back, ducking into it when anything touches [him]" (183). When his marriage ends "in part because of his frequent travels" (5), he is offered a position as personnel manager so that he can spend more time with his daughter. His wish to become "human" again makes him request that his workplace be renamed "human resources division" (97).

Our protagonist is therefore ready to step in when his company is put on trial and charged with inhumanity for ignoring the death of the cleaning lady Yulia Ragayev, one of its employees. The newspaper headline reads: "The Shocking Inhumanity behind Our Daily Bread" (5). The Gregor Samsa-like manager now becomes Joseph K., trying to clear his company's image: this is a "clerical error" (3), and the "entire accusation" is "based on a mistake" (28). The incident quickly turns into his own personal trial. Sexually repressed, like Kafka's country doctor in "A Country Doctor" ("Ein Landarzt," 1919), he lives inside himself "like a snail," whence all he can "see of goodness or beauty is its shadow" (17, 42). But this former student of Plato is not the only one who is blind.

The company's owner also lives entirely in a world of shadows and illusion. Initially, he is very "upset" (3) about the charges of inhumanity, because his bakery "was founded at the beginning of the last century by [his] grandfather" (5–6), a genealogy establishing a link with the humanist Zionism of the "founders." But his humanity is fake. He really just wants "a yes or no answer: are we guilty or not?" (90) The personnel manager immediately shifts the emphasis from "guilt" to "responsibility" (90), which involves an ethical and moral dimension that also happens to be the theme of Kafka's *Country Doctor* volume. When the old man does not see what he should be responsible for, the protagonist "gives it up" and ends their conversation.

However, there is much the owner is responsible for, because his bakery has made big profits from previous wars, the army, and the new Arab-Jewish conflict. This nightmare of a bakery, whose ovens, chimneys, and smoke rising day and night resemble the machines in Fritz Lang's futuristic dystopia *Metropolis*, also points to the shadows of the Holocaust. The more volatile the political situation, the more profit the bakery makes. The owner admits many times over that he can "afford" to atone; he never thought he would become so wealthy, "especially since the start of all this terror" (122). His company "step[s] up in production due to a closure imposed on the Palestinian territories" after the "destruction by the army of several small Palestinian bakeries suspected of harboring bomb makers" (108–9). The bakery feeds off war by feeding the war engine. Under the guise of humanity, the owner is hypocritical and opportunistic.

Otherwise, the Arab-Jewish conflict is barely mentioned, but perhaps this is the point, for the conflict is of very little concern to the bakery's owner — and by extension to society on the whole.[24] The old man thrives on human tragedy to boost his humanitarian image: he intends to exploit Yulia's tragic death for sensational purposes by using her picture for the "bakery's memorial exhibition," which is not meant only "for employees killed in action": "Terror victims deserve to be there, too" (105). Yulia's cleaning job is therefore highly symbolic, a job for a lifetime — or in

Kafka's words: "If one wished to clean it up really, there would be no end to it" (*L*, 168; translation modified).[25]

Ironically, no one sees that this woman, the lowly cleaning lady, whose body cannot be identified for the longest time, comes with a message — she is the only one who is given a name and an — albeit enigmatic, Kafkaesque — identity: she literally *incorporates* Kafkan features. Her "unusual Tatar, or perhaps Mongol eyes" (50) point to her mysterious, mixed "breeding" (92) — her Asian/Mongolian/Russian background suggests she is related to Kafka's "Crossbreed" (1917), an animal half kitten and half lamb (*KSS*, 125–27).[26] "Tatar" also alludes to a figure in Kafka's parable "Before the Law" (1915), the doorkeeper with the "black Tatar beard" (*KSS*, 68) who does not grant the "man from the country" entry to the Law.[27] Yulia is originally a "woman from the country," a little village in Russia, far from civilization. She is admitted as a temporary resident, loses her job because her supervisor falls in love with her, and patiently waits for another job opportunity. Yet, "Julia waits in vain!" (*KSS*, 74)[28] and dies not long after — the victim of a suicide bombing, with apologies to Kafka's "Fratricide" ("Ein Brudermord," 1917).

Yulia embodies the "imperial message" that in Kafka's story of 1917 never reaches its destination. No one apart from the human resources manager even bothers to think about who Yulia was, why she came, and what she represents: "What did you want from us, Yulia? What did you hope to find in the hard, sad city that killed you? What kept you there when you could have gone home with your only son?" (144). Yulia's hybridity and her decision — as a non-Jew and a non-religious Christian (82) — to make Jerusalem her home certainly raise important questions about identity and belonging. For one thing, her hybridity signifies flexibility and openness toward other possibilities. It is easy for Yulia to change identities and cross borders. In Jerusalem she lives in an orthodox neighborhood and makes friends with an orthodox family (81–83 and 130). Six orthodox girls, "like a flock of birds" (84) reminiscent of the gang of girls in the sway of Titorelli, the painter in *The Trial* (*Der Process*, 1925), tell the personnel manager that they have given Yulia a new nameplate with the Jewish name Miryam (198).

Philosophizing further about Plato and hybridity, the protagonist argues that individuals who are "divided in two" have "the human desire to unite with one's missing half, also known as love . . ." (186). Yulia may have been a mechanical engineer, but moving to Jerusalem has allowed her to connect with her spiritual, creative side. She has in her home "a sketch — done by an amateur — herself?" that depicts "a small deserted alleyway — in Jerusalem's Old City? — that curved gently to meet the silhouette of a domed and minareted mosque" (86). This "gentle curve" moving toward a meeting via a deserted path, a road not frequently taken, leads to what seems to be the Al Aqsa Mosque on the Temple Mount. This contested holy site for Jews and Moslems fell into Jewish hands after the Six Day War in 1967, when the formerly divided Jerusalem was united. Yulia's choice of subject matter for her painting is important, because Ariel Sharon's visit to the Temple Mount in 2000 allegedly provoked the Second Intifada and its explosive aftermath, in which Yulia was killed. By painting this holy site, Yulia also claims it for herself and — since she is not religious, and neither Jew nor Moslem — by extension for the whole world, crossing over religious and ethnic borders.

For the human resources manager, Yulia becomes "a subject of reflection without end."[29] Many others also notice something special about her, but the authorities care only about identifying her body and returning it to the country she came from. The bakery's owner, who wishes to atone, sends the personnel manager along as his messenger: he now becomes "an emissary. A very special one" (123). At this point, the protagonist evokes several Kafka characters at once: the family man who takes care of the crossbreed; the country doctor who tries to heal the patient (Israel) and himself; the land surveyor in *The Castle* (*Das Schloss*, 1926), who travels through a snowy, here Russian, landscape; and, at the point that the messenger delivers his final report to the old man, the ape Rotpeter. Kafka comes through in full force to make the personnel manager human again and to redeem him, his city, and his country.

The protagonist's journey with Yulia's corpse into the unknown Russian hinterlands reveals to him the importance of a global perspective. His travels disclose similarities between the two countries, most importantly the parallels in Russia's and Israel's military histories that he discovers when he agrees to make "a detour" (curve!) into Yulia's past. For her the present reality in Jerusalem has likely been a mirror image of the cold war, and she knows the lingering fear and paranoia. Given her cultural and professional background (as a mechanical engineer), Yulia is sensitive to the spiritual needs of her new country and well-suited for the "clean-up" job in a bakery that had been feeding the war engine, fueling hatred and killing.

Recognizing these parallel worlds, the protagonist has to cleanse himself of his own society. He is literally cleaned out by food poisoning and recovers deep "in the bowels of the earth" (211), in the atomic shelter underground. Miraculously, on his cell phone deep down in the atomic shelter, he manages to connect with his ex-wife in Israel, who has more insight than he: she tells him that Yulia would have wanted to be buried in Jerusalem (220). After this first "human" connection with his family, he still has to pass the last border separating him from Yulia's village. The group he travels with needs an "ice-breaker," a ferry, to cross over a big river (223), a humorous take-off on Kafka's phrase that a "book" must be like an "axe to break the frozen sea inside us."[30] In fact, the personnel manager decides that he will "cross the ice on foot," taking his first steps into a new world during a "glorious sunset" (225). Making history, he asks a "photographer" to record this event for his daughter (225).

Their final arrival at Yulia's village with the (wrong) message from the old company owner is anticlimactic. When the protagonist breaks the news to her mother "with the full authority of the company — indeed, of the entire city of Jerusalem — behind him" (229), Yehoshua's comic and ironic use of Kafka to satirize the personnel manager and his mission is quite evident! Not surprisingly, the "round little monk" (229), Yulia's mother, refuses to accept the old man's "humanitarian" gesture. She is shocked and angry that her daughter's dead body had to travel so far "for no good reason"; she should be buried in the place where she chose to live, and she insists that Jerusalem "was her city. It was everyone's" (230).

The protagonist's journey is a cyclical, macabre quest, serious and comic at the same time. The authorities in Russia and Israel are used to "dead bodies that travel in both directions" (163). But Yulia's corpse comes full circle. Like Kafka's ape, the personnel manager has "no choice" (a refrain in the text) if he wants to become human. Yulia is his cross as well as his crossbreed, and she belongs to him. She is returned to Israel precisely because, with her mixed background, her promise for the future lies here: as the night-shift supervisor puts it, it was not her smile "or even her charm, but the contradictions of a fair-complexioned Asiatic, with whom he had suddenly fallen — passively and with no hope of consummation — in love" (51). This man's Platonic love is highly ironic, not only because there is "no hope of consummation." He will not even try to love Yulia and fires her so as not to lose "control" over himself. His ultimate fear of her hybridity speaks volumes.

An identity like Yulia's that embraces contradictions presents a challenge and perhaps a cure for a homogeneous society like Israel. A national identity that embraces and welcomes otherness and diversity would be a model for this society in the future. The harmony that radiates from Yulia contrasts with "the entire false promise of Jerusalem" (193) that betrays her integrity and faith in humanity. For these symbolic reasons, the protagonist cannot abandon the crossbreed, and so he brings her back "home" to her chosen country, thereby undermining dogmatic Zionist nationalism. Israel is getting more than it asked for. Apart from Yulia's corpse, which has returned to haunt them, there are now "two new residents, an old woman and a handsome young man" (237): her old religious mother, the little monk, and Yulia's son. Tongue-in-cheek, Kafka's imperial message has finally arrived: it is for "you" (*KSS*, 120), as Yehoshua invokes Jerusalem's "global spiritual dimension."[31]

One insistent, obsessed, nameless Israeli returns with a Kafkan message of hope in this despondent contemporary climate — the very idea seems absurd in an equally Kafkaesque way. For the moment, he alone has this new "vision and initiative" (236). But the novel has two endings. For one, it concludes with the protagonist's final report to the owner of the company, who thinks his employee is out of his mind (236). Like Kafka's ape, the protagonist becomes aggressive and sarcastic when he "humbly" takes his leave: "Oh, no sir, I'm your loyal employee. I'm just surprised that a man of your wisdom and experience didn't realize that a journey like this could benefit a city we have despaired of" (236–37). The other ending shows the protagonist's metamorphosis back into a human being, his own personal redemption that opens the novel and therefore represents a new beginning. His conviction that ordinary individuals can have an impact — we may be "private individuals, but with our vision and initiative . . ." (236) — opens a door to a possible new world.

All along, this journey of redemption is accompanied by references to the sun: "the reborn sun" (127), "the ever-brighter sun" (128), the "glorious sunset" (225). The day after the protagonist returns, he is greeted with a "radiant morning" and "felt a sudden lifting of the spirits, and Jerusalem, the shabby, suffering city he had left just a week ago, was once more bathed in a glow of importance, as it had been in his childhood" (3). The symbol of the sun is linked to Yulia, whose smile was "like sunshine" (67). The reference to the protagonist's childhood takes us back to the 1960s: and here Naomi Shemer's famous song, "Jerusalem of Gold" (1967), composed just before the Six Day War, with its longing for the unification of Jerusalem, might be invoked to complete Bruckner's unfinished Ninth Symphony (89), which the bakery's owner hears on the evening when the news about Yulia's death and the company's inhumanity surfaces. Through the rising golden sun, the human resources manager's quest for redemption once more evokes the old Zionist dream of a new humanity for himself and his country.

Though Yehoshua holds up a mirror to reveal the fake, hypocritical, and debased humanism under the cracked surface, he also holds out a promise for the future. The increasing impact of multiculturalism — especially through the new immigration waves from Russia — and the effects of globalization will lead to border crossings of many kinds that can transform Israeli society into a newly energized possible world. Herzl's utopian novel *Old-New Land* (1902) already envisioned a peaceful coexistence of Arabs, Jews, men, and women in Palestine. Kafka's generation did not abandon the hope that "our humanity is our Judaism."[32] The Israeli novelist and peace activist Amos Oz, in 1982, understandably finds the humanist, spiritual Zionism of these early intellectual "dreamers" too romantic and unrealistic, but he also stresses the importance of alternate visions in the present climate of conflict: "Young people . . . have rediscovered the secret charm of the original visions," and "there is, at long last, . . . a painful reconsideration of the ideological, ethical and political propositions of the early Zionists, a growing tendency on the part of young Israelis to give a flat no to their parents — and, at the same time, to say 'perhaps' to their grandparents."[33] And if the changing nature of Israeli society indeed holds opportunities for border crossings in the future, will there perhaps be a day when at the very least a street or cul-de-sac in Israel is named after Kafka? Perhaps in Habiby and Yehoshua's Haifa or even in Jerusalem, Yehoshua's city of birth?

Notes

[1] Many thanks to Mark Gelber for this information (email correspondence 25 March 2009).

[2] In addition to S. Y. Agnon and Aaron Appelfeld, Etgar Keret and Palestinian Israeli novelist Sayed Kashua should be mentioned for the young generation.

[3] Most studies focus on Kafka and Agnon: see Robert Alter, "Kafka's Father, Agnon's Mother, Bellow's Cousins," *Commentary* 81.2 (Feb. 1986): 46–52; Arnold J. Band, "The Kafka-Agnon Polarities," in *The Dove and the Mole*, ed. M. Lazar & R. Gottesman (Malibu, CA: Undena, 1987), 151–60; Hillel Barzel, *Agnon and Kafka* (Ramat Gan, Israel: Bar Oryan, 1972); Shimon Sandbank, "History and the Law": S. Y. Agnon and Kafka," in *After Kafka: The Influence of Kafka's Fiction* (Athens: U of Georgia P, 1989), 97–111; and Gershon Shaked, "Kafka and Agnon: Their Relationship to Judaism and Zionism," in *Kafka, Zionism, and Beyond*, ed. Mark Gelber (Tübingen: Niemeyer, 2004), 239–57.

[4] "Es ist, soviel ich sehe, der absolut einzige Weg . . ., der zu einer Befreiung führen kann" (*BF*, 696–97).

[5] "allgemeine zionistische Sehnsucht" (*BF*, 595–96).

[6] Benjamin Harshav, "Introduction," in *Only Yesterday* by S. Y. Agnon (1945; Princeton, NJ: Princeton UP, 2000), ix–x. For an earlier analysis see Iris Bruce, *Kafka and Cultural Zionism: Dates in Palestine* (Madison: U of Wisconsin P, 2007), 185–88; for religious messianism and ritual see 154–56.

[7] It was well known to contemporaries that Nordau "changed his name from Südfeld (southern field) to Nordau (northern meadow)" in order to symbolize his "break with the past." George Mosse, "'Max Nordau and His Degeneration': Introduction," in *Degeneration,* by Max Nordau (Lincoln: U of Nebraska P, 1993), xiii; Bruce, *Kafka and Cultural Zionism,* 154.

[8] Arthur Holitscher, *Reise durch das jüdische Palästina* (Berlin: Fischer, 1922), 85. Holitscher reports that this "slogan" reverberated throughout Jerusalem during the November pogrom of 1921.

[9] ". . . es sind unsere Hunde; schöner als die Eurigen" (*E,* 283).

[10] "Wunderbare Tiere, nicht wahr? Und wie sie uns hassen!" (*E,* 284).

[11] Paul Mendes-Flohr, "Cultural Zionism's Image of the Educated Jew: Reflections on Creating a Secular Jewish Culture," *Modern Judaism* 18.3 (Oct. 1998): 227.

[12] For the history of the term, see Adam M. Garfinkle, "On the Origin, Meaning, Use, and Abuse of a Phrase," *Middle Eastern Studies* 27 (Oct. 1991): 539–50.

[13] Holitscher, *Reise durch das jüdische Palästina,* 79; my translation.

[14] Hugo Bergmann, "Bemerkungen zur arabischen Frage," *Palästina* 8 (1911): 191–92, and Dimitry Shumsky, "Czechs, Germans, Arabs, Jews: Franz Kafka's 'Jackals and Arabs' between Bohemia and Palestine," *AJS Review: The Journal for the Association for Jewish Studies* 33.1 (Apr. 2009) : 91–93.

[15] Shumsky, "Czechs, Germans, Arabs, Jews," 92–93.

[16] Bergmann, *Jawne and Jerusalem* (Berlin: Jüdischer Verlag, 1919), 38; my translation.

[17] "Die Hauptsache sind die Menschen, nur sie, die Menschen"; "Zionismus ist nicht etwas, was Menschen trennt, die es gut meinen" (*BF*, 694, 698).

[18] ". . . ich faßte seinen Arm" (*E*, 284).

[19] Kafka also read about Arab attacks in early "Israeli" literature by Shlomo Zemach and was familiar with the author Joseph C. Brenner, who was killed in the Arab riots of 1921. See Bruce, *Kafka and Cultural Zionism*, 173, 182.

[20] Allan Arkush, "The Jewish State and Its Internal Enemies: Yoram Hazony versus Martin Buber and His Ideological Children," *Jewish Social Studies* 7.2 (Winter 2001), 173.

[21] Arkush, "The Jewish State and Its Internal Enemies," 175.

[22] Tamar Mayer, "From Zero to Hero: Nationalism and Masculinity in Jewish Israel." In *Israeli Women Studies: A Reader*, ed. Esther Fuchs (Piscataway, NJ: Rutgers UP, 2005), 105.

[23] "Ich hatte keinen Ausweg, mußte mir ihn aber verschaffen. . . . Nur einen Ausweg; rechts, links, wohin auch immer . . ." (*E*, 326).

[24] Aluf Benn, "Sharon's Real Legacy — Keeping the Arabs out of Sight," Sun., 17 Jan. 2010, HAARETZ.com. http://www.haaretz.com/hasen/spages/1142320.html.

[25] "Wollte man wirklich reinigen, wäre ja kein Ende" (*Br*, 197).

[26] The "crossbreed" is an important metaphor in Yehoshua's writing. Many thanks to Ranen Omer-Sherman for sharing his published and unpublished research with me and discussing Yehoshua's different portrayals of hybridity, which at times even contradict one other. We produce very different accounts of Yehoshua's perspective on hybridity.

[27] "[der] schwarze[] tatarische[] Bart" (*E*, 162).

[28] "Vergebens wartet Julia!" (*E*, 262).

[29] Walter Benjamin, "Franz Kafka: On the Tenth Anniversary of His Death," in *Illuminations: Essays and Reflections*, ed. Hannah Arendt (New York: Schocken, 1968), 122.

[30] ". . . ein Buch muß die Axt sein für das gefrorene Meer in uns" (*Br*, 28).

[31] Yehoshua remarks: "I'm not a religious person. . . . But a certain religious energy erupted in this book. And through this beautiful foreign woman I also tried to restore meanings that we have lost. . . . The spiritual meaning of Jerusalem. Suddenly I noticed that Jerusalem has become rather tattered within the Jewish-Arab conflict and that both we and the Palestinians are completely losing its global spiritual dimension." A. B. Yehoshua, "A Nation That Knows No Bounds," interview by Ari Shavit. *Ha'aretz* (19 Mar. 2004), http://www89.homepage.villanova.

edu/scott.black/S04sensem/Yehoshua%20interview%20%28March%202004%29.htm.

[32] Bergmann, *Jawne und Jerusalem*, 38.

[33] Amos Oz, "Has Israel Altered Its Visions?" (1982), in *Israel, Palestine and Peace: Essays* (New York: Harcourt Brace, 1994), 16, 18.

14: Kafka and Italy: A New Perspective on the Italian Literary Landscape

Saskia Elizabeth Ziolkowski

Examining modern Italian literature is a Kafkaesque endeavor, because it is not always entirely clear if it exists. Critics have tended to concentrate on movements or smaller trends, such as *frammentismo*, *decadentismo*, *ermetismo*, *crepuscularismo*, and *futurismo*, or on particular figures, such as Luigi Pirandello, Gabriele D'Annunzio, F. T. Marinetti, Italo Svevo, and Carlo Emilio Gadda, or on regional clusters of various authors. While these approaches have offered a minute anatomy of Italy's various authors and movements, they have also isolated Italian literature from larger comparative studies and necessarily excluded certain authors from consideration. The broader term "modernism," meanwhile, which has recently been used to describe some modern Italian works,[1] frequently mischaracterizes the Italian picture.[2] This article is part of a larger project that aims to map a distinct but unexamined Kafkan tradition in Italian modern literature, a tradition that encompasses a more diverse and representative group of authors than headings such as *frammentismo* allow, without assimilating the particularity of the Italian scene to a larger modernist movement.

Reversing the clever conceit of Jorge Luis Borges's "Kafka and his Precursors," which finds Kafkan presences in the past, this study examines Kafka's presences in his Italian successors. Instead of studying direct influence, I use Ludwig Wittgenstein's idea of family resemblances to consider the Kafkan qualities these modern Italian authors share. From the use of animal imagery and oppressive spaces to representations of crises, alienation, and repressive bourgeois relations, the disparate themes of Kafka's fiction are reflected throughout modern Italian literature. By engaging the immense amount of scholarship on Kafka, the project endeavors to revisit and refine the critical understanding of twentieth-century Italian literature. A Kafkan view of Italian literature incorporates some less well known Italian texts that are currently excluded from maps of modern Italian literature at the same time as it provides new perspectives on canonical authors such as Svevo, Gadda, and Italo Calvino. In this article I first outline a distinct but unexamined Kafka tradition in Italian literature, which can reshape the critical understanding of Italian modern literature, and then provide a more detailed example of how reading Kafka with Italian authors enhances the critical understanding of them.

Although critics have called particular attention to Kafka's rise in fame in France, England, and America after the Second World War, his role in Italy has been under-examined, despite the fact that he was a critical presence there well before the war. One Italian Germanist notes that "the first non-German notice" of Kafka came from Italy.[3] Kafka's precocious appearance in the Italian literary landscape was due in part to the Austro-Hungarian and then Italian city of Trieste. The labors of the Triestine Roberto "Bobi" Bazlen, in particular, exemplify the city's role. Bazlen recommended Kafka's works to Italians who wanted to improve their German as strikingly early as 1919,[4] and to notable Italian authors, such as the poet Eugenio Montale in early 1924,[5] when one critic estimates that Kafka was so little known in the world that only two articles existed that referred to his work, both written by his good friend and constant advocate Max Brod.[6] Bazlen's friends and correspondents read like a who's who list of Italian literature, and several of them name the Prague writer as an important literary influence. They include Montale, Svevo, Umberto Saba, Natalia Ginzburg, Elsa Morante, Giani Stuparich, Alberto Savinio, Alberto Moravia, Sandro Penna, Elio Vittorini, Enrico Pea, Aldo Palazzeschi, Pier Paolo Pasolini, Giacomo Debenedetti, Carlo Emilio Gadda, and Carlo Levi.

Even outside Triestine literary circles, the early instances of Kafka's Italian presence are remarkable. In 1933, the year some of Kafka's works were being burned in Berlin and a couple of years before *The Trial* (*Der Process*, 1925) came into print in English, Frassinelli brought out an Italian translation. In 1947, Alberto Spaini, in the introduction to his translation of *Amerika: The Missing Person* (*Der Verschollene*, 1927), noted that Kafka's influence was widespread: "For more than ten years we have been invaded by ***kafkaini*** and by a ***kafkaismo*** that critics have not yet identified, perhaps because his name would not have meant anything to anyone, but which has made Kafka even more popular in Italy than one can imagine."[7] Spaini's description of a diffuse "kafkaismo" points to the difficulty of uncovering who knew Kafka's work and when: many of these traces have been lost or are impossible to locate in time. Spaini's comment may refer particularly to Dino Buzzati's vexed relationship with Kafka. When critics wrote of Buzzati's debt to the German-language writer, he responded in interviews and in print that he had not known of Kafka's work until well after having written his novels in the early 1940s. These sorts of debates often seem to circle around the concern that artistic debt somehow lessens the contributions of the later author, automatically making the second author secondary. Buzzati's anxiety that his own work could lose some of its originality, its Buzzatiness, if it were revealed to be Kafkaesque may seem misplaced, but it testifies to Kafka's powerful presence in Italian literary circles at the time.

The cultural history of Kafka's reception provides an important background for the Kafkan reading of modern Italian literature, but questions of source and influence are not decisive for the study suggested here. Instead of focusing on the positivist question of who read whom and when, I wish to emphasize the grounds of the connection and the family resemblances between the authors' works. Rather than replaying the debates about whether or not Dino Buzzati was conditioned by Kafka, scholars should explore the strong family resemblance between Kafka's *The Castle* (*Das Schloss*, 1926) and Buzzati's *Il deserto dei Tartari* (*The Tartar Steppe*), a tale of a man who waits in vain for a military invasion; or between several of Kafka's and Buzzati's short stories, many of which focus on inescapable and maddening power structures.

The question of Kafka's influence on many later writers is less problematic, since a range of authors, among them Cesare Pavese and Calvino, acknowledge Kafka as a particularly fascinating, influential, or beloved writer. The richness and variety of Kafka's presence in Italian literature is notable even in just the direct references to him made in Italian works. Montale, who, as discussed, was introduced to Kafka early, wrote a demanding poem, "Verboten," which focuses on Kafka.[8] Magris's hard-to-define *Danubio* (*Danube*) (it has been called a novel, a memoir, and a travelogue) includes numerous references to Kafka and has a chapter "Kierling, Hauptstrasse 187" that moves between the narrator's experience in the house in which Kafka died and reflections on Kafka. More playful than these two works is Tommaso Landolfi's short story, "Il babbo di Kafka" ("Kafka's Dad"), published in 1942. The narrator and his friend, Kafka, are forced to deal with the appearance of a huge spider that has the head of Kafka's father. These three very different works suggest the various ways Italian authors used Kafka in diverse genres and also reveal aspects of the Italian literary landscape.

In yet another mode of engagement with Kafka, Primo Levi, the well known author of *Se questo è un uomo (If This is a Man* in England and *Survival in Auschwitz* in America), translated *Der Process* and begins his note to the novel: "So this is it, this is human destiny: we can be persecuted and punished for a crime that has not even been committed, which is obscure and which will never be revealed to us by the 'court.'"[9] As a Holocaust survivor, his reading has striking connotations. Years after returning from Auschwitz, Levi enrolled in German courses at Turin's *Goethe-Institut* and was later asked to translate the novel for an "author translating authors" series. He was probably asked to do so partially because of the popular idea of Kafka as some sort of prophet of the Shoah. A more illuminating reason for Levi's reaction to the translation project, from which he emerged "as from an illness,"[10] relates to Ritchie

Robertson's analysis of Kafka's penetrating portrayals of institutional (broadly meant) power, authority, and violence.[11] Concentration camps are an extreme instance of the way institutions can take over all aspects of a private individual's life, and Kafka's depiction of oppressive power resonated with Levi.

Kafka's understanding and literary representations of power as central in the family, one's "first institution,"[12] in fact clarifies why a range of Italian authors whose works are often set in the home have been described as Kafkaesque. Although these three authors have not been considered together, the oppressive familial relationships depicted by Elsa Morante in *Menzogna e sortilegio* (*House of Liars*) can be compared with those depicted in Massimo Bontempelli's *Il figlio di due madri* (*The Son of Two Mothers*) and in Susanna Tamaro's "La grande casa bianca" ("The Big White House"). All three of these eerie works reveal the intense psychological power that familial relationships have in that first "institution" of one's home.

From within the vast panorama of potential Kafkan Italian authors, I want to focus on one particular encounter, because it shows how a Kafkan lens can illuminate under-studied Italian works and perhaps make them part of larger critical conversations. Although Svevo is primarily recognized for his novels, his story "Argo e il suo padrone" ("Argo and His Master") demonstrates connections to Kafka's "A Report to an Academy" ("Ein Bericht für eine Akademie," 1919). In "A Report" an ape, Rotpeter, learns to act like a man and presents a report of his process of becoming human. The story has been interpreted in a variety of ways. Rotpeter's process of human assimilation has been read as symbolizing several groups who experienced some sort of cultural shift.[13] Even when not read allegorically, "A Report" presents the crisis of human identity. The work continues to stimulate discussions about animals and their relationship to humans, especially in the growing field of animal studies.[14] Svevo's "Argo," on the other hand, has received scant attention, despite its interrogation of humans' perceptions of themselves as "human" and thus separate from animals, which could contribute to discussions of species and identity.

In "Argo," a man attempts to teach Italian to his dog, Argo, after reading about an impressively expressive German dog, who, like Rotpeter, can "talk like a human being. In fact, rather more intelligently, as they were asking its advice. The dog pronounced difficult German words which even I would hardly be able to say."[15] The ability of the German dog to learn a human language prompts the man to reflect on his own linguistic skills, and, in the end, it is he who learns a new tongue. In the first section of "Argo" the man relates the process of learning to understand Argo, and the remaining sections consist of Argo's monologues, translated by the man. Although in Kafka's story it is the animal who learns human language and in Svevo's a human who learns to understand his animal, both concentrate on the difficulties of communication between species and what this means about knowledge in general, as well as about the essence of being human.

Rotpeter's language acquisition and attempts at being human begin with a handshake: "The first thing that I learned was to shake hands; the handshake signifies openness. Now, today, at the high point of my career, let frank speech be coupled with that first handshake" (*KSS,* 77).[16] Though Rotpeter claims that his words exemplify the same openness as his first handshake, the reader soon learns that in the beginning Rotpeter did not understand the meaning of any of his actions (drinking, smoking); he simply knew that they might provide an escape. This lack of comprehension raises questions about the meaning of the first handshake, whether it was merely imitative, or had meaning for the humans but not for Rotpeter, or had a different meaning for both Rotpeter and the humans. In addition, it can be asked whether the handshake later had meaning for Rotpeter but was still viewed as imitative by humans. The same questions about meaning and for whom the act has meaning can be, and have been, asked of Rotpeter's entire report. Does he mean what he says, or is he merely imitating academic discourse? Is his audience sincerely listening to his talk, as they would a human's, or do the audience members consider his words as they would any ape's performance?[17] For whom, if anyone, Rotpeter's words have meaning and for whom they are still merely a performance are unanswerable questions.

The issue of performativity and the problem of attributing meaning to gestures are raised in "Argo" as well. Particularly when contrasted with Rotpeter's handshake, the paw-handshake in "Argo" is revealed as complex and subjective. Argo's first gesture, once his master decides to teach him to speak, is to give him his paw, to "shake hands": "The stupid animal, finding himself assailed by gestures and sounds, mustered his entire wit and gave me his paw!" (*AM,* 166; *AP,* 98). Argo does what he has been trained to do, but now the gesture, instead of being a sign of comprehension, represents the failure of Argo to understand the master's efforts: "That evening I had my hands full simply ridding him of his bad habit. If he were to become human, he would have to forget the gestures of the domesticated dog, at which he had stopped as though at the farthest limits of his education" (*AM,* 166; *AP,* 98). Argo and his master's means of communicating are based on training. Once Argo's master stops assuming that this is the only way they can interact, their relationship begins to change.

The importance of physical gestures and their shifting meanings in the two works reveals how even non-verbal communication can be interrogated by the inclusion of an animal's perspective. Both works demonstrate that the human concept of other animals' understanding is primarily due to human perspective. For Rotpeter, communication is hindered by human and other animals' established modes of interaction: "The immediate source of [Rotpeter's] confinement is not physical but epistemological; he is held captive by how humans perceive him."[18] Rotpeter is only human if he is believed to be. Similarly, Argo's master, and not Argo, has to change in order for him to understand Argo's communications. The master learns to establish a new relationship with Argo as a unique social subject, rather than as a dog to be dominated. He refers to his dog as a person and gets down on all fours, like a dog, to relate better to him.

Rotpeter portrays himself as unexcited by his new ability to speak. The ape narrator of "A Report" learns the language of another species because he sees this new kind of communication as the only possible solution to his predicament, his only way out. Rotpeter carefully qualifies this decision: his "way out" was not taken out of any desire to be like humans or interact with them — speaking was merely preferable to death. In Svevo's story, the master, as he is referred to throughout the work, does not set out to understand Argo but to teach him to speak. His resulting understanding is the only possible solution he could find for his situation: "The point was to make ourselves understood, and there were two possibilities: Argo had to learn my language or I had to learn his" (*AM,* 167; *AP,* 99). Like Rotpeter, Argo is unenthusiastic about this new ability: "Argo made his communications to me meekly and with resignation" (*AM,* 167; *AP,* 99). Rotpeter and Argo are both resigned to communicating with humans. This accomplishment, which in both stories is the subject of public attention and much human interest, is not valued especially by the animal participants.

Animals' estimation of humans is not as high as humans' estimation of themselves. Much of what Rotpeter and Argo reveal about human behavior is hard to interpret positively. "A Report" and "Argo" represent the process of learning to communicate with humans as brutal. Rotpeter, who struggles to imitate humans only so that he can leave the cage that cuts into his flesh, is burned during his attempts to learn. Argo is repeatedly hurt without reason, and the master portrays how he attempts to motivate Argo with violence. The works interrogate the divide humans often assume between bestial animals and humane humans.

Not only are human experiences made strange by the animal's perspective, but attention is also drawn to the similarities between human animals' and other animals' actions. The human handshake, both an expression of politeness and a greeting, is exposed in "Argo" as a basic physical gesture similar to ones that other species employ, just as dogs smell one another: "Men are much simpler animals than dogs, because they smell more than dogs and do so more readily. When one man meets another, they touch hands and don't seem to worry about what lies behind the other man's hand. Argo, on the other hand, when he meets another dog, cautiously advances the toothed end of his own body towards the untoothed end of the other's body and sniffs" (*AM,* 182; *AP,* 112). Argo contrasts man's seemingly detached shaking of hands with the series of ways in which his own greeting might unfold, an array which could include — (depending on the other dog) — the leading to a fight and the smell of its "untoothed" parts. All the rituals of social interactions are open to investigation in light of the outsider-perspective of an animal.

"Argo" expresses more clearly than "A Report" the similarities between humans and other animals, partially since the voice of a dog, Argo, is the focus of a large portion of the work, whereas only Rotpeter the person, not Rotpeter the ape, communicates with his human audience. In both works, though, this communication is compromised and questioned. "A Report" often highlights the instability of language by drawing attention to the language being used and to problems of expression.[19] Although Rotpeter may be mocking the academic language often used in talks, his phrasing also emphasizes that meaning is fluid, that words construct a particular reality, and that the reader or listener may not always understand what is intended. Rotpeter consistently underscores that language merely approximates what he is trying to express. This philosophical problem is aggravated by his condition of having been an ape: "Naturally, today I can only try to express my apish feelings of the time in human words, and so I misstate them" (*KSS,* 79).[20] The ape cannot discuss his animal experience, because human language lacks the proper vocabulary. As opposed to representing the ape's thoughts in human language, Kafka's story leaves openly unknowable what humans cannot know, animal life. Martin Puchner observes:

> Kafka thus does not attempt, through sympathy, to represent the ape as ape, supposedly freed from all anthropological machines. As a human writing for other humans about apes, that would be impossible or naive. Instead, his story reveals the animal as a kind of gap, a gap between the ape's mode of appearance, which is necessarily anthropomorphic — using human language, modes of address, and forms of communication — and the ape's life, the unrepresentable life which Rotpeter is trying to save by all means.[21]

Svevo constructs a similar "gap" in his story. Although it does represent an animal's point of view, these impressions are problematized because they are translated by a man, whose grasp of their meaning is imperfect. All the common problems of translation — lexical, syntactical, and hermeneutic — are compounded by the differences in species. Further complicating the transmission of Argo's thoughts, Argo's oral communications are transcribed into writing. Since Argo dies before the work is finished, the master is also translating from a lost language, so there is no way to verify his translations. The language is as foreign as a language could possibly be. Though the master claims that the "general sense" (*AM,* 167; *AP,* 99) was not affected by his misunderstandings, several moments of the narrative reveal the difference that a word can make. Although it is unlikely, the reader will never know, for instance, since Argo cannot be asked, if the master was perhaps "sniffing" a woman he had encountered: "My master had stopped to chat with a woman. [Argo asserts at this point that I 'sniffed' the lady, but this is untrue and I do not hesitate to amend his statement. Moreover, the lady was getting on in years]" (*AM*, 175; *AP*, 105–6). The master appears to resist the idea that Argo thought he was flirting with the woman. His parenthetical remarks remind the reader that the master is not an unbiased translator of Argo's words. The narrator's comments on his changing of Argo's wording highlights how differently Argo perceives the world, how language reflects these differences, and how little a reader can trust a translation of his language.

Svevo's tale contains impenetrable sentences, and the reader cannot be sure if the opacity indicates that Argo's thinking is difficult for a human to understand, Argo's master has misunderstood, or Argo's master has mistranslated Argo's words. Readers of "Argo" and "A Report" are placed in a tenuous interpretive position, not knowing when the words expressed accurately represent what has occurred, or even the true feelings of the dog or ape speaker. The stories portray something that "defeats our ordinary capacity to get our minds around reality, that is, our capacity to capture reality in language. That dislodges us from comfortably inhabiting our nature as speaking animals, animals who can make sense of things in the way the capacity to speak enables us."[22] Both works raise questions about what lies beyond human comprehension.

Argo and his master's communication is based, not on anthropomorphizing — in fact it resists anthropomorphism — but on relating to the animal. Argo even "caninizes" human behavior. Assuming that his master perceives the world in the same way he does, Argo believes that his master's most important sense is smell and, because he smells less attentively than Argo, that his master has an even more acute sense of smell: "But my master walks in the middle of the road without taking a single step aside to enjoy the smells. His senses are more powerful than Argo's and he doesn't need to go near to enjoy them" (*AM*, 178; *AP*, 109). Argo believes that all creatures, from humans to birds, perceive as he does. While this may be a cause for amusement, this cynocentrism also asks the reader to consider anthropocentrism and the distortions of anthropomorphism.

The dog in "Argo" and Rotpeter in "A Report" are certainly not the first communicating dog and ape of literature, but these stories of "realistically" communicating animals and descriptions of how they came to communicate set them apart from animal tales of other authors.[23] Both stories preclude readers from feeling as if they have truly understood an animal's worldview. Unlike most other stories of talking animals, the animals' transformations are not based on fantastic situations. Nothing unnatural — no witchcraft as in Cervantes's "A Dogs' Colloquy," no scientific experiments as in Mikail Bulgahov's *Heart of a Dog*, no mysterious circumstances as in

E. T. A. Hoffmann's "Report of an Educated Young Man" — cause the animals to speak or be understood. Rather, the isolation of Svevo's narrator and Rotpeter plays an important part in what enables Argo's owner and Rotpeter to master the others' language. While Rotpeter is taken from his home and caged, Argo's master is banished to a mountain and scorned by the small community of people that lives there. Separated from their own species, Rotpeter and Argo's master are more likely to learn to communicate with another species. While the success of the transformation may be partially due to the particular characters of those involved, it is not difficult to imagine another bored master learning to understand his dog or another trapped ape imitating and "becoming" human. This repeatable, or ordinary, element of the species' changes distinguishes both stories from most tales of talking animals. The stories are constructed so as to appear as plausible as possible. Indeed, "Argo" describes a situation that has been the focus of numerous studies in the past few years: human beings attempting to understand dog language.[24]

Dogs and apes are perhaps given the fictional power of speech especially often in literature because of their closeness to mankind, in two senses of the word "close" (man's best friend and man's precursor, respectively). This increased closeness can break down further barriers between the species. As Giorgio Agamben has discussed in detail in *The Open: Man and Animal*, this corrosion creates uncertainty: "When the difference vanishes and the two terms (man and animal) collapse upon each other — as seems to be happening today — the difference between being and nothing, licit and illicit, divine and demonic also fades away, and in its place something appears for which we seem to lack even a name."[25] As with many of the current debates on animal perception, Kafka and Svevo's realistic, talking animals create communicative confusion and raise the question of what it means to be human. Their works are early twentieth-century examples of a modernist crisis that has gained more attention in the late twentieth-and early twenty-first century.

Svevo's wife claimed that Kafka was Svevo's "last literary love."[26] Many date his reading of Kafka to 1927, a year before his death, while the few scholars who have compared the writers' work in detail often posit an earlier date, partially because Kafka's "The Judgment" ("Das Urteil"), published in 1913, and "The Death of My Father," a chapter of Svevo's *Zeno's Conscience*, contain strikingly similar scenes.[27] Although the relationship between Kafka's "A Report" and Svevo's "Argo" is not historically verifiable,[28] the fascinating connections between the stories offer one example of the riches to be found in engaging Kafka's work and criticism with readings of Italian works. The problematic historical connections between Italian authors and Kafka have discouraged scholars from working on the connections between Kafka and early twentieth-century Italian literature, but an examination of Italian modern literature in a Kafkan key can help draw attention to Italian works, like "Argo," whose 'Kafkan' qualities are one of the reasons they should be read and considered.

Whereas several scholars have examined what Kafka took from his Italian experiences,[29] few have scrutinized what Kafka gave to Italy and its literature.[30] A Kafkan line of exploration helps to refine and broaden the critical understanding of Italian modern literature. The topics of study are as varied as what makes Kafka modern, from alienated figures to surreal encounters to claustrophobic rooms to crises of identity. Ritchie Robertson's observation in 1992 that "Kafka studies form a good barometer for the development of literary studies in general"[31] continues to be true, as the importance of Kafka in the growing field of animal studies attests. The vast international audience and immense body of Kafka criticism stand in great contrast to those of most Italian modernist literary works. Italian literary criticism is often isolated from, and therefore sometimes lags behind, other literary studies. A study of Italian literature that includes Kafka and Kafka criticism can help engage Italian literature in larger critical debates, as well as add to them.

Comparative studies of modern European literature often relegate Italian literature to a brief mention or addendum. When cited, Italian authors are regularly compared, generally to their disadvantage, with French and English-language ones; and authors like Svevo, Gadda, and Luigi Pirandello are frequently omitted from the canon of modern writers, in which James Joyce, Marcel Proust, and Kafka generally reside. While Kafka has been mobilized and deployed in discourses on minor and world literature, this project uses him instead to examine the dimensions of an often questioned and ignored literary formation. This investigation of a Kafkan tradition, which draws attention to unnoted aspects of well-known Italian authors and some lesser-studied ones, suggests one way to construct a possible identity of modern Italian literature.

Notes

[1] See, for instance, Robert Dombroski, "The Foundations of Italian Modernism: Pirandello, Svevo, Gadda," in *The Cambridge Companion to the Italian Novel*, ed. Peter Bondanella and Andrea Ciccarelli (Cambridge: Cambridge UP, 2003), 89–103; Luca Somigli and Mario Moroni, "Modernism in Italy: An Introduction," in *Italian Modernism: Italian Culture between Decadentism and Avant-Garde*, ed. Somigli and Moroni (Toronto: U of Toronto P, 2004), 3–32; Luca Somigli, "In the Shadow of Byzantium: Modernism in Italian Literature" in *Modernism*, vol. 2, ed. Astradur Eysteinsson and Vivian Liska (Amsterdam: John Benjamins, 2007), 911–30; and Gino Tellini, *The Invention of Modern Italian Literature: Strategies of Creative Imagination* (Toronto: U of Toronto P, 2007).

[2] A brief consideration of Dombroski's title, "The Foundations of Italian Modernism: Pirandello, Svevo, Gadda," reveals the particularly vexed issue of chronology when describing Italian modernism. The works of these "foundational" authors problematically cover over sixty years, spanning from the late nineteenth century to the second half of the twentieth. A modernism that not only encompasses but supposedly begins with these three authors is more diffuse than many other national modernisms. Adding Gabriele D'Annunzio (1863–1938) or Pier Paolo Pasolini (1922–75) to the picture, as is often done, only exacerbates the problem.

[3] Lavinia Mazzucchetti, *Novecento in Germania* (Milan: Mondadori, 1959), 188.

[4] See Stelio Mattioni, *Storia di Umberto Saba* (Milan: Camunia, 1989), 82; and Manuel La Ferla, *Diritto al silenzio: vita e scritti di Roberto Bazlen* (Palermo: Sellerio, 1994).

[5] Eugenio Montale, *Eugenio Montale Lettere a Italo Svevo: Con gli scritti di Montale su Svevo* (Bari, Italy: De Donato, 1966), 178.

[6] Paul Kurt Ackermann, "A History of Critical Writing on Kafka," *The German Quarterly* 23.2 (Mar. 1950): 106.

[7] Alberto Spaini, "Prefazione" in *America*, by Franz Kafka (Turin: Frassinelli, 1947), vii.

[8] See Eugenio Montale's *New Poems*, trans. G. Singh (New York: New Directions, 1972), 83.

[9] Primo Levi, "Note to Franz Kafka's *The Trial*," in *The Black Hole of Auschwitz*, ed. Marco Belpoliti, trans. Sharon Wood (Cambridge: Polity, 2005), 140.

[10] Levi, "Note to Franz Kafka's *The Trial*," 140.

[11] Ritchie Robertson, chapter 8 in this volume.

[12] Ibid.

[13] Partly because of Kafka's background, Rotpeter, with all his contradictions, has been viewed by some critics as an allegory for an assimilated Jew. See, for instance, William C. Rubinstein, "A Report to an Academy," in *Franz Kafka Today*, ed. Angel Flores and Homer Swander (Madison: U of Wisconsin P, 1968), 55–60. Walter Sokel's "Identity and the Individual or Past and Present: Franz Kafka's 'A Report to an Academy' in a Psychoanalytic and a Sociohistorical Context," in *The Myth of Power and the Self: Essays on Franz Kafka* (Detroit: Wayne State UP, 2002), 268–91, concentrates on "A Report" as an illustration of the problems of adapting to Western society in general.

[14] For example, "A Report" is used as a grounding text for Nigel Rothfels's *Savages and Beasts: The Birth of the Modern Zoo* (Baltimore: Johns Hopkins UP, 2002). The piece also plays an important role in Marian Scholtmeijer, "What is 'Human'? Metaphysics and Zoontology in Flaubert and Kafka," in *Animal Acts: Configuring the Human in Western History*, eds. Jennifer Ham and Matthew Senior (New York: Routledge, 1997), 127–44; and Amy Gutmann, ed., *The Lives of Animals* (Princeton, NJ: Princeton UP, 1999) which includes J. M. Coetzee's two Tanner lectures and the essays of the respondents, Marjorie Garber, Barbara Smuts, Wendy Doniger, and Peter Singer.

[15] Italo Svevo, "Argo and his Master," in *Short Sentimental Journey and Other Stories,* trans. Beryl de Zoete, L. Collison-Morley, and Ben Johnson (Berkeley: U of California P, 1967), 165. Hereafter referred to as *AM.* The Italian original will be referred to as *AP.* See Italo Svevo, "Argo e il suo padrone," in *Tutte le opere di Italo Svevo: Racconti e scritti autobiografici* (Milan: Mondadori, 2004), 97.

[16] "Das erste, was ich lernte, war: den Handschlag geben; Handschlag bezeugt Offenheit; mag nun heute, wo ich auf dem Höhepunkt meiner Laufbahn stehe, zu jenem ersten Handschlag auch das offene Wort hinzukommen" (*DL,* 303).

[17] For recent treatments of Rotpeter as an artist-poet-performer see Miguel Tamen's "The Ape Speaks" and Stanley Corngold's "Kafka's 'A Report to an Academy' with Adorno," in *Aesthetics and the Work of Art: Adorno, Kafka, Richter,* ed. Peter de Bolla and Stefan H. Uhlig (New York: Palgrave Macmillan, 2009), 113–25 and 147–66 respectively.

[18] Philip Armstrong, *What Animals Mean in the Fictions of Modernity* (London: Routledge, 2008), 203.

[19] Rotpeter frequently refers to the words he chooses by commenting on his own use of metaphors, idioms, and images: for instance, "to continue the metaphor" (*KSS,* 77; um in Bilde zu bleiben, *DL,* 299 and "There is an excellent German saying" (*KSS,* 83; Es gibt eine ausgezeichnete deutsche Redensart, *DL,* 312). Rotpeter also uses the word "sense (or meaning)" (Sinn) repeatedly to clarify the exact significance of his words.

[20] "Ich kann natürlich das damals affenmäßig Gefühlte heute nur mit Meschenworten nachzeichnen und verzeichnen und verzeichne es infolgedessen" (*DL,* 303; translation modified).

[21] Martin Puchner, "Performing the Open: Actors, Animals, Philosophers," *The Drama Review* 51.1 (Spring 2007): 28.

[22] John McDowell, "Comment on Stanley Cavell's 'Companionable Thinking,'" in *Philosophy and Animal Life* (New York: Columbia UP, 2008), 134.

[23] For an overview of dog stories (including Svevo's and with an emphasis on Kafka's "Investigations of a Dog") see "Talking Dogs: The Caninization of Literature," in Theodore Ziolkowski's *Varieties of Literary Thematics* (Princeton, NJ: Princeton UP, 1983), 86–122.

[24] "In the language I am developing here [between the author of the article, Barbara Smuts, and her dog], relating to other beings as persons as nothing to do with whether or not we attribute human characteristics to them. It has to do, instead, with recognizing that they are social subjects, like us, whose idiosyncratic, subjective experience of us plays the same role in their relations with us that our subjective experience of them plays in our relations with them." Barbara Smuts, "Reflections," in *The Lives of Animals,* ed. Amy Gutmann (Princeton, NJ: Princeton UP, 1999), 118. Elvio Guagnini's introduction to a Portuguese translation of Svevo's shorter works contrasts Argo's speech with modern canine language experiments. See Elvio Guagnanini, "Svevo: A arte do conto," in *Argo e seu dono,* by Italo Svevo, trans. Liliana Laganá (Sao Paulo, Brazil: Berlendis & Vertecchia, 2001), 13–14.

[25] Giorgio Agamben, *The Open: Man and Animal,* trans. Kevin Attell (Stanford, CA: Stanford UP, 2004), 22.

[26] Livia Veneziani Svevo, *Vita di mio marito* (Pordenone, Italy: Arti Grafiche Fratelli Cosarini, 1958), 144.

[27] See Peter E. Bondanella, "Franz Kafka and Italo Svevo," in *Proceedings of the Comparative Literature Symposium: "Franz Kafka: His Place in World Literature,"* ed. Wolodymir T. Zyla (Lubbock, TX: Interdepartmental Committee on Comparative Literature, Texas Tech U, 1971), 24; and Peter Scharer von Aurau, *Zur psychischen Strategie des schwachen Helden: Italo Svevo im Vergleich mit Kafka, Broch und Musil* (Thusis, Switzerland: Buchdruckerei Werner Roth, 1978), 114–24.

[28] Many works mention, but do not explore, the connections between the two men and their works. Bondanella's is the most thorough piece on the two authors and their work to date. More concentrated works on the two authors also include, in chronological order: Giuseppe Antonio Camerino, *Italo Svevo e la crisi della Mitteleuropa* (Florence: Le Monnier, 1974), 135–52; Scharer, *Zur psychischen Strategie des schwachen Helden,* 114–26; M. Jeuland Meynaud, *Zeno e i suoi fratelli: La creazione del personaggio nei romanzi di Italo Svevo* (Bologna: Pàtron, 1985), 306–7; Giuseppe Antonio Camerino "Italo Svevo: Significato e caratteri di una poetica mitteleuropea," in *Italo Svevo: Scrittore europeo,* ed. N. Cacciaglia and Guzzetta L. Fava (Florence: Olschki, 1994), 15–29; Lynn Lara Westwater, "Franz Kafka and Italo Svevo: 'A Blur of Languages,'" *RLA Archive* (1996) Purdue U, 5 Dec. 2007, http://tell.fll.purdue.edu/RLA-Archive/1996/italian.html.

[29] Maria Luisa Caputo-Mayr summarizes and comments on Kafka's four trips to Riva and Brescia (1909), Lugano, Milan, and Stresa (1911), Trieste, Venice, Verona, Riva, and Desenzano (1913), and Merano (1920). See Caputo-Mayr, "Kafka and Romance Languages: A Preliminary Survey," *Journal of the Kafka Society of America: New International Series* 27.1–2 (2003): 4–20. Guido Crespi also describes and summarizes the mentions of Italian and Italian things in general in Kafka's work. See Guido Crespi, "Kafka e l'Italia," in *Miti e contromiti: Cent'anni di relazioni culturali italo-austriache dopo il 1861,* ed. Alida Fliri (Fasano, Italy: Schena, 1990), 107–12. Peter Demetz's *The Air Show at Brescia, 1909* (New York: Farrar, Straus, & Giroux, 2002) treats Kafka's significant visit to Brescia and its effect on Kafka — the man and his work.

[30] For articles that include a discussion of Kafka's Italian reception see Caputo-Mayr, "Kafka and Romance Languages"; Johannes Hösle, "Italien," in *Kafka-Handbuch,* ed. Hartmut Binder (Stuttgart: Alfred Kröner, 1979), 519–29; Giorgio Cusatelli, "Kafka e i suoi lettori italiani," in *Kafka Oggi,* ed. Giuseppe Farese (Bari, Italy: Adriatics, 1986), 1–10.

[31] Ritchie Robertson, "In Search of the Historical Kafka: A Selective Review of Research, 1980–92," *Modern Language Review* 89.1 (Jan. 1994): 107.

Bibliography

Abraham, Karl. “Erstes Korreferat.” In *Zur Psychoanalyse der Kriegsneurosen*, 31–41. Leipzig: Internationaler Psychoanalytischer Verlag, 1919.

Abraham, Nicolas, and Maria Torok. *The Shell and the Kernel.* Vol. 1. Edited and translated by Nicholas T. Rand. Chicago: U of Chicago P, 1994.

Ackermann, Paul Kurt. “A History of Critical Writing on Kafka.” *German Quarterly* 23.2 (March 1950): 105–13.

Adelman, Gary. “Double on the Rocks: Ishiguro’s *The Unconsoled*.” *Critique* 42.2 (2001): 166–79.

Adler, Max. *Neue Menschen: Gedanken über sozialistische Erziehung*. Berlin: E. Laub, 1924.

Adorno, Theodor W. “Notes on Kafka.” In *Prisms*, translated by Samuel Weber and Shierry Weber, 243–71. London: Neville Spearman, 1967.

———. “The Position of the Narrator in the Contemporary Novel.” In *Notes to Literature*, vol. 1, edited by Rolf Tiedemann, translated by Shierry Weber Nicholsen, 30–36. New York: Columbia UP, 1991.

Agamben, Giorgo. *The Open: Man and Animal.* Translated by Kevin Attell. Stanford, CA: Stanford UP, 2004.

Allbutt, Clifford. “Nervous Disease and Modern Life.” *Contemporary Review* 67 (1895): 214–15.

Alt, Peter-André. *Franz Kafka: Der ewige Sohn; Eine Biographie.* Munich: C. H. Beck, 2005.

———. “Im Kino.” In *Franz Kafka: Der ewige Sohn; Eine Biographie*, 214–19.

———. *Kafka und der Film: Über kinematographisches Erzählen.* Munich: C. H. Beck, 2009.

Alter, Robert. *Imagined Cities: Urban Experience and the Language of the Novel.* New Haven, CT: Yale UP, 2005.

———. “Kafka: Suspicion and the City.” In *Imagined Cities: Urban Experience and the Language of the Novel*, 141–59.

———. “Kafka’s Father, Agnon’s Mother, Bellow’s Cousins.” *Commentary* 81.2 (1986): 46–52.

Amichai, Yehuda. “Anniversaries Of War”: *Huleikat — The Third Poem About Dicky.* In *Even a Fist Was Once an Open Palm with Fingers: Recent Poems*, translated by Barbara Benjamin Harshav, 9–10. New York: Harper Perennial, 1991.

Anders, Günther. *Kafka Pro und Contra.* Munich: Beck, 1951.

Anderson, Mark M. *Kafka's Clothes: Ornament and Aestheticism in the Habsburg Fin de Siècle.* Oxford: Clarendon, 1992.

Arkush, Allan. "The Jewish State and Its Internal Enemies: Yoram Hazony versus Martin Buber and His Ideological Children." *Jewish Social Studies* 7.2 (2001): 169–90.

Armstrong, Philip. *What Animals Mean in the Fictions of Modernity.* London: Routledge, 2008.

Auden, W. H. *Prose, 1939–1948.* Volume 2 of *The Complete Works of W. H. Auden*, edited by Edward Mendelson. Princeton, NJ: Princeton UP, 1986.

Augustin, Bettina. "Raban im Kino: Kafka und die zeitgenössische Kinematographie." *Schriftenreihe der Franz-Kafka-Gesellschaft* 2. Vienna: Braumüller, 1987.

Babrius and Phaedrus. Edited by Ben Edwin Perry. London: William Heinemann, 1965.

Bal, Mieke. *Narratology: Introduction to the Theory of Narrative.* 3rd ed. 1985. Reprint, Toronto: U of Toronto P, 2009.

Band, Arnold J. "The Kafka-Agnon Polarities." In *The Dove and the Mole*, edited by M. Lazar & R. Gottesman, 151–60. Malibu, CA: Undena, 1987.

Barthes, Roland. "La mort de l'auteur" (1968). Reprinted in *Le bruissement de la langue.* Paris: Seuil, 1984.

Barzel, Hillel. *Agnon and Kafka.* Ramat Gan, Israel: Bar Oryan, 1972.

Baudelaire, Charles. *The Painter of Modern Life and Other Essays.* Edited and translated by Jonathan Mayne. 2nd ed. New York: Phaidon, 1995.

Beard, George. *American Nervousness: Its Causes and Consequences.* New York: G. P. Putnam's Sons, 1881.

Beck, Evelyn. "Kafka's Traffic in Women: Gender, Power, and Sexuality." *Literary Review* 26 (1983): 577–87.

Beicken, Peter. *Franz Kafka: Eine kritische Einführung in die Forschung.* Frankfurt am Main: Athenaion, 1974.

———. *Franz Kafka: Der Process.* 2nd rev. ed. 1999. Reprint, Munich: Oldenbourg, 2005.

———. "Kafka's Gaze/Gays." *Journal of the Kafka Society of America* 23.1 and 2 (1999 [2002]): 3–22.

———. "Kafka's Mise-en-Scène: Literary and Cinematic Imaginary." *Journal of the Kafka Society of America* 24.1 and 2 (2000 [2003]): 4–11.

———. "Kafkas visuelle Methode." In *Franz Kafka: Der Proceß*, 162–71.

———. "Le flâneur de Kafka: Regard, image, vision cinématographique." *Europe* 84.923 (2006): 160–83.

———. "Perspektive und Sehweise bei Kafka." PhD dissertation, Stanford U, 1971.

Beißner, Friedrich. *Der Erzähler Franz Kafka und andere Vorträge.* Frankfurt am Main: Suhrkamp, 1983.

Bell, Vikki. "On Speech, Race and Melancholia: An Interview with Judith Butler." *Theory, Culture & Society* 16.2 (1999): 163–74.

Benbennick, David. *Picture of a Mobius Strip.* 14 March 2005. Wikimedia Commons, http://en.wikipedia.org/wiki/File:M%C3%B6bius_strip.jpg.

Benjamin, Walter. *The Arcades Project.* Translated by Howard Eiland and Kevin McLaughlin. Cambridge, MA: Harvard UP, 1999.

———. *Charles Baudelaire: Ein Lyriker im Zeitalter des Hochkapitalismus.* Frankfurt am Main: Suhrkamp, 1955.

———. "The Flâneur." In *The Arcades Project,* 416–55.

———. "Franz Kafka: On the Tenth Anniversary of His Death." In *Illuminations: Essays and Reflections,* edited by Hannah Arendt, 111–40. New York: Schocken, 1968.

———. *Illuminations.* Translated by Harry Zohn. London: Fontana, 1973.

———. *Selected Writings. Vol. 2, 1927–1934.* Translated by Rodney Livingstone, edited by Michael W. Jennings, Howard Eiland, and Gary Smith. Cambridge, MA,: Harvard UP, 1999.

Benn, Aluf. "Sharon's Real Legacy — Keeping the Arabs out of Sight" (Sun., 17 January 2010). HAARETZ.com. http://www.haaretz.com/hasen/spages/1142320.html.

Bennett, Alan. *Two Kafka Plays.* London: Faber, 1987.

Benson, Stephen. "Words without Song: Kafka and *The Unconsoled.*" In *Literary Music: Writing Music in Contemporary Fiction,* 141–60. Burlington, VT: Ashgate, 2006.

Bergmann, Hugo. "Bemerkungen zur arabischen Frage." *Palästina* 8 (1911): 190–95.

———. *Jawne und Jerusalem.* Berlin: Jüdischer Verlag, 1919.

Bernheimer, Charles. *Flaubert and Kafka: Studies in Psychopoetic Structure.* New Haven, CT: Yale UP, 1982.

Bernstein, Michael. *Foregone Conclusions: Against Apocalyptic History.* Berkeley: U of California P, 1994.

Bezzel, Chris. *Kafka Chronik, zusammengestellt von Chris Bezzel.* Munich: Hanser, 1975.

Bhabha, Homi K. *The Location of Culture.* New York: Routledge, 1994.

Binder, Hartmut, ed. *Kafka-Handbuch.* Vol. 1. Stuttgart: Alfred Kröner, 1979.

———. *Kafka-Kommentar zu sämtlichen Erzählungen.* Munich: Winkler, 1975.

Birnbaum, Nathan. *Ausgewählte Schriften: Zur jüdischen Frage*. Vol. 2. Czernowitz, Austria-Hungary: Birnbaum & Kohut, 1910.

Blumenberg, Hans. *Arbeit am Mythos*. Frankfurt am Main: Suhrkamp, 1984. In English, *Work on Myth*. Translated by Robert M. Wallace. Cambridge, MA: MIT Press, 1985.

Boa, Elizabeth. "The Castle." In *The Cambridge Companion to Kafka*, edited by Julian Preece, 61–79. Cambridge: Cambridge UP, 2002.

Bokhove, Niels. "'The Entrance to the More Important': Kafka's Personal Zionism." In *Kafka, Zionism and Beyond*, edited by Mark H. Gelber, 23–58. Tübingen: Niemeyer, 2004.

Bondanella, Peter E. "Franz Kafka and Italo Svevo." In *Proceedings of the Comparative Literature Symposium: Franz Kafka: His Place in World Literature*, edited by Wolodymir T. Zyla, 17–34. Lubbock, TX: Interdepartmental Committee on Comparative Literature, Texas Tech U.

Bontempelli, Massimo. *Il figlio di due madri*. Macerata, Italy: Liberilibri, 2005. In English, "The Son of Two Mothers." In *Separations: Two Novels of Mothers and Children*, translated by Estelle Gilson. Kingston, NY: McPherson, 2000.

Borges, Jorge Luis. "Kafka and His Precursors." In *Labyrinths*, 199–201. New York: New Directions, 2007.

Born, Jürgen. *Kafkas Bibliothek: Ein beschreibendes Verzeichnis*. Frankfurt am Main: S. Fischer, 1990.

Bourdieu, Pierre. *The Rules of Art: Genesis and Structure of the Literary Field*. Cambridge: Polity, 1996.

Brabandt, Anne. *Franz Kafka und der Stummfilm: Eine intermediale Studie*. Munich: Meidenbauer, 2009.

Brod, Max. *Franz Kafka, A Biography*. Translated by G. Humphrey Robert. New York: Schocken Books, 1970.

———. *Paganism, Christianity, Judaism: A Confession of Faith*. Translated by William Wolf. Tuscaloosa, AL: U of Alabama P, 1970.

———. *Über Franz Kafka*. Frankfurt am Main: Fischer Bücherei, 1966

Brod, Max, and Franz Kafka. *Eine Freundschaft*. Vol. 1, Reiseaufzeichnungen. Edited by Malcolm Pasley. Frankfurt am Main: Fischer, 1987.

Bruce, Iris. *Kafka and Cultural Zionism: Dates in Palestine*. Madison: U of Wisconsin P, 2007.

Buber, Martin. *On Judaism*. Edited by Nahum N. Glatzer. New York: Schocken, 1996.

Butler, Judith. *Gender Trouble: Feminism and the Subversion of Identity*. New York: Routledge, 1990.

———. *The Psychic Life of Power: Theories in Subjection*. Stanford, CA: Stanford UP, 1997.

Buzzati, Dino. *Il deserto dei Tartari.* Milan: Mondadori, 1989. In English, *The Tartar Steppe.* Translated by Stuart C. Hood. Jaffrey, NH: David R. Godine, 2005.

Camerino, Giuseppe Antonio. *Italo Svevo e la crisi della Mitteleuropa.* Florence: Le Monnier, 1974.

———. "Italo Svevo: Significato e caratteri di una poetica mitteleuropea." In *Italo Svevo: Scrittore europeo*, edited by N. Cacciaglia and Guzzetta L. Fava, 15–29. Florence: Olschki, 1994.

Campe, Rüdiger. "Kafkas Fürsprache." In Höcker and Simons, *Kafkas Institutionen*, 189–212.

———. "Kafkas Institutionenroman: *Der Proceß, Das Schloß.*" In *Gesetz, Ironie: Festschrift für Manfred Schneider*, edited by Rüdiger Campe and Michael Niehaus, 197–208. Heidelberg: Synchron, 2004.

Caputo-Mayr, Maria Luisa. "Kafka and Romance Languages: A Preliminary Survey." *Journal of the Kafka Society of America: New International Series* 27.1–2 (2003): 4–20.

Caruth, Cathy, ed. *Trauma: Explorations in Memory.* Baltimore: Johns Hopkins UP, 1995.

Cervantes, Miguel de. "The Dogs' Colloquy." In *Exemplary Stories,* translated by C. A. Jones, 195–252. New York: Penguin, 1972.

Chamberlain, Houston. *Die Grundlagen des 19. Jahrhunderts.* Vol. 1. 4th ed. Munich: Bruckmann, 1904.

Charcot, Jean-Martin. "A propos de six cas d'hystère chez l'homme." In *J. M. Charcot: L'Hystérie*, edited by E. Trillat, 157–58. Toulouse: Privat, 1971.

———. *Poliklinische Vorträge (Leçons du mardi).* Vol. 1. Translated by Sigmund Freud. Leipzig: Deutike, 1892.

Chenu, Marie-Dominique. *Nature, Man, and Society in the Twelfth Century.* Edited and translated by Jerome Taylor and Lester K. Little. Toronto: U of Toronto P, 1997.

Claudin, Gustave. *Paris.* Paris: Faure, 1867.

Cohen, Jean. *Structure du langage poétique.* Paris: Flammarion, 1999.

Cohn, Dorritt. "Kafka and Hofmannsthal." *Modern Austrian Literature* 30.1 (1997): 1–19.

Corngold, Stanley. *The Commentators' Despair: The Interpretation of Kafka's "Metamorphosis."* Port Washington, NY: Kennikat, 1973.

———. *Franz Kafka, The Necessity of Form.* Ithaca, NY: Cornell UP, 1988.

———. "Kafka and the Ministry of Writing." In *Franz Kafka: The Office Writings,* edited by Corngold, Jack Greenberg, and Benno Wagner, translated by Eric Patton and Ruth Hein, 1–18. Princeton, NJ: Princeton UP, 2009.

———. "Kafka and the Philosophy of Music; or, des Kommas Fehl hilft." *Journal of the Kafka Society of America* 28.1–2 (2004): 4–16

———. "Kafka's 'A Report to an Academy' with Adorno." In de Bolla and Uhlig, *Aesthetics and the Work of Art: Adorno, Kafka, Richter*, 147–66.

———. "Kafka's *The Metamorphosis*: Metamorphosis of the Metaphor." In Kafka, *The Metamorphosis*, 79–107.

———. *Lambent Traces: Franz Kafka*. Princeton, NJ: Princeton UP, 2004.

Corngold, Stanley, and Benno Wagner. *Franz Kafka: The Ghosts in the Machine*. Evanston, IL: Northwestern UP, 2011.

Cowan, Michael. *Cult of the Will: Nervousness and German Modernity*. University Park, PA: Pennsylvania State UP, 2008.

Crespi, Guido. "Kafka e l'Italia." In *Miti e contromiti: Cent'anni di relazioni culturali italo-austriache dopo il 1861*, edited by Alida Fliri, 107–12. Fasano, Italy: Schena, 1990.

Cusatelli, Giorgio . "Kafka e i suoi lettori italiani." In *Kafka Oggi*, edited by Giuseppe Farese, 1–10. Bari, Italy: Adriatics, 1986.

De Bolla, Peter, and Stefan H. Uhlig, eds. *Aesthetics and the Work of Art: Adorno, Kafka, Richter*. New York: Palgrave Macmillan, 2009.

Deleuze, Gilles, and Félix Guattari. *Kafka: Towards a Minor Literature*. Minneapolis: U of Minnesota P, 1986.

Demetz, Peter. *The Air Show at Brescia, 1909*. New York: Farrar, Straus, & Giroux, 2002.

Derlien, Hans-Ulrich. "Bürokratie in der Literatur und Soziologie der Moderne: Über Kafka und Max Weber." In *Die Modernität des Expressionismus*, edited by Thomas Anz and Michael Stark, 44–61. Stuttgart: Metzler, 1994.

Derrida, Jacques. "Architecture: Where the Desire May Live." In *Rethinking Architecture: A Reader in Cultural Theory*, edited by Neil Leach, 300–328. New York: Routledge, 1997.

Dombroski, Robert. "The Foundations of Italian Modernism: Pirandello, Svevo, Gadda." In *The Cambridge Companion to the Italian Novel*, edited by Peter Bondanella and Andrea Ciccarelli, 89–103. Cambridge: Cambridge UP, 2003.

Drinka, George Frederick. *The Birth of Neurosis: Myth, Malady, and the Victorians*. New York: Simon & Schuster, 1984.

Duttlinger, Carolin. "Film und Fotografie." In Engel and Auerochs, *Kafka-Handbuch: Leben, Werk, Wirkung*, 72–79.

———. *Kafka and Photography*. New York; Oxford UP, 2007.

Eagleton, Terry. *Criticism and Ideology*. London: New Left Books, 1976.

Eghigian, Greg A. "The German Welfare State as a Discourse of Trauma." In *Traumatic Pasts: History, Psychiatry, and Trauma in the Modern Age, 1870–*

1930, edited by Mark S. Micale and Paul Lerner, 92–112. Cambridge: Cambridge UP, 2001.

Eissler, K. R. *Freud as Expert Witness: The Discussion of War Neuroses between Freud and Wagner-Jauregg*. Translated by Christine Trollope. Madison, CT: International UP, 1986.

Emrich, Wilhelm. *Franz Kafka*. Bonn: Athenäum, 1958.

Engel, Manfred, and Bernd Auerochs, eds. *Kafka-Handbuch: Leben, Werk, Wirkung*. Stuttgart: J. B. Metzler, 2010.

Erichsen, John Eric. *On Railway and other Injuries of the Nervous System*. 1866. Reprint, Philadelphia: Henry C. Lea, 1867.

Etkind, Efim. "Kafka in sowjetischer Sicht." In *Franz Kafka: Themen und Probleme*, edited by Claude David, 229–37. Göttingen: Vandenhoeck & Ruprecht, 1980.

Ewald, François. *L'état Providence*. Paris: Grasset & Fasquelle, 1986.

Faith, Nicholas. *Derail: Why Trains Crash*. London: Macmillan, 2000.

Fischer-Homberger, Esther. "Railway Spine und traumatische Neurose — Seele und Rückenmark." *Gesnerus* 27 (1970): 96–111.

———. *Die traumatische Neurose: Vom somatischen zum sozialen Leiden*. Bern: Verlag Hans Huber, 1975.

Flaubert, Gustave. *Briefe über seine Werke*. Edited by F. P. Greve. Translated by E. Greve. Minden: Bruns, 1904 (=*Gustave Flauberts Gesammelte Werke*, edited by E. W. Fischer, vol. 7).

Foucault, Michel. *Discipline and Punish: The Birth of the Prison*. Translated by Alan Sheridan. New York: Vintage Books, 1995.

———. *Language, Counter-Memory, Practice*. Edited by Donald F. Bouchard. Translated by Donald F. Bouchard and Sherry Simon. Ithaca, NY: Cornell UP, 1977.

———. "What is an Author?" In *Language, Counter-Memory, Practice*, 113–38.

Freud, Sigmund. "Three Essays on the Theory of Sexuality [1905]." In *The Standard Edition of the Complete Psychological Works*, translated by James Strachey, edited by Anna Freud. London: Hogarth Press & the Institute of Psycho-analysis, 1953–1974. Original German, "Drei Abhandlungen zur Sexualtheorie," in *Gesammelte Werke*, edited by Anna Freud. London: Imago, 1940–52.

———. *The Standard Edition of the Complete Works of Sigmund Freud*. 24 volumes. Edited by James Strachey et al. London: Hogart and the Institute of Psychoanalysis, 1953–74.

Friedberg, Anne. *Window Shopping: Cinema and the Postmodern*. Berkeley: U of California P, 1993.

Garfinkle, Adam M. "On the Origin, Meaning, Use, and Abuse of a Phrase." *Middle Eastern Studies* 27 (Oct. 1991): 539–50.

Garloff, Katja. "Kafka's Crypt: W. G. Sebald and the Melancholy of Modern German Jewish Culture." *Germanic Review* 82.2 (Spring 2007): 123–40.

Gilman, Sander. *Franz Kafka, the Jewish Patient.* New York: Routledge, 1995.

———. "The Image of the Hysteric." In Gilman et al., *Hysteria beyond Freud*, 345–452.

———. *The Jew's Body.* New York: Routledge, 1991.

Gilman, Sander, Helen King, Roy Porter, G. S. Rousseau, and Elaine Showalter, eds. *Hysteria beyond Freud.* Berkeley: U of California P, 1993.

Goffman, Erving. *Asylums.* 1961; Harmondsworth, UK: Penguin, 1968.

Goldstücker, Eduard, ed. *Franz Kafka aus Prager Sicht.* Berlin: Voltaire Verlag, 1966.

Gotthilf, Otto. "Wie schützt man sich beim Eisenbahnfahren gegen Gesundheitsschädigungen." *Deutsche Alpenzeitung*, vol. 9 1901/02, 17–18.

Grass, Günter. *The Tin Drum.* Translated by Ralph Manheim. London: Secker & Warburg, 1965.

The Greek Anthology. Translated by W. R. Paton. Vol. 4. London: William Heinemann, 1916.

Gross, Ruth V. "Rich Text, Poor Text: A Kafkan Confusion." *PMLA* 95 (1980): 168–82.

Guagnanini, Elvio. "Svevo: A arte do conto." In *Argo e seu dono*, 13–14. Sao Paulo, Brazil: Berlendis & Vertecchia, 2001.

Gullberg, Jan. *Mathematics: From the Birth of Numbers.* New York: W. W. Norton, 1997.

Gutmann, Amy, ed. *The Lives of Animals.* Princeton, NJ: Princeton UP, 1999.

Habiby, Emile. *The Secret Life of Saeed: The Pessoptimist.* Translated by Salma Khadra Jayyusi. 1974. Reprint, New York: Interlink Books, 2002.

Harman, Mark. "'At least he could garden': Beckett and Kafka," in *Partisan Review* 66.4 (1999): 574–79.

———. "Biography and Autobiography: Necessary Antagonists?" *Journal of the Kafka Society* 10.1/2 (1986): 56–62.

———. "Circus Rider on Two Horses? Franz Kafka and Literary Translation." *Times Literary Supplement* 5590 (2010), 14–15.

———. "Life into Art: Kafka's Self-Stylization in the Diaries." In *Franz Kafka (1883–1983): His Craft and Thought*, edited by Roman Struc and J. C. Yardley, 101–16. Waterloo, ON: Wilfrid Laurier UP, 1986.

———. "Terminal Fantasies: Beckett and Kafka." In *That Other World: The Supernatural and the Fantastic in Irish Literature and Its Contexts*, edited by Bruce Stewart, 2:177–87, Princess Grace Irish Library 12. Gerrards Cross, UK: Colin Smythe, 1998.

Harrington, Ralph. "Trains, Technology and Time-Travellers: How the Victorians Re-invented Time" (2003). http://harringtonmiscellany.wordpress.com/essays/time-travellers/ (retrieved 24 October 2010).

Harshav, Benjamin. "Introduction." In *Only Yesterday,* by S. Y. Agnon, vii–xxix. 1945. Reprint, Princeton, NJ: Princeton UP, 2000.

Haviland, Alfred. *Hurried to Death or, a Few Words of Advice on the Danger of Hurry and Excitement, Especially Addressed to Railway Travellers* (London: Renshaw & Mitchell, 1868.

Hawes, James. *Excavating Kafka.* London: Quercus, 2008.

Heinemann, Richard. "Kafka's Oath of Service: 'Der Bau' and the Dialectic of Bureaucratic Mind," *PMLA* 111.2 (March 1996). http://www.jstor.org/stable/463105.

———. "The Rhetoric of Kafka's *Amtliche Schriften." Journal of the Kafka Society of America* 15.1–2 (1991): 29–36.

Herman, Luc, and Bart Vervaeck. *Handbook of Narrative Analysis.* Lincoln: U of Nebraska P, 2005.

Hermsdorf, Klaus. "Schreibanlässe und Textformen der amtlichen Schriften Franz Kafkas: Eine Einführung." In Kafka, *Amtliche Schriften,* edited by Hermsdorf and Benno Wagner, 11–104. Frankfurt am Main: S Fischer, 2004.

Hinderer, Walter. "'Kleist bläst in mich wie in eine alte Schweinsblase.'" In *Kafka und die Weltliteratur,* edited by Manfred Engel und Dieter Lamping. Göttingen: Vandenhoeck & Ruprecht, 2006.

Hirsch, Max. "Reisekrankheiten." *Therapeutische Rundschau* (Halle) 2.19 (10 May 1908): 301–4.

Höcker, Arne, and Oliver Simons, eds. *Kafkas Institutionen.* Bielefeld: Transcript, 2007.

Hoffmann, E. T. A. *The Golden Pot and Other Tales.* New translation by Ritchie Robertson. Oxford: Oxford UP, 1992.

———. "My Cousin's Corner Window." In *The Golden Pot and Other Tales,* 377–401.

———. "Report of an Educated Young Man." In *E. T. A. Hoffmann's Musical Writings: Kreisleriana, The Poet and the Composer, Music Criticism,* edited by David Charlton, 136–43. Cambridge: Cambridge UP, 2003.

Hofmannsthal, Hugo von. "Ein Brief." In *Erzählungen, Erfundene Gespräche und Briefe, Reisen,* vol. 7 of *Gesammelte Werke in Einzelausgaben,* edited by Herbert Steiner, 461–72. Frankfurt am Main: Fischer 1979. In English, "A Letter." In *The Lord Chandos Letter and Other Writings,* edited and translated by Joel Rotenberg, 117–28. New York: New York Review of Books, 2005.

Hofstader, Douglas. *Gödel, Escher, Bach: An Eternal Golden Braid*. New York: Basic Books, 1999.

———. *I Am A Strange Loop*. New York: Basic Books, 2007.

Holitscher, Arthur. *Reise durch das jüdische Palästina*. Berlin: Fischer, 1922.

Hösle, Johannes. "Italien." In Binder, *Kafka-Handbuch*, 519–29.

Hughes, Kenneth, ed. *Franz Kafka: An Anthology of Marxist Criticism*. Hanover, NH, 1981.

Ishiguro, Kazuo. *The Unconsoled*. New York: Vintage Books, 1995.

Jaggi, Maya."Kazuo Ishiguro with Maya Jaggi." In *Conversations with Kazuo Ishiguro*, edited by Brian W. Schaffer and Cythia F. Wong, 110–19. Oxford: UP of Mississippi, 2008.

Jahn, Wolfgang. *Kafkas Roman "Der Verschollene" ("Amerika")*. Stuttgart: Metzler, 1965.

Jahraus, Oliver. "Kafka und der Film." In *Kafka Handbuch*, edited by Bettina von Jagow and Oliver Jahraus, 224–36. Göttingen: Vandenhoeck & Ruprecht, 2008.

Janouch, Gustav. *Gespräche mit Franz Kafka*. Frankfurt am Main: Fischer, 1961. In English, *Conversations with Kafka*. Translated by Goronwy Rees. New York: New Directions, 1971.

Joerges, Bernhard. *Körper der Gesellschaft: Arbeiten zur Techniksoziologie*. Frankfurt am Main: Suhrkamp, 1996.

Kafka, Franz. *Amtliche Schriften*, Edited by Klaus Hermsdorf and Benno Wagner. Frankfurt am Main: S. Fischer, 2004.

———. *The Blue Octavo Notebooks*. Translated by Ernst Kaiser and Eithne Wilkins. Cambridge: Exact Change, 1991.

———. *Briefe, 1902–1924*. Edited by Max Brod. Frankfurt am Main: Fischer, 1958.

———. *Briefe an Milena*. Expanded edition. Edited by Jürgen Born and Michael Müller. Frankfurt am Main: Fischer, 1999.

———. *The Castle*. Translated by Mark Harman. New York: Schocken, 1998.

———. *Complete Stories*. Translated by Edwin Muir and Willa Muir. New York: Schocken, 1971.

———. *Diaries, 1919–1923*. Edited by Max Brod. New York: Schocken, 1976.

———. *The Diaries of Franz Kafka, 1910–1923*. Edited by Max Brod. New York: Schocken Books, 1975.

———. *The Diaries of Franz Kafka, 1910–1923*. Edited by Max Brod. London: Minerva, 1992.

———. *Drucke zu Lebzeiten*. Edited by Wolf Kittler, Hans-Gerd Koch, and Gerhard Neumann. Frankfurt am Main: S. Fischer, 1994.

———. *Erzählungen und andere ausgewählte Prosa.* Edited by Roger Hermes. Frankfurt am Main: Fischer, 1996.

———."Der Fahrgast." In *Drucke zu Lebzeiten*, 27–28.

———. *Gesammelte Werke in zwölf Bänden.* Nach der kritischen Ausgabe. Edited by Hans-Gerd Koch. Frankfurt am Main: Fischer Taschenbuch Verlag, 1994.

———. "An Introductory Talk on the Yiddish Language." In *Reading Kafka: Prague, Politics, and the Fin de Siècle*, edited by Mark M. Anderson, 265–66. New York: Schocken, 1989.

———. *Kafka's Selected Stories.* Translated and edited by Stanley Corngold. Boston: Norton, 2007.

———. *Letters to Felice.* Edited by Erich Heller and Jürgen Born. Translated by James Stern and Elisabeth Duckworth. New York: Schocken, 1973.

———. *Letters to Friends, Family, and Editors.* Translated by Richard Winston and Clara Winston. New York: Schocken Books. 1977.

———. *Letters to Milena.* Translated by Philip Boehm. New York: Schocken, 1990.

———. *The Metamorphosis.* Translated and edited by Stanley Corngold. New York: Norton, 1996.

———. *Nachgelassene Schriften und Fragmente I in der Fassung der Handschrift.* Edited by Malcolm Pasley. Frankfurt am Main: S. Fischer, 1990.

———. *Nachgelassene Schriften und Fragmente II in der Fassung der Handschrift.* Edited by Jost Schillemeit. Frankfurt am Main: S. Fischer, 1992.

———. *The Office Writings.* Edited by Stanley Corngold, Jack Greenberg, and Benno Wagner. Translated by Eric Patton and Ruth Hein. Princeton, NJ: Princeton UP, 2009.

———. *Der Proceß.* Edited by Malcolm Pasley. Frankfurt am Main: S. Fischer, 1990.

———. *Der Proceß: Apparatband.* Edited by Malcolm Pasley. Frankfurt am Main: S. Fischer, 1990.

———. *Der Process.* In *Die historisch-kritische Ausgabe sämtlicher Handschriften, Drucke und Typoskripte*, edited by Roland Reuß in cooperation with Peter Staengle. Frankfurt am Main: Stroemfeld, 1997.

———. *Sämtliche Erzählungen.* Edited by Paul Raabe. Frankfurt am Main: Fischer, 1970.

———. *Das Schloß.* Edited by Malcolm Pasley. Frankfurt am Main: S. Fischer, 1982.

———. *Tagebücher in der Fassung der Handschrift.* Edited by Michael Müller. Frankfurt am Main: S. Fischer, 1990.

———. *The Trial.* Translated by Breon Mitchell. New York: Schocken, 1998.

———. *Der Verschollene in der Fassung der Handschrift*. Edited by Jost Schillemeit. Frankfurt am Main: S. Fischer, 1983.

Kaschuba, Wolfgang. *Die Überwindung der Distanz: Zeit und Raum in der europäischen Moderne*. Frankfurt am Main: Fischer, 2004.

Kellner, Douglas. "Virilio on Vision Machines." *Film-Philosophy* 2.30 (October 1998) http://www.film-philosophy.com/vol2–1998/n30kellner.

Killen, Andreas. *Berlin Electropolis: Shocks, Nerves, and German Modernity*. Berkeley: U of California P, 2005.

Kittler, Friedrich A. *Aufschreibesysteme*. 4th ed. Munich: Fink, 2003.

———. *Grammophon, Film, Typewriter*. Berlin: Brinkmann & Bose, 1986.

Kittler, Wolf. "Schreibmaschinen, Sprechmaschinen: Effekte technischer Medien im Werk Franz Kafkas." In Kittler and Neumann, *Franz Kafka: Schriftverkehr*, 75–163.

Kittler, Wolf, and Gerhard Neumann. *Franz Kafka: Schriftverkehr*. Freiburg: Rombach, 1990.

Koch, Hans-Gerd, and Klaus Wagenbach, eds. *Kafkas Fabriken*. (Marbacher Magazin 100) Marbach: Deutsche Schillergesellschaft, 2002.

Koelb, Clayton. *Kafka's Rhetoric: The Passion of Reading*. Ithaca, NY: Cornell UP, 1989.

Köhn, Eckhardt. *Straßenrausch: Flanerie und kleine Form; Versuch zur Literaturgeschichte des Flaneurs bis 1933*. Berlin: Das Arsenal, 1989.

Kraft, Herbert. *Kafka: Wirklichkeit und Perspektive*. Bebenhausen: Lothar Rotsch, 1972.

Kurz, Gerhard. "Einleitung: Der junge Kafka im Kontext." In Kurz, *Der junge Kafka*, 7–39.

———, ed. *Der junge Kafka*. Frankfurt am Main: Suhrkamp, 1979.

La Ferla, Manuel. *Diritto al silenzio: Vita e scritti di Roberto Bazlen*. Palermo: Sellerio, 1994.

Landolfi, Tommaso. "Il babbo di Kafka." In *Le più belle pagine scelte da Italo Calvino*, 242–43. Milan: Adelphi, 2001.

Lange-Kirchheim, Astrid. "Franz Kafka: 'In der Strafkolonie' und Alfred Weber: 'Der Beamte.'" *Germanisch-Romanische Monatsschrift* 27 (1977): 202–21.

Lehmann, Hans-Thies. "Der buchstäbliche Körper: Zur Selbstinszenierung der Literatur bei Franz Kafka." In Kurz, *Der junge Kafka*, 213–41.

Lerner, Paul. *Hysterical Men: War, Psychiatry, and the Politics of Trauma in Germany, 1890–1930*. Ithaca, NY: Cornell UP, 2003.

Levi, Primo. *If This Is a Man*. Translated by Stuart Woolf. London: Abacus, 1987.

———. *Il processo*. Turin: Einaudi, 1983.

———. "Note to Franz Kafka's *The Trial*." In *The Black Hole of Auschwitz*, edited by Marco Belpoliti, translated by Sharon Wood, 140–41. Cambridge: Polity, 2005.

———. *Se questo è un uomo*. Turin: Einaudi, 1958.

———. *Survival in Auschwitz: The Nazi Assault on Humanity*. Translated by Stuart Woolf. New York: Simon & Schuster, 1996.

Lewis, Barry. *Kazuo Ishiguro*. Manchester: Manchester UP, 2000.

Leys, Ruth. *Trauma: A Genealogy*. Chicago: U of Chicago P, 2000.

Liska, Vivian. *When Kafka Says We: Uncommon Communities in German-Jewish Literature*. Bloomington: Indiana UP, 2009.

Lyotard, Jean-François. "Answering the Question: What is Postmodernism?" In *The Postmodern Condition: A Report on Knowledge*, translated by Geoff Bennington and Brian Massumi, 71–84. Minneapolis: U of Minnesota P, 1979 and 1984.

Magris, Claudio. *Danubio*. Milan: Garzanti, 1991. In English, *Danube*. New York: Farrar, Straus & Giroux, 1989.

Marx, Karl. *Das Kapital*. Vol. 2. In *Marx Engels Werke*, 24:160. Berlin: Dietz, 1956–1990.

Mattioni, Stelio. *Storia di Umberto Saba*. Milan: Camunia, 1989.

Mayer, Tamar. "From Zero to Hero: Nationalism and Masculinity in Jewish Israel." In *Israeli Women's Studies: A Reader*, edited by Esther Fuchs, 97–120. Piscataway, NJ: Rutgers UP, 2005.

Mazzucchetti, Lavinia. *Novecento in Germania*. Milan: Mondadori, 1959.

McDowell, John. "Comment on Stanley Cavell's 'Companionable Thinking.'" In *Philosophy and Animal Life*, 127–38. New York: Columbia UP, 2008.

Mendes-Flohr, Paul. "Cultural Zionism's Image of the Educated Jew: Reflections on Creating a Secular Jewish Culture." *Modern Judaism* 18.3 (October 1998): 227–39.

Meynaud, M. Jeuland. *Zeno e i suoi fratelli: La creazione del personaggio nei romanzi di Italo Svevo*. Bologna: Pàtron, 1985.

Micale, Mark S. *Hysterical Men: The Hidden History of Male Nervous Illness*. Cambridge, MA: Harvard UP, 2008.

Micale, Mark S., and Paul Lerner, eds. *Traumatic Pasts: History, Psychiatry, and Trauma in the Modern Age, 1870–1930*. (Cambridge: Cambridge UP, 2001.

Miron, Dan. *From Continuity to Contiguity: Toward a New Jewish Literary Thinking*. Stanford, CA: Stanford UP, 2010.

Mombauer, Annika. *Helmuth von Moltke and the Origins of the First World War*. Cambridge: Cambridge UP, 2001.

Montale, Eugenio. *Eugenio Montale Lettere a Italo Svevo: Con gli scritti di Montale su Svevo*. Bari, Italy: De Donato, 1966.

———. *New Poems*. Translated by G. Singh. New York: New Directions, 1972.

Morante, Elsa. *House of Liars*. Translated by Adrienne Foulke. New York: Harcourt Brace, 1951.

———. *Menzogna e sortilegio*. Turin: Einaudi, 1994.

Mosse, George. "'Max Nordau and His Degeneration': Introduction." In *Degeneration,* by Max Nordau, xiii–xxxvi. Lincoln: U of Nebraska P, 1993.

Muir, Edwin. *Essays on Literature and Society*. London: Hogarth, 1949.

Mulvey, Laura. "Visual Pleasure and Narrative Cinema." *Screen* 16.3 (1975): 6–18.

Nägele, Rainer. "Kafkaesk." In *Odradeks Lachen: Fremdheit bei Kafka,* edited by Hansjörg Bay and Christof Hamann, 21–39. Freiburg im Breisgau: Rombach Verlag, 2006.

Nekula, Marek. *Franz Kafkas Sprachen "... in einem Stockwerk des innern babylonischen Turmes ..."* Tübingen: Niemeyer, 2003.

Neumann, Gerhard. "'Ein Bericht für eine Akademie': Erwägungen zum 'Mimesis'-Charakter Kafkascher Texte." *Deutsche Vierteljahrsschrift für Literaturwissenschaft und Geistesgeschichte* 49 (1975): 166–83.

———. "Franz Kafka: Der Name, die Sprache und die Ordnung der Dinge." In Kittler and Neumann, *Franz Kafka: Schriftverkehr*, 11–29.

———. "Kafka und Goethe." In *Franz Kafka und die Weltliteratur*, edited by Manfred Engel and Dieter Lamping, 48–65. Göttingen: Vandenhoeck & Ruprecht, 2006.

———. "Literature as Historiography: Franz Kafka's Concept of the 'Diary-Keeping of a People.'" *Journal of the Kafka Society of America* 26.1–2 (2002): 35–41.

———. "'Nachrichten vom 'Pontus'": Das Problem der Kunst im Werk Franz Kafkas." In Kittler and Neumann, *Franz Kafka: Schriftverkehr*, 164–98.

Nietzsche, Friedrich. *Also sprach Zarathustra*. In *Werke in drei Bänden,* edited by Karl Schlechta, 3:28. Munich: Hanser, 1954.

———. *Basic Writings of Nietzsche*. Edited and translated by Walter Kaufmann. New York: Modern Library, 1968.

———. *Beyond Good and Evil*. Translated by Marion Faber. Oxford: Oxford UP, 1998.

———. *The Gay Science*. Translated by Josephine Nauckhoff. Cambridge: Cambridge UP. 2001.

———. *The Portable Nietzsche*. Edited and translated by Walter Kaufmann. New York: Viking, 1969 and 1982.

———. *Werke in drei Bänden*. Edited by Karl Schlechta. Munich: Hanser, 1999.

Nonne, Max. Report on Walter Cimbal's 1915 lecture, "Die seelischen und nervösen Erkrankungen seit der Mobilmachung." In "Ärztlicher Verein in Hamburg: Sitzung vom 23. Februar 1915." *Neurologisches Zentralblatt* 34 (1915): 408–15.

Nordau, Max. *Entartung*. Berlin: Duncker, 1892.

Nyíri, J. C. "Einleitung." In *Der Selbstmord als sociale Massenerscheinung der modernen Civilisation,* by Thomas G. Masaryk, 5–21. Munich: Philosophia Verlag, 1982.

Olney, James. *Metaphors of Self: The Meaning of Autobiography*. Princeton, NJ: Princeton UP, 1972.

Oppenheim, Hermann. "Der Krieg und die traumatischen Neurosen." *Berliner klinische Wochenschrift* 52 (15 March 1915): 257–61.

———. *Die traumatischen Neurosen nach den in der Nervenklinik der Charité in den letzten 5 Jahren gesammelten Beobachtungen*. Berlin: Hirschwald, 1889.

Oschmann, Dirk. "Kafka als Erzähler." In Engel and Auerochs, *Kafka-Handbuch: Leben, Werk, Wirkung*, 438–49.

Oz, Amos. "Has Israel Altered Its Visions?" (1982). In *Israel, Palestine and Peace: Essays*, 4–18. New York: Harcourt Brace, 1994.

Pape, Klaus. *Sprachkunst und Kunstsprache bei Flaubert und Kafka*. St. Ingbert, Germany: Röhrig, 1996.

Pater, Walter. *The Renaissance: Studies in Art and Poetry*. Edited by Adam Phillips. Oxford: Oxford UP, 1986.

Peters, Paul. "Witness to the Execution: Kafka and Colonialism." *Monatshefte* 93 (2001): 401–25.

Prümm, Karl. "Intermedialität und Multimedialität: Eine Skizze medienwissenschaftlicher Forschungsfelder." In *Ansichten einer künftigen Medienwissenschaft*, edited by Rainer Bohn, Eggo Müller, and Rainer Ruppert, 195–200. Berlin: Edition Sigma Bohn, 1988.

Puchner, Martin. "Performing the Open: Actors, Animals, Philosophers." *The Drama Review* 51.1 (2007): 21–32.

Radkau, Joachim. *Das Zeitalter der Nervosität: Deutschland zwischen Bismarck und Hitler*. Munich: Carl Hanser, 1998.

Rajewsky, Irina O. *Intermedialität*. Tübingen: A. Francke/UTB, 2002.

Reitano, Natalie. "The Good Wound: Memory and Community in *The Unconsoled*." *Texas Studies in Language and Literature* 49.4 (2007): 361–86.

Reuß, Roland, and Peter Staengle, eds. *Die historisch-kritische Ausgabe sämtlicher Handschriften, Drucke und Typoskripte Franz Kafkas*. Frankfurt am Main: Stroemfeld, 1995–.

Reynolds, J. Russell. "Travelling: Its Influence on Health." In *The Book of Health*, edited by Malcolm Morris, 559–88. London: Castle, 1884.

Ricoeur, Paul. "The Metaphorical Process as Cognition, Imagination, and Feeling." In *On Metaphor*, edited by Sheldon Sacks, 141–58. Chicago: U of Chicago P, 1979.

Robertson, Ritchie. "In Search of the Historical Kafka: A Selective Review of Research, 1980–92." *The Modern Language Review* 89.1 (January 1994): 107–37.

———. *The "Jewish Question" in German Literature, 1749–1939: Emancipation and Its Discontents.* New York: Oxford UP, 1999.

———. "Proposal" for the Princeton-Oxford-Humboldt Kafka Consortium. http://www.princeton.edu/international/doc/GCRF-KAFKA-network.pdf.

Robinson, Richard. *Narratives of the European Border: A History of Nowhere.* Basingstoke, UK: Palgrave Macmillan, 2007.

Rorem, Ned. "Fiction in Review." *Yale Review* 84.2 (1996): 154–59.

Rosenzweig, Franz. *Der Stern der Erlösung.* 3rd ed. Frankfurt am Main: Suhrkamp, 1990.

Roskothen, Johannes. *Verkehr: Zu einer poetischen Theorie der Moderne.* Munich: Fink, 2003.

Rubinstein, William C. "A Report to an Academy." In *Franz Kafka Today,* edited by Angel Flores and Homer Swander, 55–60. Madison: U of Wisconsin P, 1968.

Ryan, Judith. "The Maze of Misreadings: Thoughts on Metaphor in Kafka." *Journal of the Kafka Society of America* 7.2 (1983): 38–43.

Sandbank, Shimon. "History and the Law": S. Y. Agnon and Kafka." In *After Kafka: The Influence of Kafka's Fiction*, 97–111. Athens: U of Georgia P, 1989.

Santner, Eric. "Kafka's *Metamorphosis* and the Writing of Abjection." In Kafka, *The Metamorphosis*, 195–210.

Schaffer, Brian W. *Understanding Kazuo Ishiguro.* Columbia: U of South Carolina P, 1998.

Schäffner, Wolfgang. "Event, Series, Trauma: The Probabilistic Revolution of the Mind in the Late Nineteenth and Early Twentieth Centuries." In Micale and Lerner, *Traumatic Pasts: History, Psychiatry, and Trauma in the Modern Age, 1870–1930*, 81–91.

Scharer von Aurau, Peter. *Zur psychischen Strategie des schwachen Helden: Italo Svevo im Vergleich mit Kafka, Broch und Musil.* Thusis, Switzerland: Buchdruckerei Werner Roth, 1978.

Schings, Dietmar. *Franz Kafka und der Mann ohne Schatten. "Eiserne Fensterläden" — Kafka und das Kino.* Berlin: Vorwerk 8, 2004.

Schivelbusch, Wolfgang. *Geschichte der Eisenbahnreise: Zur Industrialisierung von Raum und Zeit im 19. Jahrhundert.* Munich: Hanser, 1977.

Schlingmann, Carsten. "Die Verwandlung." In *Interpretationen zu Franz Kafka: Das Urteil, Die Verwandlung, Ein Landartzt, Kleine Prosastücke.* Munich: Oldenbourg, 1968.

Schmeling, Manfred. "Kafka und Flaubert: Perspektive, Wirklichkeit, Welterzeugung." In *Kafka und die Weltliteratur*, edited by Manfred Engel and Dieter Lamping, 109–24. Göttingen: Vandenhoeck & Ruprecht, 2006.

Schnitzler, Arthur. *Gesammelte Werke.* Frankfurt am Main: Fischer, 1961.

Scholtmeijer, Marian. "What is 'Human'? Metaphysics and Zoontology in Flaubert and Kafka." In *Animal Acts: Configuring the Human in Western History*, edited by Jennifer Ham and Matthew Senior, 127–44. New York: Routledge, 1997.

Schopenhauer, Arthur. *Die Welt als Wille und Vorstellung.* Vol. 2/2. Edited by Rolf Toman. Dortmund: Könemann, 1997.

Schulze, F. K. A. *Die ersten deutschen Eisenbahnen.* 2nd ed. Leipzig: Voigtländer, 1917.

Shaked, Gershon. "Kafka and Agnon: Their Relationship to Judaism and Zionism." In *Kafka, Zionism, and Beyond*, edited by Mark Gelber, 239–57. Tübingen: Niemeyer, 2004.

Sheppard, Richard. *On Kafka's Castle: A Study.* London: Croom Helm, 1973.

Showalter, Dennis. "Railroads, the Prussian Army, and the German Way of War in the Nineteenth Century." In *Railways and International Politics: Paths of Empire, 1848–1945*, edited by T. G. Otte and Keith Neilson, 21–44. New York: Routledge, 2006.

Showalter, Elaine. "Hysteria, Feminism, Gender." In Gilman et al., *Hysteria beyond Freud*, 286–344.

Shumsky, Dimitry. "Czechs, Germans, Arabs, Jews: Franz Kafka's 'Jackals and Arabs' between Bohemia and Palestine." *AJS Review: The Journal for the Association for Jewish Studies* 33.1 (April 2009): 71–100.

Siegert, Bernhard. *Relays: Literature as an Epoch of the Postal System.* Translated by Kevin Repp. Stanford, CA: Stanford UP, 1999.

Sim, Wai-Chew. *Globalization and Dislocation in the Novels of Kazuo Ishiguro.* Lewiston, NY: Edwin Mellen, 2006.

Simmel, Georg. *Aufsätze und Abhandlungen, 1901–1908.* Edited by Rüdiger Kramme, Angela Rammstedt, and Otthein Rammstedt. Vol. 1. Vol. 7 of *Georg Simmel Gesamtausgabe*, edited by Otthein Rammstedt. Frankfurt am Main: Suhrkamp, 1995.

———. "The Metropolis and Mental Life." 1903. In *The Sociology of Georg Simmel*, edited by Kurt H. Wolff, 409–24. London: Free Press of Glencoe, 1950.

———. *Simmel on Culture.* Edited by David Frisby and Mike Featherstone. London: Sage Publications, 1997.

Simons, Oliver. "Schuld und Scham: Kafkas episches Theater." In *Kafkas Institutionen*, edited by Arne Höcker and Oliver Simons, 269–93. Bielefeld: Transcript, 2007).

Smuts, Barbara. "Reflections." In *The Lives of Animals*, edited by Amy Gutmann, 107–20. Princeton, NJ: Princeton UP, 1999.

Sokel, Walter H. "Identity and the Individual or Past and Present: Franz Kafka's 'A Report to an Academy' in a Psychoanalytic and a Sociohistorical Context." In *The Myth of Power and the Self: Essays on Franz Kafka*, 268–91. Detroit: Wayne State UP, 2002.

———. "Kafka as a Jew." *New Literary History* 30.4 (1999): 837–53.

———. "On the Dionysian in Nietzsche." *New Literary History* 36 (2005): 501–20.

———. "Zur Sprachauffassung und Poetik Franz Kafkas." In *Franz Kafka: Themen und Probleme*, 26–47. Göttingen: Vandenhoeck, 1980.

Somigli, Luca. "In the Shadow of Byzantium: Modernism in Italian Literature." In *Modernism*, vol. 2, edited by Astradur Eysteinsson and Vivian Liska, 911–30. Amsterdam: John Benjamins, 2007.

Somigli, Luca, and Mario Moroni. "Modernism in Italy: An Introduction." In *Italian Modernism: Italian Culture between Decadentism and Avant-Garde*, edited by Somigli and Moroni, 3–32. Toronto: U of Toronto P, 2004.

Spaini, Alberto. "Prefazione." In *America,* by Franz Kafka, ii–viii. Turin: Frassinelli, 1947.

Spiegel, Alan. *Fiction and the Camera Eye: Visual Consciousness in Film and the Modern Novel.* Charlottesville: U of Virginia P, 1976.

Stach, Rainer. *Kafka: Die Jahre der Erkenntnis.* Frankfurt am Main: Fischer, 2008.

Stanzel, Franz K. *A Theory of Narrative.* Translated by Charlotte Goedsche. Cambridge: Cambridge UP, 1984.

Steiner, Andreas. *Das nervöse Zeitalter: Der Begriff der Nervosität bei Laien und Ärzten in Deutschland und Österreich um 1900.* Zurich: Juris-Verlag, 1964.

Steiner, George. "K." In *Language and Silence: Essays, 1958–1966*, 141–49. London: Faber, 1967.

———. *Real Presences.* Chicago: U of Chicago P, 1991.

Stierle, Karlheinz. "Möglichkeiten des dunklen Stils in den Anfängen moderner Lyrik in Frankreich." In *Immanente Ästhetik — Ästhetische Reflexion: Lyrik als Paradigma der Moderne*, edited by Wolfgang Iser, 157–94. Munich: Fink, 1966 (=Poetik und Hermeneutik, vol. 2).

Straus, Nina Pelikan. "Transforming Franz Kafka's *Metamorphosis.*" In Kafka, *The Metamorphosis,* 126–40.

Stüssel, Kerstin. *In Vertretung: Literarische Mitschriften von Bürokratie zwischen früher Neuzeit und Gegenwart.* Tübingen: Niemeyer, 2004.

Svevo, Italo. "Argo and His Master." In *Short Sentimental Journey and Other Stories,* translated by Beryl de Zoete, L. Collison-Morley, and Ben Johnson, 163–94. Berkeley: U of California P, 1967.

———. "Argo e il suo padrone." In *Tutte le opere di Italo Svevo: Racconti e scritti autobiografici,* 95–118. Milan: Mondadori, 2004.

———. *La coscienza di Zeno.* Rome: Edizioni di storia e letteratura, 2008.

———. *Zeno's Conscience.* Translated by William Weaver. New York: Vintage International, 2003.

Sweeney, Kevin W. "Competing Theories of Identity in Kafka's *The Metamorphosis.*" In Kafka, *The Metamorphosis,* 152.

Tabori, George. "Liebeserklärung: Dankrede." *Jahrbuch der deutschen Akademie für Sprache und Dichtung Darmstadt* (1992): 133–37.

Tamaro, Susanna. "La grande casa bianca." *Panta* 5 (1991): 117–26. In English, "The Big White House." In *The Quality of Light,* edited by Ann and Michael Caesar, 59–69. London & New York: Serpent's Tail, 1993.

Tamen, Miguel. "The Ape Speaks." In de Bolla and Uhlig, *Aesthetics and the Work of Art: Adorno, Kafka, Richter,* 113–25.

Taylor, A. J. P. *War by Timetable: How the First World War Began.* London: MacDonald, 1969.

Tellini, Gino. *The Invention of Modern Italian Literature: Strategies of Creative Imagination.* Toronto: U of Toronto P, 2007.

The Influence of Railway Travelling on Public Health. Published by the *The Lancet.* London, 1862.

Thomas, Dylan. *The Collected Letters.* Edited by Paul Ferris. London: J. M. Dent, 1985.

Theweleit, Klaus. *buch der könige,* vol. 1. Basel: Stroemfeld, 1988.

Timms, Edward. "Musil's Vienna and Kafka's Prague: The Quest for a Spiritual City." In *Urban Experience in Modern European Literature and Art,* edited by Edward Timms and David Kelly, 260–61. New York: St. Martin's, 1985.

Todorov, Tzvetan. *The Fantastic: A Structural Approach to a Literary Genre.* Translated by Richard Howard. Ithaca, NY: Cornell UP, 1975.

Torres, Amanda. "Kafka and the Common Law: The Roots of the 'Kafkaesque' in *The Trial,*" unpublished seminar paper for "Kafka and the Law." Columbia U School of Law, 7 May 2007.

Turner, Alison. "Kafka's Two Worlds of Music." *Monatshefte* 55.5 (October 1963): 265–76.

Urban Experience in Modern European Literature and Art. Edited by Edward Timms and David Kelly. New York: St. Martin's, 1985.

Urzidil, John. "Recollections." In *The Kafka Problem,* edited by Angel Flores, 20–24. New York: New Directions, 1946.

Veneziani Svevo, Livia. *Vita di mio marito.* Pordenone, Italy: Arti Grafiche Fratelli Cosarini, 1958.

Virilio, Paul. *Open Sky* Translated by Julie Rose. London: Verso, 1997.

———. "The Third Interval: A Critical Transition." In *Rethinking Technologies*, edited by Verena Andermatt Conley, 3–12. Minnesota: U of Minnesota P, 1993.

Voigt, Fritz. *Die Entwicklung des Verkehrssystems.* Berlin: Duncker & Humblot, 1965.

———. *Die Theorie der Verkehrswirtschaft.* Berlin: Duncker & Humblot, 1973.

Wagenbach, Klaus, ed. *In der Strafkolonie: Eine Geschichte aus dem Jahre 1914.* Expanded edition. Berlin: Wagenbach, 1995.

Wagner, Benno. "'Beglaubigungssorgen': Zur Problematik von Verfasserschaft, Autorschaft und Werkintegration im Rahmen der *Amtlichen Schriften* Franz Kafkas." *Editio*: *International Yearbook of Scholarly Editing* 17 (2003): 155–69.

———. "Der Bewerber und der Prätendent: Zur Selektivität der Idee bei Platon und Kafka." *Hofmannsthal Jahrbuch zur europäischen Moderne* 8 (2000): 274.

———. "'. . . in der Fremde, aus der Sie kommen . . .': Die Geburt des Schreibens aus der Statistik des Selbstmords." In *Odradeks Lachen: Fremdheit bei Kafka*, edited by Hansjörg Bay and Christof Hamann, Litterae 136, 193–228. Freiburg: Rombach, 2006.

———. "Kafkas phantastisches Büro." In *Kontinent Kafka: Mosse-Lectures an der Humboldt-Universität zu Berlin*, edited by Klaus R. Scherpe and Elisabeth Wagner, 104–18. Berlin: Vorwerk 8, 2006.

Wagner, Rudolf. "Simulation im Bahnbetriebe mit besonderer Berücksichtigung der sogenannten 'traumatischen Neurose.'" *Aerztliche Sachverständigen Zeitung* 6 (1900): 47–52, 69–73.

Walser, Martin. *Beschreibung einer Form: Versuch über Franz Kafka.* Munich: Hanser, 1961.

Warwar, Max. "Die Flucht vor dem Typus." *Selbstwehr* 3 (30 April 1909): 1–2.

Weber, Max Maria von. "Die Abnutzung des physischen Organismus beim Fahrpersonal der Eisenbahnen." *Wieck Deutsche Illustrirte Gewerbezeitung* 25 (1860): 228.

Weißler, Adolf. *Geschichte der Rechtsanwaltschaft.* Leipzig: C. E. M. Pfeffer, 1905.

Westwater, Lynn Lara. "Franz Kafka and Italo Svevo: 'A Blur of Languages.'" *RLA Archive* (1996) Purdue U. 5 Dec. 2007. http://tell.fll.purdue.edu/RLA-Archive/1996/italian.html.

Westwood, John. *Railways at War.* San Diego, CA: Howell-North, 1980.

Winn, J. M. "Railway Traveling, and Its Effects on Health." *The Journal of Public Health* 4 (December 1855): 425.

Woods, Gregory. *A History of Gay Literature: The Male Tradition.* New Haven, CT: Yale UP, 1998.

Yeats, W. B. *Collected Poems.* London: Macmillan, 1961.

Yehoshua, A. B. "A Nation That Knows No Bounds." Interview by Ari Shavit. *Ha'aretz* (19 Mar. 2004). http://www89.homepage.villanova.edu/scott.black/S04sensem/Yehoshua%20interview%20%28March%202004%29.htm.

———. *A Woman in Jerusalem.* Translated by Hillel Halkin. 2004. Reprint, Orlando: Harcourt, 2007.

Zilcosky, John. *Kafka's Travels: Exoticism, Colonialism, and the Traffic of Writing.* New York: Palgrave-Macmillan, 2003.

Ziolkowski, Theodore. "Talking Dogs: The Caninization of Literature." In *Varieties of Literary Thematics,* 86–122. Princeton, NJ: Princeton UP, 1983.

Zischler, Hanns. *Kafka Goes to the Movies.* Translated by Susan H. Gillespie. Chicago: U of Chicago P, 2003.

Contributors

PETER BEICKEN got his PhD at Stanford University (1971) and has taught at Princeton University. He is currently a professor at the University of Maryland, College Park, where he teaches German literature, culture, and film. Among his specialties are Ingeborg Bachmann (two books, 1988 and 2001), Anna Seghers, and German film (*The Films of Wim Wenders*, coauthored 1993; *Wie interpretiert man einen Film*, 2004). His book publications on Kafka include *Franz Kafka: Eine kritische Einführung in die Forschung* (1974), *Franz Kafka. "Die Verwandlung": Dokumente und Erläuterungen* (1983), *Franz Kafka: Leben und Werk* (1986), and *Franz Kafka: "'Der Process": Interpretation* (1995).

IRIS BRUCE is associate professor of German and comparative literature at McMaster University in Hamilton, Ontario, Canada. Her research interests are Kafka in his time and contemporary popular culture, German-Jewish studies, and Israel studies: the literature of Israel and Palestine. She is the author of *Kafka and Cultural Zionism: Dates in Palestine* and has published many articles on Kafka and Yiddish literature, Jewish folklore, Zionism, and Kafka in popular culture.

JACOB BURNETT received a BA in mathematics from the University of Chicago and an MA in English literature from North Carolina State University. He is currently pursuing a PhD in comparative literature at the University of North Carolina, Chapel Hill. His primary research involves the examination of the literary and aesthetic aspects of mathematical texts and, conversely, the underlying mathematical aspects of literary texts, particularly in (though — as is obvious from his work on Kafka — not limited to) the early modern period.

STANLEY CORNGOLD is professor emeritus of German and Comparative Literature at Princeton University, where he taught for over forty years. He is the author of *Lambent Traces: Franz Kafka* (2004), translator of *Kafka's Selected Stories* (2006), and coeditor of *Franz Kafka: The Office Writings* (2009). Together with Benno Wagner, he has written a new book titled *Franz Kafka: The Ghosts in the Machine* (due out in 2011). He recently founded the Princeton-Oxford-Humboldt Kafka Consortium and also continues to work on the late German Enlightenment, translating and editing Goethe's *The Sufferings of Young Werther* (also due out in 2011). He is a Fellow of the American Academy of Arts and Sciences.

UTA DEGNER studied at the Universities of Konstanz, Bologna, and Berlin, earning a doctorate in German literature. Later she held a postdoctoral position at the Freie Universität Berlin. Currently she is a member of the German faculty at the University of Salzburg (Austria). Her publications on Kafka include "Kafka's 'écriture automatique': Zur intermedialen Dimension seines Erzählens" and "'Was ich berühre zerfällt': Gesichter der Handschrift in Kafkas Oktavheften."

DOREEN DENSKY is a PhD candidate in the Department of German and Romance Languages and Literatures at the Johns Hopkins University. She is currently working on her dissertation, examining the rhetoric of "speaking-for" in modern literature, particularly in Franz Kafka.

KATJA GARLOFF is associate professor of German and Humanities at Reed College, where she teaches courses on German Jewish culture, critical theory, and eighteenth- to twentieth-century German literature. She is the author of *Words from Abroad: Trauma and Displacement in Postwar German Jewish Writers* and of articles on many authors, including G. E. Lessing, Achim von Arnim, Robert Walser, Joseph Roth, Peter Weiss, Theodor Adorno, and W. G. Sebald. She is currently working on a new book project titled *Mixed Feelings: Tropes of Love in German Jewish Culture, 1800/1900.*

ROLF J. GOEBEL holds degrees from Brown University, the University of Kiel, and the University of Maryland. He is professor of German at the University of Alabama in Huntsville. His research focuses on German modernism and contemporary literature; metropolitan space, especially post-reunification Berlin; and cultural theory (hermeneutics, postcolonialism, media competition). His publications include: *Constructing China: Kafka's Orientalist Discourse* (1997) and *Benjamin heute: Großstadtdiskurs, Postkolonialität und Flanerie zwischen den Kulturen* (2001). He is also coauthor of *A Franz Kafka Encyclopedia* (2005) and editor of *A Companion to the Works of Walter Benjamin* (2009).

RUTH V. GROSS studied German and comparative literature at Northwestern and received her PhD from Yale University. She has taught at the University of Rochester and the University of Texas at Arlington and is currently head of the Department of Foreign Languages and Literatures and professor of German at North Carolina State University. She is the author of *PLAN and the Austrian Rebirth* (1982) and the editor of *Critical Essays on Franz Kafka* (1990). She is coauthor and editor of *A Franz Kafka Encyclopedia* (2005). Her recent publications, in addition to those on Kafka, deal with the works of the Austrian novelist Albert Drach.

MARK HARMAN is professor of English and German at Elizabethtown College. His translation of *The Castle* (Schocken) won the Modern Language Association's Lois Roth Award. He has written widely on Kafka and other modern German-language and Irish authors for scholarly journals, literary reviews, and newspapers in the United States, Britain, Ireland, and Germany, and has translated Hermann Hesse's selected letters, various works by contemporary German-language authors, and (with Walter Arndt) the volume *Robert Walser Rediscovered*, which he also edited. In 2008 Schocken published his translation of Kafka's *Amerika: The Missing Person.*

ROBERT LEMON is assistant professor of German at the University of Oklahoma. He received his BA in Modern Languages (German) from the University of Oxford and his MA and PhD from Harvard University. He has published the following articles on Kafka: "Cargo Colonies and Penal Cults: Ethnology and Ethnocentrism in Kafka's 'In der Strafkolonie,'" in *Colloquia Germanica*, and "'Die alten, alten Geschichten': The Relevance of Ancient History for Franz Kafka," in the *Journal of the Kafka Society of America*. His book on orientalist fiction in the Habsburg *fin-de-siècle*, *Imperial Messages*, which will appear in 2011 with Camden House, includes two chapters on Kafka's short stories.

ROLAND REUß is professor of German literature at the University of Heidelberg and honorary professor at the Freie Universität Berlin. He is founder and chair of the *Institut für Textkritik* in Heidelberg and head of the program of "Editionswissenschaft und Textkritik" at the University of Heidelberg. He is also editor of the *Historisch-kritische Franz Kafka-Ausgabe*, the *Historisch-kritische Brandenburger Kleist-Ausgabe*, and the annual journal *TEXTkritische Beiträge*. His major areas of interest are textual criticism, Hölderlin, Kafka, Kleist, romantic literature, Paul Celan, and digital media.

RITCHIE ROBERTSON is a graduate of Edinburgh and Oxford Universities. He was a fellow and tutor in German at St John's College, Oxford, from 1989 to 2010, when he became Taylor Professor of German at Oxford. His books include *Kafka: Judaism, Politics, and Literature* (1985), *The "Jewish Question" in German Literature, 1749–1939* (1999), *Kafka: A Very Short Introduction* (2004), and *Mock-Epic Poetry from Pope to Heine* (2009). In 2004 he became a Fellow of the British Academy. He is a director of the Oxford Kafka Research Centre.

WALTER H. SOKEL was born in Vienna. During his career he taught at Columbia, Stanford, and the University of Virginia, with guest professorships at Harvard, Rutgers, and the universities of Hamburg, Freiburg, and Graz. Since 1994 he has been Commonwealth Professor Emeritus of German and English Literature at the University of Virginia. He now resides in San Francisco. He has served on the Executive Committee of the MLA and is a Fellow of the American Academy of Arts and Sciences and the Pen Club (Austria). He has received fellowships from the National Endowment of the Humanities and the Alexander von Humboldt Foundation, an honorary doctorate from the University of Graz, and the Cross of Merit, First Class, of the Federal Republic of Austria. He is the author of *German Expressionist Literature* and three books on Franz Kafka; and he has edited *Anthology of German Expressionist Drama* (in English translation) and published numerous scholarly articles on topics of German and European literature and philosophy, ranging chronologically from Schiller to Peter Handke.

JOHN ZILCOSKY is chair of the Department of German and member of the Centre for Comparative Literature at the University of Toronto. He is the author of *Kafka's Travels: Exoticism, Colonialism, and the Traffic of Writing*, which won the MLA's 2004 Scaglione Prize. He has written widely on modern European literature, travel writing, psychoanalysis, and literary theory, and is the editor of *Writing Travel: The Poetics and Politics of the Modern Journey*. He has lectured in Germany, Italy, France, Sweden, Ireland, China, and Brazil. His work has been supported by the Fulbright and Humboldt foundations, as well as by Canada's Social Sciences and Humanities Research Council.

SASKIA ELIZABETH ZIOLKOWSKI is a Mellon Postdoctoral Fellow in the Humanities at the University of California, Berkeley. She holds a PhD in Italian and Comparative Literature and Society from Columbia University. Her dissertation, *Trieste and the Migrations of Modernism: Fin-de-siècle Austria in the Italian Literary Landscape*, uses Trieste to focus an examination of the relationships between key Austro-Hungarian authors (Kafka, Musil, Rilke, Roth) and Italian modernists (Svevo, Saba, Slataper, Quarantotti Gambini). Several of these chapters have been published. She is working on a book entitled *Kafka's Progeny: For a New Genealogy of Modern Italian Literature.*

Index

Abraham, Nicolas, 90
"Absent-minded Window-gazing," 77–81, 170–71
Abu Ghraib, 139, 140
Adorno, Theodor, 3, 122, 147
"Advocates," 122, 128, 132
aesthetics: community and, 208–9; Ishiguro and, 208–9, 218; Nietzsche and, 66; *vs.* realism in Kafka's early writing, 11, 75–88
Agamben, Giorgio, 245
alienation, 68, 153, 159, 169, 188; narrative, 208, 215–16
allegorical self-reflection, 79–80
alliteration, 78
Alt, Peter-André, 148
Amerika: The Missing Person, 2, 24–25, 158–59, 172–73, 179, 215; cinematic effects and, 172–73
Anders, Günther, 48
animal imagery, 17, 100–101, 183; animal protagonists (*see* "Josefine, the Singer"; "A Report to an Academy"; *Researches of a Dog*); Italian authors and, 237, 240–41; in "Jackals and Arabs," 223–24; in *The Metamorphosis*, 168; in *The Trial*, 54; in *Wedding Preparations*, 168
anonymity, 125–27, 129
anti-Semitism: blood libel and, 101n2; as Kafka's context, 4, 6, 12, 101n2, 223; racialization and, 11–12, 93, 95, 100–101
aphorisms, 4–5, 13, 18, 145
apparatus, use of term, 144
"Argo and His Master" (Svevo), 17, 240–46
assimilation: as choice, 93–94, 226, 232; Jewish, 12, 89, 100–101, 226–28; mimicry and, 12, 100–101
Auden, W. H., 18
audience / readership: Kafka's global readership, 2; lay *vs.* academic, 136; readers, realistic *vs.* aesthetic types of, 79–80; the reader's agency, 116
authenticity: media and loss of authentic experience of reality, 160–61; sincerity, 50; writing as artificial, 57
author-function *vs.* author-subject, 127
authority: acquiescence or obedience to, 70, 141–43, 145–46; author as, 126, 134n18; deferral and bureaucratic hierarchy, 127; father as familial, 70, 82–83, 142; hierarchy and, 143; and the institution, 120, 143; invisibility of institutional, 144–45; Kafka and resistance to personal, 126–27; machines as tyrannical, 156–57; parlographs (dictating machines) and subversion of, 154–55; resistance to, 145–47; and *Schriftstellersein*, 126–27, 132; "strange loops" and disappearance of hierarchy, 107, 113; in *The Trial*, 127–28, 142–44; violence as foundation for, 144
authorship, 125–27, 132

backshadowing, 18
Balfour declaration, 223–24
Barthes, Roland, 12
Bauer, Felice, 134n25, 148, 154; correspondence with, 1, 75, 76, 126–27
Baum, Oskar, 193, 195
Bazlen, Roberto "Bobi," 238

Beer-Hoffmann, Richard, 77
Begley, Louis, 21n20
Beicken, Peter, 15; article by, 165–74; cited, 151, 205n76
Beißner, Friedrich, 131–32
Bell, Vikki, 90–91
Benjamin, Walter, 141–42, 225
Benn, Gottfried, 77
Bennett, Alan, 136
Berdyczewski, Micha, 225
Bernstein, Michael, 18
Bhabha, Homi, 92
Birnbaum, Nathan, 96
The Birth of Tragedy (Nietzsche), 64–66, 71
Blei, Franz, 77, 125
blood, as metaphor for race, 12, 89–90, 95–101
"The Blood of the Walsungs" (Mann), 5–6
Boa, Elizabeth, 110
the body: Freud and traumatic neurosis, 192–94; the Jewish body as biologically different, 89, 95, 97–98; telecommunication technology and, 151–52, 154–56, 158–59; transportation technology and "natural" presence, 179; travel and mechanically damaged bodies, 179–85, 188–94; as unreadable sign, 179–96
Bontempelli, Massimo, 240
Borges, Jorge Luis, 237
Bourdieu, Pierre, 11, 75–76, 81
Brod, Max: on *The Castle*, 146; correspondence with, 51, 56–57; as editor, 9, 25, 35, 38; on Kafka, 3; on Nietzsche and Kafka, 10; titles assigned by, 35, 122
Bruce, Iris, 16–17; article by, 222–34
Buber, Martin, 99–100, 225
"Building the Great Wall of China," 208, 213, 217–18
bureaucracy, 14; bureaucratic writing, 121–27; and erasure of human agency, 156–57, 159; in Habiby, 226–27; institutions and, 137, 143–44; Kafka's work within, 1, 6–7, 121–27, 137
Burnett, Jacob: article by, 105–19
Butler, Judith, 89–91
Buzzati, Dino, 17, 238–39

Calvino, Italo, 239
Campe, Rüdiger, 120–21
The Castle: authority or hierarchy in, 14, 146–47; the erotic in, 114–15; family in, 114–15, 146; indeterminate setting of, 215; land surveying and, 8; metaphor in, 56–57; modernity and, 110–11; as novel of the institution, 120–21; observational mode and, 166; and parabolic strange loops, 109–16; resistance in, 146–48; sexual exploitation in, 146–47
castration imagery, 91–92
Chamberlain, Houston Stewart, 96
Chenu, Père, 110, 112
"The Child and the City," 52–53
childhood: issues explorations, 57–58; Kafka's critiques of child-rearing, 141–42; and *The Metamorphosis*, 67; and Nietzsche's Zarathustrian morality, 67–68
Chinese stories, 18, 143, 213–14
cinematic effects, 151, 163n20; Kafka's use contrasted with that of his contemporaries, 174n6; and narrative structure, 165, 168–74 (*see also* cinematic gaze)
cinematic gaze, 15, 169; in "Absent-minded Window-gazing," 170–71; character as focalizer, 165, 168–71; in "The Passenger," 168–70; stasis and, 167; and zooming effects, 169–71
circumcision, 97–98, 100
Cohen, Jean, 51
colonial mimicry, 92
colonialism, 92, 144
communication technology, 162n1; in *The Castle*, 110–11; conversation between apparatuses, 156–57, 159; as dehumanizing, 159; parlographs (dictating machines), 134n25, 154–58, 179; as spectral or ghostly, 157–58, 179

concentration camps, 1, 138, 140, 145, 240
Conrad, Joseph, 144
Conversations with Kafka (Janouch), 49, 163n27
Corngold, Stanley, 50, 63n55, 110, 126, 201n38, 210; introductory essay by, 1–23
correspondence, 56–57; as erotic, 196; Flaubert as model for, 75; letters as spectral or ghostly, 152–54, 157, 197n3; letter-writing in fiction, 81–82; with Pollak, 50–51, 206n78; as preferred means of interaction, 50; as site of metaphor, 50–51. *See also specific correspondents*
A Country Doctor: Little Stories, 24, 38, 229
crisis of language, 50
"Crossbreed," 230
culture: institutions/machinery, 9

Danube (Magris), 239
"dead bride" metaphor, 53
death: Kafka's illness and, 1, 6
Degner, Uta, 11; article by, 75–88
Deleuze, Gilles, 96
Densky, Doreen, 12–13; article by, 120–35
Derrida, Jacques, 57
"Description of a Struggle," 165–67; Nietzsche and, 5
Diaries, 96; metaphor training and discipline, 51; as self-surveillance, 52; workshop selves, 52; writing experimentation in, 49–51
the Dionysian: in *The Metamorphosis*, 69; and Nietzschean aestheticism, 65–66; and "oneness of being" in Nietzsche, 64–65; in "A Report to an Academy," 93
Discipline and Punish (Foucault), 137, 178n46
doubling: phonetic repetition in style, 78–79; in "A Report to an Academy," 95
dreams: art and communal, 72–73; dream-like quality of writing and imagination, 7, 148, 214, 216–17; Kafka's accounts of, 155; as symptoms in *The Metamorphosis*, 15, 184, 188; travel-induced trauma and, 184, 188, 190–92
Dymant, Dora, 148

Eagleton, Terry, 147
education, 141–42, 148
Eliot, T. S., 108
emigration, 148
England global echoes, 9
the erotic: in "Description of a Struggle," 166–67; gaze and, 151–55, 166–74; and media technologies, 151–55, 171–74; power and, 70–71, 114–15; in "A Report to an Academy," 89–93, 96, 99, 102n14; writing or correspondence as erotic act, 196
Escher, M. C., 108
ethnographic stance, 208–9, 212–14, 218, 243

family: in *The Castle*, 114–15, 146; as institution, 14, 137, 140–42, 240; in "The Judgment," 70–71, 84, 141; in *The Metamorphosis*, 11, 14, 68–69, 141, 195–96; patriarchal authority and, 142. *See also* childhood
father: Kafka's relationship with his, 1, 4, 14, 141–42
father figures in Kafka, 11, 68, 70–71, 77, 81–85, 141, 195, 213–14
"feedback loops," 197n3
first-person narrators, 30–31, 35, 52–54, 166–67, 169, 172; in Ishiguro, 172, 207, 216–17
Fischer edition, 30
Flaubert, Gustave: and contest between realism and aestheticism, 75–76; and generic hybridity, 75–76; literary identification with, 75–76; metaphor and, 10; on style and intent, 76–77; as stylistic influence, 10, 19, 75–77, 81
Fortmann, Patrick, 151

Foucault, Michel, 126, 134n19, 137–38
Freud, Sigmund: on malingering, 190; on mechanical shock and traumatic neurosis, 181, 189, 192–94, 199n21, 203n62; mourning *vs.* melancholia, 90; and psychoanalysis as medical practice, 202n50; and Simmel's theories, 192, 204n64; speech acts, 26
futurism, 13–14; and morality of the artist, 66–67

Garloff, Katja, 11; article by, 89–104
gaze: in "Absent-minded Window-gazing," 170–71; and character as focalizer, 165, 168–71; cinematic, 15, 165, 167–71, 169; clarity of, 4; desire and the voyeuristic, 154, 166–68; erotic desire and the, 166–70; narrator as observer, 38, 165–66; in "The Passenger," 168–70; and perception through the object, 38; stasis and, 167; in *The Trial*, 173–74; writing process and, 38; and zooming effects, 169–71
gender: gender melancholy, 11–12, 89–95; identity, 173; Zionism as gendered culture, 225
Gilman, Sander, 95–96, 205n69
Glass, Philip, 2
Goebel, Rolf, 13, 14; article by, 151–64
Goffman, Erving, 14, 138–40
gramophones, 151, 156–57
"gray ecology," 160
Greenberg, Jack, 8–9
Grelling's paradox, 109
Gross, Otto, 26, 142
Gross, Ruth, vii, 63n55; introductory essay by, 1–23; preface by, vii–ix
Guattari, Félix, 96

Haam, Ahad, 225
Habiby, Emile, 17, 223, 225–28
Halley's comet, 51–52
handwritten texts, 9; errors engendered during editing, 24; insertion signs in, 30; material parameters and, 25, 35, 42, 47; notebook pages pictured, 27–29, 39–41; omissions and cancellations, 25; restitution signs in, 46; separation lines in, 36, 38; sequencing of passages as editorial decision, 30, 46
Harman, Mark, 3, 10; article by, 48–63
"harmonic opposition," 78
Hauptmann, Gerhart, 77, 195
Heart of Darkness (Conrad), 144
Heraclitus, 70–71
Hermann, Elli, 148
Herzl, Theodor, 224, 225, 233
hierarchy: and man-machine relationships, 156–57; "strange loops" and disappearance of, 107, 113; in *The Trial*, 127–28, 142–44
Hoffmann, E. T. A., 143–44, 171
Hofmannsthal, Hugo von, 50, 77, 80
Hofstader, Douglas, 107–9
Holitscher, Arthur, 224
Holocaust, 1, 136, 229, 239
House of Liars (Morante), 240
humiliation, 138, 140
humor, 53–54
"The Hunter Gracchus," 18, 193; Nietzsche and, 5; writing process and, 30–35, 43
hybridity, 12; "crossbreeds" in Kafka, 230, 235n26; Jews as crossbreeds, 96; of texts, 15, 207–8; in Yehoshua's *A Woman in Jerusalem*, 230–32
Hyperion (journal), 77

identity: ambiguity of human, 244–45; cinematic gaze and loss of, 160; colonial mimicry and construction of the Other, 92; fluidity of narrator, 81; gender identity, 89–90, 173, 205n69; Habiby and constructions of, 226–28; human, 69, 91, 210, 240, 245; hybridity or crossbreed, 230, 232; Jewish racial, 89–90, 95–96, 100; metaphor and, 49, 53; minor literatures and the formation

of national, 97–98; as writer, 3–4; Yehoshua and constructions of, 228–33
"In the Penal Colony," 144–46, 159, 191, 193, 208
In the Penal Colony (Glass), 2
"In the Penal Colony" (Müller-Seidel), 136–37
individuation: the ego as illusion, 65, 68–69, 71–74; suppression of individuality by authority, 141–42
influenza pandemic, 6
institution(s): acquiescence to, 14, 141–43, 145; as *Anstalt*, 137; hierarchy and, 142–43; as inescapable, 14; Kafka and desire to reform, 148; Kafka and poetics of the, 120–21; Kafka's employment with Workmen's Accident Insurance Institute, 1, 6–7, 121–27, 137; Kafka's works as "novels of the institution," 120–21; lack of direct communication in, 131; logic of, 145; split between inmates and staff in, 139; structure of, 138; the teletoptical city as virtual, 14; "total," 14, 138–39, 148
insurance, Kafka's work in, 1, 7, 15, 121–27, 132, 188–90, 193
intercourse, 11, 70–72, 179, 195–96
interiority, 167–68
intermarriage, 89
intermediality, 15, 157, 165, 174, 178n49
intermediaries, 121–22, 128; proxies contrasted with, 121–22
interpretation: in Kafka's fiction, 5; misreadings and, 9, 24; print layouts and, 46; sequence of passages and, 30; writing process and, 12, 35
intertextuality: Kafka's erudition, 5–6
irony, 11, 56–57, 115, 195; Flaubert's influence and, 81; metaphor and, 49
Isiguro, Kazuo, 16, 207–19; appropriation of *2001: A Space Odyssey* by, 216
Israel, and Kafka as heritage, 16–17
Italian literature, 9, 17; Kafkan tradition and, 237–46

"Jackals and Arabs," 212–13, 223–25; conflict in Palestine as context, 17, 223, 225
Janouch, Gustav, 49, 163n24
Jarrell, Randall, 137
Jesenská, Milena, 1, 141; correspondence with, 7, 89, 152, 154
"Josefine, the Singer," 69, 72–74, 208, 211–12, 218
Judaism: and "community of blood," 12, 89, 95–99, 100–101; as feminized, 205n70; Jewish assimilation, 12, 89, 100–101, 226–28; Jews as crossbreeds, 96; racialization of Jewish identity, 11–12, 90–91, 93, 95. *See also* Zionism
"The Judgment": authority or hierarchy in, 14; the Dionysian and, 69–72, 74; family in, 70–71, 84, 141; "negative contact" in, 81; observational mode and, 166; structure of, 71–72; style in, contest of realistic and aesthetic, 11, 81–85

"K" (alphabet letter), 129
Kafka, biographical information: childhood, 57–58; emigration, 148; employment with Workmen's Accident Insurance, 1, 6–7, 121–27, 132, 137, 188–90, 193; familial relationships, 1, 2, 4, 14, 141–42; physical description, 2; self-identification as poet, 10
Kafka, Ottla, 1, 25, 193–94, 195
Kafka and His Precursors (Borges), 136
Kafkaesque, as term, 16, 207
Kafkan literature, 14, 15, 17; Habiby's *The Secret Life of Saeed* as, 223, 225–28; Ishiguro's *The Unconsoled* as, 207–19; Italian authors and, 237–46; Yehoshua's *A Woman in Jerusalem* as, 223, 228–33
"Kafka's Dad" (Landolfi), 239
Kafka's Dick (Bennett), 136

Kittler, Wolf, 159
"The Knock at the Courtyard Gate," 35, 38
Koelb, Clayton, 201n38
Kurtág, György, 2
Kurz, Gerhard, 80

Landolfi, Tommaso, 239
language: animals and human speech, 17, 240–45, 248n24; communication technology and, 156–57; decomposition and loss of coherence, 90; distrust of, 50, 52; Grelling's paradox, 109; human agency and communication, 159; misunderstanding in Svevo's "Argo," 243–44; social subjects and, 248n24; translation and, 98–99, 157, 239–40, 243–44; Yiddish, 96, 98–100
legal discourse, 2–3
Lemon, Robert, 16; article by, 207–21
Letter to Lord Chandos (Hofmannsthal), 50, 80, 83
"Letter to My Father," 14, 142
Levi, Primo, 17, 239–40
"Little Automobile Story," 151
Lyotard, Jean-François, vii, 16, 218
lyricism, 14, 76–77, 78, 148

machinery, 9; animal life and freedom from, 243; "apparatus" and, 144; cinematic vision, 160–61; as dehumanizing or alienating, 158–59; "ghostly" media, 197n2; and the human body as commodity, 187; humans as parts or appendages of, 180–81, 187; impacts of mechanization and speed on the human body, 15–16, 179–97, 180–81, 187, 191; and instrumentalization of the human, 157, 159–60; Kafka and abandonment of subject of, 193; machine language, 157, 159; man-machine interface, 154, 159–61; the office or bureaucracy as machine, 226–27; and pace or speed, 155; as tyrannical authority, 155–57; writing and transportation, 196. *See also* communication technology
Madame Bovary (Flaubert), 76
Magris, Claudio, 17, 239
Mallarmé, Stéphane, 44, 80
Mann, Thomas, 5–6, 21n14, 77
marginality: minor literatures and, 96–98
Marschner, Robert, 123
media technologies: audiovisual, 151; communication, 151
"Meditation" (*Betrachtung*), 55, 77, 176n25
melancholy, 12, 89–92
memory, 54
The Metamorphosis: authority or hierarchy in, 14; childhood in, 67; diary explorations and, 52; the Dionysian in, 69; family in, 11, 14, 68–69, 141, 195–96; and imagery in *Wedding Preparations*, 168; as influence on Yehoshua's *A Woman in Jerusalem*, 228–29; music in, 5–6; Nietzsche's Zarathustrian thought and, 67–69; Thomas Mann and, 5–6; travel-induced trauma in, 181–90, 194–95
metaphor: aversion to, 10, 58; childhood and emotional tenor of, 52–53; diaries and exploration of, 49–51, 54; and disjunction of vehicle and tenor, 55; as inadequate, 49–50; indeterminate or fluid nature of, 201n38; interchangability of, 58; Kafka on, 48–49, 57, 58; Kafka's cognitive process as image-oriented, 50–51, 63n54; literalization of, 12, 100–101, 165; Nietzsche on, 59; "obsessive" metaphors, 48, 52; personal obsessions as, 58; as resistant to interpretation, 55–56; universalizing the personal, 48
metrical repetition, 78
mimicry, 12, 100–101, 241; machines as parody of human agents, 157
mirrors as narrative screens, 171–72
misrecognition, 8
Möbius, Paul Julius, 189, 202n47

Möbius strip, 107–8
modernity, 6; Kafka as exemplar of, 18
monoperspective, 131–32, 166, 174
Montale, Eugenio, 238, 239
morality, political or ethical appropriation of Kafka, 157
Morante, Else, 17, 238, 240
mortification and the total institution, 138
Muir, Edwin, 106–7, 110
Müller-Seidel, Walter, 137–38
music: compositions as readings of Kafka's works, 2; in Ishiguro's *The Unconsoled*, 209–11, 220n19; in "Josephine, the Singer," 69, 72–73, 211–12; in *The Metamorphosis*, 5–6, 69; in *Researches of a Dog*, 210–11; writing process compared with musical composition, 42–43
myth, engagement with, 18, 19, 145

Nägele, Rainer, 207
narrative structure: Ishiguro's contrasted with Kafka's, 16; myth and, 18; resolution and consolation, 207, 208, 218–19
narrators or narrative mode: breaks in perspective, 125n39, 131–32; figural narrative perspective, 13, 166–67; first-person, 165–66; fusion with textual structure, 122; interpolated narratives, 217; monoperspective and, 131–32, 166, 174; multifaceted narrative mode, 132; narrative authority, 120; objectival perspective, 35; proxies and (*see* proxies); shifts in, 122, 168; third-person, 13, 166
"negative contact," in "The Judgment," 81
Nekula, Marek, 129
Neumann, Gerhard, 157
"The New Lawyer," 24, 38
Nietzsche, Friedrich, 58–59; aestheticism and, 66; and the death of God, 105–6; and Greek tragedy, 65; Kafka's engagement with, 5; and morality of the artist, 66–67; the Will and, 65, 66, 69
Nordau, Max, 181, 185, 194, 223–24, 234n7
North, Paul, 7

O'Brien v. Henderson, 2–3
"Observation" (*Betrachtung*), 55–56, 77, 176n25
office, as figure, 7, 226–27
Office Writings, 7, 121–27
Old-New Land (Herzl), 224, 233
Olney, James, 54
On Parables, 107, 109–10
"On Truth and Lie in an Extra-Moral Sense" (Nietzsche), 58–59
The Open: Man and Animal, 245
Oppenheim, Hermann, 189, 192, 200n26
originality, 17, 77, 165, 238–39
Oz, Amos, 233

Paganism, Christianity, Judaism (Brod), 18
"A Page from and Old Document," 143
Palestine: emigration to, 148, 223; "Jackals and Arabs" and racial conflict in, 17–18, 223, 225
Panizza, Oskar, 89
parlographs, 134n25, 154–58, 179
"The Passenger," 168–70, 195
passive voice, 58
Pavese, Cesare, 239
persona, development of literary, 52–53
phonetic repetition, 78–79
Pictures from an Institution (Jarrell), 137
poetics: "harmonic opposition," 78; phonetic repetition in style, 78
Pollak, Oskar, 50–51
postmodernity, 154, 161, 217, 218
power: of composition writing process, 42; institutional, 140, 239–40; in "Jackals and Arabs," 212–13; Kafka's interest in the will to, 26; and resistance in "A Report to an Academy," 94; and sexual exploitation in *The Castle*, 146–47; violence and, 14, 137. *See also* authority

professional writing, 121–27; anonymity of, 125–27; linked to fiction, 124; and role as proxy, 120, 122–27
"Prometheus," 26, 30
pronomial shifts, 122
"The Propertyless Workforce," 148
prophetic, Kafka as prescient or, 13, 136–37
Proust, Marcel, 10
proxies, 12–13; and the absent author, 13; authorization of, 120, 123; contrasted with intermediaries, 121; as *Fürsprecher* (narrator representative), 120, 128; Josef K., 127–28, 132; "K.," 129–32; Kafka as *Koncipist* for Workmen's Accident Insurance Institute, 122–27; narrators as, 121, 123; parlographs as, 134n25; as representative of institution, 121–22
Puchner, Martin, 243
punishment machine, 2, 144, 145, 191

quarries, 7–8

Raabe, Paul, 24
racial melancholy, 89–101
racialization, 11–12, 93, 95; displacement and, 90–91; racism, 16–17 (*see also* anti-Semitism)
realism, 75, 165; speech acts and relationship between language and reality, 84; *vs.* aestheticism in Kafka's early writing, 11
reception of works, 2–3
Reitano, Natalie, 221n23
"Report of an Educated Young Man" (Hoffmann), 244–45
"A Report to an Academy": assimilation as choice in, 93–94, 226, 232; as captivity narrative, 241–42; compared and contrasted with Svevo's "Argo," 241–46; human identity and, 240; as parody or satire on Jewish assimilation, 89, 227; Rotpeter and decision to assimilate, 93–94, 226, 232; Rotpeter and human speech, 240–45
reproduction, media and, 151, 158, 160–61, 162n1
Researches of a Dog, 210–11, 213, 218
resistance, 14, 141, 148; in *The Castle*, 146–48; as futile, 146–47
resolution, absence of narrative, 207
Reuß, Roland, 9; article by, 24–47
Richard and Samuel, 179
Ricoeur, Paul, 49
Rilke, Rainer Maria, 77
risk, calculation of, 122–25
Robertson, Ritchie, viii, 13–14, 89; article by, 136–50; cited, 89, 239–40, 246
Rolleston, James, vii, 63n55
Romanticism, 50
Rosenzweig, Franz, 100
Rossmann, Karl, 174n6
Roth, Philip, 19
Rules of Art (Bourdieu), 75–76
running texts, 9, 24–47
Russell's paradox, 108–9

sadism, 136, 144
satire, social: "A Report to an Academy" as, 89, 227; use of Kafka by authors of, 17, 222–34
Schnitzler, Arthur, 185
Schopenhauer, Arthur, 64–65, 68, 70, 210
Schriftstellersein, 126–27, 132
The Secret Life of Saeed: The Pessoptimist (Habiby), 223, 225–28
self-obliteration, 54–55, 69
semblance (*Schein*), 72–73
setting, as indeterminate, 207
sex or sexuality: castration imagery, 91–92; homosexuality, 90, 144, 166; intercourse, traffic as symbol or metaphor for, 11, 196; in *The Metamorphosis*, 196; power and sexual exploitation in *The Castle*, 146–47; in "A Report to an Academy," 11–12, 90–92, 94–95
Sheppard, Richard, 146, 148
signatures, signing, 126–27, 129
Simmel, Georg, 168–69, 192, 204n64
social criticism in Kafka, 53–54

Sokel, Walter, viii, 10–11, 50, 63n55; article by, 64–74; cited, 26, 50
space: communication technology and, 152–54; ideological, 147
Spaini, Alberto, 238
speed: modernity and acceleration, 14–16, 152; pace of urban life, 168–69; relative to observer, 79; telecommunication technology and, 154–55, 158–59; and the teleoptic city, 152; of thought, 58; transportation technology and, 158, 179–80, 185; vision and cinematic images, 15, 163n27, 185
standardization, 122, 160, 185–86
statistics, 4–5
Steiner, George, 106–7, 110, 136
"The Stoker," 172–73
"strange loops": *The Castle* and parabolic, 109–16; defined and described, 107–9; irony and, 115; Möbius strips as example of, 12, 107–8, *108*
"The Street Window," 171
Stroemfeld edition, 35, 38
style: cinematic quality of Kafka's prose, 15, 151, 165–74; contest between realistic and aesthetic, 11, 75–88; Kafka and fusion of, 80; Kafka on Flaubert's, 76–77; "Meditation" ("Observation") as experiments in, 77–78; phonetic repetition, 78–79; self-reflexivity and, 161; Virilo's, 161
suicide, 4–5, 185, 214
surveillance, 137, 140, 167, 173; diaries as self-surveillance, 52
surveying, land surveyors, 7–8, 148, 231

Tabori, George, 102
Tagger, Theodore, 24
Tamaro, Susanna, 240
the teletoptical city, 13–14, 151–61
temporality. *See* time
Thus Spoke Zarathustra (Nietzsche), 5
time: institutions and, 140; "railway" time and psychic trauma, 185–93, 200n29, 203n62; and spatial location, 153, 159, 161, 216–17; temporal nature of writing process, 38; war and timetabling, 191–93
Timms, Edward, 176n25, 177n31
Torok, Maria, 90
total institutions, 14, 138, 139, 148
traffic, 11, 70–72, 85, 151, 153, 156, 158, 169, 179, 195–96
trains: "railway" time, 185–93, 200n29, 203n62; "traumatic neurosis" caused by travel, 15–16, 181, 184, 188–93, 199n21, 203n62
translation, 24, 98–99, 157, 239–40, 243–44
transportation technologies: impacts of mechanization and speed, 15–16, 179–97
"traumatic neurosis," 181, 184, 188–93, 189, 199n21, 203n62
"travel phobia," 193–95
"The Trees," 55
The Trial, 2; authority or hierarchy in, 14, 127–28, 142–44; diary explorations and, 52, 54; gaze in, 173–74; indeterminate setting of, 215; as influence on Yehoshua's *A Woman in Jerusalem*, 229, 230; Levi's translation of, 239–40; as novel of the institution, 120–21, 136–45; and proxies, 121–22, 124, 127–32; variations among editions of, 25–26, 30; work experiences and, 8–9, 121–22, 124
Turner, Alison, 210
2001: A Space Odyssey (film), 216

The Unconsoled (Isiguro), 16, 207–19
"Unhappiness," 172
uniqueness of the individual, 72–73
unity, oneness of being, 64–65, 71, 73
unpublished texts, 9, 25, 120
Urzidil, Johannes, 10, 49

"Verboten" (Montale), 239

violence, 14; institutional power and, 137, 140, 144, 240; Kafka on "normal," 1; mechanization and trauma, 191; metaphors and, 53–54, 99, 220n19
Virilio, Paul, 13–14, 151–61
vision or visual perception: cinematic, 160–61, 165; mechanical travel as harmful to, 184–85; postmodernity and visual orientation, 154; visual commodification, 169–70; and writing practices, 38, 151. *See also* gaze
Vitesse de liberation (Virilio), 152
voyeurism, 92, 154, 166–70, 171, 195

Wagner, Benno, 4–5
Warwar, Max, 96
Wassermann, Jakob, 21n14, 77, 86n13
Wedding Preparations in the Country, 166, 167, 168, 180–85, 199n19, 201n33
the Will, 65, 66, 68, 69, 70
windows as narrative screens, 171–72
"Wish to be a Red Indian," 143
Wohryzek, Julie, 1
A Woman in Jerusalem, 223, 228–33
work life, relationship of writing to, 4–9, 12–13, 21n20, 120–35; business travel as context for writing, 199n19
Workmen's Accident Insurance Institute for the Kingdom of Bohemia, 1, 6–7, 121–27, 132, 137, 188–90, 193
workshop selves, 52
World War I: Kafka on war as "normal," 1; Kafka's work during, 6–7, 193; "timetabling" and, 191–93; "war tremblers" and traumatic shock, 180, 189–90, 192–93, 204n48; Zionism and context of, 222–24
World War II, 224. *See also* Holocaust
writing process: experimentation and, 25–27, 42–43, 48, 58, 159; handwritten texts and revelation of, 24–47; as interpretive, 12, 35; literary experimentation and, 26; material parameters and, 25–26, 42–43, 46–47; as non-intentional, 26, 42; the reader's agency and, 116; temporality and, 38; visual perception and, 38, 151

Yeats, W. B., 48
Yehoshua, A. B., 17, 223, 228–34, 235n26, 235n31
Yiddish, 96, 98–100

Zeno's Conscience (Svevo), 245–46
Zilcosky, John, 15–16, 63n55; article by, 179–206
Ziolkowski, Saskia Elizabeth, 17; article by, 237–50
Zionism, 89, 148, 222–25, 227, 229, 233

Printed and bound by CPI Group (UK) Ltd, Croydon, CR0 4YY

07/07/2026

14916224-0001